Charles Spurgeon, 1854

the LOST SERMONS *of*
C. H. SPURGEON

the LOST SERMONS *of*

C. H. SPURGEON

His Earliest Outlines and Sermons
Between 1851 and 1854   *Vol. 1*

Edited with Introduction and Notes by CHRISTIAN T. GEORGE

B&H
ACADEMIC
NASHVILLE, TENNESSEE

The Lost Sermons of C. H. Spurgeon, Volume 1
Copyright © 2016 by Christian George and Spurgeon's College
Published by B&H Academic
Nashville, Tennessee

Standard Edition ISBN: 978-1-4336-8681-8
Collector's Edition ISBN: 978-1-4336-4908-0

Dewey Decimal Classification: 252
Subject Heading: SPURGEON, CHARLES H. \ SERMONS \ CHRISTIAN LIFE–SERMONS

Special thanks to Spurgeon's College, spurgeons.ac.uk

The web addresses referenced in this book were live and correct at the time of the book's publication but may be
subject to change.

The marbled paper for the cover of the collector's edition was created by Lesley Patterson-Marx,
lesleypattersonmarx.com
Interior Design by Roy Roper, wideyedesign

Printed in China

1 2 3 4 5 6 7 8 9 10 · 21 20 19 18 17 16

RRD

For the rising generation of pastors, scholars, students,
and all to whom Spurgeon—though being dead—still speaks

CONTENTS

CONTENTS

CONTENTS

FOREWORD

In 1856 Elias Lyman Magoon, pastor of Oliver Street Baptist Church, New York, published a collection of the sermons of Charles Haddon Spurgeon. Magoon had visited Britain in the previous decade and continued to be supplied with newspapers from the United Kingdom. He had written two books on oratorical achievements past and present. The New York pastor was therefore fascinated to discover that a youthful preacher of his own denomination had taken London by storm. Spurgeon, though only a teenager when he accepted the pulpit of New Park Street Baptist Chapel, Southwark, in 1854, was the talk of the British capital. His chapel was thronged every Sunday; his services were sought throughout the land; and his sermons flooded from the press. Magoon decided to publish a sample for consumption in the United States. Spurgeon, according to the American, was "as original in his conceptions as he is untrammeled in their utterance."[1] Over the years down to his death in 1892, Spurgeon was to prove to be the greatest preacher of the century. What, asked Magoon, was the explanation of his powers?

In the first place, Magoon explained, there was Spurgeon's intelligence. Mental ability, honed by a dedication to education, allowed the London preacher to provide a wealth of rich illustrations. Magoon's estimate has been confirmed by later scholarship. Spurgeon was an avid reader, amassing a personal library of over 12,000 volumes. Each month his church magazine, *The Sword and the Trowel*, contained perceptive critical evaluations of his latest reading. It is true that he did not overvalue the classical authors of antiquity, then the basis of an elite education, remarking that "Wisdom does not always speak Latin."[2] Yet, as Magoon noticed, Spurgeon could allude knowledgeably in a sermon to Homer and Virgil. Later, in 1869, he was to be held up to ridicule by the essayist Matthew Arnold as a man who did not appreciate the sweetness and light to be derived from classical sources,

1   E. L. Magoon, ed., *'The Modern Whitfield': Sermons of the Rev. C. H. Spurgeon, of London, with an Introduction and Sketch of His Life* (New York: Sheldon, Blakeman, & Co., 1856), v.
2   C. H. Spurgeon, *John Ploughman's Talk* (London: Passmore & Alabaster, 1868), 177.

a denier of the value of culture.[3] Yet that was entirely unfair. Spurgeon respected learning and had imbibed a great deal of it. Magoon was nearer the mark when he declared that the London preacher acquired an "early and varied culture."[4]

Secondly, according to Magoon, Spurgeon was notable for his independence. The American contrasted the originality of Spurgeon's sermons with the standard views expressed in the pulpit by the bulk of preachers. He was willing to speak his mind, expressing sturdy opinions that diverged from the predominant views of the day. He was a product of rural East Anglia, gladly challenging the values of the capital where he preached. "As a general rule," Spurgeon was to tell the students at the college he founded, "I hate the fashions of society, and detest conventionalities."[5] He repudiated the notion that ministers should belong to a refined class, distinct from the common people. His students were required to live in the homes of ordinary church members rather than together in a residential college so that they should not adopt the airs of a separate class of men. The Victorian idea of a gentleman, possessing a polished lifestyle superior to that of his fellows, was anathema to him. Against the model of the gentleman Spurgeon set the image of a man. "Scarcely one man in a dozen in the pulpit," he complained, "talks like a man."[6] That quality brought him condemnation in many quarters, but it appealed to his congregations.

In the third place, Magoon singled out Spurgeon's honesty of purpose. He was a preacher of the gospel with a "frank, open-heartiness of manner."[7] Unlike most of his contemporaries, Spurgeon was prepared to introduce humor into the pulpit. "There is no commandment in the Bible," he observed, "which says 'Thou shalt not laugh.'"[8] He was also prepared to denounce views which he considered wrong. He often censured the clergy of the Church of England, even criticizing evangelicals within its ranks for remaining loyal to an institution which taught that infants were born again in baptism. He was particularly hostile to the Roman Catholic Church as a sinister force in the world, past and present. If people are often best understood through their heroes, it is useful to note that Spurgeon lavished praise on Martin

3   Matthew Arnold, *Culture and Anarchy*, ed. J. Dover Wilson (Cambridge: Cambridge University Press, 1935), 173.
4   Magoon, '*Modern Whitfield*,' xix.
5   C. H. Spurgeon, *Lectures to My Students* (London: Marshall, Morgan & Scott, 1954), 21.
6   Ibid., 111.
7   Magoon, '*Modern Whitfield*,' xxxi.
8   Ibid.

Luther, a man "always himself."[9] Luther was unafraid to voice his authentic opinions whatever the cost. That was true of Spurgeon too.

This remarkable preacher—intelligent, independent, and honest in purpose—is still widely read. This series of volumes includes 400 hitherto unpublished sermons, the earliest that Spurgeon preached. He was a precocious genius, his first sermon delivered when he was only sixteen. The volumes will print not just what Spurgeon wrote, for the commentary will set the sermons in their context. Detailed notes will allow the reader to understand Spurgeon's developing mind. It is shown in this first volume, for example, that Spurgeon drew 44 percent of his earliest texts from the Old Testament. A comparison with a sample of American evangelical sermons in the twenty-first century, when only 31 percent were based on Old Testament texts, suggests food for thought.[10] Perhaps Spurgeon was more familiar with his whole Bible than many preachers of a later date. The editor, Christian George, as the curator of The Spurgeon Library at Midwestern Baptist Theological Seminary, is uniquely qualified for his task, for he has many of Spurgeon's own volumes in his care. Magoon imagined himself telling Spurgeon that through his selection of sermons published in the United States, the English preacher would "soon . . . be read . . . from the Eastern Atlantic to the great Pacific of the West."[11] Now Spurgeon's first addresses will be available to the same audience—and to an even wider one.

DAVID BEBBINGTON
August 2016
University of Stirling

---

9   *The Freeman*, 7 December 1883, 803.
10   Personal notes on 200 sermons.
11   Magoon, *'Modern Whitfield,'* xxxvi.

EDITOR'S PREFACE

In 1859, an American minister named "Rev. H." traveled to London to meet the famous pastor of the New Park Street Chapel. When Spurgeon discovered his guest was from Alabama, his "cordiality sensibly diminished." A six-month American preaching tour would expedite the construction of the Metropolitan Tabernacle, but could Southerners tolerate Spurgeon's stance against slavery? When Spurgeon asked his guest this question, the Alabamian said he "had better not undertake it."[1]

This advice might have saved Spurgeon's life. The same year, S. A. Corey, pastor of Eighteenth Street Baptist Church in New York City, invited the twenty-four-year-old to preach at the Academy of Music opera house for $10,000.[2] News of Spurgeon's visit was met with anticipation in the North and hostility in the South. According to an Alabama newspaper, Spurgeon would receive a beating "so bad as to make him ashamed."[3] On February 17, 1860,[4] citizens of Montgomery, Alabama, publicly protested the "notorious English abolitionist"[5] by gathering in the jail yard to burn his "dangerous books"[6]:

---

1 "Spurgeon's Anti-Slavery Mission to America," *The Times-Picayune* (October 22, 1859).
2 See "Spurgeon and His $10,000 Offer," *The Brooklyn Daily Eagle* (February 5, 1859).
3 "They Want Spurgeon," *Daily Confederation* (October 30, 1858).
4 There is some confusion about the date of the Montgomery burning. Some British newspapers claimed it occurred on January 17 ("Mr. Spurgeon's Sermons Burned by American Slaveowners," *The Southern Reporter and Daily Commercial Courier* [April 10, 1860]). American sources reveal the more likely date of February 17 ("Book Burning," *Pomeroy Weekly Telegraph* [March 13, 1860]).
5 The full quote is, "A gentleman of this city requests us to invite, and we do hereby invite all persons in Montgomery who possess copies of the sermons of the notorious English abolitionist, Spurgeon, to send them to the jail-yard to be burned, on next Friday (this day week). A subscription is also on foot to buy of our booksellers all copies of said sermons now in their stores to be burnt on the same occasion" (*Montgomery Mail*, repr. in "Spurgeon's Sermons—a Bonfire," *Nashville Patriot* [March 15, 1860]). See also "The Barbarism of Slavery," *The Cleveland Morning Leader* (July 3, 1860), and *Randolph County Journal* (July 5, 1860). The burning of Spurgeon's sermons in Montgomery solicited caustic responses in Northern states, such as in New York's *Poughkeepsie Eagle*: "There will—unless this fanaticism is soon checked—be a general bonfire of another Book, which has something of a circulation [in the] south, and which declares it to be every man's duty to 'let the oppressed go free'" (March 8, 1860).
6 For a more comprehensive account of the burning of Spurgeon's sermons at the Montgomery, Alabama, jail yard, see "Burning Spurgeon's Sermons," *The Burlington Free Press* (March 30, 1860).

Last Saturday, we devoted to the flames a large number of copies of Spurgeon's Sermons. . . . We trust that the works of the greasy cockney vociferator may receive the same treatment throughout the South. And if the Pharisaical author should ever show himself in these parts, we trust that a stout cord may speedily find its way around his eloquent throat.[7]

On March 22, a "Vigilance Committee"[8] in Montgomery followed suit and burned Spurgeon's sermons in the public square. A week later Mr. B. B. Davis, a bookstore owner, prepared "a good fire of pine sticks" before reducing about sixty volumes of Spurgeon's sermons "to smoke and ashes."[9] British newspapers quipped that America had given Spurgeon a warm welcome, "a literally brilliant reception."[10]

Anti-Spurgeon bonfires illuminated jail yards, plantations, bookstores, and courthouses throughout the Southern states. In Virginia, Mr. Humphrey H. Kuber, a Baptist preacher and "highly respectable citizen" of Matthews County, burned seven calf-skinned volumes of Spurgeon's sermons "on the head of a flour barrel."[11] The arson was assisted by "many citizens of the highest standing."[12] In North Carolina, Spurgeon's famous sermon "Turn or Burn"[13] found a similar fate when a Mr. Punch "turned the second page and burned the whole."[14] By 1860, slave-owning pastors were "foaming with rage because they [could not] lay hands on the youthful Spurgeon."[15] His life was threatened, his books burned,

---

7 "Mr. Spurgeon's Sermons Burned by American Slaveowners." See also *The Morning Advertiser* (April 2, 1860). A similar statement is found in a letter from Virginia minister James B. Taylor: "Wonder that the earth does not open her mouth, and swallow up Spurgeon. . . . Pity that that cord from the South is not applied to his eloquent throat!" ("Review of a Letter from Rev. Jas. B. Taylor, of Richmond, Va.," *The Liberator* [July 6, 1860], 108).

8 "News from All Nations," *The Bradford Reporter* (March 22, 1860).

9 "Book-Burning in Montgomery, Ala.," *Randolph County Journal* (March 29, 1860). See also "Another Bonfire of Spurgeon's Sermons," *The Wilmington Daily Herald* (March 12, 1860).

10 *The Morning Advertiser* (April 2, 1860). See also "The Rev. C. H. Spurgeon in Scotland," *The Morning Advertiser* (March 11, 1861).

11 For a more accurate version of this account, see "Mr. Spurgeon's Sermons: Why They Were Burned by Virginians," *The New York Times* (July 9, 1860).

12 "Virginia News," *Alexandria Gazette and Virginia Advertiser* (June 22, 1860). See also "Burning Spurgeon," *Richmond Dispatch* (June 5, 1860), and *Brooklyn Evening Star* (June 22, 1860).

13 Spurgeon preached the sermon "Turn or Burn" (*NPSP* 2, Sermon 106) on December 7, 1856.

14 "Our Politeness Exceeds His Beauty," *North Carolina Christian Advocate* (July 10, 1857).

15 "Espionage in the South," *The Liberator* (May 4, 1860).

his sermons censured,[16] and below the Mason-Dixon Line, the media catalyzed character assassinations. In Florida, Spurgeon was a "beef-eating, puffed-up, vain, over-righteous pharisaical, English blab-mouth."[17] In Virginia, he was a "fat, overgrown boy";[18] in Louisiana, a "hell-deserving Englishman";[19] and in South Carolina, a "vulgar young man" with "(soiled) sleek hair, prominent teeth, and a self-satisfied air."[20] Georgians were encouraged to "pay no attention to him."[21] North Carolinians "would like a good opportunity at this hypocritical preacher" and resented his "fiendish sentiments, against our Constitution and citizens."[22] *The Weekly Raleigh Register* reported that anyone selling Spurgeon's sermons should be arrested and charged with "circulating incendiary publications."[23]

Southern Baptists ranked among Spurgeon's chief antagonists.[24] *The Mississippi Baptist* hoped "no Southern Baptist will now purchase any of that incendiary's books."[25] The Baptist colporteurs of Virginia were forced to return all copies of his sermons to the publisher.[26] *The Alabama Baptist* and *Mississippi Baptist* "gave the Londoner 4,000 miles of an awful raking" and "took the hide off him."[27] The *Southwestern Baptist* and

16 The following reports suggest that the censuring of Spurgeon's sermons became widely publicized in American newspapers: "Beecher has charged that the American edition of Spurgeon's sermons, does not contain his sentiments on slavery as the English edition does. A comparison of the editions has been made, and the charge has been found correct" ("Spurgeon Purged," *Ashtabula Weekly Telegraph* [November 26, 1859]). In April of the following year, the newspaper reported that "grave charges have been made of interpolations and modifications in the American edition of his sermons, to suit American squeamishness, and secure currency to his works" (April 14, 1860). See also "Ex-Spurgeon," *Ohio State Journal* (November 29, 1859).

17 "A Southern Opinion of the Rev. Mr. Spurgeon," *The New York Herald* (March 1, 1860).

18 "The Great Over-Rated," *The Daily Dispatch* (August 17, 1858).

19 "Spurgeon on Slavery," *The Bossier Banner* (February 24, 1860).

20 "Spurgeon and the Lady," *Charleston Courier* (June 15, 1858).

21 *Macon Weekly Telegraph* (February 25, 1860).

22 "Rev. Mr. Spurgeon," *The North Carolinian* (February 18, 1860).

23 "Rev. Mr. Spurgeon," *The Weekly Raleigh Register* (February 15, 1860).

24 Spurgeon was ten years old when tensions over slavery resulted in Baptists from the Southern state conventions gathering in Augusta, Georgia, to form the Southern Baptist Convention in 1845 (see A. H. Newman, *A History of the Baptist Churches in the United States* [New York: The Christian Literature Co., 1894], 443–47). On June 20–22, 1995, the SBC adopted a resolution in Atlanta, Georgia, acknowledging that "our relationship to African-Americans has been hindered from the beginning by the role that slavery played in the formation of the Southern Baptist Convention," and "Many of our Southern Baptist forbears defended the right to own slaves, and either participated in, supported, or acquiesced in the particularly inhumane nature of American slavery." It also stated that they "unwaveringly denounce racism, in all its forms, as deplorable sin" ("Resolution on Racial Reconciliation on the 150th Anniversary of the Southern Baptist Convention," 1995; accessed May 18, 2016, www.sbc.net/resolutions/899/resolution-on-racial-reconciliation-on-the-150th-anniversary-of-the-southern-baptist-convention).

25 *The Weekly Mississippian* (March 14, 1860).

26 "Spurgeon Repudiated," *Newbern Weekly Progress* (March 20, 1860). See also "Spurgeon Rejected in Virginia," *Cincinnati Daily Press* (March 28, 1860).

27 "Prof. J. M. Pendleton of Union University, Tenn., and the Slavery Question," *The Mississippian* (April 4, 1860).

other denominational newspapers took the "spoiled child to task and administered due castigation."[28]

In the midst of this mayhem, Spurgeon attempted to publish several notebooks of sermons from his earliest ministry. His promise to his readers in 1857 would not be fulfilled, however, due to difficult life circumstances in London. How poetic, then, that 157 years after *The Nashville Patriot* slandered Spurgeon for his "meddlesome spirit,"[29] a publishing house from Nashville would complete the task he failed to accomplish. How symmetrical that Spurgeon's early sermons would be published not by Passmore & Alabaster in London but by Americans. And not only Americans, but *Southern* Americans. And not only Southern Americans, but Southern *Baptist* Americans with all the baggage of their bespeckled beginnings.

As a Southern Baptist from Alabama, allow me to confess my own bias. I have spent the majority of my vocational life studying Spurgeon. I have found in him (and share with him) a genuine commitment to making Jesus Christ known to the nations. Like him, I too am deeply invested in the church and claim the same evangelical impulses that fueled Spurgeon's ministry. I admire his stance for social justice, love for the marginalized, and commitment to biblical orthodoxy.

Spurgeon's language is not always theologically precise. At times his colorful, allegorical, and experimental rhetoric make academic treatments challenging. However, Spurgeon was not a theologian in the systematic sense and never claimed to be. He was a preacher. And as such his ultimate concern was not crafting perfect manuscripts—though he spent a great deal of time redacting his sermons for publication. His greatest concern was, as his famous title hinted, becoming a *Soul Winner*. With pen and pulpit, Spurgeon indentured his literary and intellectual abilities to service of the church. His uncanny gift for rendering complex ideas in the working class vernacular distinguished him from many of his contemporaries and gave him instant audiences.

Spurgeon's preaching emerged not in the ivory towers of Cambridge but in the lowly villages surrounding it. He was more concerned with feeding sheep than giraffes.[30] Spurgeon started his ministry as a country, not city, preacher. His

28 "Mr. Spurgeon," *The Edgefield Advertiser* (February 22, 1860).
29 "Spurgeon's Sermons—a Bonfire," *Daily Nashville Patriot* (March 15, 1860).
30 "We must preach according to the capacity of our hearers. The Lord Jesus did not say, 'Feed my giraffes,' but 'Feed my sheep.' We must not put the fodder on a high rack by our fine language, but use great plainness of speech" (C.H. Spurgeon, *The Salt-Cellars: Being a Collection of Proverbs, Together with Homely Notes Thereon* [New York: A. C. Armstrong and Son, 1889], 56); "Some brethren put the food up so high that the poor sheep cannot possibly feed upon it. I have thought, as I have listened to our eloquent friends, that they imagined that our Lord had said, 'Feed my camelopards.' None but giraffes could reach the food when placed in so lofty a rack. Christ says, 'Feed my sheep,' place the food among them, put it close to them" (*MTP* 56: 406).

congregants at Waterbeach Chapel were farmers and laborers. Even after moving to London, Spurgeon retained his early earthy idioms and used illustrations common to the Victorian experience.

His preaching flourished in cholera-ravaged Southwark near London's warehouses, distilleries, and factories. This gave Spurgeon a finger on the pulse of the population that, when combined with his own physical and mental ailments, produced a level of empathy uncommon to his contemporaries. Spurgeon "never suffered from having never suffered."[31]

At the height of my illness in 2013, Spurgeon's earliest sermons had a profound effect on me. During a series of surgeries, my eyes chanced upon a phrase in Notebook 1: "Think much on grace, Christian."[32] Over the twelve months of my recovery, these words brought such encouragement that I doubt they shall ever be forgotten.

Whenever new discoveries are made—whether lost diaries, letters, hymns, poems, or sermons—there is an opportunity to further our knowledge of a particular subject or person. In 2011, only a handful of doctoral students in the world were writing on Spurgeon. Today roughly two dozen are entering the field. Much work is yet to be done. Caverns of untapped resources await exploration. My hope is that the publication of Spurgeon's lost sermons will inspire future generations of scholars to mine the theological treasures still untapped.

I am also hopeful that this project will promote a reinvigorated sense of unity, mission, and Christian witness throughout evangelicalism. The recent surge of interest in Spurgeon could and should be leveraged for the kingdom. Spurgeon can become an agent of healing. Everyone can, and does, claim him, regardless of theological stripe, tribe, or camp. Spurgeon's appeal extends not only across denominational barriers, but also into the broader evangelical tradition. With the upcoming accessibility of Spurgeon's sermons on the revamped website www.spurgeon.org and also with the advances in scholarship at The Spurgeon Library of Midwestern Baptist Theological Seminary, younger and older generations face exciting new opportunities to stand together as witnesses to the world in celebration of what God has accomplished in history. Who knows? Perhaps it was for this reason that the sermons were lost in the nineteenth century and found in the twenty-first.

In 1860, an article entitled "Mr. Spurgeon and the American Slaveholders" offered the following words: "Southern Baptists will not, hereafter, when they

---

31 Christian George, "Raising Spurgeon from the Dead," Desiring God, December 5, 2015; accessed May 18, 2016. http://www.desiringgod.com/articles/raising-spurgeon-from-the-dead.
32 See "God's Grace Given to Us" (Sermon 14).

visit London, desire to commune with this prodigy of the nineteenth century. We venture the prophecy that his books in [the] future will not crowd the shelves of our Southern book merchants. They will not; they should not."[33] In 1889, Spurgeon uttered a prophecy of his own: "For my part, I am quite willing to be eaten of dogs for the next fifty years; but the more distant future shall vindicate me."[34]

The more distant future *did* vindicate Spurgeon. His sermons *do* crowd the shelves of Southern bookstores. As Carl F. H. Henry rightly noted, Spurgeon has become "one of evangelical Christianity's immortals."[35] Throughout Alabama, Virginia, and the United States of America, the books of "the notorious English abolitionist" still burn—casting light and life in a dark and dying world.

After the Emancipation Proclamation of 1863, Spurgeon's reputation improved among Southern Baptists. Many of their churches were named after Spurgeon's Metropolitan Tabernacle, like Mark Dever's Capitol Hill Baptist Church in Washington, DC, which originally was called "Metropolitan Baptist Church."[36] Southern Baptists like John A. Broadus, founder of The Southern Baptist Seminary in Louisville, Kentucky, flocked to Elephant & Castle to hear Spurgeon preach. After his 1891 visit, Broadus said, "The whole thing—house, congregation, order, worship, preaching, was as nearly up to my ideal as I ever expect to see in this life."[37] In June 1884, the faculty of that seminary penned a collective letter of commendation to Spurgeon:

> We thank God for all that he made you and has by his grace enabled you to become and achieve. We rejoice in your great and wonderful work as preacher and pastor, and through your Orphanage and your Pastor's [*sic*] College; as also your numerous writings, so sparkling with genius, so filled with the spirit of the gospel . . . . And now, honored brother, we invoke upon you the continued blessings of our covenant God. May your life and health be long spared, if it be his will; may Providence still smile on your varied work, and the Holy Spirit richly bless your spoken and written messages to mankind.[38]

---

33 *The Christian Index*, repr. in "Mr. Spurgeon and the American Slaveholders," *The South Australian Advertiser* (June 23, 1860).

34 "The Preacher's Power, and the Conditions of Obtaining It" (*ST*, August 1889), 420.

35 Carl. F. H. Henry, quoted in Lewis Drummond, *Spurgeon: Prince of Preachers* (3rd ed.; Grand Rapids, MI: Kregel, 1992), 11.

36 See Timothy George, "Puritans on the Potomac," *First Things*, May 2, 2016; accessed May 18, 2016.

37 A. T. Robertson, *Life and Letters of John Albert Broadus* (Philadelphia: American Baptist Publication Society, 1910), 243.

38 Ibid., 342.

In 1892, B. H. Carroll, founder of Southwestern Baptist Theological Seminary in Fort Worth, Texas, reflected on Spurgeon's enduring legacy: "The fire has tried his work. It abides unconsumed." He added, "When Bonaparte died, Phillips said: 'He is fallen.' When Spurgeon died, the world said: 'He is risen.'"[39] The notable theologian Augustus Hopkins Strong had such admiration for Spurgeon that, on June 17, 1887, he brought John D. Rockefeller to London to meet him. After two hours of fellowship, the two Americans concluded that "the secret of Mr. Spurgeon's success was his piety and his faith. Above all else, he seemed to be a man of prayer."[40]

In 1934, George W. Truett, pastor of First Baptist Church, Dallas, Texas, was the only speaker invited to deliver a fifty-five minute address at the Royal Albert Hall in London for the Centenary of Spurgeon's birth.[41] Truett's successor at First Baptist Dallas, W. A. Criswell, once claimed that Spurgeon was "the greatest preacher who has ever lived." He added, "When I get to Heaven, after I see the Saviour and my own dear family, I want to see Charles Haddon Spurgeon."[42] Billy Graham once applauded Spurgeon for being "a preacher who extolled Christ—everlastingly."[43]

Charles Spurgeon *has* come to America. Through the rotations of a thousand gears of grace, his early sermons have spanned a century and a sea to be read by new audiences. Like Abel, who "still speaks, even though he is dead" (Heb 11:4 NIV), Spurgeon still has something to say. "I would fling my shadow through eternal ages if I could,"[44] he once declared. And indeed, his shadow has spilled into our age. Few preachers are as frequently cited, "memed," tweeted, and quoted (or misquoted) as Spurgeon is. Future historians will be right to see the publication of his *Lost Sermons* as belonging to an extraordinary and unexpected narrative of redemption.

The publication of these sermons will reach full potential when they guide readers not just *to* Spurgeon but *through* Spurgeon to Jesus Christ. Insomuch as John the Baptist's words become our own, "[Christ] must increase, but I must decrease" (John 3:30 ESV), and insomuch as the sermons inform minds, reform hearts, and

---

39 These two quotations come from B. H. Carroll's 1892 address "The Death of Spurgeon" (J. B. Cranfill, comp., *Sermons and Life Sketch of B. H. Carroll* [Philadelphia: American Baptist Publication Society, 1895], 25, 44).

40 Crerar Douglas, ed., *Autobiography of Augustus Hopkins Strong* (Valley Forge, PA: Judson Press, 1981), 300. See also *ST*, July 1887: 369.

41 See Keith E. Durso, *Thy Will Be Done: A Biography of George W. Truett* (Macon, GA: Mercer University Press, 2009), 214. Truett had also delivered an address entitled "Spurgeon: Herald of the Everlasting Evangel" at the Marble Collegiate Church in New York City on May 8, 1934 (see "Centenary Program in Honor and Recognition of Charles Haddon Spurgeon" in The Spurgeon Library archives).

42 W. A. Criswell, quoted in *NPSP*, 1:book jacket.

43 Billy Graham, quoted in *NPSP*, 3:book jacket.

44 W. A. Fullerton, *C. H. Spurgeon: A Biography* (London: Williams and Norgate, 1920), 181.

transform lives, then the energy will be worth the expenditure, and future generations will glimpse not only Spurgeon's shadow but the *Son* that caused the shadow.[45]

B. H. Carroll once said, "The great crying want of this day in our churches is *fire*."[46] If we can share Carroll's desire for fire, then Helmut Thielicke's words will still ring true of Spurgeon: "This bush from old London still burns and shows no signs of being consumed."[47]

Christian T. George
Assistant Professor of Historical Theology
Curator of The Spurgeon Library
Midwestern Baptist Theological Seminary
Kansas City, Missouri

---

45 I have used some of the verbiage in this paragraph and in the preceding one on numerous occasions in interviews, blogs, social media, and in my interview for Stephen McCaskell's documentary on Spurgeon, *Through the Eyes of Spurgeon*; accessed May 18, 2016, www.throughtheeyesofspurgeon.com. However, I originally wrote this material for the contextual introduction of the timeline "The Man and His Times: Charles Haddon Spurgeon" that hangs on the wall in the entrance of The Spurgeon Library at Midwestern Baptist Theological Seminary in Kansas City, Missouri.

46 Cranfill, *Sermons and Life Sketch of B. H. Carroll*, 42, emphasis added.

47 Helmut Thielicke, *Encounter with Spurgeon* (trans. John W. Doberstein; Stuttgart, Germany: Quell-Verlag, 1961), 4.

ACKNOWLEDGMENTS

O ver the past seven years, I have become indebted to numerous individuals who have lent time and talent to the formation and publication of this project:

David Bebbington took an interest in this project from the beginning, and I am grateful for the encouraging way he has shepherded these sermons. Steve Holmes, my doctoral supervisor at the University of St. Andrews, has also provided timely advice and guidance over the years. Tom Wright, Ian Randall, Mark Elliot, and Ian Bradley were instrumental in sharpening my writing and honing my thoughts on Spurgeon's Christology. Timothy Larson, Brian Stanley, Mark Hopkins, Michael Haykin, and Tom Nettles widened my understanding of nineteenth-century evangelicalism in ways that directly benefited this present volume.

J. I. Packer, Chuck Colson (1931–2012), and Mark Dever have offered broad direction to my research. I am indebted to their mentorship, support, and investment in my life. To those at St. Andrews who witnessed the embryonic stage of this research, I also remain grateful: Liam Garvey, pastor at St. Andrew's Baptist Church at the time; my doctoral colleagues at the Roundel; the students I tutored at St. Mary's College; and also Lawrence Foster (1991–2010), whose winsome conversations about Spurgeon on the Eden Golf Course made my frequent excavations of its bunkers always worth the dig.

When Nigel Wright and Andy Brockbank at Spurgeon's College first contracted with me in 2010 to publish Spurgeon's sermons, I could not have envisioned the scope of this project. Nigel's timely emails over the years are among my most cherished correspondences. Peter Morden, acting principal of Spurgeon's College, is a Spurgeon scholar of the highest caliber whose friendship I value. I am also indebted to the librarian of the College for many years, Judy Powles, who aided my research in the Heritage Room Archives and, along with Mary Fugill, made arrangements for prolonged research visits.

Roger Standing, Helen Stokley, Annabel Haycraft, the board of governors, and all those who serve in the administration of Spurgeon's College have also garnished my gratitude. Their continued partnership with B&H Academic and The Spurgeon Library is accomplishing much in keeping Spurgeon's legacy alive for rising generations of scholars, pastors, and students. London-based photographer Chris Gander also deserves special acknowledgment for his indefatigable resolve in photographing every single page of Spurgeon's notebooks.

After moving from St. Andrews to teach at Oklahoma Baptist University, the project benefited from the leadership of President David Whitlock, Provost Stan Norman, and Dean Mark McClellan. My colleagues in the Herschel H. Hobbs College of Theology and Ministry and in other departments offered helpful feedback in the initial editing and organization of the sermons. I am also grateful for the research assistants who offered their time in assisting me on the original proposal: Cara Cliburn Allen, Justine Kirby Aliff, Kasey Chapman, Raliegh White, and Christina Perry.

During my last semester in Shawnee, Oklahoma, Jim Baird, vice president of B&H Academic, expressed interest in publishing these sermons. Jim's enthusiasm, commitment to Christian publishing, and courage for undertaking a one-million-word project have not escaped me. He and his capable team in Nashville stand in direct continuity with Spurgeon's original London publisher, Passmore & Alabaster, who would have published these sermons in 1857–1858 if Spurgeon had completed his editing process. Special thanks goes to Chris Thompson, Dave Schroeder, Mike Cooper, Audrey Greeson, Jade Novak, Chris Stewart, Steve Reynolds, India Harkless, Debbie Carter, Judi Hayes, Lesley Patterson-Marx, Jason Jones, Ryan Camp, Roy Roper, and Jennifer Day for shaping the project thus far. I am also grateful for Trevin Wax, Chris Martin, and Brandon Smith. I am also deeply thankful for my literary agent, Greg Johnson, a friend and fellow laborer.

A turning point in the project came in 2014 when Jason Allen, president of Midwestern Baptist Theological Seminary, hired me to teach historical theology and serve as curator of The Spurgeon Library. His allocation of resources and excitement for these sermons allowed me to undertake a publication of this scope. I am grateful for his friendship, leadership, initiative, and vision for all that God has in store for this seminary. Connie and Bill Jenkins gave generously for the construction of The Spurgeon Library, and their support has provided a platform on which this project can stand. The opportunity to curate the thousands of volumes Spurgeon owned and often annotated has added innumerable layers of unexpected value to the research. Spurgeon owned some of the books in this collection during the writing of his early sermons.

The faculty, administration, and staff of Midwestern Seminary have been instrumental in creating an environment where scholarship and collegiality excel. I am particularly grateful to Provost Jason Duesing, Deans Thor Madsen and John Mark Yeats, Vice President for Institutional Relations Charles Smith, and all those who work in the Communications Office, seminary library, and bookstore who daily embody the kind providence of God.

I have discovered a lifelong friend in Jared Wilson, director of Content Strategy and Managing Editor of "For the Church" (www.ftc.co). Jared is a wordsmith par excellence who won't shut up about grace and whose weekly conversations have sustained me through the editing of these sermons. I am grateful for Jared and the "thinklings" who join our weekly discussions and for all those associated with The Spurgeon Library. I am appreciative of Brian Albert, David Conte, and research assistants Ronni Kurtz, Adam Sanders, Tyler Sykora, and Phillip Ort, a recent but essential addition who has selflessly exceeded the call of duty and without whom I could not have pushed this present volume to deadline. I am also grateful for the team of Spurgeon Scholars who have worked in some capacity on the project: Allyson Todd, Cody Barnhart, Colton Strother, Austin Burgard, Gabriel Pech, and Jordan Wade. I am also thankful for Chad McDonald, my pastor at Lenexa Baptist Church, whose sermons rarely suffer from the absence of a poignant Spurgeon quotation.

During my research in Oxford, Cambridge, and London in November and December 2014, the following librarians offered me their expertise:

Emily Burgoyne, library assistant, The Angus Library and Archive, Regent's Park College, University of Oxford;

Yaye Tang, archives assistant, Cambridgeshire Archives and Local Studies, Shire Hall;

Josh E. Acton, Myles Greensmith, Celia Tyler, and Mary Burgess, local studies assistants with the Cambridgeshire Collection, Central Library;

Anne Taylor, head of the Map Department, and Ian Pittock, assistant librarian, Maps Room, Cambridge University Library;

Stephen Southall, Dorrie Parris, Marion Lemmon, and Anne Craig, Waterbeach Independent Lending Library;

John Matthews, archivist, St. Andrew's Street Baptist Church;

The librarians of Cherry Hinton Public Library, Bottisham Community Library Association, and Suffolk County Council Information and Library Service;

The librarians of Dr. Williams's Library and John Harvey Library, London.

I am thankful for the tremendous hospitality of Osvaldo and Kristen Padilla, and their son Philip, during this season of research in the UK.

I am also grateful for assistance provided by Taylor Rutland, Pam Cole, and Amanda Denton of the New Orleans Baptist Theological Seminary, along with Jeff Griffin, Eric Benoy, and Kyara St. Amant. Numerous individuals also contributed to this project from a distance and deserve acknowledgment: Peter Williams at Tyndale House, Cambridge; Charles Carter, Robert Smith Jr., Gerald Bray, Paul House, Vickie Gaston, and Le-Ann Little at Beeson Divinity School; and David Dockery, Thomas Kidd, Nathan Finn, David Crosby, Fred Luter, and my longtime pilgrim friend, David Riker. I am also grateful for Stephen McCaskell whose documentary *Through the Eyes of Spurgeon* (www.throughtheeyesofspurgeon.com) remains second to none, and Jeff Landon, who champions Spurgeon through www.missionalwear.com.

This project also found support in those who are historically and even biologically connected with Spurgeon. I am grateful for Darren Newman and Mary McLean, current residents of the Teversham cottage where Spurgeon preached his first sermon; Martin Ensell, pastor of Waterbeach Chapel, and his wife, Angela, for their hospitality; and also Peter Masters, senior pastor of the Metropolitan Tabernacle.

I am humbled to know Spurgeon's living descendants: David Spurgeon (great-grandson), whom I met shortly before his passing in 2015. His wife, Hilary, and their two children, Susie (along with her husband, Tim, and children, Jonah, Lily, Juliet, and Ezra) and Richard (along with his wife, Karen, and daughter, Hannah), have become family to me.

I would especially like to acknowledge my father, who first inspired me to read Spurgeon on a pilgrimage to England and who continues to model scholarship, preaching, fatherhood, and Christian hospitality at their very best. My mother is one of the best writers I know, and her encouragements along the way have allowed me to better undertake this project. Bayne and Jerry Pounds have been prayer warriors for us from the beginning and would require additional paragraphs to acknowledge all they have done. Hannah and Jerry (and Luke and Caroline) Pounds are family who have become precious friends, and I am also grateful for the friendship of Stephanie and Nic Francis (and Andrew, Ella Grace, and Caleb). I am so thankful for Jane and Jack Hunter and for Dorothy Smith, an editor extraordinaire who worked tirelessly on the sermons during the early stages of editing.

The warmest words of gratitude I reserve for my wife, Rebecca—a writer, editor, and scholar of uncanny ability. Rebecca's companionship has made this road worth walking. When I first encountered the sermons in London, Rebecca was with me.

Since then she has sacrificed greatly in donating hundreds of hours to copyediting, proofreading, researching, brainstorming, and improving every aspect of this project. Were it not for Rebecca's fearless resolve in 2013 during my illness, the *Lost Sermons* would have remained as lost today as when Spurgeon abandoned them in 1857 when his own life circumstances gridlocked the publication. To Rebecca I give full credit, not only for saving the life of this project, but also for saving the life of its editor.

When the first copy of his seven-volume commentary on the Psalms, *The Treasury of David*, was bound, Spurgeon "looked at it as fondly as he might have done at a favourite child."[1] The release of this present volume has solicited a similar sentiment in us and in many who have played roles in the stewardship of these sermons. To them, and to all those yet to join our journey, I remain a grateful bondservant.

---

1   Eric Hayden, introduction to *The Treasury of David*, by C. H. Spurgeon (London: Passmore & Alabaster ed.; Pasadena, TX: Pilgrim Publications, 1983), 1:iii.

ABBREVIATIONS

Autobiography   *C. H. Spurgeon's Autobiography. Compiled from His Diary, Letters, and Records, by His Wife, and His Private Secretary.* 4 vols. London: Passmore & Alabaster, 1899–1900. The Spurgeon Library.

Lectures   *Lectures to My Students: A Selection from Addresses Delivered to the Students of the Pastors' College, Metropolitan Tabernacle.* London: Passmore & Alabaster, 1893. The Spurgeon Library.

MTP   *The Metropolitan Tabernacle Pulpit: Sermons Preached and Revised by C. H. Spurgeon.* Vols. 7–63. Pasadena, TX: Pilgrim Publications, 1970–2006.

Notebook   *Spurgeon Sermon Outline Notebooks.* 11 vols. Heritage Room, Spurgeon's College, London. K1/5, U1.02.

NPSP   *The New Park Street Pulpit: Containing Sermons Preached and Revised by the Rev. C. H. Spurgeon, Minister of the Chapel.* 6 vols. Pasadena, TX: Pilgrim Publications, 1970–2006.

ST   *The Sword and the Trowel; A Record of Combat with Sin & Labour for the Lord.* 37 vols. London: Passmore & Alabaster, 1865–1902. The Spurgeon Library.

TD   C. H. Spurgeon, *The Treasury of David: Containing an Original Exposition of the Book of Psalms; A Collection of Illustrative Extracts from the Whole Range of Literature; A Series of Homiletical Hints Upon Almost Every Verse; And Lists of Writers Upon Each Psalm.* 7 Vols. London: Passmore & Alabaster, 1869–1885. The Spurgeon Library.

TIMELINE 1800–1910*

Entries related to Spurgeon are red. Contextual entries are black.

1800	Baptist missionary William Carey and the Serampore Trio see first convert in India.
1800	The Library of Congress is founded in Washington, DC, as a reference library for Congress.
Jan. 1, 1801	The Act of Union joins Ireland with Britain to form the United Kingdom of Great Britain and Ireland.
March 10, 1801	UK Census reveals a population of nine million in England and Wales.
1802	Factory Act 1802 limits a child's working day in a textile mill to twelve hours.
March 1802	The Treaty of Amiens brings temporary peace between Britain and France during the French Revolutionary Wars.
April 30, 1803	The United States purchases 530 million acres from France for $15 million in the Louisiana Purchase.
May 18, 1803	Britain again declares war on France.
May 14, 1804	Lewis and Clark set off from St. Louis in search of a water route connecting the Missouri and Columbia rivers.
Dec. 2, 1804	Napoleon Bonaparte crowns himself emperor in a coronation ceremony at Notre Dame Cathedral in Paris.
Nov. 20, 1806	Isaac Backus, Baptist pioneer of American religious liberty, dies.
March 1807	In the UK, William Wilberforce's campaign succeeds in passing the Slave Trade Act 1807 in the same month the US passes the Act Prohibiting Importation of Slaves.
1807	In response to British and French disrespect of US merchant ships, Thomas Jefferson puts an embargo on US exports, hoping to weaken the economies of France and Britain during the Napoleonic Wars.

July 15, 1810	John Spurgeon, Charles's father, is born in Clare, Suffolk.
1810	Sixteen-year-old Cornelius Vanderbilt begins his career by purchasing a periauger and establishing a ferry service between Staten Island and Manhattan.
Feb. 19, 1812	America's first commissioned missionaries, Ann and Adoniram Judson, sail for India and eventually Burma.
June 18, 1812	The US declares war on Britain, beginning the War of 1812.
Jan. 28, 1813	Jane Austen publishes *Pride and Prejudice*.
1813	The Baptist Union of Great Britain is founded.
1814	Francis Scott Key writes "The Star-Spangled Banner."
May 3, 1815	Eliza Jarvis, Charles's mother, is born in Belchamp Otten, Essex.
May 7, 1815	Andrew Fuller dies.
June 18, 1815	Napoleon is defeated at the Battle of Waterloo and within days is exiled to the island of Saint Helena, where he eventually dies.
Jan. 1818	Mary Shelley publishes *Frankenstein*.
Jan. 29, 1820	British King George III dies after fifty-nine years on the throne.
1821	Friedrich Schleiermacher publishes *The Christian Faith*.
Feb. 1821	Under the Adams-Onís Treaty of 1819, Spain sells Florida to the US for $5 million.
1822	Using the Rosetta Stone, French Egyptologist Jean-François Champollion deciphers Egyptian hieroglyphs and publishes his initial findings in *Lettre à M. Dacier*.
March 1830	Joseph Smith publishes the first edition of the Book of Mormon.
March 1831	Victor Hugo publishes *The Hunchback of Notre Dame*.
Dec. 1831	With twenty-two-year-old Charles Darwin as the ship's naturalist, the HMS *Beagle* sets sail for a five-year expedition to the Southern Hemisphere.
Jan. 15, 1832	Susannah Thompson, Spurgeon's future wife, is born.
1833	The Oxford Movement begins.
1833	The Slavery Abolition Act passes in the UK.

1833	The New Hampshire Baptist Confession is written.
June 9, 1834	William Carey dies in Serampore, India.
June 19, 1834	Charles Haddon Spurgeon, the eldest of seventeen children, is born in Kelvedon, Essex.
August 3, 1834	Spurgeon is baptized as an infant by his grandfather, James Spurgeon, in Stambourne.
1835	Spurgeon's parents move to Colchester while Spurgeon moves to Stambourne to live with his grandparents, discovering Puritan tomes in the attic.
1835	Charles G. Finney publishes *Lectures on Revivals*.
March 6, 1836	Davy Crockett and nearly 200 Texians are killed in the Battle of the Alamo.
March 30, 1836	Charles Dickens begins serial publication of his first fictional work, *The Pickwick Papers*.
1836	Mary and George Müller establish, in their home in London, the first of several orphanages, eventually caring for more than 10,000 orphans in five orphan houses.
1837	Oberlin College becomes the first coeducational college in the US to grant bachelor's degrees to women.
1838	Eighteen-year-old Victoria becomes queen of England.
Sept. 1839	Edgar Allan Poe publishes *The Fall of the House of Usher*.
1840	Spurgeon returns to Colchester to live with his parents.
1841	John Leland, Baptist pioneer of American religious liberty, dies.
Dec. 1843	Charles Dickens publishes *A Christmas Carol*.
1844	"This child will one day preach the gospel, and he will preach it to great multitudes." —Richard Knill, prophesying about Charles Spurgeon
June 6, 1844	Eleven friends join twenty-two-year-old George Williams to found the YMCA in London.
1845	The potato famine devastates Ireland.
May 1845	The Southern Baptist Convention is formed in Augusta, Georgia.

April 1846	Spurgeon's earliest known writing, a handmade magazine entitled *Home Juvenile Society*, is written in Colchester.
1846	George Eliot (Marian Evans) publishes *The Life of Jesus*, an English translation of *Leben Jesu* by German scholar David Friedrich Strauss.
1846	The Evangelical Alliance is formed.
Jan. 24, 1848	The California Gold Rush begins.
Feb. 1848	Karl Marx publishes *The Communist Manifesto*.
1848	Spurgeon attends All Saints' Augustine's College, Maidstone, Kent.
June 19, 1849	Spurgeon celebrates his fifteenth birthday.
August 17, 1849	Spurgeon attends Newmarket Academy as a pupil and tutor.
Likely 1849	Spurgeon sketches bird drawings in his notebook "Notes on the Vertebrate Animals Class Aries."
Sept. 10, 1849	Spurgeon delivers his first public speech at a missionary meeting.
Nov. 1849	Charles Dickens publishes *David Copperfield* in book form.
Dec. 23, 1849	Spurgeon completes the 295-page handwritten essay "Antichrist and Her Brood; or, Popery Unmasked."
Jan. 6 (or 13), 1850	Spurgeon is converted at the Primitive Methodist Artillery Street Chapel, Colchester.
1850	The US Congress passes the Fugitive Slave Act.
March 1850	Nathaniel Hawthorne publishes *The Scarlet Letter*.
April 4, 1850	Spurgeon applies for church membership at Newmarket.
April 23, 1850	English Romantic poet William Wordsworth dies at the age of eighty.
May 3, 1850	Spurgeon is baptized in the River Lark at Isleham Ferry by W. H. Cantlow.
May 5, 1850	Spurgeon's first Communion; he begins teaching Sunday school.
June 17, 1850	Spurgeon moves from Newmarket to Cambridge.
June 19, 1850	Spurgeon celebrates his sixteenth birthday.
August 1850	Spurgeon preaches his first sermon at a cottage in Teversham, near Cambridge.

Sept. 1850	Harriet Tubman leads nearly seventy slaves to freedom on the Underground Railroad.
Oct. 3, 1850	Spurgeon is received as a member of St. Andrew's Street Baptist Church, Cambridge.
1851	Irish in London now number 108,000.
Feb. 1851	Spurgeon delivers "An Essay Read February 1851: Depravity."
Feb. 9, 1851	Spurgeon begins writing his sermon Notebook 1 and preaches his fourth sermon ("Necessity of Purity for an Entrance to Heaven," Sermon 2) in Barton, near Cambridge.
Feb. 23, 1851	Spurgeon preaches "Necessity of Purity for an Entrance to Heaven" (Sermon 2) in Grantchester.
March 9, 1851	Spurgeon preaches "Condescending Love of Jesus" (Sermon 5) in Comberton.
March 30, 1851	The United Kingdom Census of 1851 reveals a UK population of 21 million.
April 13, 1851	Spurgeon preaches "Adoption" (Sermon 1) in Barton and Toft.
April 20, 1851	Spurgeon preaches "Adoption" (Sermon 1) in Cherry Hinton.
May 11, 1851	Spurgeon preaches "A Contrast" (Sermon 4) in Comberton.
May 11, 1851	Spurgeon preaches "Future Judgment" (Sermon 6) in Comberton.
May 18, 1851	Spurgeon preaches "Final Perseverance" (Sermon 8) in Barton.
May 18, 1851	Spurgeon preaches "Sinners Must Be Punished" (Sermon 9) in Barton.
May 25, 1851	Spurgeon preaches "Death, the Consequence of Sin" (Sermon 12) in Coton.
June 1851	Spurgeon attends the Great Exhibition at Hyde Park, London.
June 1, 1851	Spurgeon preaches "Salvation" (Sermon 11) in Cherry Hinton.
June 2, 1851	Spurgeon delivers "An Essay Read June 2."
June 5, 1851	Harriet Beecher Stowe begins her serial publication of *Uncle Tom's Cabin*.
June 15, 1851	Spurgeon preaches "Free Grace" (Sermon 13) in Milton.
June 19, 1851	Spurgeon celebrates his seventeenth birthday.

June 29, 1851	Spurgeon preaches "Free Grace" (Sermon 13) in Tollesbury.
July 1, 1851	Spurgeon preaches "God's Grace Given to Us" (Sermon 14) in Hythe.
July 8, 1851	Spurgeon preaches "Christ About His Father's Business" (Sermon 15) in Hythe.
July 13, 1851	Spurgeon preaches "Christian and His Salvation" (Sermon 17) in Layer Breton.
July 13, 1851	Spurgeon preaches "God's Sovereignty" (Sermon 18) in Layer Breton.
July 15, 1851	Spurgeon preaches "Adoption" (Sermon 1) in Hythe.
July 24, 1851	**The British Window Tax is repealed.**
July 27, 1851	Spurgeon preaches "Making Light of Christ" (Sermon 21) in Balsham.
August 3, 1851	Spurgeon preaches "Christian and His Salvation" (Sermon 17) in Coton.
August 3, 1851	Spurgeon preaches "Christ Is All" (Sermon 22) in Coton.
August 10, 1851	Spurgeon preaches "Faith Precious" (Sermon 23) in Barton.
August 10, 1851	Spurgeon preaches "Salvation in God Only" (Sermon 24) in Barton.
August 17, 1851	Spurgeon preaches "The Peculiar People" (Sermon 25) in Milton.
August 31, 1851	Spurgeon preaches "Christian and His Salvation" (Sermon 17) in Dunmow.
August 31, 1851	Spurgeon preaches "Paul's Renunciation" (Sermon 27) in Dunmow.
August 31, 1851	Spurgeon preaches "Heaven's Preparations" (Sermon 28) in Dunmow.
Sept. 6, 1851	Spurgeon preaches "Christian and His Salvation" (Sermon 17) in West Wratting.
Sept. 6, 1851	Spurgeon preaches "Beginning at Jerusalem" (Sermon 29) in Balsham.
Sept. 13, 1851	Spurgeon preaches "Christian and His Salvation" (Sermon 17) in Toft.
Oct. 3, 1851	Spurgeon preaches at Waterbeach Chapel for the first time.
Oct. 12, 1851	Spurgeon preaches "Christian and His Salvation" (Sermon 17) in Waterbeach.
Oct. 18, 1851	**Herman Melville publishes *Moby Dick*.**
Oct. 1851	Spurgeon becomes pastor of Waterbeach Chapel.

Oct. 19, 1851	Spurgeon preaches "Necessity of Purity for an Entrance to Heaven" (Sermon 2) in Waterbeach.
Dec. 1851	Spurgeon records his first convert, "Mr. Charles" ("The Little Fire and Great Combustion," Sermon 54).
Feb. 1852	Spurgeon misses his interview with Joseph Angus, tutor of Stepney College.
Feb. 1852	Spurgeon has a mystical experience in Midsummer Common, Cambridge.
Feb. 1852	"Mrs. Spalding" is converted ("Sinners Must Be Punished," Sermon 9).
Feb. 1852	Spurgeon begins preaching sermons from Notebook 2.
March 5, 1852	Spurgeon preaches "Christian and His Salvation" (Sermon 17) in Trumpington.
June 19, 1852	Spurgeon celebrates his eighteenth birthday.
July 5, 1852	Frederick Douglass delivers his famous speech "The Meaning of July Fourth for the Negro."
Feb. 7, 1853	Spurgeon sends a letter to Richard Knill, the man who prophesied over him when he was a child.
June 6, 1853	Waterbeach Chapel hosts a jubilee service, and Spurgeon's hymn "The One Request" is sung.
June 19, 1853	Spurgeon celebrates his nineteenth birthday.
1853	Spurgeon publishes his Waterbeach Tracts.
Oct. 1853	The Crimean War begins.
Dec. 18, 1853	Spurgeon preaches for the first time at New Park Street Chapel, Southwark, London, his 673rd sermon ("The Father of Light").
1854	Japan opens trade to the West.
March 1, 1854	Missionary Hudson Taylor arrives in China.
April 20, 1854	Spurgeon gives Susannah Thompson a copy of John Bunyan's *The Pilgrim's Progress*.
April 28, 1854	Spurgeon accepts the invitation to serve as pastor of New Park Street Chapel.
June 10, 1854	The Crystal Palace opens in its new location in Sydenham.
June 19, 1854	Spurgeon celebrates his twentieth birthday.

August 2, 1854	Spurgeon proposes to Susannah Thompson in her grandfather's garden.
1854	Cholera outbreak in London; more than 10,000 die.
August 1854	Spurgeon meets George Müller for the first time near Bristol.
Jan. 1855	Spurgeon publishes the first volume of *The New Park Street Pulpit*, later called *The Metropolitan Tabernacle Pulpit*, with subsequent volumes following until May 10, 1917, when a shortage of paper in Britain prohibits further printing.
Feb. 1855	Spurgeon preaches for the first time at Exeter Hall, the Strand, London.
April 21, 1855	Dwight L. Moody is converted to Christianity.
1855	The Earl of Shaftesbury passes a bill in Parliament legalizing Anglican clergyman to "imitate Spurgeon" by preaching outdoors.
June 19, 1855	Spurgeon celebrates his twenty-first birthday.
July 1855	Spurgeon preaches in Scotland for the first time.
July 1855	Thomas Medhurst begins studying under Spurgeon's supervision, the beginnings of the Pastors' College.
1855	David Livingstone discovers Victoria Falls.
1855	Benjamin Jowett publishes *Essays and Dissertations*.
Sept. 4, 1855	Spurgeon preaches in the open air at King Edward's Road, Hackney, to 14,000 people.
1855	Edward Bouverie Pusey publishes *The Doctrine of the Real Presence*.
Oct. 1855	Spurgeon republishes the Baptist Confession of 1689.
Nov. 1855	The "Rivulet Controversy" is sparked by the publication of Thomas Toke Lynch's *Hymns for Heart and Voice, The Rivulet*.
Jan. 8, 1856	Spurgeon marries Susannah Thompson and embarks upon a ten-day honeymoon in Paris, France.
Feb. 1856	The Crimean War ends.
June 16, 1856	The Metropolitan Tabernacle Building Committee holds its first meeting.
Sept. 20, 1856	Spurgeon's twin sons, Thomas and Charles, are born.
Oct. 19, 1856	In the Surrey Gardens Music Hall disaster, seven people are killed, twenty-eight are injured, and Spurgeon subsequently falls into a deep depression.

Nov. 23, 1856	His ministry restored, Spurgeon returns to the pulpit.
1856	Membership of the New Park Street Chapel reaches 860.
Oct. 7, 1857	Spurgeon preaches to 23,654 people at the Crystal Palace, Sydenham, his largest gathering.
1857	E. J. Silverton is accepted as the second student of the Pastors' College.
1857	Spurgeon publishes *The Saint and His Saviour*.
1858	Spurgeon visits Ireland for the first time.
1858	Renowned artist John Ruskin visits Spurgeon during his illness.
April 2, 1858	A makeshift structure collapses in Halifax, West Yorkshire, during Spurgeon's preaching; while there are no deaths, many are injured.
June 1858	Spurgeon preaches at the Epsom Race Course to 10,000 people.
1858	John L. Dagg publishes *A Treatise on Church Order*.
1859	The Southern Baptist Theological Seminary is founded.
1859	James Baldwin Brown sparks controversy with the publication of *Divine Life in Man*.
1859	Charles Darwin publishes his *Origin of Species*.
Feb. 1859	An architecture competition is held at the Newington Horse and Carriage Repository for renderings of the proposed Metropolitan Tabernacle.
July 10, 1859	Spurgeon preaches under a tree at Clapham Common to 10,000 people.
August 16, 1859	The foundation stone is laid for the Metropolitan Tabernacle.
Dec. 8, 1859	South Carolina fugitive slave John Andrew Jackson shares the platform with Spurgeon at the Metropolitan Tabernacle, and, consequently, Spurgeon's sermon sales drop in the United States.
1860	Spurgeon's worship services are now held at Exeter Hall.
1860	Florence Nightingale opens the first scientifically based training school for nurses.
1860	Spurgeon preaches in John Calvin's gown in Geneva.
1860	John William Parker's *Essays and Reviews* is published.

Feb. 1860	Spurgeon's sermons are censured and destroyed in the Southern states of the US.
June–July 1860	Spurgeon takes a tour of continental Europe.
August 2, 1860	The first meeting is held in the unfinished Metropolitan Tabernacle for the purpose of thanksgiving and fund-raising.
Nov. 6, 1860	**Abraham Lincoln is elected sixteenth president of the United States.**
March 18, 1861	The Metropolitan Tabernacle is opened, debt free, with a congregation of 1,200 people.
April 12, 1861	**The US Civil War begins.**
Oct. 1, 1861	Spurgeon delivers the lecture "On the Gorilla and the Land He Inhabits" in response to Paul B. Du Chaillu's publication of *Explorations and Adventures in Equatorial Africa*.
Dec. 6, 1861	Spurgeon delivers his lecture "The Two Wesleys."
Dec. 14, 1861	**Albert, prince consort of the United Kingdom and husband of Queen Victoria, dies.**
1861	The Pastors' College holds classes in the basement of the Metropolitan Tabernacle.
1862	**Victor Hugo publishes *Les Misérables*.**
1861–1863	David Livingstone pens in his African dairy "Very good" in regard to Spurgeon's sermon "Accidents, Not Punishments."
July 1–3, 1863	**The Battle of Gettysburg is fought.**
1863	The Pastors' College has sixty-six students; one million copies of Spurgeon's sermons are sold annually.
June 5, 1864	Spurgeon preaches his controversial "Baptismal Regeneration" sermon, which sells 300,000 copies by the end of the year and half a million copies by the end of the century.
1864	Membership of the Metropolitan Tabernacle totals 2,900.
1865	Spurgeon withdraws from the Evangelical Alliance but later rejoins.
1865	Susannah Spurgeon, age thirty-three, undergoes a cervical operation and is rendered unable to conceive additional children.
1865	Spurgeon celebrates his thirtieth birthday.

Jan. 1, 1865	Spurgeon publishes the first issue of *The Sword and the Trowel* magazine.
April 14, 1865	President Lincoln is assassinated by John Wilkes Booth at the Ford Theater in Washington, DC.
May 25, 1865	The US Civil War ends.
1865	Membership in the Metropolitan Tabernacle's Young Ladies Bible Study class totals 700.
1865	The Thirteenth Amendment to the US Constitution abolishes slavery.
July 2, 1865	Catherine and William Booth establish the Christian Mission, which is later known as the Salvation Army.
1866	Spurgeon publishes *Morning by Morning*.
July 27, 1866	A telegraph cable is stretched across the Atlantic Ocean, connecting Newfoundland to Ireland.
August 1866	Anne Hillyard, the widow of an Anglican clergyman, donates £20,000 for the development of the Stockwell Orphanage.
Nov. 1, 1866	The Metropolitan Tabernacle Colportage Association is formed for the distribution and sale of Christian literature.
March 24–April 21, 1867	Sunday services are held at the Agricultural Hall, Islington, with crowds of 20,000 in each service, during the renovation of the Metropolitan Tabernacle.
August 4, 1867	James A. Garfield, later the twentieth president of the United States, hears Spurgeon preach at the Metropolitan Tabernacle.
Oct. 1867	Spurgeon experiences his first attack of Bright's disease, an inflammation of the kidneys.
Jan. 6, 1868	James Archer Spurgeon becomes assistant pastor of the Metropolitan Tabernacle.
Feb. 1868	Gale-force winds sweep through southern England, damaging the Stockwell Orphanage.
1868	Louisa May Alcott begins publishing *Little Women* in serial form.
1868	Spurgeon publishes *Evening by Evening*.
Dec. 3, 1868	William Gladstone begins the first of four tenures as British prime minister.

1869	Spurgeon publishes the first of seven volumes of *The Treasury of David*, a commentary on the Psalms that takes twenty years to complete; Spurgeon keeps the price at eight shillings to "reach as large a number of students of the Word as I could."
1869	Harvard University changes its motto from "Veritas pro Christo et ecclesia" (truth for Christ and church) to one word, "Veritas" (truth).
May 10, 1869	The first transcontinental railroad is completed in the United States.
1869	The Spurgeon family moves into the Helensburgh House on Nightingale Lane, Clapham.
Sept. 9, 1869	Stockwell Orphanage for boys officially opens.
Nov. 1869	The Suez Canal is opened.
Dec. 1869	Spurgeon suffers from neuralgia, or smallpox.
Dec. 8, 1869	Pope Pius IX convenes the First Vatican Council in Rome, Italy.
1870	Spurgeon's sermons sell 25,000 copies per week.
1870	John A. Broadus publishes *On the Preparation and Delivery of Sermons*.
Dec. 10, 1870	*Vanity Fair* publishes a satirical caricature of Spurgeon.
1871	Spurgeon visits Mentone, France, for relief from illness.
1871	Charles Darwin publishes *The Descent of Man*.
Oct. 8, 1871	The Great Chicago Fire kills roughly 300 people and causes more than $200 million in damages.
March 1, 1872	The US Congress establishes Yellowstone, the first national park in the world.
1872	Claude Monet paints *Impression, Sunrise*, ushering in the Impressionist movement.
1872	Friedrich Nietzsche publishes *The Birth of Tragedy*.
April 1, 1873	Russian composer and pianist Sergei Rachmaninoff is born.
May 8, 1873	English philosopher John Stuart Mill dies.
Oct. 14, 1873	The foundation stone of the new Pastors' College building is laid.
Nov. 2, 1873	Queen Victoria slips undetected into a Presbyterian church in Crathie, Scotland, to take Communion, adding plausibility to the rumor that she also snuck undetected into the Royal Surrey Gardens Music Hall to hear Spurgeon preach.

1873	Spurgeon is invited by Yale University to give the Lyman Beecher Lectures on Preaching, but he refuses the invitation.
1873	**David Livingstone dies.**
1874	The Pastors' College migrates to Temple Street in south London.
April 1874	George Rogers, a Congregationalist, is selected as principal of the Pastors' College.
June 19, 1874	Spurgeon celebrates his fortieth birthday.
Sept. 21, 1874	Spurgeon's twin sons are baptized at the age of eighteen.
1875	Susannah Spurgeon inaugurates a book fund.
1875	Spurgeon publishes the first volume of *Lectures to My Students*.
1875	Thomas Johnson, a former slave from Virginia, matriculates at the Pastors' College.
1876	Spurgeon publishes *Commenting and Commentaries*.
1876	**Samuel Clemens (Mark Twain) publishes *The Adventures of Tom Sawyer*.**
Feb. 14, 1876	Alexander Graham Bell submits a patent for a method of transmitting sounds that would eventually become the telephone.
March 20, 1876	Hudson Taylor visits the Metropolitan Tabernacle for the third time.
July 1878	Spurgeon publishes *The Bible and the Newspaper*.
July 28, 1878	Spurgeon preaches to a crowd of approximately 20,000 people at Rothesay, Isle of Bute, Scotland.
1878	Spurgeon publishes *Speeches at Home and Abroad*.
1878	Ninety-four colporteurs have sold £78,276 of Christian literature and paid 926,290 visits through the Metropolitan Tabernacle Colportage Association.
1878	**Julius Wellhausen develops his Documentary Hypothesis.**
1879	The girls' wing of the Stockwell Orphanage opens.
Jan. 15, 1879	Spurgeon again visits Mentone, France.
May 20, 1879	Spurgeon completes his twenty-fifth year as pastor of the Metropolitan Tabernacle.
August 17, 1879	Mark Twain attends a service at the Metropolitan Tabernacle to hear Spurgeon preach.

Oct. 1879	A soldier in India circulates Spurgeon's weekly sermons to the men of his 73rd division; the sermons return "all black and fringed through the wear and tear."
1880	The Spurgeon family moves their residence to Westwood on Beulah Hill in Upper Norwood.
August 1880	*John Ploughman's Pictures* is published.
Jan. 10, 1881	The Spurgeons celebrate their twenty-fifth wedding anniversary.
1881	Thomas Spurgeon is accepted as pastor of Wellesley Baptist Church, which had been renamed Auckland Tabernacle, in Auckland, New Zealand.
1881	The Savoy Theatre in London becomes the first public building in the world to use electricity for lighting.
1881	J. Gresham Machen is born.
May 17, 1881	The Revised Version of the New Testament is published, with the Old Testament being released four years later.
Nov. 20, 1881	D. L. Moody preaches at the Metropolitan Tabernacle at Spurgeon's request.
Jan. 8, 1882	Prime Minister William Gladstone attends an evening service at the Metropolitan Tabernacle.
April 29, 1882	John Nelson Darby dies.
June 1882	Spurgeon publishes his *Farm Sermons*.
1883	Spurgeon's sermons are transmitted by telegraph to Boston, Chicago, Philadelphia, and St. Louis.
Jan. 1883	A man in Jamaica reads an excerpt from Spurgeon's sermon just before he is hanged, saying "it had been a great blessing to him in his terrible condition."
May 24, 1883	The Brooklyn Bridge opens as the world's longest suspension bridge.
1883	Robert Louis Stevenson publishes *Treasure Island*.
Jan. 2, 1884	Johann Oncken, pioneer Baptist missionary to Europe, dies.
March 1884	Spurgeon publishes *The Clue of the Maze*.
June 18, 1884	A Jubilee Celebration is held at the Metropolitan Tabernacle.
June 19, 1884	Spurgeon celebrates his fiftieth birthday.

1884	Lord Rosebery is the first to describe the British Empire as a "commonwealth of nations."
1885	Spurgeon publishes the last volume of *The Treasury of David*.
Jan. 29, 1886	German engineer Karl Friedrich Benz patents the Benz Patent-Motorwagen, the world's first gasoline-powered automobile.
April 1886	Spurgeon preaches at the Wesleyan Missionary Society.
May 10, 1886	Karl Barth is born in Basel, Switzerland.
June 1886	Spurgeon publishes *All of Grace*.
1886	Augustus H. Strong publishes *Systematic Theology*.
Oct. 28, 1886	President Grover Cleveland dedicates the Statue of Liberty.
June 20, 1887	Queen Victoria's two-day Golden Jubilee celebration begins.
July 1887	Augustus Hopkins Strong and John D. Rockefeller spend two hours with Spurgeon and donate funds for the Stockwell Orphanage.
August 1887	Spurgeon writes his first "Down-grade" paper in *The Sword and the Trowel*.
Sept. 15, 1887	"Lottie" Moon writes a letter from China appealing to Southern Baptist women in the US to collect a Christmas offering for international missions.
1887	B. B. Warfield is appointed as Charles Hodge Chair at Princeton Theological Seminary.
Jan. 13, 1888	A Baptist Union delegation asks Spurgeon to reconsider his withdrawal; Spurgeon proposes that the Union adopt an evangelical statement of faith.
Jan. 18, 1888	The Baptist Union Council accepts Spurgeon's withdrawal and votes to censure him.
Feb. 1888	Spurgeon pens a Declaration of Faith; it is opposed by eighty alumni of the Pastors' College.
April 1888	Spurgeon withdraws from the London Baptist Association.
May 1888	Women delegates from twelve states establish the Executive Committee of the Woman's Mission Societies, Auxiliary to the Southern Baptist Convention, with Annie Armstrong elected as the first corresponding secretary.

May 23, 1888	Spurgeon's mother, Eliza Jarvis, dies.
August 31, 1888	"Jack the Ripper" murders his first victim in London.
1889	Fifteen-year-old Oswald Chambers is converted after hearing Spurgeon preach.
June 1889	Spurgeon publishes his first volume of *Salt-Cellars*, with the second volume following in November.
Oct. 15, 1889	Spurgeon attends an All Day Missions Convention in support of young men and women missionaries departing for China.
1890	Spurgeon publishes *Around the Wicket Gate*.
May 1891	Spurgeon travels to Stambourne to visit his childhood haunts.
1891	Canadian athlete and future minister James Naismith invents the game of basketball at a YMCA college in Massachusetts.
June 7, 1891	Spurgeon preaches his last sermon at the Metropolitan Tabernacle.
1891	The Sunday School Board of the Southern Baptist Convention is founded.
Oct. 26, 1891	Spurgeon departs for Mentone, France, for the final time.
Nov. 1891	Spurgeon publishes *Memories of Stambourne*.
1891	Sigmund Freud publishes his first book, *On Aphasia*.
Jan. 1, 1892	Ellis Island opens as a reception station for immigrants to the US.
Jan. 8, 1892	Spurgeon poses in Mentone, France, for his last photograph.
1892	The Pastors' College has trained 900 students who have baptized more than 100,000 people since 1865.
Jan. 31, 1892	At 11:05 PM, fifty-seven-year-old Spurgeon falls into a coma at the Hotel Beau-Rivage in Mentone, France, and does not recover.
Feb. 11, 1892	Spurgeon is interred at Norwood Cemetery.
May 1, 1893	The World's Fair is held in Chicago, Illinois.
1893	Spurgeon's commentary on Matthew, *The Gospel of the Kingdom*, is completed by Susannah and published.
1895	The National Baptist Convention is formed.
April 6, 1896	The first modern Olympic Games are held in Athens, Greece.

June 20, 1897	Queen Victoria celebrates her Diamond Jubilee.
1897	George W. Truett is called as pastor of First Baptist Church, Dallas, Texas.
April 20, 1898	The Metropolitan Tabernacle burns.
1900	Orville and Wilbur Wright test their biplane glider in Kitty Hawk, North Carolina.
1900	The Boxer Rebellion begins in China.
Sept. 19, 1900	Thomas Spurgeon reopens the Metropolitan Tabernacle.
Jan. 22, 1901	Queen Victoria dies on the Isle of Wight, ending her sixty-three-year reign; her son Albert Edward becomes King Edward VII.
March 31, 1901	In fifty years, the population of the United Kingdom has nearly doubled to 38 million.
Oct. 2, 1903	Susannah Spurgeon dies.
1904	The Sunday School Board of the Southern Baptist Convention publishes its first hymnal.
1905	Albert Einstein publishes five new scientific theories, including special relativity and $E=mc^2$.
July 1905	The Baptist World Alliance is formed in London during the first meeting of the Baptist World Congress; Alexander Maclaren is elected as its first president.
1905	The Welsh Revival begins.
1908	Henry Ford introduces his Model T.
1908	B. H. Carroll forms Southwestern Baptist Theological Seminary.
1909	Spurgeon's student Thomas Johnson publishes his memoir, *Twenty-Eight Years a Slave.*
March 31, 1909	Construction begins on the RMS *Titanic* in Belfast, Northern Ireland.
1909	C. I. Scofield publishes his *Scofield Reference Bible.*
1910	D. W. Griffith directs Hollywood's first film, *In Old California.*
June 1910	The ten-day Edinburgh Missionary Conference is held.

INTRODUCTION

"LORD, SPEAK
BY ME TO SOME, TO MANY."
Charles Spurgeon

(Notebook 3, Sermon 175, 1853)

Charles Haddon Spurgeon was born into an age of upgrade and downgrade.[1] Over the course of his life, lightbulbs replaced gas lamps, engines replaced animals, and with the publications of *Essays and Reviews*, *The Life of Jesus*, and *On the Origin of Species*, nineteenth-century evangelicalism sparked as much controversy as electricity. A crisis of faith[2]—or better yet, a crisis of *doubt*[3]—walked the aisles of England's newly lit chapels. Was Jesus God? Did miracles happen? Can faith and science coexist?

By the time Queen Victoria was crowned in 1838, the world of Wesley and Whitefield was vanishing. Gear-driven gadgets and inventions of all types alleviated the discomforts previous generations had tolerated. It was the age of rubber bands and safety pins. Sewing machines could stitch an astonishing 1,000 yards of fabric each day.[4] Lawn mowers and "clod crushers" revolutionized agriculture.[5] Photography, still an industry in infancy, captured history as it happened.

1 Some of this material has been adapted from Christian T. George, "The Man and His Times: Charles Haddon Spurgeon," a contextual timeline that hangs on the wall in the entrance of The Spurgeon Library at Midwestern Baptist Theological Seminary in Kansas City, Missouri. This introduction also contains reworked material from the introduction of Christian T. George, "Jesus Christ, The 'Prince of Pilgrims': A Critical Analysis of the Ontological, Functional, and Exegetical Christologies in the Sermons, Writings, and Lectures of Charles Haddon Spurgeon (1834–1892)" (PhD thesis, University of St. Andrews, 2012), 1–9.
2 See Richard J. Helmstadter and Bernard Lightman, eds., *Victorian Faith in Crisis: Essays on Continuity and Change in Nineteenth-Century Religious Belief* (London: The MacMillan Press, 1990).
3 Timothy Larsen, *Crisis of Doubt: Honest Faith in Nineteenth-Century England* (Oxford: Oxford University Press, 2006).
4 "Sewing Machine," *The Stirling Observer* (May 2, 1850).
5 "To Farmers and Agriculturalists," *Nottingham Guardian* (September 6, 1860).

In medicine, bloodletting became widely discredited. Hypodermic syringes improved disease control. Symbolic and Boolean algebras expanded the field of mathematics. Calculation machines like Charles Babbage's "difference engine" laid the groundwork for later inventions like the modern computer. In music Beethoven and Schubert gave way to the rising talents of Wagner, Chopin, Strauss, Debussy, and Liszt. In 1846, Adolphe Sax invented a brand-new instrument that combined all the power of brass with all the complexities of a woodwind.

In the home, new appliances lessened labor-intensive duties. Dishes could be washed by cranking a lever. Meats could be refrigerated; vegetables, canned. In 1851, it took only one minute to chill a bottle of water in the "cooling funnel."[6] The population was eating better and living longer. The life expectancy of William Carey's generation was thirty-four years. For Andrew Fuller's, that number rose by four. Spurgeon was promised forty years when he was born in 1834 (he outlived his life expectancy by seventeen years).[7] By the end of the nineteenth century, a newborn baby could hope for fifty long years of life.

London was due for a makeover. Public executions, once a social pastime, had fallen out of fashion. The decapitated grimaces of traitors and criminals, displayed in previous generations, no longer greeted visitors. Founded in AD 43, the Roman fort of Londinium overtook Peking (now Beijing) in the 1820s to become the largest and most powerful city in the world,[8] an accomplishment surpassed only by New York City a full century later.[9] Spurgeon's claim in 1871 that London was a "three-million city"[10] proved accurate with 3.2 million in London County and 3.8 million in greater London.[11] By the end of Spurgeon's life, an urban superpower had emerged, adding new meaning to William Cowper's famous line "God made the country, and man made the town."[12]

But forging a nineteenth-century metropolis with an eighteenth-century infrastructure would not be easy. Sustainability became the question of the day,

6 "A Modern Luxury Always at Hand," *Bell's Life in London and Sporting Chronicle* (July 27, 1851).
7 Max Roser, "Life Expectancy," *OurWorldInData.org*, 2016, accessed May 18, 2016, www.ourworldindata.org/life-expectancy.
8 David Satterthwaite, "The Transition to a Predominantly Urban World and Its Underpinnings" in Human Settlements Discussion Paper Series: Theme: Urban Change—4 (International Institute for Environment and Development, 2007), 9.
9 "Growth of the World's Urban and Rural Population: 1920–2000" (Department of Economic and Social Affairs, Population Studies 44, United Nations, 1969), 36.
10 *MTP* 17:179.
11 P. J. Waller, *Town, City, and Nation: England 1850–1914* (Oxford: Oxford University Press, 1983), 25.
12 Jennifer Speake and John Simpson, eds., *The Oxford Dictionary of Proverbs* (6th ed.; Oxford: Oxford University Press, 2015), 129.

one technology was sure to answer. Gardens replaced marshy mews and greens. Public squares were paved and historic monuments erected. In Trafalgar Square, four bronze lions were tasked with guarding Horatio Nelson's towering statue. Even cemeteries like "Bone Hill" (later named Bunhill Fields) were landscaped and memorialized. All three of Spurgeon's pastoral predecessors were buried there—John Gill, John Rippon, and Benjamin Keach. He likely visited their tombs on May 21, 1860, before giving an address at the unveiling of John Bunyan's refurbished tomb.

London's pilgrimage to urbanization witnessed some sectors progressing more slowly than others. Even up until the mid-nineteenth century, human excrement was still deposited in "dry closets" (essentially buckets) that were emptied beneath the floorboards of houses. "Wet closets" improved sanitation, but their pipes concluded in cesspools instead of sewers. With the Nuisance Removal and Contagious Diseases Act in 1848 and additional legislation, Londoners were encouraged to rid their houses of "nuisance." As a result, the River Thames—once blue and brimming with salmon—became an open sewer. During Spurgeon's first year in London, a cholera outbreak killed 10,000 people. The pandemic, originally thought to be the result of airborne disease, actually spread through contaminated water and devastated Spurgeon's congregation. He recounted: "All day, and sometimes all night long, I went about from house to house, and saw men and women dying, and, oh, how glad they were to see my face. When many were afraid to enter their houses lest they should catch the deadly disease, we who had no fear about such things found ourselves most gladly listened to when we spoke of Christ and of things Divine."[13]

Biographers have yet to realize fully how Spurgeon survived the pandemic. Instead of drinking from the 60 million gallons of river water pumped into neighborhoods surrounding his church, Spurgeon's water came from deep wells tapped by the Kent Company near Greenwich—the only unpolluted source in Southwark.[14] When cholera struck again in 1866, Spurgeon stated: "It seems to me that this disease is to a great extent in our own hands, and that if all men would take scrupulous care as to cleanliness, and if better dwellings were provided for the poor, and if overcrowding were effectually prevented, and if the water supply could be larger, and other sanitary improvements could be carried out, the disease, most probably, would not occur."[15]

---

13 *Autobiography* 1:371.

14 Noel A. Humphreys, ed., *Vital Statistics: A Memorial Volume of Selections from the Reports and Writings of William Farr* (London: The Sanitary Institute of Great Britain, 1885), 361. See also *Annual Summary of Births, Deaths, and Causes of Death in London, and Other Large Cities* (London: George E. Eyre and William Spottiswoode, 1871), xxxii–xxxiv.

15 *MTP* 12:445.

The Thames that once "glideth at his own sweet will,"[16] as William Wordsworth wrote in 1802, had, in Spurgeon's day, soured. In 1858, exactly one century after Robert Binnell called its water "exceeding wholsome [*sic*],"[17] the satirical paper *Punch* depicted a skeleton rowing down the river in search of life to steal.[18] Spurgeon painted a similar picture in his 1866 sermon "Fields White for Harvest": "You may look upon this great city as the harvest-field, and every week the bills of mortality tell us how steadily and how surely the scythe of death moves to and fro, and how a lane is made through our population, and those who were once living men are taken like sheaves to the garner, taken to the graveyard and laid aside. You cannot stop their dying."[19]

The newly installed sewage system of 1870 could not have come soon enough. The welcomed addition unburdened the metropolis of her odoriferous reputation and assured the population that sweltering summers like the "Great Stink" of 1858[20] would never happen again.

The currents of language were also shifting. In rural and religious communities where the King James Bible and Puritan literature prevailed, archaic pronouns could still be heard. But in nineteenth-century cities, "thy" had become "your," "thine" had become "yours," and "thou" (the informal of "you") had, for the most part, abandoned the vocabulary. Joseph Worcester updated Samuel Johnson's groundbreaking dictionary,[21] and by the end of the century, a cluster of colorful idioms had been grafted into the vernacular.

If a Victorian desired to ride in a three-horsed carriage, a "unicorn carman"[22] was summoned. One might fancy a glass of "balloon-juice" (a carbonated beverage)[23] or "belly-washer" (lemonade).[24] Instead of saying "Excuse me," a Victorian might

16 William Wordsworth, "Composed upon Westminster Bridge, September 3, 1802" in *The Collected Poetry of William Wordsworth: With an Introduction and Biography*, The Wordsworth Poetry Library (Ware, Hertfordshire: Wordsworth Editions, Ltd., 1994), 269.

17 Robert Binnell, *A Description of the River Thames, &c. with the City of London's Jurisdiction and Conservacy* (London: T. Longman, 1758), 4.

18 "The 'Silent Highway'—Man," *Punch* (July 10, 1858).

19 *MTP* 12:466.

20 See Stephen Halliday, *The Great Stink of London: Sir Joseph Bazalgette and the Cleaning of the Victorian Metropolis* (new ed.; Gloucestershire: The History Press, 2001).

21 Samuel Johnson's *Dictionary* is cited throughout Spurgeon's early sermons given its prominence before Worcester's updated dictionary. See Abbreviations and also Henry Hitchings, *Defining the World: The Extraordinary Story of Dr. Johnson's Dictionary* (New York: Picador, 2005).

22 J. Redding Ware, *Passing English of the Victorian Era* (London: George Routledge & Sons, Limited, n.d., likely 1909), 255.

23 Ibid., 17.

24 Ibid., 25.

mumble, "Mind the grease."[25] A well-dressed lady was said to be "afternoonified."[26] If a woman was too talkative, she was a "church-bell."[27] Poor breeding could produce a "half-hour gentleman"[28] or a "broad faker" (a dubious card player).[29] A mediocre carpenter was a "wood-spoiler";[30] a policeman, a "mutton shunter."[31] If an actor forgot his lines, the audience might say he is a "Captain Macfluffer."[32] To thrash about was to "batty-fang,"[33] and too much batty-fanging could produce "enthuzimuzzy."[34] A Victorian might "chuck a dummy" (faint),[35] "give beans" (chastise),[36] or "face the music" (accept a challenge).[37] In courtship, no proper gentlemen would "tip the velvet" (kiss)[38] with his "sauce box" (mouth)[39] before he could "hang up the ladle" and marry.[40]

Another word—"progress"—became the quintessential Victorian virtue. One year before Spurgeon was born, the Slavery Abolition Act passed in the UK. The first prepaid postage stamp, the "Penny Black," entered circulation when Spurgeon was five; the word "dinosaur" was coined around his eighth birthday. At eleven, Spurgeon could walk on pavement instead of cobblestone, and as a teenager he might have even flushed the first public toilet at the Great Exhibition of 1851, which he attended in June of that year.[41]

Two years after Spurgeon "hung up the ladle," Victoria telegraphed US President James Buchanan via a copper cable that stretched from Ireland to Newfoundland. Spurgeon was twenty-eight when the world's first subway wormholed its way beneath the streets of London. He could place a telephone call by age forty-two, read by an incandescent lightbulb by forty-three, and by

25 Ibid., 176.
26 Ibid., 3.
27 Ibid., 77.
28 Ibid., 149.
29 Ibid., 49.
30 Ibid., 268.
31 Ibid., 179.
32 Ibid., 63.
33 Ibid., 21.
34 Ibid., 124.
35 Ibid., 75.
36 Ibid., 22.
37 Ibid., 126.
38 Ibid., 246.
39 Ibid., 215.
40 Ibid., 150.
41 For Charles's visit to the Great Exhibition of 1851, see the first sermon he preached upon his return, "Making Light of Christ" (Sermon 21).

1885, he could ride the new "safety bicycle" instead of the high-wheeled "penny farthing"—a daunting challenge for the man who stood only five feet and five inches tall.[42] The advances of the age astonished him. When Spurgeon heard Thomas Edison's voice emerge from the tubes of the phonograph in 1888, the pastor "felt lost in the mystery."[43]

There is, of course, a temptation to overromanticize the Romantic Era—to view it through rose-colored glasses and ignore the dark smog that settled over the century. The Industrial Revolution promised exciting possibilities, but poorer populations absorbed its cost. Demand for labor widened class divisions. Social, economic, and administrative challenges went unsolved. Child labor, overpopulation, slum life, and crime were still very much part of the Victorian experience.

Three years into Spurgeon's pastorate in London, there were 8,600 known prostitutes, or "fallen" women, living in his city.[44] England's brilliant inventions needed hardworking hands to manufacture them. By the ages of three and four, children often labored alongside their parents in textile factories, mills, and coal mines.[45] Cleaning London's narrow flues and chimneys required small bodies. Cancers, ulcers, and respiratory illnesses shortened the lives of "sweeps." According to a prison report from 1837, a "ragged, barefoot" chimney sweep was incarcerated for committing a misdemeanor. When forced to take a bath, the sixteen-year-old was "delighted." When offered socks and shoes, he was filled with "most amazement." "Am I really to wear this?" he enquired. When escorted to his cell, the teenager's "joy reached its height" when he saw the bed and realized he would sleep the night in comfort.[46]

---

42 According to Mr. Fulton, editor of *The Baltimore American* who traveled to London to visit New Park Street Chapel, Spurgeon was "about five feet five inches high, rather stout, with a round fair smooth, full face, and low forehead" ("The Rev. Mr. Spurgeon. Described by an American Editor," *The Times-Picayune* [July 31, 1859]). Spurgeon inherited his height from his mother, Eliza, not his father, John, who stood almost six feet tall (Henry Davenport Northrop, *Life and Works of Rev. Charles H. Spurgeon: Being a Graphic Account of the Greatest Preacher of Modern Times* [n.p.: Memorial Publishing Co., 1892], 21, 22).

43 *MTP* 34:532. Given his description of Edison's "childish ditty," Spurgeon likely listened to Edison's 1877 wax cylinder recording of "Mary Had a Little Lamb" (Thomas A. Edison, "Mary Had a Little Lamb" [West Orange, NJ: August 12, 1927, Golden Jubilee Ceremony, originally recorded in 1877]). To listen to Edison's recording, visit www.archive.org/details/EDIS-SCD-02; accessed May 18, 2016.

44 E. M. Sigsworth and T. J. Wyke, "A Study of Victorian Prostitution and Venereal Disease," in *Suffer and Be Still: Women in the Victorian Age*, Routledge Revivals (ed. Martha Vicinus; Methuen and Co., 1972; repr., New York: Routledge, 2013), 79. See also Judith R. Walkowitz, *Prostitution and Victorian Society: Women, Class, and the State* (Cambridge: Cambridge University Press, 1980).

45 Edward Royle, *Modern Britain: A Social History 1750–1997* (3rd ed.; London: Bloomsbury Academic, 2012), 111. See also John Rule, *The Labouring Classes in Early Industrial England, 1750–1850* (London: Longman Group Limited, 1986), 147.

46 Benita Cullingford, *British Chimney Sweeps: Five Centuries of Chimney Sweeping* (Chicago: New Amsterdam Books, 2000), 93.

Charles Dickens aptly described the life many Victorians were forced to live in his 1854 publication *Hard Times*. Congested neighborhoods struggled to cope with expanding populations, especially when Irish immigrants fled the famines caused by *phytophthora infestans*—a water-born fungus that decimated Ireland's potato crop.[47] Economic disparity and systemic poverty prevailed throughout the nineteenth century.

However, even in the midst of London's growing pains—especially in the decades between the hungry 1840s and the Great Depression of 1873[48]—there was a real sense that life was improving. The opening lines of Dickens's 1859 novel *A Tale of Two Cities*, though written about the French Revolution, might also describe Spurgeon's London: "It was the best of times, it was the worst of times."[49] England was not yet Edwardian, but nor was she Georgian. A new day had dawned for the empire on which the sun never set.

---

47 Susan Campbell Bartoletti, *Black Potatoes: The Story of the Great Irish Famine, 1845–1850* (Boston: Houghton Mifflin Co., 2001), 36.

48 See Geoffrey Best, *Mid-Victorian Britain: 1851–75* (London: Fontana Press, 1988), 19.

49 Dickens's novel was published in parts. This quote is found in "A Tale of Two Cities: In Three Books. Book the First. Recalled to Life. Chapter 1. The Period," *All the Year Round, A Weekly Journal Conducted by Charles Dickens* (April 30, 1859), 1.

A MAN *of* HIS TIME

Three men named Charles ascended to prominence in the nineteenth century—Charles Dickens, Charles Darwin, and Charles Spurgeon. Each popularized his profession, and although they likely never met,[1] they became paragons of Victorian literature, science, and preaching. A motley "unicorn carman" had been harnessed, and together they would tug the century into an age of optimism and skepticism.

Spurgeon was twenty-one years old when his first biography was written.[2] By the end of 1857, both sides of the Atlantic knew his name.[3] By the end of the decade,

---

1   For Spurgeon's citation of Dickens, see C. H. Spurgeon, *The Soul-Winner; or, How to Lead Sinners to the Saviour* (New York: Fleming H. Revell, 1895), 98. For Dickens's citation of Spurgeon, see Charles Dickens and Wilkie Collins, *The Lazy Tour of Two Idle Apprentices; No Thoroughfare; The Perils of Certain English Prisoners* [London: Chapman and Hall, 1890], 7, 22, and 92). Spurgeon owned nearly twenty novels by Dickens in his personal library, including *Christmas Stories, Little Dorrit, Great Expectations, Bleak House,* and *The Adventures of Oliver Twist.* The light pencil markings in *Sketches by Boz* might have belonged to Spurgeon (see "Black Sheep! by the Author of 'Land at Last,' 'Kissing the Rod,' &c., &c., Book III, Chapter III, On the Balcony," *All the Year Round, a Weekly Journal Conducted by Charles Dickens* [December 29, 1866, The Spurgeon Library], 1–4).

2   See Magoon (ed.), *'The Modern Whitfield,'* v–xxxvi.

3   "[Spurgeon] stands in a lofty pulpit, and already has a nation for his audience!" ("Spurgeon, by Theodore L. Cuyler," *Kalamazoo Gazette,* [November 13, 1857]).

he had become the most popular preacher in the world.[4] Spurgeon's baritone voice was described as "clear and ringing as a bell"[5] and could reach audiences of 3,000 or 23,000.[6] He was compared to George Whitefield,[7] Henry Ward Beecher,[8] and John Albert Broadus.[9] An American schoolboy once assumed Spurgeon was the prime minister of England.[10]

Spurgeon's popularity in the pulpit was matched by his productivity in the press. His Sunday morning sermons were published in *The New Park Street Pulpit* and *The Metropolitan Tabernacle Pulpit* and eventually totaled sixty-three volumes.[11] In 1917, a shortage of paper caused by World War I prevented the further publication of his weekday sermons. Spurgeon also published a monthly magazine, approximately 140 books, and his magnum opus, a commentary on the Psalms entitled *The Treasury of*

4 This claim was reported by numerous newspapers, including "The Beginning of the World," *The South-Western* (June 15, 1859). A newspaper in Wales claimed Spurgeon was "the most popular preacher of the present generation" ("The Rev. C. H. Spurgeon's First Visit to Wales," *The Cardiff Times and Newport and South Wales Advertiser* [July 23, 1859]). According to the *Louisville Daily Courier*, Spurgeon had "been heard by more people in the last few years than any other living preacher" (*Louisville Daily Courier* [May 15, 1858]).

5 *Eclectic Review* (Vol. XII—New Series, London: Jackson, Walford, & Hodder; Edinburgh: W. Oliphant and Son; Aberdeen: G. and R. King; Glasgow: G. Gallie; and Manchester: Bremner, January–June, 1867), 359. *The Liverpool Daily Post* claimed "one of his chief qualifications was a voice of bell-like clearness and wonderful resonancy" ("Mr. Spurgeon," [September 6, 1870]).

6 On October 7, 1857, Queen Victoria sanctioned a national day of prayer in which Spurgeon addressed an audience of 23,654 people at the Crystal Palace. See footnotes in "Making Light of Christ" (Sermon 21) and in "The Peace of God" (Sermon 60). See also Arthur Christopher Benson and Viscount Esher, eds., *The Letters of Queen Victoria: A Selection from Her Majesty's Correspondence Between the Years 1837 and 1861, Published by Authority of His Majesty the King* (London: John Murray, 1908; repr., Teddington, UK: The Echo Library, 2010), 3:227.

7 E. L. Magoon included Spurgeon's response: "I have been puffed off as being a Whitfield, the greatest preacher of the age, which certainly I am not, and never professed to be" [Magoon (ed.) 'The Modern Whitfield,' xxvi]. See also Spurgeon's use of Whitefield in his sermon "What Think Ye of Christ?" (Sermon 71).

8 "Compared with Mr. Beecher, Mr. Spurgeon is more religious, more spiritual, less profound, less of the philosopher, but more of the saint. Beecher is like Shakespeare, or any other great social philosopher, while Spurgeon is like John Bunyan. You may go away from Beecher impressed with the greatness of the man; you go away from Spurgeon, impressed with the searching greatness of the Gospel" (W. W. Barr, ed., *The Evangelical Repository and United Presbyterian Worker* [First Series, Vol. LI.—Fourth Series, Vol. I, Philadelphia, PA: Young and Ferguson, 1874], 301). See also "An American View of Spurgeon," *The Boston Recorder* (September 2, 1858) and "The Rev. C. H. Spurgeon," *The Essex Standard* (April 18, 1855).

9 "Broadus was more like Spurgeon and [Alexander] Maclaren than any of the others. He lacked Spurgeon's intensity of experience in a continued pastorate, but he surpassed Spurgeon in Biblical learning and general culture" (A. T. Robinson, *The Minister and His Greek New Testament* [Eugene, OR: Wipf & Stock, 2011], 139).

10 Rev. O. P. Gifford, pastor of Warren Avenue Baptist Church in Boston, Massachusetts, quoted in C. H. Spurgeon, *Mr. Spurgeon's Jubilee: Report of the Proceedings at the Metropolitan Tabernacle on Wednesday and Thursday Evenings, June 18th and 19th 1884* (London: Passmore & Alabaster, n.d.), 34.

11 Over the course of Spurgeon's ministry, his Sunday morning sermons were edited and published. After his death in January 1892, Joseph Passmore and James Alabaster continued the process of revising and publishing the sermons Spurgeon had preached on Sunday evenings and throughout the week. An additional forty-five sermons taken from *The Baptist Messenger* were published in 2009 (see Terence Peter Crosby, *C. H. Spurgeon's Sermons Beyond Volume 63, An Authentic Supplement to The Metropolitan Tabernacle Pulpit* [Day One Publications, 2009]).

David that took twenty years to complete. The sum of Spurgeon's published words exceeded that of the famed 1875–89 ninth edition of the *Encyclopædia Britannica.*[12]

By 1857, Spurgeon's sermons had doubled in sales.[13] American tradeshows were selling a thousand copies of his books per minute.[14] Copycats soon discovered that by using Spurgeon's name they could generate revenue. An Irish gentleman who "passed himself off as Spurgeon"[15] received royal treatment at a hotel. A lecturing con artist in Ohio claimed to be "E. H. Spurgeon," the brother of Charles. When the audience confronted him, the gentleman "abruptly scooted" into anonymity.[16]

Even the Anglicans envied his success. By the mid-nineteenth century, it had become illegal (though rarely enforced) for established churches to conduct services in nonreligious spaces to crowds totaling more than twenty persons. In 1855, the Earl of Shaftesbury muscled the Religious Worship Bill[17] through Parliament, enabling clergymen to "imitate Spurgeon."[18] Some tried but discovered that no one could generate the crowds the newfangled Baptist on New Park Street could marshal. Even the most spacious venues in the world's largest city—the Surrey Garden Music Hall, Exeter Hall, and the Crystal Palace—could not adequately accommodate his ever-expanding audiences. In a letter to his brother, Spurgeon wrote, "I believe I could secure a crowded audience at dead of night in a deep snow."[19]

By 1858, Americans returning from London faced two questions: "Did you see the queen?" and "Did you hear Spurgeon?"[20] Victoria herself likely attended a sermon disguised in pedestrian garb, a behavior not uncommon to the queen.[21]

12 Eric W. Hayden, "Did You Know?" *Christian History* Issue 29. 2. In his *Christian History* article, Hayden notes the total number of volumes in the ninth edition of the *Encyclopædia Britannica.* In actuality, the ninth edition contains twenty-four volumes with the additional index volume, not twenty-seven volumes as indicated in Hayden's research and John Piper's article "Preaching Through Adversity" (John Piper, "Preaching Through Adversity," *Founder's Journal*, 23 [Winter 1996]). For more information, see www.britannica.com/EBchecked/topic/186618/Encyclopaedia-Britannica/2107/Ninth-edition; accessed May 18, 2016.

13 *NPSP* 3:preface.

14 "Upwards of 100,000 copies of Spurgeon's sermons have been sold in the United States. On Wednesday evening, at the trade sale, when the list of Sheldon, Blakeman & Co. was reached, 20,000 copies were sold in twenty-minutes. No book ever published in this country has had so large a sale" (*Daily Confederation* [vol. 1, no. 215]).

15 "A False Spurgeon at Limerick," *Daily National Intelligencer* (August 30, 1861).

16 "Splurgin' by a Spurgeon," *Plain Dealer* (November 7, 1857), 3.

17 See Edwin Hodder, *The Life and Work of the Seventh Earl of Shaftesbury, K. G.* (London: Cassell & Company, 1887), 510–18.

18 Owen Chadwick, *The Victorian Church: An Ecclesiastical History of England* (New York: Oxford University Press, 1966), 1:525.

19 *Autobiography* 2:99.

20 A. P. Peabody, "Spurgeon," *North American Review* 86 (1858), 275.

21 *Autobiography* 4:183. On November 2, 1873, Victoria attended a Presbyterian service in a church at Crathie, Scotland. Unnoticed, she "stepped quietly among the communicants" (Chadwick, 2:320–21).

Spurgeon constantly switched hats among pastor, president, editor, author, and traveling evangelist. The once-dwindling congregation on New Park Street soon became the largest in Protestant Christendom and had to move to a larger building, the Metropolitan Tabernacle, which eventually baptized nearly 15,000 members,[22] maintained weekly attendances of 6,000 people, and, by June 1884, had spawned sixty-six parachurch ministries, including a theological college, two orphanages, a book fund, a clothing drive, a Sunday school for the blind, nursing homes, and ministries to policemen, among dozens more.[23] Much of the revenue generated by his sermon sales was funneled back into these ministries. Unlike his much wealthier Roman Catholic contemporary Henry Edward Manning, Spurgeon died with only £2,000 to his name.[24]

In many ways Spurgeon represented the ideals of his day. He was "manly,"[25] ambitious, entrepreneurial, well connected, well written, influential, and heavily involved in politics. In 1880, he single-handedly swung an election in favor of his favorite candidate.[26] One biographer described him as "not a reed to be shaken by the wind, but a wind to shake the reeds."[27] And indeed, his religious and social influence is difficult to overestimate. To borrow from one of David Bebbington's widely accepted distinctives of evangelicals, Spurgeon was deeply invested in social reform, an *activist* filled with "eagerness to be up and doing."[28] This impulse resulted in his combat against opium trading in the East, anti-Semitism in the North, economic poverty in the South, and human trafficking in the West.

Nowhere was Spurgeon's opposition to slavery more pronounced than in Thomas L. Johnson's memoir, *Twenty-Eight Years a Slave*. Johnson overheard his

---

22 The archives of the Metropolitan Tabernacle contain unpublished interview questions for those who were baptized under Spurgeon's ministry.

23 C. H. Spurgeon, *The Metropolitan Tabernacle: Its History and Work* (Pasadena, TX: Pilgrim Publications, 1990), 7.

24 "Mrs. Spurgeon has communicated to the *Baptist* the fact that the money left by Mr. Spurgeon was really about £2,000. The £10,643 represented by the probate of his will covers a life insurance policy for £1,000, with bonus additions, and the valuations of all Mr. Spurgeon's copyrights; also the furniture, library, and other effects at Westwood. These items in themselves amount to over £8,000. Mrs. Spurgeon will not continue to reside in Westwood" ("Mr. Spurgeon's Property," *The Nottingham Evening Post* [March 31, 1892]).

25 "Ministerial Elocution," *The Boston Recorder* (August 21, 1862), 133.

26 Albert R. Meredith, "The Social and Political Views of Charles Haddon Spurgeon 1834–1892" (PhD diss., Michigan State University, 1973), 66–67. See also Christian T. George, "How Would Spurgeon Vote?" (The Ethics & Religious Liberty Commission of the Southern Baptist Convention, December 17, 2015; accessed May 18, 2016, www.erlc.com/article/how-would-spurgeon-vote).

27 William Williams, *Spurgeon: Episodes and Anecdotes of His Busy Life: With Personal Reminiscences by Thomas W. Handford* (Chicago: Morrill, Higgins, 1892), 10. This phrase, attributed to John the Baptist in Matt 11:7 and Luke 7:24, was commonly used throughout Victorian literature.

28 David W. Bebbington, *Evangelicalism in Modern Britain: The Age of Spurgeon and Moody* (Leicester: InterVarsity Press, 2005), 36.

masters in Virginia talking about Spurgeon, though the preacher "did not stand very high"[29] in their estimations. After his emancipation in 1865, Johnson traveled to Denver, Colorado, where he encountered Spurgeon's pamphlet "Preachers' Prayers." Johnson wrote, "No book that I possessed at the time, apart from the Bible, gave me such assistance."[30] He then traveled to London to meet Spurgeon and enrolled as a student in the Pastors' College before becoming a missionary to Africa.

Spurgeon was not the only notable preacher in the nineteenth century. It was, after all, the era of "sermon tasting."[31] Saint Paul's Cathedral had Henry Liddon. Westminster Chapel claimed G. Campbell Morgan. City Temple boasted of Joseph Parker. Baptists like Alexander Maclaren and John Clifford also achieved notoriety but not to the international extent of Spurgeon. Had he desired it, Spurgeon could have launched a denomination and almost inadvertently did.[32]

His sermons were translated into nearly forty languages including German, Spanish, French, Japanese, and Portuguese.[33] A diaspora of documents circumnavigated the world—books, commentaries, pamphlets, and magazines. The affordable "penny pulpits" were found in the hands of fishermen in the Mediterranean, coffee farmers in Sri Lanka, sailors in San Francisco, and even Catholics on pilgrimage. In May 1884, a Chinese Christian preferred to "go without a meal than miss this spiritual food."[34] After fifty to sixty troops of the 73rd Regiment handled one of his sermons in India, they returned the manuscript "all black and fringed."[35] D. L. Moody once commented, "It is a sight in Colorado on Sunday to see the miners come out of the bowels of the hills and gather in the schoolhouses or under the trees while some old English miner stands up and reads one of Charles Spurgeon's

29 Thomas L. Johnson, *Twenty-Eight Years a Slave; or, the Story of My Life in Three Continents* (London: Christian Workers' Depot, 1909), 102.

30 Ibid., 69.

31 Robert H. Ellison, *The Victorian Pulpit: Spoken and Written Sermons in Nineteenth-Century Britain* (London: Associated University Press, 1998), 44.

32 See "Spurgeonism Again" (*ST* June 1866:281–84); "Spurgeonism," *The Nation* (June 13, 1857) 9; and "Spurgeonism," *Dundee, Perth, and Cupar Advertiser* (April 2, 1861).

33 *Autobiography* 4:291. Translations of Spurgeon's sermons include: *Die Wunder unfres Hernn und Heilandes in 52 Predigten von C. H. Spurgeon* (Hamburg: Verlagsbuchhandlung von J. B. Oncken Machfolger, 1897); *Walda Predifningar af C. H. Spurgeon, Brebifant mib Metropolitan Tabernacle i London* (Stockholm: B. Balmqmifts Förlag, 1867); and *Pulpito Metropolitano Do Revdo Carlos Haddon Spurgeon* (Spurgeon Scrapbooks, comp. Susannah Spurgeon, Heritage Room, Spurgeon's College, London).

34 *ST* May 1884:246.

35 *ST* October 1879:496.

sermons."[36] In Australia an escaped convict was converted to Christianity after reading a "blood-stained" sermon looted from the pocket of his murdered victim.[37]

Spurgeon's popularity was meteoric and expansive, and when coupled with the geographical trajectory of his teenage years, the silhouette of an ideal Victorian takes shape. With the invention of steam locomotion, industrial opportunities pulled England's population out of the farms and into the factories. By 1859, half of London's citizens under the age of twenty had been born outside the city.[38] Spurgeon's transition to London mimicked the population distribution of the day. As a nineteen-year-old, he too transitioned from the pastoral landscapes of Cambridgeshire to the factory-fogged neighborhoods of the metropolis.

The city offered Spurgeon more resources and opportunities than could the country. The global reach of his sermons would not have been possible had he remained in Waterbeach. Nor would he have met his publishers, Joseph Passmore and James Alabaster. Spurgeon never sought a transition to London, but four years after being baptized in the meandering stream of Isleham, he moored his ministry to the southern bank of the well-trafficked Thames, the waters of which opened directly into the sea.

---

36 William R. Moody, *The Life of Dwight L. Moody* (New York: Fleming H. Revell, 1900), 456.
37 Cranfill, 29.
38 Chadwick, *The Victorian Church*, 1:325.

A MAN *Behind* HIS TIME

Meanwhile the Mississippi River was producing its own author, Samuel Clemens (Mark Twain). Before becoming the celebrated American novelist, Clemens—who was not even two years Spurgeon's younger—worked as a riverboat captain navigating the often-treacherous waters of "Big Muddy." On Sunday morning, August 17, 1879, the paths of these two men intersected at the Metropolitan Tabernacle.

It was a pivotal year for the Missouri native. His book *The Adventures of Tom Sawyer* had just been published, and his mind was occupied with an upcoming novel, *A Tramp Abroad*. The European tour that had occupied eighteen months of his life had come to a close. Soon he would depart for home on Cunard's newest addition, the RMS *Gallia*. That morning, Clemens documented his experience in his diary:

> Sunday Aug 17/79. Raw & cold, & a drenching rain. Went over to the Tabernacle & heard Mr. Spurgeon. House ¾ full—say 3,000 people. 1st hour, lacking 1 minute, taken up with two prayers, two ugly hymns, & Scripture-reading. Sermon ¾ of an hour long. A fluent talk. Good sonorous voice. Topic treated in the unpleasant old fashion—man a mighty bad child, God working at him in forty ways & having a world of trouble about him. A wooden faced congregation. . . . English sacred music seems to be always the perfection of the ugly—the music to-day could not be worsted. It neither touched nor pleased. It is a slander to suppose that God could

enjoy *any* congregational singing. . . . Spurgeon was not at his best, to-day, I judge—he was probably even at his worst. It was so cold I was freezing—the pouring rain made everything gloomy—the wooden congregation was not an inspiration—the music was depressing . . . so the man *couldn't* preach well.[1]

The "two ugly hymns" Clemens referenced were written by Isaac Watts and Robert Grant (a third hymn by John Newton was also sung). Before the sermon Spurgeon read from Isaiah 57:15–21 and also chapter 58. The reading was likely punctuated with his usual extemporaneous expositions. The topic that Spurgeon "treated in the unpleasant old fashion" is summarized by the title of his sermon: "Contention Ended and Grace Reigning."[2]

Spurgeon's first point was, "Divine contention is well deserved."[3] To the "*seeking sinner*"[4] he said, "I do not care who you are, you are guilty. . . . You have committed treason against God and you are condemned already by his unquestionable justice."[5] He implored God to "bring you down to this prostrate condition if he has not done so."[6] Aiming his words at God's people, he continued: "Surrender unconditionally, be thou saint or sinner: throw down the weapons of rebellion, doff the plumes of pride, and sue out a pardon on thy bended knee. . . . Majesty is ever pitiful to misery."[7] Then he added, "Be humble because you are a nobody."[8]

Encouragements were sure to come, for "God himself finds reasons for ending the contention"[9] and "it is never his intention to destroy his own children."[10] Spurgeon's fourth point assured the congregation that God "invents and proposes another method for ending his contentions,"[11] namely the applying of mercy and grace to the plight of the sinner. Spurgeon concluded his forty-five-minute message with the exhortation:

> Oh, come, ye wanderers, and rest in Jesus. Come, ye most lost, most ruined, most hopeless, and find heaven begun in Christ. Oh, you that sit on the

---

1   Frederick Anderson, Lin Salamo, and Bernard L. Stein, eds., *Mark Twain's Notebooks & Journals (1877–1883)* (Berkeley: University of California Press, 1975), 2:338–39, italics in the original.
2   "Contention Ended and Grace Reigning" (*MTP* 25, Sermon 1490).
3   *MTP* 25:469.
4   Ibid., 25:470, italics in the original.
5   Ibid., 25:471.
6   Ibid.
7   Ibid., 25:473.
8   Ibid., 25:474.
9   Ibid., 25:475.
10 Ibid., 25:477.
11 Ibid., 25:478.

verge of perdition, who have made a covenant with death and a league with hell, whose death warrant seems to be signed, and put into your hands, so that you read it by the flames of hell whose fury you anticipate, come to Jesus and that handwriting of death shall be blotted out. The impending judgment seems even now to scorch your souls; come and find deliverance from it, for God himself invites you. Tarry no longer. May Jesus sweetly lead you to himself. Amen.[12]

Two days later a steamboat transported Clemens to Windermere Lake to meet "the great Darwin."[13] The English naturalist would have certainly sympathized with Clemens's assessment of Spurgeon. In the eyes of many modern scientists, Spurgeon's theology was unpleasant and old-fashioned. Had not science moved beyond miracles, myths, and superstitions? Could concepts like sin, judgment, hell, and eternal damnation still be held? The earth was no longer believed to be 6,000 years old. Natural selection, not *super*natural selection, determined the destiny of mankind. To many, Spurgeon's theology looked like a fossil from a bygone age, a thing best studied or pitied.

William Gladstone was not altogether wrong in calling Spurgeon the last of the Puritans,[14] though his descriptor is historically problematic. Spurgeon's theological convictions were forged not in the halls of Germany but in the fens of England. Puritanism had been baked into his boyhood ever since he first encountered the tomes in his grandfather's attic in Stambourne. While other boys occupied themselves with playful adventures, Spurgeon enjoyed the writings of John Bunyan, Richard Baxter, Thomas Manton, and John Owen.

Raised as an Independent, educated in an Anglican school, and converted in a Methodist chapel, Spurgeon was a unique amalgamation of nonconformist sentiment. After his conversion Spurgeon's mother said, "Ah, Charles! I often prayed the Lord to make you a Christian, but I never asked that you might become a Baptist." Spurgeon replied, "Ah, mother! the Lord has answered your prayer with His usual bounty, and given you exceeding abundantly above what you asked or thought."[15] When later asked by a student if there were a book that detailed the doctrine of believer's baptism,

12 Ibid., 25:480.

13 Anderson, Salamo, and Stein, *Mark Twain's Notebooks & Journals*, 2:339.

14 The term "last of the Puritans" is widely attributed to William Gladstone, though it was likely first coined by William Clarke (see William Clarke, *William Clarke: A Collection of His Writings with a Biographical Sketch* [London: Swan Sonnenschein & Co., 1908], 278). This title can be misleading since it requires a relaxation of the definition of Puritanism. Spurgeon may have been puritanical, but most scholars date the end of Puritanism to the early eighteenth century at the latest.

15 *Autobiography* 1:69.

Spurgeon replied, "Yes, there is a little book you may buy . . . the New Testament."[16] Through the prism of the Baptist tradition, Spurgeon illuminated the doctrines that had been rediscovered by the Protestant Reformers, appropriated by the English Puritans, and realized in the evangelical awakenings. The works of Matthew Henry, Charles Simeon, and John Gill were never far from reach. Spurgeon also reached deeper into history to consult the writings of Augustine of Hippo, Bernard of Clairvaux, and Madame Guyon.

Spurgeon was seven years old when Marian Evans translated into English Ludwig Feuerbach's *Das Wesen des Christentums.*[17] Her translation of David Strauss's *Das Leben Jesu* followed five years later. In Strauss's work the author argued, "It was time to substitute a new mode of considering the life of Jesus, in the place of the antiquated systems of supranaturalism and naturalism."[18] English-bred scholars like Frederick Maurice, John Colenso, Charles Gore, Benjamin Jowett, and Thomas Huxley each contributed to the dislodging and demythologizing of the core axioms of orthodox Christianity.

The outbreak of what Spurgeon deemed the "bloodless neology of modern thought"[19] left many, like Charles Babbage, scrambling to accommodate the ascendency of rationalism, skepticism, and secularization. In the same year Babbage devised the "differential engine," he also published an essay entitled *The Ninth Bridgewater Treatise* in which he attempted to "devise a novel picture of God"[20] that was compatible with the advances in science.

For Spurgeon, however, there would be no accommodation. To him modern theology was rooted in Gnosticism,[21] a separation of humanity from divinity. Spurgeon's 1888 prediction, "We shall see the monkey-god go down yet, and evolution will be ridiculed as it deserves to be,"[22] would not come true in his lifetime, at least not in mainline denominations. When he criticized the theory of evolution in a public lecture in October 1861 (accompanied on the stage by an oversized stuffed gorilla), the newspapers took to the offensive: "We are now to be entertained by Mr. Spurgeon's

16 Charles Spurgeon, *Speeches by C. H. Spurgeon: At Home and Abroad* (London: Passmore & Alabaster, 1878, The Spurgeon Library), 18.

17 Some of this material has been adapted from Christian T. George, "Downgrade: 21st-Century Lessons from 19th-Century Baptists," in *The SBC and the 21st Century: Reflection, Renewal, and Recommitment* (ed. Jason K. Allen; Nashville, B&H Academic, 2016), 127–37.

18 David Friedrich Strauss, *The Life of Jesus Critically Examined* (trans. Marian Evans; New York: Calvin Blanchard, 1860), 1:5.

19 *MTP* 55:224.

20 Anthony Hyman, *Charles Babbage: Pioneer of the Computer* (Princeton: Princeton University Press, 1982), 139. See also Charles Babbage, *The Ninth Bridgewater Treatise: A Fragment* (London: John Murray, 1837).

21 *MTP* 11:365.

22 Ibid., 34:664.

lecture on the gorilla, but, in after ages,—according to the development theory,—we shall doubtless have a gorilla lecturing on Mr. Spurgeon."[23]

Other than occasional outbursts of resistance, Spurgeon left no lasting legacy on the development of higher critical scholarship. In *Commenting and Commentaries* he evidences familiarity with some German authors, but their dismissal of doctrines like the atonement made Spurgeon "feel really ill."[24] In 1887, a controversy erupted when he removed his membership from the Baptist Union. His own brother James and many of his students at the Pastors' College rejected Spurgeon's decision. According to Susannah the controversy claimed his life.[25] In an article entitled "Another Word on the Down Grade," Spurgeon lamented: "The Atonement is scouted, the inspiration of Scripture is derided, the Holy Spirit is degraded into an influence, the punishment of sin is turned into fiction, and the resurrection into a myth. . . . Germany was made unbelieving by her preachers and England is following in her tracks."[26]

Germany had indeed done her damage. Nonconformity assumed the defensive. And the irony should not be lost that, on July 17, 1944, fifty-two years after Spurgeon died, a German V-1 rocket (*Vergeltungswaffen*, or "vengeance weapon") detonated near his tomb in West Norwood Cemetery. The blast not only left Spurgeon's coffin exposed to the elements, but it also detached the Bible cemented to the tomb and deposited it on the ground.

It can be difficult for those living in the twenty-first century to share in the bright optimism of those in the nineteenth. The lacuna separating the centuries is filled with two world wars, the Great Depression, carpet bombing, poison gas, the Cold War, communism, Vietnam, the Rwandan genocide, ISIS, and numerous other filters that darken the perspective. Somewhere between the horrors of the Holocaust and the threat of nuclear annihilation, modernity acquired a prefix: *post*. Postmodernism, or better yet, *anti*modernism, has become the attitude of the age.

But Spurgeon never knew a world at war. Most Victorians could not have imagined their inventions would produce some of the worst atrocities in history.

23 *Autobiography* 3:51.
24 *MTP* 34:178.
25 See *Autobiography* 4:255.
26 Charles Spurgeon, "Another Word on the Down Grade," *ST* (August 1887), handwritten notes from the personal collection of Dr. Jason K. Allen, Midwestern Baptist Theological Seminary, Kansas City, MO.

The Victorians were busy discovering atoms, not splitting them. Imperial Britain remained virtually unchallenged for the entirety of his ministry. Napoleon had been defeated in 1815 when Spurgeon's mother, Eliza, was born. Occasional conflicts emerged in Crimea, India, and the Middle East, but the dreaded air raids, bomb sirens, and the trench warfare that C. S. Lewis and others would come to know were dots in the distance. Winston Churchill was seventeen years old when Spurgeon died. Adolf Hitler was still in diapers.

The borders of Britain were dissolving. Steam-powered locomotion could transport the population to places previously only imagined, to the uncolonized edges of civilization. A premium on speed produced unprecedented nautical innovations. The sluggish ships John Newton had known were replaced with faster, center-wheeled paddle steamers. The invention of the screw propeller later opened a world of seagoing tourism; it no longer took a full month to cross the Atlantic Ocean. In 1873, D. L. Moody could sail from Liverpool to New York City in eight days.[27] An obsession with speed soon morphed into an obsession with size. Half a decade after Susannah Spurgeon died, construction began on a ship so large—so *Titanic*—that God himself could not sink her.

Victorians could not help but raise their gaze. In 1843, Neptune was discovered. The first piloted glider debuted a decade later. In 1889, Gustave Eiffel constructed the tallest tower of the time, a title Paris flaunted for forty-one years until New York City's Chrysler Building reached into the sky.

Through the lens of the telescope, large things became little. Through the lens of the microscope, little things became large. At both ends of existence, in the blackness of space and sea, uncharted adventures awaited. Within five years Jules Verne launched his readers *From the Earth to the Moon* before the *Nautilus* plunged them *20,000 Leagues Under the Sea*.

---

27 A. W. Williams, *The Life and Work of Dwight L. Moody: The Great Evangelist of the 19th Century: The Founder of Northfield Seminary, Mount Hermon School for Boys and the Chicago Bible Institute* (n.p., 1900), 173.

The LOST SERMONS

The nineteenth century has correctly been called an "ocean of expanding horizons."[1] Lytton Strachey challenges the Victorian scholar to "row out over that great ocean of material, and lower down into it, here and there, a little bucket, which will bring up to the light of day some characteristic specimen, from those far depths, to be examined with a careful curiosity."[2]

With the publication of this present volume, the first of twelve "buckets" containing the earliest unpublished sermons of Charles Spurgeon, and additional analysis, will be retrieved. The volumes will follow in regular installments over the next several years.[3] By the end of the expedition, a total of 400 sermons filling 1,127 pages, and also additional material, will be offered for scholarship.[4] A prequel to *The New Park Street Pulpit*, *The Lost Sermons of C. H. Spurgeon* constitutes the first critical

---

1   Owen Chadwick, *The Victorian Church: An Ecclesiastical History of England* (New York: Oxford University Press, 1966), 1:1.

2   Lytton Strachey, *Eminent Victorians: Cardinal Manning—Florence Nightingale—Dr. Arnold—General Gordon* (London: Chatto & Windus, 1918), vii.

3   The first nine volumes of *The Lost Sermons* contain the sermons Spurgeon preached from 1851 to 1854. The subsequent three volumes contain theological essays, hand-sketched illustrations, prayers, early grammars, and additional material dating to 1849.

4   In this first volume Spurgeon's sermons consist of outlines or "skeletons," as he called them. As the notebooks progress, the outlines expand in length before resulting in full manuscripted sermons in the ninth volume.

edition of any of his works and adds approximately 10 percent more material to the total sum of his sermons.

Spurgeon began writing the sermons in Notebook 1 as a sixteen-year-old itinerate preacher in Cambridgeshire approximately one year after his conversion in January 1850. He continued writing sermons throughout his pastorate at Waterbeach Chapel and concluded his ninth and final sermon notebook in 1854 as a nineteen-year-old pastor of London's New Park Street Chapel. His notebooks have remained in the archives of Spurgeon's College in London and received only passing mention.[5]

To be clear, Spurgeon's sermons were never actually "lost" to history. But they were lost to *publishing* history. Until now the only attempt at their publication was undertaken by Spurgeon himself in 1857, an attempt he abandoned for reasons Susannah articulated in his *Autobiography*:

> The first volume of Outlines must have been commenced very soon after Mr. Spurgeon began to preach, for the second written in it was only the *fourth* discourse delivered by the youthful evangelist. The text was Revelation xxi. 27, and it was preached at Barton, near Cambridge, on February 9th, 1851.[6] This fact fixes, approximately, the date of the commencement of that wonderful world-wide ministry which the Lord so long and so greatly blessed, and which He still continues most graciously to own and use. Such intense interest attaches to these early records, that the *Autobiography* would be incomplete unless it included at least a few specimens of the beloved preacher's first homiletic efforts. Mr. Spurgeon had himself intended, long ago, to publish a selection from them; in the Preface to *The New Park Street Pulpit* for 1857, he announced that he hoped shortly to issue a volume of his earliest Sermons, while Pastor at Waterbeach, but this was prevented by the pressure of his rapidly-increasing work.[7]

The initial impulse of this editor was to fulfill Spurgeon's 1857 promise to publish his sermons. However, it soon became clear that a tremendous amount of time, energy, resources, and sacrifice would be required to finish what the Victorian had started. Fresh out of doctoral work, the "rapidly increasing work" of a first-year

---

5   For a recent mention of the notebooks, see Patricia Stallings Kruppa, "Charles Haddon Spurgeon: A Preacher's Progress" (PhD diss., Columbia University, 1968), 47, and Peter J. Morden, "*Communion with Christ and His People": The Spirituality of C. H. Spurgeon*, (vol. 5, Centre for Baptist History and Heritage Studies; Oxford: Regent's Park College, 2010), 51.

6   See "Necessity of Purity for an Entrance to Heaven" (Sermon 2).

7   *Autobiography* 1:213, italics in the original.

assistant professor doldrumed the dream. But even still the work progressed in spurts of growth between academic semesters. Seven years later, after having traveled from St. Andrews, Scotland, to Shawnee, Oklahoma, and eventually to Kansas City, Missouri, the project took permanent residence in Nashville, Tennessee, with B&H Academic.[8]

This publication is best viewed as an act of stewardship, not ownership. As carriers of the collection, the editor and publisher have sought to transmit the sermons as transparently as possible—the less interference between the reader and the text, the better. However, it soon became apparent that the sermons demanded a docent, for

> the great problem of studying the past is that you and I are tethered to the present. In 21st-century America, we are separated from Spurgeon by two intimidating barriers: chronology and geography. To scale them, the historian must live in two worlds. He must live in the world he knows and he must live in the world he wants to know. . . . It is not enough to hold the Bible in one hand and a newspaper in the other. This project demands a Bible in one hand and two newspapers in the other—one from the past and one from the present.[9]

The gap separating the reader and the sermons could not be spanned responsibly by a mere transcription, though that would have been easier to produce. Cultural, political, and theological references need context. Mistakes in grammar, punctuation, and syntax require explanation. Spurgeon's erratic use of punctuation is difficult to interpret. His periods, commas, dashes, and ellipses served as little more than visual cues. At times Spurgeon scribbled his words so poorly they are difficult to decipher. Occasionally, his marginal notations leave the reader guessing as to where the author intended to insert them. Had Spurgeon published the sermons with Passmore & Alabaster, as he did with his later multivolume work *My Sermon Notes*, he certainly would have edited the collection. Pencil redactions in Notebook 1 suggest

---

8   The actual notebooks of sermons reside in the Heritage Room Archives of Spurgeon's College in London. With the exception of return visits to the College, the editor has worked with high-quality facsimiles of the originals.

9   Christian T. George, "Spurgeon's Enduring Ministry in the 21st Century: An Interview with Christian George," (October 15, 2015; accessed May 18, 2016, http://ftc.co/resource-library/blog-entries/spurgeons-enduring-ministry-in-the-21st-century).

Spurgeon may have attempted an editorial revision,[10] but his work is sparse and leaves the majority of his idiosyncrasies and textual problems untreated.

For these reasons it was decided that a critical edition, not a popular abridgement, would allow twenty-first-century readers to engage meaningfully with the material. Full-color facsimiles have also been included to allow transcriptions to be cross-examined against their original sources. Unlike Susannah, who took great liberties in transcribing the outlines she prepared for the *Autobiography*,[11] a strict fidelity to the text has been prioritized with the belief that Spurgeon's typographical errors—his misspellings, strikethroughs, and grammatical mistakes—better illuminate the mechanisms of his mind.

If twentieth-century literature failed Spurgeon anywhere, it failed to produce scholars interested in constructing three-dimensional portraits of the preacher, flaws and all.[12] Warts can be as informative as dimples. Yet in the aftermath of the Downgrade Controversy, Spurgeon's biographers (many were among his friends) sensed the need to bolster his besmirched reputation. Their apotheosis resulted in decades of hagiographic accounts that exaggerated his strengths while underplaying his weaknesses.

However, Spurgeon is not—and should not be—immune to critique. He was capable of both weakness and greatness. His dependency on the Holy Spirit is evident

---

10 For pencil redactions in Notebook 1, see the notes for "K1/5" on the first page and also the following sermons: "Adoption" (Sermon 1); "Future Judgment" (Sermon 6); "Regeneration" (Sermon 7); "Final Perseverance" (Sermon 8); "Sinners Must Be Punished" (Sermon 9); "Love Manifest in Adoption" (Sermon 16); "Christian and His Salvation" (Sermon 17); "The Plant of Renown" (Sermon 20); "Salvation in God Only" (Sermon 24); "Paul's Renunciation" (Sermon 27); "Heaven's Preparations" (Sermon 28); "The Fight" (Sermon 37b); "God's Estimation of Men" (Sermon 41); "Josiah" (Sermon 66); "The Saints' Justification and Glory" (Sermon 68); "The Men Possessed of the Devils" (Sermon 70); and "The Physician and His Patients" (Sermon 74). For a step-by-step analysis of Spurgeon's later editorial process, see the display in The Spurgeon Library, located on the campus of Midwestern Baptist Theological Seminary in Kansas City, Missouri.

11 Susannah recorded the following sermon outlines in the first volume of the *Autobiography*: "Adoption" (Sermon 1, *Autobiography* 1:214); "Necessity of Purity for an Entrance to Heaven" (Sermon 2, *Autobiography* 1:216); "Abraham Justified by Faith" (Sermon 3, *Autobiography* 1:216); "Salvation from Sin" (Sermon 33, *Autobiography* 1:229–30); "By Faith Jericho Fell" (Notebook 2, Sermon 133, *Autobiography* 1:218–19); "The Church of Antioch" (Notebook 3, Sermon 172, *Autobiography* 1:223–25); "Nowise Cast Out" (Notebook 4, Sermon 212, *Autobiography* 1:225–26); "Christ Our Surety" (Notebook 5, Sermon 243, *Autobiography* 1:277–79); "Christ Is Precious" (Notebook 6, Sermon 311, *Autobiography* 1:279–81); and "Praise Ye the Lord" (Notebook 7, Sermon 327, *Autobiography* 1:282–84). For an analysis of her transcriptions in the outlines of this volume, see "Adoption" (Sermon 1), "Necessity of Purity for an Entrance to Heaven" (Sermon 2), and "Abraham Justified by Faith" (Sermon 3).

12 Recent publications that offer a more critical analysis of Spurgeon include Morden, *Communion with Christ and His People*; Mark Hopkins, *Nonconformity's Romantic Generation: Evangelical and Liberal Theologies in Victorian England*, Studies in Evangelical History and Thought (Waynesboro, GA: Paternoster, 2004); Timothy Larson, *A People of One Book: The Bible and the Victorians* (Oxford: Oxford University Press, 2011); and Tom Nettles, *Living by Revealed Truth: The Life and Pastoral Theology of Charles Haddon Spurgeon* (Ross-shire, Scotland: Christian Focus Publications, 2013).

throughout his sermons and reveals the force of his spirituality. On the title page of Notebook 1, beneath the words "Skeletons I to LXXVII," he wrote, "And only skeletons without the Holy Ghost." The prayers Spurgeon scripted at the conclusion of his sermons are also illuminating. Some of these prayers include: "God, help me, a poor thing,"[13] "Oh Father, help thro' Jesus,"[14] "God, my Father, help me, I entreat thee,"[15] "Lord, help thy weakling,"[16] "Lord, revive both me and the people,"[17] and "Lord, revive my stupid soul!"[18] Here is a preacher in progress and regress. Some of his early habits he retained for the rest of his life; others were abandoned. Spurgeon's witticism, command of language, spiritual vitality, metaphors, illustrations, applications, and exhortations are as evident in 1851 as they are in 1891. Nevertheless, it becomes obvious to those familiar with his style that the early Spurgeon had yet to fully hone his homiletic. In fact, some of his experimental exegesis might even raise the eyebrow of the iron-sighted expositor, especially sermons like "Regeneration,"[19] which contains not even a single reference to Scripture.

More than a handful of sermons were not even original to Spurgeon. He lifted them directly from the works of John Gill, Philip Doddridge, Richard Baxter, John Bunyan, Charles Simeon, George Whitefield, Jean Claude, John Stephenson, and others.[20] Spurgeon retained this tendency after moving to London, once saying, "He who will not use the thoughts of other men's brains, proves that he has no brains of his own."[21] On another occasion Spurgeon was about to reprimand a young preacher at the Pastors' College caught preaching from Spurgeon's outline. In his book *Preaching and Preachers*, Martyn Lloyd-Jones narrated the exchange:

> "Well now," said Mr. Spurgeon, "you need not be frightened. If you are honest you will not be punished. We are all sinners, but we do want to get at the facts. You have been preaching a sermon on such and such a text?"

13 "The Tabernacle of Jacob and Mount Zion Blessed of God" (Notebook 3, Sermon 145).
14 "The Joy of Heaven" (Notebook 3, Sermon 147).
15 "Open Profession Required" (Notebook 3, Sermon 158).
16 "I Glory in Infirmities" (Notebook 3, Sermon 165).
17 "God's Visits and the Effects Thereof" (Notebook 2, Sermon 113).
18 "The Meekness of Moses" (Notebook 3, Sermon 179).
19 See "Regeneration" (Sermon 7).
20 The following sermons in Notebook 1 were not original to Spurgeon: "Adoption" (Sermon 1, John Gill); "Regeneration" (Sermon 7, John Gill); "Final Perseverance" (Sermon 8, John Gill); "Salvation" (Sermon 11, Philip Doddridge); "Making Light of Christ" (Sermon 21, Richard Baxter); "Beginning at Jerusalem" (Sermon 29, John Bunyan); "The Son's Love to Us Compared with God's Love to Him" (Sermon 38, Charles Simeon); "Regeneration, Its Causes and Effects" (Sermon 46, Charles Simeon); "What Think Ye of Christ?" (Sermon 71, George Whitefield); and "The Church and Its Boast" (Sermon 75, John Stephenson).
21 *MTP* 9:668.

"Yes sir." "And you have divided up the subjects as follows?" "Yes, sir." "And you say that you have not been preaching my sermons?" "That is so, sir." . . . "Well, are you saying, then, that it is your sermon?" "Oh no, sir," said the young man. "Well, then, whose sermon is it?" "It is a sermon of William Jay of Bath, sir" said the student. . . . The fact was that Mr. Spurgeon had also preached William Jay's sermon and had actually put it into print with other sermons of his.[22]

Some may decry plagiarism in Spurgeon's early sermons, but it should be remembered that before the mid-nineteenth century, intellectual property was far more flexible than it is today. Some Victorians doubted the idea of originality was even possible. Robert Macfarlane has noted that Samuel Johnson offered in his dictionary a third definition, "first copy," beneath the word "original"[23] to suggest that "the writer is merely a rearranger of bits and pieces: an administrator rather than a producer."[24]

Spurgeon's occasional borrowing reveals an overlooked feature in the development of his preaching, namely that he did not originate a new style; he adopted an older one and adapted it to suit his context. His appropriation of Reformation and Puritan doctrine is commonly known. But less explored are the actual machinations of that appropriation. Spurgeon's sermon structure (introduction, primary divisions and subdivisions, and final exhortation) may be largely credited to his interaction with *Essay on the Composition of a Sermon* by Jean Claude (1619–1687), pastor of the French Reformed Church at Charenton, near Paris, who emphasized that "a sermon should be like a telescope," and primary divisions are like lenses that "bring the subject of your text nearer."[25] Spurgeon's use of Claude's work in his sermon "The Treasure in Earthen Vessels" from Notebook 2[26] reveals as much about the development of his style as does "The Eloquence of Jesus" from Notebook 1, in which Spurgeon analyzes the qualities and characteristics of Jesus's own homiletic, which featured "simplicity," "seriousness," "earnestness," and "directness."[27]

---

22 Martyn Lloyd-Jones, *Preaching and Preachers* (Grand Rapids, MI: Zondervan, 1971), 294.

23 "3. First Copy; archetype; that from which any thing is transcribed or translated" (Johnson's *Dictionary*, s.v. "origin; original").

24 Robert Macfarlane, *Original Copy: Plagiarism and Originality in Nineteenth-Century Literature* (Oxford: Oxford University Press, 2007), 4.

25 Hugh Evans Hopkins, *Charles Simeon of Cambridge* (Hodder and Stoughton, 1977; repr., Eugene, OR: Wipf & Stock, 2012), 59.

26 "The Treasure in Earthen Vessels" (Notebook 2, Sermon 80).

27 "The Eloquence of Jesus" (Sermon 49).

Spurgeon's sermons did not emerge ex nihilo, nor did he merely parrot the Puritans. In a unique and innovative way, he rendered their expositions in a language that common Victorians could comprehend. In this sense Spurgeon was not a creator; he was a converter. His preaching upcycled older expressions of evangelicalism and transferred them to new audiences. In the same way that water absorbs the properties of its conduit, the traditional axioms of biblical orthodoxy were not altered by Spurgeon, only flavored. It is no small wonder that Spurgeon gained a reputation as "boy preacher of the fens."[28] His formative years were spent immersed in the sermons, commentaries, and writings of England and France's greatest divines.

The most obvious characteristic of Spurgeon's earliest sermons is the dynamic progression of page length. Notebooks 1 and 2 contain simple skeletal outlines, often no more than one or two pages in length. However, as the notebooks progress, the page count increases so that by Notebooks 8 and 9, Spurgeon displays an unusual practice for him of penning full-length manuscripts that often occupy eight to twelve pages per sermon. After accepting the pastorate of the New Park Street Chapel in London, however, Charles reverted to preaching from bare outlines, likely because of the constraints on his time.[29] In this way his earliest sermons in Notebook 1 resemble those that characterize his later ministry, while the sermons in Notebooks 2–9 are substantially longer. Spurgeon continued producing outlines for the remainder of his ministry. He once said, "Much hard labour have I spent in manipulating topics, ruminating upon points of doctrine, making skeletons out of verses, and then burying every bone of them in the catacombs of oblivion. . . . I believe that, almost any Saturday in my life, I prepare enough outlines of Sermons, if I felt at liberty to preach them, to last me for a month."[30]

The final volume of the *Lost Sermons* will bring into sharper focus the historical context of mid-nineteenth Cambridgeshire with an emphasis on the political, social, geographical, and homiletic influences that shaped Spurgeon's earliest ministry. In that volume, a deeper analysis of all 400 of Spurgeon's early sermons will also be offered with special attention given to the development of Spurgeon's soteriology, ecclesiology, eschatology, and other theological categories.

---

28 *Autobiography* 1:99.
29 See ibid., 3:293.
30 Ibid., 1:207.

SOURCES *and* METHOD

Awide range of primary and secondary sources has been consulted in addition to the eleven handwritten journals. These sources include unpublished letters,[1] original pulpit notes, redacted stenographer's notes, annotated typeset galleys,[2] newspaper clippings,[3] books Spurgeon owned and annotated housed

---

1 I have consulted letters and miscellaneous materials contained in box D/SPU 1 in the Angus Library and Archive at Regent's Park College, Oxford University, and also the three bound volumes of letters: "Original Correspondence of Charles Haddon Spurgeon" 1851–1893 (vol. 1); 1863–1868 (vol. 2); and 1887–1892 (vol. 3) at Spurgeon's College Heritage Room Archives (4G).

2 For analytical comparisons, a wide range of unpublished pulpit notes, redacted stenographer's notes, and redacted, typeset galleys have been consulted.

3 "Spurgeon's Scrapbooks, Numbered Volumes," "Spurgeon's Scrapbooks, Two Unnumbered Volumes," "Loose-Leaf Scrap Folders," and four volumes of "Maroon Bound Scrapfolders," Spurgeon's College, Heritage Room.

at The Spurgeon Library,[4] *The New Park Street Pulpit* and *The Metropolitan Tabernacle Pulpit* series, academic and popular books, maps, monographs, essays, journal articles, doctoral dissertations and master's theses, and church records.

The publications of Spurgeon's sermons usually fall into two camps: either they are presented as exact reproductions[5] or as contemporized abridgements.[6] Both treatments contain strengths and weaknesses. Exact reproductions are valuable for scholars because they constitute unedited primary sources, but they do require some familiarity with Victorianisms and archaic uses of language. Contemporized

4   The Spurgeon Library at Midwestern Baptist Theological Seminary in Kansas City, Missouri, contains helpful information and marginal annotations that benefited this project. The following history of the library is taken from a wall display: "By the time of his death in 1892, Charles Spurgeon had marshaled approximately 12,000 books in his personal library at his Westwood residence in south London. While many of the volumes were theological, his collection also contained a great number of interdisciplinary offerings, including popular literature, novels, travel guides, biographies, scientific and historical tomes, and books on hymnody. In 1904, Spurgeon's sons bestowed the bulk of their father's library upon the care of an agent who attempted to sell the collection to a British college. The attempt was unsuccessful, and in the following year the Missouri Baptist General Association expressed interest in its acquisition. Led by J. T. M. Johnson, John E. Franklin, John Priest Greene, and J. E. Cook, the Association raised $2,500 for the purchase of the library, which sold for 50 cents per volume. Under the supervision of Dr. J. W. Thirtle, Spurgeon's library was packaged in 38 cases lined with waterproof canvas, loaded onto the SS *Cuba*, and shipped across the Atlantic Ocean on December 16. After arriving in New Orleans, Louisiana, the library was transported to Kansas City, Missouri, by the Illinois Central Railroad before traveling some 20 miles to Liberty, Missouri, where it was presented as a gift from the Missouri Baptist Association to William Jewell College. For 100 years, the collection remained on display in the lower level of the Curry Library. In a blind auction on October 10, 2006, Midwestern Baptist Theological Seminary purchased the library of over 6,000 volumes, many of them heavily annotated by Spurgeon. In 2014, under the leadership of Dr. Jason K. Allen, the Seminary's fifth president, a generous donation was given for the founding of the Spurgeon Center. Renovations to transform the Seminary's former chapel were completed in July 2015, with its dedication following that October. Today, The Spurgeon Library contains the largest collection in the world of Spurgeon's personally owned works and is committed to advancing Spurgeon scholarship, promoting biblical preaching, and bringing theological higher education into the service of the church."

5   *The New Park Street Pulpit* and *The Metropolitan Tabernacle Pulpit*, printed by Pilgrim Publications, are examples of facsimile reproductions from Passmore & Alabaster. Nonfacsimile reproductions are also found in *Spurgeon's Sermon Notes: Over 250 Sermons Including Notes, Commentary and Illustrations* (Peabody, MA: Hendrickson Publishers, 1997); *Spurgeon's Sermons on the Death and Resurrection of Jesus* (Peabody, MA: Hendrickson Publishers, 2005); Kerry James Allen, ed., *Call unto Me: Twenty Selected Sermons on the Topic of Prayer from the Works of Charles Haddon Spurgeon* (Romeoville, IL: Fox River Press, 2007); The Spurgeon Collection vols. 1–7 (Belfast, Northern Ireland and Greenville, SC: Emerald House, 1998), in which the titles include *Comfort and Assurance, Evangelism, Miracles, Parables, Prayer, Psalms*, and *Revival*; and Kregel Publications' C. H. Spurgeon Sermon Series (Grand Rapids, MI) including *Spurgeon's Sermons on Christmas and Easter, Spurgeon's Sermons on Soulwinning, Spurgeon's Sermons on New Testament Women* (2 vols.), *Spurgeon's Sermons on New Testament Men* (2 vols), *Spurgeon's Sermons on the Parables of Christ, Spurgeon's Sermons on Great Prayers of the Bible, Spurgeon's Sermons on Angels*, and *Spurgeon's Sermons on the Cross of Christ*.

6   Whitaker House has published an anthology of Spurgeon's sermons that has been "edited for the modern reader" (*Charles Spurgeon, Power Over Satan* [New Kensington, PA: Whitaker House, 1997], editor's note). Their titles include *All of Grace, Faith* (previously titled *Strong Faith*), *Spurgeon on the Holy Spirit, Being God's Friend, God's Grace to You, Joy in Your Life, How to Have Real Joy* (previously titled *The Joy of the Lord*), *Spurgeon on Prayer & Spiritual Warfare, The Power in Praising God*, and *Morning by Morning*, among others. In 1981, Baker Books released the *Spurgeon Devotional Bible: Selected Passages from the Word of God with Running Commentary* (Grand Rapids, MI: Baker Books, 1981) in which "the passages omitted are almost always summarized wherever possible" (preface). An exception is found in *Letters of Charles Haddon Spurgeon: Selected with Notes by Iain H. Murray* (Edinburgh: Banner of Truth Trust, 1992) in which the editor offers commentary.

abridgements are more accessible for the popular market and generate broader readership, but they alter the verbiage to the point that Spurgeon's original wording cannot be distinguished from that of the editor. In this edition the editor has attempted to offer the reader a third presentation of Spurgeon's sermons: a critical work that can be accessed by academics and laity alike. This has been accomplished by rolling the annotations onto additional pages so the full transcription of each sermon is offered opposite its facsimile. In this way the casual reader and the scholar can both navigate the sermons, depending on their intended use of the material.

Technical adjustments and textual interpolations are kept intentionally minimal so that Spurgeon's style, idiom, and sermon structure are retained. Periods have been added in the place of dashes and other improvised punctuation devices Spurgeon used to signal pauses. When necessary, colons are inserted prior to lists. Where possible, spacing between lines has been preserved, as have pagination, word clusters, and marginal notations. One additional space has been added prior to primary divisions for clarity. Major headings have been indicated in red for readability and Scripture quotations and paraphrases immediately following headings are italicized. At the top of each transcription, sermon titles are capitalized with the exception of italicized articles and prepositions.

Archaic words are not modernized. Revisions, typographical errors, strike-throughs, and errors in punctuation and grammar are retained but explained. Orthographic contractions such as "call'd" are kept in the text. Abbreviations like "Xian" or "Xn" (Christian), "emp" (emphasis) and "inf" (inference), among others, are noted. The Puritan "s" has been modernized. Excessive dotting is explained, as well as Spurgeon's use of symbols. Ampersands have been replaced with the word "and." At times the lack of apostrophes leaves the reader guessing whether Spurgeon intended the word to be plural or possessive. In most instances the context determines its correct usage; however, alternative readings are offered where appropriate.

Spurgeon's numbering techniques are not always consistent. When absent from the text or confusing, the editor has included numbers in brackets. Each detail on the page has been deemed worthy of analysis; ink smears, splotches, fingerprints, and stains caused by the aging process of the manuscript are explained. Emphasizing devices such as underlining, italicizing, bolding, and capitalizing are indicated either in the transcription or footnotes. The hand-drawn illustrations and notations Spurgeon wrote on the title pages of Notebooks 1 and 2 are also analyzed and compared to the content of the sermons.

Original spellings of unusual words are retained but analyzed. Words possibly unfamiliar to the modern reader have been defined from the copy of Samuel Johnson's dictionary that Spurgeon owned in his personal library. In the rare instances in which

Johnson's definitions do not assist the analysis, Joseph Worcester's 1859 dictionary has been consulted.[7] Cultural references are explained using secondary literature and newspapers dating to the time when Spurgeon preached the sermon. On occasion the editor offers commentary about the development of particular doctrines, themes, or topics that reoccur throughout the sermons and occasionally directs the reader to additional literature. Dating the sermons required a triangulation of sources, including letters Spurgeon wrote to family members, autobiographical references, and dates written at the conclusion of his sermons.[8] For references to specific individuals, genealogical records have been accessed.

Of interest to the editor are the Scripture references from Spurgeon's early sermons that he preached again later in his ministry. The editor has indicated the sermons in which this occurs and offers a judgment as to whether the structural similarities between the sermons are close enough to suggest that Spurgeon might have used the early outline for his later exposition. Further scholarship is required to complete a thorough comparative analysis, but it is hoped that the inclusion of this information will expose patterns in Spurgeon's rhetoric and preaching that will assist the scholar in answering the question, How did Spurgeon's early sermons compare to his later ones?

In the introduction the editor has opted to use the name Spurgeon to refer to the preacher. However, in the sermon analysis itself, Spurgeon's first name, Charles, is preferred. At the beginning of the sermons, the title of the sermon is centered and bolded for clarity. Beneath it the Scripture reference is written, taken from the King James Bible Spurgeon owned in his personal library.[9] The sermon numbers, which Spurgeon justified either to the top right or left, have been centered. Scripture references have been added when the editor suspects Spurgeon was drawing from or indirectly alluding to doctrines, biblical characters, or other noncited instances in Scripture.

The following is a breakdown of the sermon notebooks currently housed in the Heritage Room Archives at Spurgeon's College in London:[10]

7   See "Salvation in God Only" (Sermon 24).
8   See "Christian and His Salvation" (Sermon 17).
9   Spurgeon used the King James Bible in his early sermons and also later in his ministry (see *The Illustrated Family Bible, Containing the Old and New Testaments, &c., &c., with the Self-Interpreting and Explanatory Notes, and Marginal References, of the Late Rev. John Brown, Minister of the Gospel at Haddington: to Which Is Appended, a Complete Concordance to the Old and New Testaments* [London: Fisher, Son, and Co., n.d., The Spurgeon Library]). He lionized it as the "thrice precious version, which, take it for all in all, remains the Queen of all the versions" (*MTP* 36:206).
10 The sermon notebooks are categorized as "Notebook Containing Early Sermon Skeletons, Vol. 1," (K1.5); "Notebooks with Sermon Outlines, Vols. 2–9" (U1.02). Volumes 10–12 of *The Lost Sermons* will include the following nonsermon material: "French Grammar," "Parable of the Sower," "The Talents," "Misc.," "An Essay Read February 1851: Depravity," "An Essay Read June 2, 1851," "Antichrist and Her Brood; or, Popery Unmasked," "Notes on the Vertebrate Animal Class Aries," and "Waterbeach Dream."

Notebook 1: 90 total pages

(81 pages of sermon text, 4 blank pages,[11] and 5 miscellaneous[12] pages)

Notebook 2: 140 total pages

(135 pages of sermon text, 2 blank pages, and 3 miscellaneous pages)

Notebook 3: 140 total pages

(135 pages of sermon text, 3 blank pages, and 2 miscellaneous pages)

Notebook 4: 123 total pages

(114 pages of sermon text, 7 blank pages, and 2 miscellaneous pages)

Notebook 5: 123 total pages

(115 pages of sermon text, 5 blank pages, and 3 miscellaneous pages)

Notebook 6: 128 total pages

(120 pages of sermon text, 6 blank pages, and 2 miscellaneous pages)

Notebook 7: 125 total pages

(113 pages of sermon text, 11 blank pages, and 1 miscellaneous page)

Notebook 8: 178 total pages

(167 pages of sermon text, 11 blank pages, and 0 miscellaneous pages)

Notebook 9: 164 total pages

(147 pages of sermon text, 17 blank pages, and 0 miscellaneous pages)

Total number of sermons: 400[13]

Total number of pages of sermon text: 1,127

---

11 By using the word "blank," I am referring to pages within the notebooks that do not primarily contain text. Some of these pages do contain trace amounts of information that could hold significance for the text and this is noted.

12 "Miscellaneous" pages include title pages, indices, and pages that contain concluding hymns.

13 This number also includes the following eighteen sermons that Spurgeon began writing but did not complete: "Son, Be of Good Cheer" (Notebook 4, Sermon 225); "He Filleth the Hungry with Good Things" (Notebook 4, Sermon 226); "He Will Bring Every Work into Judgment" (Notebook 4, Sermon 228); "As One Whom His Mother Comforteth" (Notebook 4, Sermon 229); "Feast for Boys and Girls" (Notebook 5, Sermon 239); "Feast for Young Believers" (Notebook 5, Sermon 240); "Job the Perfect Man" (Notebook 5, Sermon 263); "As the Rain Cometh Down and the Snow from Heaven" (Notebook 6, Sermon 291); "Oh Lord, Be Gracious unto Us" (Notebook 6, Sermon 295); "Partaking Other Men's Sins" (Notebook 7, Sermon 324); "How to Meet Evil Tidings" (Notebook 7, Sermon 325); "The Means of the Blessing" (Notebook 7, Sermon 336); "The Two Birds" (Notebook 8, Sermon 352); "Inner Court Worship" (Notebook 8, Sermon 379); "Paul's Commission" (Notebook 9, Sermon 385); "A Glad Congregation" (Notebook 9, Sermon 386); "Untitled" (Notebook 9, Sermon 388); and "Untitled" (Notebook 9, Sermon 393).

SERMON ANALYSIS: NOTEBOOK 1
(Sermons 1–77)

Throughout the seventy-seven sermons[1] contained in Notebook 1, Spurgeon incorporated a variety of literary habits. Some of these include abbreviations,[2] repetition devices,[3] numbering techniques,[4] stippling,[5]

---

1   There are actually seventy-eight sermons when counting sermons 37a and 37b.

2   Abbreviations are found in the following sermons: "Necessity of Purity for an Entrance to Heaven" (Sermon 2); "Future Judgment" (Sermon 6); "Regeneration" (Sermon 7); "Election" (Sermon 10); "Free Grace" (Sermon 13); "Christ Is All" (Sermon 22); "Salvation in God Only" (Sermon 24); "Ignorance, Its Evils" (Sermon 31); "The Son's Love to Us Compared with God's Love to Him" (Sermon 38); "Pharisees and Sadducees Reproved" (Sermon 39); "Regeneration, Its Causes and Effects" (Sermon 46); "Pleasure in the Stones of Zion" (Sermon 53); "The Affliction of Ahaz" (Sermon 57); "The Improvement of Our Talents" (Sermon 61); "Can Two Walk Together Unless They Are Agreed?" (Sermon 76); and "The Lepers" (Sermon 77).

3   Examples of repetition devices are found in the sermons "Future Judgment" (Sermon 6) and "Beginning at Jerusalem" (Sermon 29).

4   A variety of numbering techniques are found in the following sermons: "Condescending Love of Jesus" (Sermon 5); "Regeneration" (Sermon 7); "Christ About His Father's Business" (Sermon 15); "God's Sovereignty" (Sermon 18); "Christian Prosperity and Its Causes" (Sermon 51); "The Peace of God" (Sermon 60); and "The Physician and His Patients" (Sermon 74).

5   Examples of stippling are found in the following sermons: "Adoption" (Sermon 1); "Necessity of Purity for an Entrance to Heaven" (Sermon 2); "Condescending Love of Jesus" (Sermon 5); "Future Judgment" (Sermon 6); "Sinners Must Be Punished" (Sermon 9); "Beginning at Jerusalem" (Sermon 29); "The Lamb and Lion Conjoined" (Sermon 34); "The Fight and the Weapons" (Sermon 37a); "The Men Possessed of the Devils" (Sermon 70); and "An Exhortation to Bravery" (Sermon 72).

strikethroughs,[6] brackets,[7] dittography,[8] underscoring,[9] misspellings,[10] superscripts,[11] miscellaneous markings,[12] and fingerprints.[13] Spurgeon's halfhearted attempt at indexing the sermons in Notebook 1 contains numerous errors and might explain the discontinuation of the practice in subsequent notebooks.[14]

Notebook 1 also reveals the influences, pressures, personalities, and politics that shaped Spurgeon's early ministry. Some of these cultural allusions and extrabiblical references include India's gold mines;[15] boatsmen;[16] sandalwood and cow trees;[17] fires

6   Examples of strikethroughs are found in the following sermons: "Future Judgment" (Sermon 6); "Making Light of Christ" (Sermon 21); "Despisers Warned" (Sermon 26); "Paul's Renunciation" (Sermon 27); "Salvation from Starvation" (Sermon 30); "The Path of the Just" (Sermon 35); "The Son's Love to Us Compared with God's Love to Him" (Sermon 38); "Christian Joy" (Sermon 40); "Elijah's Faith and Prayer" (Sermon 44); "He Took Not Up Angels" (Sermon 52); "The Wise Men's Offering" (Sermon 58); "Gethsemane's Sorrow" (Sermon 63); "The Men Possessed of the Devils" (Sermon 70); "Slavery Destroyed" (Sermon 73); and "The Physician and His Patients" (Sermon 74).

7   Spurgeon uses brackets in the following sermons: "Necessity of Purity for an Entrance to Heaven" (Sermon 2); "Abraham Justified by Faith" (Sermon 3); "Salvation from Sin" (Sermon 33); "Josiah" (Sermon 66); and "Slavery Destroyed" (Sermon 73).

8   Examples of dittography are found in the following sermons: "Jesus, the Shower from Heaven" (Sermon 43); "The Little Fire and Great Combustion" (Sermon 54); "The Affliction of Ahaz" (Sermon 57); "Imitation of God" (Sermon 69); and "Can Two Walk Together Unless They Are Agreed?" (Sermon 76).

9   Examples of underscoring are found in the following sermons: "Necessity of Purity for an Entrance to Heaven" (Sermon 2); "Christ About His Father's Business" (Sermon 15); "Heaven's Preparations" (Sermon 28); "Elijah's Faith and Prayer" (Sermon 44); "The Authors of Damnation and Salvation" (Sermon 45); "Regeneration, Its Causes and Effects" (Sermon 46); "God, the Guide of His Saints" (Sermon 62); and "The Physician and His Patients" (Sermon 74).

10   Examples of Spurgeon's misspellings are found in the following sermons: "Regeneration" (Sermon 7); "The Plant of Renown" (Sermon 20); "Making Light of Christ" (Sermon 21); "Salvation in God Only" (Sermon 24); "Beginning at Jerusalem" (Sermon 29); "Salvation from Sin" (Sermon 33); "The Fight" (Sermon 37b); "Pharisees and Sadducees Reproved" (Sermon 39); "King of Righteousness and Peace" (Sermon 42); "The Eloquence of Jesus" (Sermon 49); "God Glorified in the Saved" (Sermon 56); "The Affliction of Ahaz" (Sermon 57); "The Wise Men's Offering" (Sermon 58); "The First Promise" (Sermon 59); "Josiah" (Sermon 66); "The Men Possessed of the Devils" (Sermon 70); "What Think Ye of Christ?" (Sermon 71); and "The Physician and His Patients" (Sermon 74).

11   Examples of superscripts are found in the following sermons: "Adoption" (Sermon 1); "Abraham Justified by Faith" (Sermon 3); "Christ About His Father's Business" (Sermon 15); "An Answer Required" (Sermon 19); "Salvation from Starvation" (Sermon 30); "The Wrong Roads" (Sermon 32); "Salvation from Sin" (Sermon 33); "Repentance and Salvation" (Sermon 50); "He Took Not Up Angels" (Sermon 52); "The Affliction of Ahaz" (Sermon 57); "The Wise Men's Offering" (Sermon 58); "The Peace of God" (Sermon 60); "The Improvement of Our Talents" (Sermon 61); "God, the Guide of His Saints" (Sermon 62); "Gethsemane's Sorrow" (Sermon 63); and "Josiah" (Sermon 66).

12   For examples of miscellaneous markings, see "Adoption" (Sermon 1); "Necessity of Purity for an Entrance to Heaven" (Sermon 2); "The Wise Men's Offering" (Sermon 58); and "God, the Guide of His Saints" (Sermon 62).

13   For one example of a fingerprint on the pages of the manuscript, likely belonging to Spurgeon, see the final page of the notebook.

14   Spurgeon's front and final indices contain numerous errors in Scripture referencing, titling of sermons, and proper placement. For instance, Spurgeon did not include forty-one of his sermon titles in his final index. In Notebook 2, Spurgeon ceased indexing his sermons after his only entry, "Self Deception" (Notebook 2, Sermon 78).

15   See "Condescending Love of Jesus" (Sermon 5).

16   See "An Answer Required" (Sermon 19).

17   See "The Plant of Renown" (Sermon 20).

in America;[18] chemistry, plasters, cordials, bitters, and catholicons;[19] nurses, doctors, sextons, and sailors;[20] rainmakers and Gypsies ("gipsies");[21] Arabians, Persians, Zoroaster, Virgil, Suetonius, Tacitus, and the Sybils;[22] and French politics.[23] This notebook also contains the discovery that Spurgeon's first recorded convert, "Mr. Charles," likely apostatized,[24] which might explain why Spurgeon later claimed that his second recorded convert, "Mrs. Spalding,"[25] was actually his first. Spurgeon also alluded to religious movements he encountered like Roman Catholicism and Puseyism,[26] Atheism and Deism,[27] Arminianism, Antinomianism, and Socinianism,[28] Sophistry,[29] Mormons and Arians,[30] and Islam ("Mahometanism").[31]

Notebook 1 records Spurgeon's transition from preaching itinerantly with the Lay Preachers' Association connected with St. Andrew's Street Baptist Church[32] to serving as pastor of Waterbeach Chapel. Many of the first thirty-two sermons in Notebook 1 were preached in cottages and chapels in the following villages: Balsham, Barton, Cherry Hinton, Comberton, Coton, Dunmow, Grantchester, Hythe, Layer Breton, Milton, Teversham, Toft, Tollesbury, Trumpington, Waterbeach, and West Wratting. The distances Spurgeon traveled from his residence near the town center in Cambridge to these villages range from 2.5 miles (Cherry Hinton, Grantchester, and Trumpington) to 105 miles (Hythe). In October 1851, Spurgeon preached his first sermon as pastor of Waterbeach Chapel ("Salvation from Sin," Sermon 33). He remained in Waterbeach until April 28, 1854 when he accepted the pastorate of New Park Street Chapel in London.

18 See "The Little Fire and Great Combustion" (Sermon 54).
19 See "The Physician and His Patients" (Sermon 74).
20 See "The Affliction of Ahaz" (Sermon 57).
21 See "Imitation of God" (Sermon 69).
22 See "The Wise Men's Offering" (Sermon 58).
23 See "The Peace of God" (Sermon 60).
24 See "The Little Fire and Great Combustion" (Sermon 54).
25 See "Sinners Must Be Punished" (Sermon 9).
26 See "Salvation in God Only" (Sermon 24).
27 See "Ignorance, Its Evils" (Sermon 31).
28 See "Pleasure in the Stones of Zion" (Sermon 53).
29 See "Offending God's Little Ones" (Sermon 67).
30 See "What Think Ye of Christ?" (Sermon 71).
31 See "The Little Fire and Great Combustion" (Sermon 54).
32 *Autobiography* 1:200.

Below is a listing of the distances Spurgeon traveled to preach:[33]

Balsham — 10.0 mi
Barton — 4.1 mi
Cherry Hinton — 2.5 mi
Comberton — 5.7 mi
Coton — 3.2 mi
Dunmow — 28.4 mi
Grantchester — 2.5 mi
Hythe — 105 mi

Layer Breton — 46.8 mi
Milton — 3.5 mi
Teversham — 3.4 mi
Toft — 6.8 mi
Tollesbury — 49.7 mi
Trumpington — 2.5 mi
Waterbeach — 6.1 mi
West Wratting — 11.2 mi

The average distance traveled is 16.0 miles.

DISTANCES *from* CAMBRIDGE TOWN CENTRE *to* VILLAGES WHERE SPURGEON PREACHED *(in miles)*

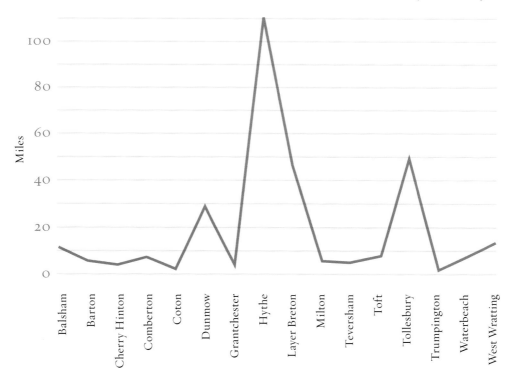

33 These distances were calculated using Google Maps to generate the shortest walking directions from the Cambridge City Centre to the center of each village. The exception is Waterbeach, which was calculated using the specific address of Waterbeach Baptist Church on Chapel Street. These routes are modern and may not reflect the actual footpaths Spurgeon took. To reach some of the villages, particularly Dunmow, Layer Breton, Tollesbury, and Hythe, Spurgeon traveled by train or carriage.

In Notebook 1, Spurgeon wrote forty-three sermons (55 percent) on New Testament texts, thirty-four sermons (44 percent) on Old Testament texts, and one sermon without a Scripture text. The total number of sermons in Notebook 1 is seventy-seven (seventy-eight when Sermons 37a and 37b are counted as two separate sermons).

In his earliest notebook, Spurgeon preached more sermons from Matthew than any other biblical book (nine sermons), followed by the books of Psalms (eight sermons) and Proverbs (six sermons). He preached forty-three sermons from the New Testament. Of his New Testament sermons, 21 percent are from Matthew; 9 percent (four sermons) from Ephesians; 7 percent (three sermons) each from Mark, John, 2 Corinthians, Philippians, Hebrews, and Revelation; 5 percent (two sermons) each from Luke and Colossians; and 2 percent (one sermon) each from Romans, 1 Corinthians, Galatians, 1 Timothy, James, 1 Peter, 2 Peter, and 1 John.[34] Spurgeon preached from eighteen of the twenty-seven books of the New Testament (67 percent). He did not preach any sermons from Acts, 1 Thessalonians, 2 Thessalonians, 2 Timothy, Titus, Philemon, 2 John, 3 John, or Jude (33 percent of the New Testament books).

Spurgeon also preached thirty-four sermons from the Old Testament. Of his Old Testament sermons in Notebook 1, 24 percent are from Psalms (eight sermons); 18 percent from Proverbs (six sermons); 9 percent from Isaiah (three sermons); 6 percent (two sermons) each from Genesis, Deuteronomy, 2 Samuel, 2 Kings, and Ezekiel; and 3 percent (one sermon) each from Exodus, Joshua, 1 Kings, 2 Chronicles, Jeremiah, Hosea, and Amos. Spurgeon preached from fifteen of the thirty-nine books of the Old Testament (38 percent). He did not preach any sermons from the Old Testament books of Leviticus, Numbers, Judges, Ruth, 1 Samuel, 1 Chronicles, Ezra, Nehemiah, Esther, Job, Ecclesiastes, Song of Solomon, Lamentations, Daniel, Joel, Obadiah, Jonah, Micah, Nahum, Habakkuk, Zephaniah, Haggai, Zechariah, or Malachi (62 percent of the Old Testament books). In total, Spurgeon preached from thirty-three of the sixty-six books of the Bible (50 percent).

All of the sermons in Notebook 1 are outlines (or "skeletons," as Spurgeon called them).[35] These outlines range in word count from 85 words (Sermon 14, "God's Grace Given to Us") to 571 words (Sermon 74, "The Physician and His Patients"). These word counts include Roman numerals and other outlining mechanisms for headings and subheadings, but they do not include sermons titles, Scripture

---

34 All percentages have been rounded.
35 See the title page of Notebook 1.

references, Scripture texts, references to villages or dates, or marginal notations written on the sermon page. Below is the word count for the sermons in Notebook 1:

Sermon 1 = 265 words

Sermon 2 = 152 words

Sermon 3 = 143 words

Sermon 4 = 117 words

Sermon 5 = 157 words

Sermon 6 = 173 words

Sermon 7 = 159 words

Sermon 8 = 116 words

Sermon 9 = 98 words

Sermon 10 = 150 words

Sermon 11 = 119 words

Sermon 12 = 134 words

Sermon 13 = 116 words

Sermon 14 = 85 words

Sermon 15 = 145 words

Sermon 16 = 102 words

Sermon 17 = 152 words

Sermon 18 = 130 words

Sermon 19 = 161 words

Sermon 20 = 119 words

Sermon 21 = 135 words

Sermon 22 = 93 words

Sermon 23 = 129 words

Sermon 24 = 137 words

Sermon 25 = 131 words

Sermon 26 = 142 words

Sermon 27 = 129 words

Sermon 28 = 144 words

Sermon 29 = 143 words

Sermon 30 = 124 words

Sermon 31 = 134 words

Sermon 32 = 192 words

Sermon 33 = 221 words

Sermon 34 = 200 words

Sermon 35 = 185 words

Sermon 36 = 212 words

Sermon 37a = 173 words

Sermon 37b = 213 words

Sermon 38 = 271 words

Sermon 39 = 154 words

Sermon 40 = 196 words

Sermon 41 = 168 words

Sermon 42 = 257 words

Sermon 43 = 194 words

Sermon 44 = 248 words

Sermon 45 = 187 words

Sermon 46 = 296 words

Sermon 47 = 179 words

Sermon 48 = 266 words

Sermon 49 = 254 words

Sermon 50 = 185 words

Sermon 51 = 283 words

Sermon 52 = 315 words

Sermon 53 = 276 words

Sermon 54 = 251 words

Sermon 55 = 165 words

Sermon 56 = 327 words   Sermon 67 = 188 words
Sermon 57 = 247 words   Sermon 68 = 133 words
Sermon 58 = 540 words   Sermon 69 = 283 words
Sermon 59 = 202 words   Sermon 70 = 328 words
Sermon 60 = 335 words   Sermon 71 = 274 words
Sermon 61 = 310 words   Sermon 72 = 289 words
Sermon 62 = 255 words   Sermon 73 = 215 words
Sermon 63 = 280 words   Sermon 74 = 571 words
Sermon 64 = 284 words   Sermon 75 = 321 words
Sermon 65 = 193 words   Sermon 76 = 328 words
Sermon 66 = 171 words   Sermon 77 = 152 words

When excluding the two longest sermons, "The Wise Men's Offering" (Sermon 58, 540 words) and Sermon 74, "The Physician and His Patients" (571 words), the average word count of the sermons in Notebook 1 is 196 words. The general trend appears to indicate that the longer Spurgeon preached, the more words he wrote for each sermon.

WORD COUNT *per* SERMON:

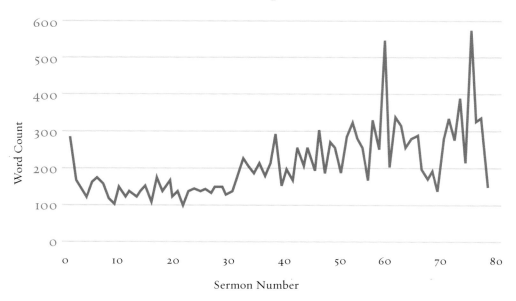

WORD COUNT DISTRIBUTION
of ALL SERMONS *in* NOTEBOOK 1

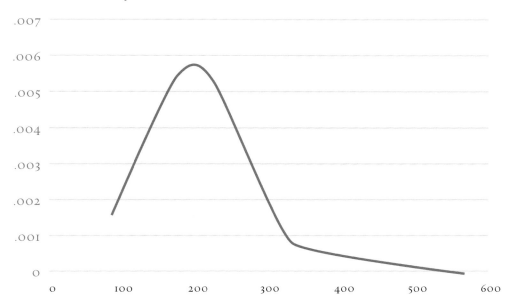

WORD COUNT DISTRIBUTION
EXCLUDING SERMONS 58 *and* 74 [36]

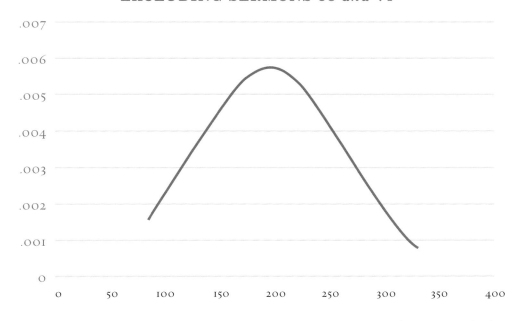

36 Of note to the statistician, when excluding Sermons 58 and 74, the sermon word count in Notebook 1 forms a nearly perfect normal distribution ("bell curve") with a mean of 196 and a standard deviation of 69. The x-axis represents word count and the y-axis represents probability.

PERCENTAGE *of* SERMONS
from OLD *and* NEW TESTAMENTS

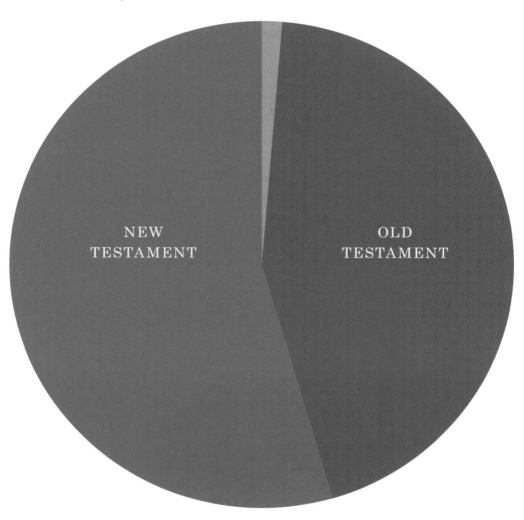

Percentages of Sermons:
- Old Testament – 44% (34 sermons)
- New Testament – 55% (43 sermons)
- No Text – 1% (1 sermon)

Length of Sermons:
Longest Sermon – 571 words
Shortest Sermon – 85 words
Average Sermon – 196 words

Books Most Frequently Preached:
Matthew – 9 times
Psalms – 8 times
Proverbs – 6 times

PERCENTAGE *of* OLD TESTAMENT SERMONS
Preached from Each Book

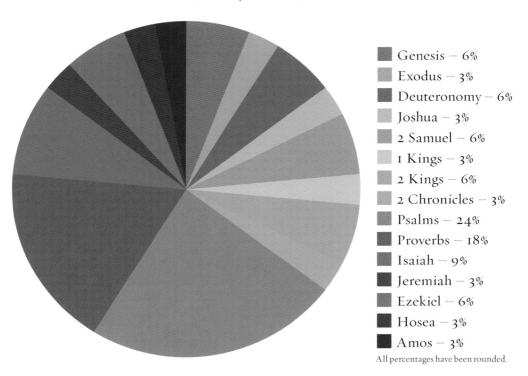

- Genesis – 6%
- Exodus – 3%
- Deuteronomy – 6%
- Joshua – 3%
- 2 Samuel – 6%
- 1 Kings – 3%
- 2 Kings – 6%
- 2 Chronicles – 3%
- Psalms – 24%
- Proverbs – 18%
- Isaiah – 9%
- Jeremiah – 3%
- Ezekiel – 6%
- Hosea – 3%
- Amos – 3%

All percentages have been rounded.

NUMBER *of* PREACHING OCCASIONS USING
OLD TESTAMENT TEXTS

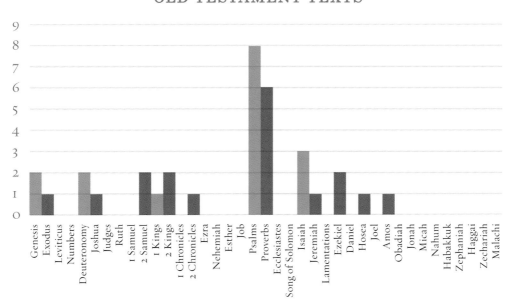

PERCENTAGE *of* NEW TESTAMENT SERMONS
Preached from Each Book

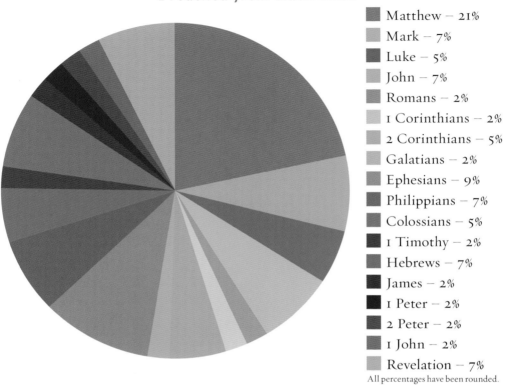

Matthew – 21%
Mark – 7%
Luke – 5%
John – 7%
Romans – 2%
1 Corinthians – 2%
2 Corinthians – 5%
Galatians – 2%
Ephesians – 9%
Philippians – 7%
Colossians – 5%
1 Timothy – 2%
Hebrews – 7%
James – 2%
1 Peter – 2%
2 Peter – 2%
1 John – 2%
Revelation – 7%

All percentages have been rounded.

NUMBER *of* PREACHING OCCASIONS USING
NEW TESTAMENT TEXTS

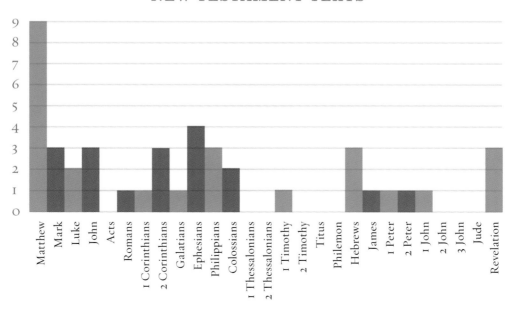

WORD CLOUD *of* TOPICAL FREQUENCY

In this word cloud, the larger the word, the more frequently it appears in Notebook 1.

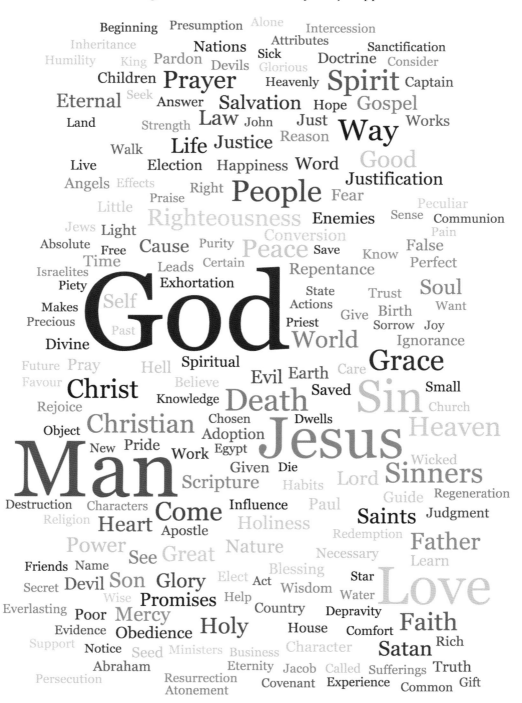

The final word is reserved for Spurgeon. In the preface of his later work *My Sermon-Notes*, he sheds light on his vision for his sermon outlines:

> I have prepared these frameworks, not to encourage indolence, but to help bewildered industry; and I hope that I have not written so much as to enable any man to preach without thought, nor so little as to leave a weary mind without help. . . . As we pour a little water down a pump to help it to draw up a stream from below, so may "My Sermon-notes" refresh many a jaded mind, and then set it working so as to develop its own resources. May the Holy Spirit use these outlines for the help of His busy servants. To Him shall be all the praise, and to His Church the prophet.[37]

And now, for the first time in 160 years, we—the misplaced audience of a long-lost promise—can hear Spurgeon's words, originally offered to his age but divinely detoured to ours:

> "I shall soon issue a volume of my earliest productions,
> while Pastor of Waterbeach . . .
> and would now bespeak for it a favourable reception."[38]

CHARLES SPURGEON, *December 1857*

---

37   C. H. Spurgeon, *My Sermon-Notes: A Selection from Outlines of Discourses Delivered at the Metropolitan Tabernacle with Anecdotes and Illustrations, from Genesis to Proverbs—I to LXIV* (New York: Robert Carter & Brothers, 1885, The Spurgeon Library), iii–v.

38   *NPSP* 3:preface.

Charles Spurgeon, 1854–1855, preaching from "The Lamb and Lion Conjoined" (Sermon 34)

THE SERMONS

NOTEBOOK 1 (SERMONS 1–77)

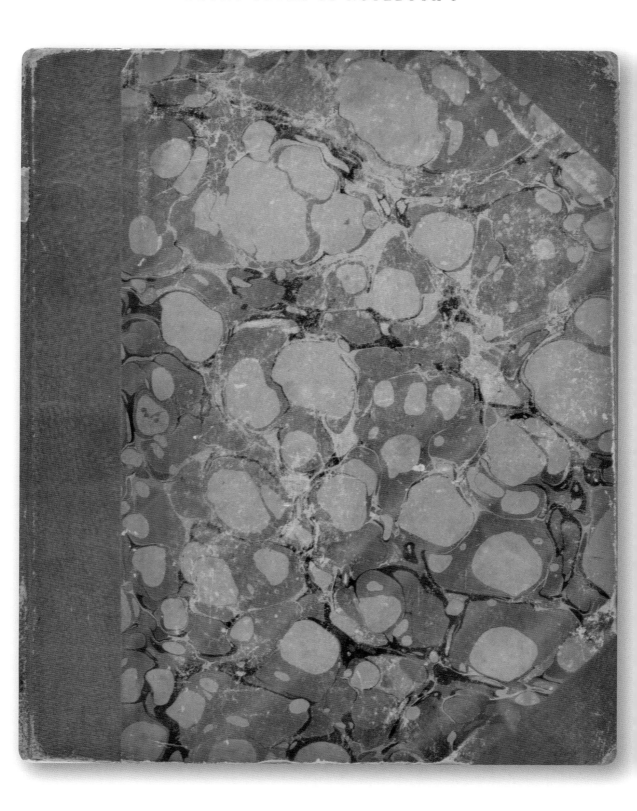

K1/5[1]

1. The inscription "K1/5" was written in pencil and corresponds to the grey box/folder in which Notebook 1 is kept in the Heritage Room Archives at Spurgeon's College in London. The other box/folder in which the notebooks are contained is labeled "U1.02." There is evidence that some of the pencil redactions within the sermons were written by Charles as he prepared his sermons for publication in 1857 (see *Autobiography* 1:213 and *NPSP* 3:vi); however, the inscription above does not appear to be in the hand of Charles and was likely written during the cataloguing process of the archives. The following inscriptions are found in the front of the notebooks: "A2.6" appears on the inside front cover of the 1849 notebook entitled "Antichrist and Her Brood; or, Popery Unmasked." The front cover of Notebook 2 is partially missing and may have contained a similar inscription. The Roman numeral III appears at the top of the title page in Notebook 3. A circled Roman numeral IV appears on the second page of Notebook 4. The Roman numeral V appears on the second page of Notebook 5. A circled Roman numeral VI appears on the second page of Notebook 6. A circled Roman numeral VII appears on the second page of Notebook 7. Two inscriptions are found on the inside front cover of Notebook 8: the Roman numeral VIII in the upper left corner and "Vol. VIII" in the upper right. The front cover of Notebook 9 is partially missing; however, the inscription "VOL IX" appears in the remaining space at the top of the truncated flap.

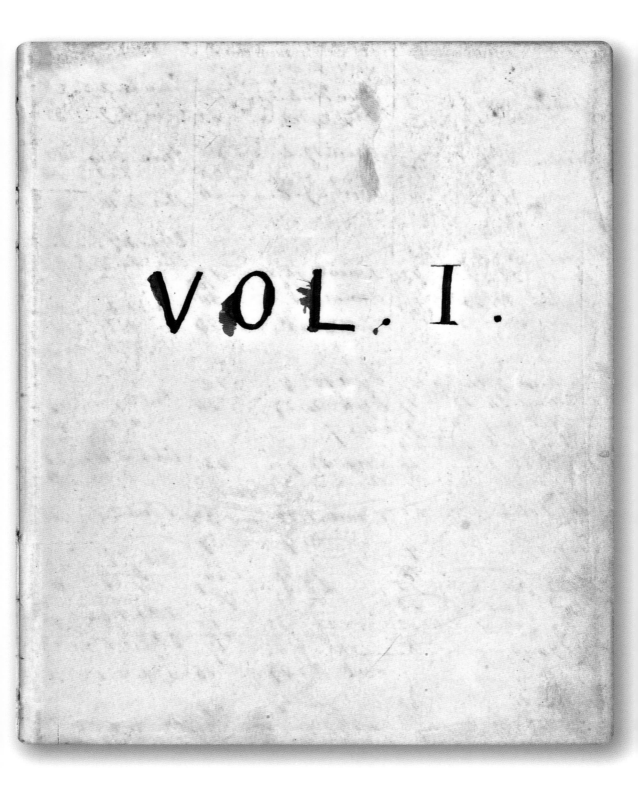

VOL. I.[1]

1.   Abbr., "Volume 1." For similar block lettering, see Charles's 1849 notebook containing his French grammar and also the inside front cover of Notebook 2. The ink in the letters is smeared toward the left side of the page and may have been the source of the two fingerprints on the page. A fingerprint with sharper definition is found on the final page of this notebook to the right of the word "Ghost" in the last line of the Doxology.

Gen . 3.15 . . . 59	Prov 4.18 35	John . 7. 46 ~ 49
Genesis . 15.16. . . . 3	Prov 10.3 - . . 30	John 14. 2 . . 28
	Prov 14.12 . . . 32	John 15. 9. . 38
Exodus . 11.7 . . . 41	Prov. 19.2 . . . 31	Rom. 2.16. 52
	Prov 28.26 . . 65	— 8 .17 . 73
	Prov 29.1 . . . 26	1 Cor.15.10 . , 14
		2 Cor. 8.7 . . 5
Deut . 14. 2 . . .25		2 Cor. 10.4 . . 37
Deut . 20 . 1 ~ 72	Isaiah 45.17 . . 17	
Joshua . 21.45 .	46. 25 . . 68	Ephes 1.4 . 10
	Isaiah 55 . 7 . . 50	— 1.5 . . 1
	Jer. 3. 23 . . 24	— 4.8 . . 4
		— 5. 1 ~ 69
2 Samuel 7.14 . . . 47	Ezek 18. 4 . . . 12	
2 Samuel 24. 13 . . 19	Ezek 34.29 . . . 20	Phil 3.7 . . . 27
2. Kings . 7 . 3.4 . 77	after 7	— 4.4 . . 49
1 Kings . 18. 43 . . 44		— 4.7 . . 60
2 Kings 22. 2 . . . 66	Hos. 13. 9 . . . 45	Colos. 3.11 . . 22
2. Chron . 28. 22 ~ 57	Amos. 3. 3 . . ~ 76	— 3. 25 . . 6
Psal 1. 1-3 . . . 51	Matt. 1.12 . . . 33	1 Tim 2.1 . . 48
	— 3. 7 . . 39	
Ps. 9. 17 9	— 2. 11 . . 58	Heb. 7. 2 . . 42.
Ps. 10. 16 . . . 18	— 13. 25 . . 64	— 7. 25 . . 11
Ps. 22 . 3 . . . 75	— 22. 3 . . 21	
Ps. 72 . 6 . . . 43	— 23 . 42 . ~ 71	
Ps. 73 . 24 . . . 62	— 25 . 19 ~ 61	1 Pet. 1. 3. 5 ~ 46
Ps. 94. 14 . . . 8	— 26 . 38 . 63	2 Pet. 1. 1 . . 23
	Mk. 5. 15 ~ 70 67	
	Luke 2. 49 . . 15	1 John 3. 1 ~ 16
Ps 102. 14 . . . 53	— 24 .17 29	
	Mk. 2.17 — 74	Rev 21.6 . . 13
		— 21. 27 . . 2

1. With the exception of the last page of Notebook 2, which contains the one entry of "Self Deception" (Notebook 2, Sermon 78), the two indices in this notebook constitute Charles's only attempts at organizing his early sermons. In the above index Charles arranged the sermons in biblical sequence with three vertical lines drawn in pencil that separate the data into three columns. To the right of the Scripture references, Charles listed the corresponding sermon number that appears at the top of each sermon in this notebook. In contrast the index at the end of this notebook contains sermons arranged by subject/title with two vertical lines drawn in pencil that separate the title of the sermon from the Scripture reference. Inaccuracies exist in both indices and reveal that Charles did not apply a careful method to either, possibly a reason he discontinued indexing his sermons in Notebook 2. Susannah noted, "At the beginning of Vol. I is a *textual* index, showing that the seventy-seven Outlines were based upon passages taken from fifteen Books in the Old Testament, and sixteen in the New Testament" (*Autobiography* 1:213, italics in the original). Susannah correctly counted the Old and New Testament Scripture references; however, she failed to account for the two sermons that Charles wrote on 2 Cor 10:4: "The Fight and the Weapons" (Sermon 37a) and "The Fight" (Sermon 37b). The total sermon count for this notebook is seventy-eight, not seventy-seven. In the index above, Charles listed only seventy-three sermons. The four missing sermons (with the exclusion of either 37a or 37b) are "The Lamb and Lion Conjoined" (Sermon 34); "The Little Fire and Great Combustion" (Sermon 54); "Rest for the Weary" (Sermon 55); and "God Glorified in the Saved" (Sermon 56). In the index at the end of this notebook, Charles did not list forty-one sermons.

2. For consistency, all Scripture references have been abbreviated.

3. The correct Scripture reference for "Abraham Justified by Faith" (Sermon 3) is Gen 15:6, not Gen 15:16.

4. The correct Scripture reference for "He Took Not Up Angels" (Sermon 52) is Heb 2:16, not Rom 2:16. Beneath the title of the sermon itself, Charles wrote, "~~Rom~~ Hebrews 2:16."

5. Although Charles connected the three ellipses that separate the number 1 from 72, an en dash was likely unintended. Cf. dashes beneath "Isaiah," "Matthew," "Luke," etc. A similar use of ellipses precedes the number 74 at the end of the second column.

6.   The correct sermon number for "Certain Fulfilment of Promises" is 36. It is unclear why Charles did not include this number.

7.   The correct Scripture reference for "Condescending Love of Jesus" (Sermon 5) is 2 Cor 8:9, not 2 Cor 8:7. In his index at the end of this notebook, Charles listed the correct Scripture reference.

8.   The number 9 was smudged toward the bottom of the page.

9.   The correct Scripture reference for "The Saints' Justification and Glory" (Sermon 68) is Isa 45:25, not Isa 46:25. In the sermon itself, Charles wrote "Isaiah 46:25"; however, the number 5 was written in pencil above 6 to construct the correct Scripture reference.

10. Charles preached two sermons on 2 Cor 10:4: "The Fight and the Weapons" (Sermon 37a) and "The Fight" (Sermon 37b). His reason for not distinguishing between these two sermons is unclear; however, in the index at the end of this notebook Charles listed only "The Fight." Perhaps he preferred his second sermon on 2 Cor 10:4 to his first.

11. The phrase "77 after 7" signifies the location of the final sermon of Notebook 1, "The Lepers" (Sermon 77). Charles inserted this sermon in the empty space beneath the conclusion of "Regeneration" (Sermon 7). Charles identified the location of this sermon again in "Can Two Walk Together Unless They Are Agreed?" (Sermon 76) with the words "For 77 see 7." Sermon 7 is the only sermon in this notebook without a Scripture reference.

12. Charles abbreviated the word "Ephesians" by writing "Ephes." For an additional example of this abbreviation, see the index at the end of this notebook.

13. This Scripture reference, "1 Kgs 18:43," is out of sequence and should be located above 2 Kgs 7:3–4.

14. The letters "VOL. 1" bled through the page and can be seen behind the Scripture references.

15. "Adoption" (Sermon 1) was actually the third sermon Charles preached, not the first as the numerical sequence in this notebook suggests. Susannah recorded, "The

first volume of Outlines must have been commenced very soon after Mr. Spurgeon began to preach, for the second written in it was only the *fourth* discourse delivered by the youthful evangelist. The text was Revelation xxi. 27, and it was preached at Barton, near Cambridge, on February 9th, 1851" (*Autobiography* 1:213, italics in the original). The first sermon Charles preached in Teversham was not recorded in this notebook given its impromptu delivery. The text he selected on that occasion was 1 Pet 2:7, "Unto you therefore which believe he is precious." Charles recounted, "I do not think I could have said anything upon any other text, but Christ was precious to my soul, and I was in the flush of my youthful love, and I could not be silent when a precious Jesus was the subject" (*Autobiography* 1:202–3; see also 1:199–202). Charles preached six additional sermons from 1 Pet 2:7 throughout his ministry: "Christ Precious to Believers" (*NPSP* 5, Sermon 242); "Three Precious Things" (*MTP* 16, Sermon 931); "Jesus, the Stumbling Stone of Unbelievers" (*MTP* 21, Sermon 1224); "Christ Precious to Believers" (*MTP* 36, Sermon 2137); "A Sermon from a Sick Preacher" (*MTP* 52, Sermon 3014); and "A Sermon and a Reminiscence" (*MTP* 54, Sermon 3112).

16.   The correct Scripture reference for the sermon "A Contrast" (Sermon 4) is Eph 5:8, not Eph 4:8. In the sermon itself the number 4 was struck through in pencil and replaced with 5. Charles did not correct this mistake in the index at the end of this notebook.

17.   The correct Scripture reference for "Paul's Renunciation" (Sermon 27) is Phil 3:9, not Phil 3:7. In the index at the end of this notebook, Charles incorrectly wrote "Philippians 3:11." In the sermon itself Charles listed the Scripture reference correctly.

18.   Charles inserted a period between the numbers 1 and 6. However, the correct Scripture reference for "God's Sovereignty" (Sermon 18) is Ps 10:16, not Ps 10:1,6 or 10:1–6.

19.   The correct Scripture reference for "Salvation from Sin" (Sermon 33) is Matt 1:21, not Matt 1:12. In the index above, the number 12 was struck through in pencil and replaced with 21. This was the first sermon Charles preached as pastor of Waterbeach Chapel.

20.   The number 31 was smudged toward the right side of the page.

21. The Scripture reference Matt 2:11 is out of sequence. It should be located above Matt 3:7.

22. The number 7 was smudged toward the top left side of the page.

23. The size and location of "Mark 5:15" suggests Charles added this Scripture reference after he had written "Mark 9:42."

24. The correct Scripture reference for "Beginning at Jerusalem" (Sermon 29) is Luke 24:47, not Luke 24:17. In the index at the end of this notebook, Charles recorded the correct Scripture reference.

25. The Scripture reference Mark 2:17 is out of sequence. It should be located above Mark 5:15.

Blow ye the trumpet in Zion.[1]

Ye shall mount as on Wings of Eagles.[2]
Holiness unto the Lord.[3]
I am ever with you even unto the end of the world.[4]
JUBILEE.[5]
Jesus Christ and him crucified.[6]

SKELETONS

I *to* LXXVII [7]

and only SKELETONS *without the* HOLY GHOST.[8]

Not unto us.
Not unto us, but unto thy name be all the Glory.[9]
Who maketh his angels spirits.
His ministers, a flame of Fire.[10]
Peace.[11] FREE GRACE.[12]
By grace, I am what I am.[13]
Where is boasting then?
It is excluded.[14]
Less than the least of all Saints.[15]

Designed and Engraved by William Smith.[16]

1. Joel 2:1, "Blow ye the trumpet in Zion, and sound an alarm in my holy mountain: let all the inhabitants of the land tremble: for the day of the LORD cometh, for it is nigh at hand." According to a letter from "S. J. C.," Joel 2:1 was one of Charles's favorite verses of Scripture (*Autobiography* 2:237). Susannah included a facsimile of this title page in *Autobiography* 1:215. With the exceptions of the cross and crown, all the illustrations on this page were predrawn by the manufacturer of the notebook. Charles spiritualized these illustrations by writing Scripture verses around them. Given their potential to shed light onto Charles's thought, his writings on this page are noted below. For comparable illustrated pages, see Notebooks 2, 3, 4, 5, 6, and 7. The similarities among these seven notebooks suggest they were part of the same printed series. Only in Notebooks 1 and 2 did Charles embellish the title pages with his own illustrations and script. A smudge appears at each corner of this title page and also on either side of the center. The source of these smudges is unknown, but their symmetry may suggest intention.

2. Isa 40:31, "But they that wait upon the LORD shall renew their strength; they shall mount up with wings as eagles; they shall run, and not be weary; and they shall walk and not faint." Spurgeon changed the words of the KJV to "Ye shall mount as on wings of eagles." The angel's wing was likely the inspiration for his reference to Isa 40:31.

3. Zecheriah 14:20, "In that day shall there be upon the bells of the horses, HOLINESS UNTO THE LORD; and the pots in the LORD's house shall be like bowls before the alter." Charles may have had in mind Jer 2:3, "Israel was holiness unto the LORD, and the first-fruits of his increase: all that devour him shall offend; evil shall come upon them, saith the LORD."

4. Matthew 28:20, "Teaching them to observe all things whatsoever I have commanded you: and, lo, I am with you alway even unto the end of the world. Amen." Charles altered the wording of the KJV with the words "I am ever with you even unto the end of the world."

5. Charles may have had in mind Lev 25:9, "Then shalt thou cause the trumpet of the jubilee to sound on the tenth day of the seventh month, in the day of atonement shall ye make the trumpet sound throughout all your land."

6. First Corinthians 2:2, "For I determined not to know any thing among you, save Jesus Christ, and him crucified." By positioning the phrase "Jesus Christ

and him crucified" after the bell of the trumpet, Charles may have had in mind the announcement of Jesus Christ in the Old Testament and his advent in the New Testament.

7.   The equivalent of Roman numeral LXXVII is 77, which corresponds to the total number of sermons contained in this notebook. This number does not include one of the two sermons Charles wrote for 2 Cor 10:4: "The Fight and the Weapons" (Sermon 37a) or "The Fight" (Sermon 37b).

8.   The inscription "and only skeletons without the Holy Ghost" was likely a reference to Ezek 37:1–10. Additional pneumatological statements include "The Gospel provisions will be of no avail unless applied by the Spirit" ("The Authors of Damnation and Salvation" [Sermon 45]) and "Holy Spirit, blow through me" ("No Condemnation to Christians" [Notebook 3, Sermon 174]). See also "The Teaching of the Holy Ghost" (*NPSP* 6, Sermon 315); "A Most Needful Prayer Concerning the Holy Spirit" (*MTP* 16, Sermon 954); "The Paraclete" (*MTP* 18, Sermon 1074); and Zachery W. Eswine, "The Role of the Holy Spirit in the Preaching Theory and Practice of Charles Haddon Spurgeon" (PhD diss., Regent University, 2003).

9.   Psalm 115:1, "Not unto us, O LORD, not unto us, but unto thy name give glory for thy mercy, and for thy truth's sake." Charles altered the wording of the KJV with the words "Not unto us. Not unto us, but unto thy name be all the Glory."

10.   The cherub/angel at the bottom of the page was likely the inspiration for his reference to Ps 104:4, "Who maketh his angels spirits; his ministers a flaming fire." The predrawn, curling lines that flank the angel were likely intended by the manufacturer to represent clouds; however, given Charles's reference to Ps 104:4, these lines may have represented fire in his mind.

11.   The characteristics of the word "peace" resemble those of "FREE GRACE" near the forearm of the angel and are best grouped together.

12.   Charles may have had in mind Rom 3:24, "Being justified freely by his grace through the redemption that is in Christ Jesus." The positioning of the words "FREE GRACE" may hold theological significance. Their location above the angel's forearm suggests directionality toward the cross that Charles illustrated.

That is to say, free grace is found at the cross. Charles's diary entry for May 25, 1850, suggests this idea had been on his mind during the months leading up to the writing of this notebook: "Free grace, sovereign love, eternal security are my safeguards" (*Autobiography* 1:140). On the title page of Notebook 2, Charles wrote, "Grace through Jesus to me, to sinner[s]. Praise ought to and shall be given to God's free grace and unchanging love." See also "Free Grace" (Sermon 13). The cross may have been inspired by Christian's conversion experience in Charles's favorite book, John Bunyan's *The Pilgrim's Progress* (see John Bunyan, *The Pilgrim's Progress: From This World to That Which Is to Come. Delivered Under the Similitude of a Dream. Wherein Is Discovered, the Manner of His Setting Out; His Dangerous Journey, and Safe Arrival at the Desired Country. Accurately Printed from the First Edition, with Notices of All the Subsequent Additions and Alterations Made by the Author Himself. Edited for The Hanserd Knollys Society, with an Introduction by George Offor* [London: J. Haddon, 1847, The Spurgeon Library], 39–40). Charles sketched a crown above the cross, which may have represented the kingship/lordship of Jesus Christ. In 1875, Charles said, "But, rest assured that the old motto, 'No cross, no crown,' is certainly true, and those who refuse to carry the cross after Christ on earth shall never be permitted to wear the crown with Christ in the land that is beyond the stars" (*MTP* 51:361). Charles also said, "There are no crown-wearers in heaven who were not cross-bearers here below" (C. H. Spurgeon, *Gleanings Among the Sheaves* [2nd ed.; New York: Sheldon and Company, 1869], 57). See also "The Saviour's Many Crowns" (*NPSP* 5, Sermon 281).

13. First Corinthians 15:10, "But by the grace of God I am what I am: and his grace which was bestowed upon me was not in vain; but I labored more abundantly than they all: yet not I, but the grace of God which was with me." For Charles's sermon on 1 Cor 15:10, see "God's Grace Given to Us" (Sermon 14).

14. Romans 3:27, "Where is boasting then? It is excluded. By what law? Of works? Nay; but by the law of faith."

15. Ephesians 3:8, "Unto me, who am less than the least of all the saints, is this grace given, that I should preach among the Gentiles the unsearchable riches of Christ."

16. In a letter likely to his father, Charles took inventory of the expenses he incurred in Cambridge. In addition to "Hair Cuttings," "Piece of Riband for my Watch," "Tincture of Iodine for my chillblains," and "Gave to a poor Black man," among others, Charles also listed the following entry: "a Writing Book 1" (Angus Library

and Archive, Regent's Park College, Oxford University, D/SPU 1). There is no date on the letter itself; however, the information "Now I had asked Mr. L. to buy me a Horace, a book I very much wanted, and he has bought me one at a sale" is revealing. The signature "C. H. Spurgeon" and "Cambridge, 1850" are found on the inside front cover of William Baxter's *Horace* in The Spurgeon Library. If the inventory is from 1850, then Notebook 1 is likely "Writing Book 1." The words "Designed & Engraved by William Smith" at the bottom of this title page surely refer to Cambridge bookseller William Haddon Smith, the precursor to WH Smith, whose business in 1850 was located at 7 Rose Crescent (*Slater's Royal National and Commercial Directory and Topography of the Counties of Bedfordshire, Cambridgeshire, Huntingdonshire, Lincolnshire, Norfolk, Northamptonshire, and Suffolk* [Manchester, England: Isaac Slater, 1850, Cambridgeshire Collection, Cambridge]). Similar title pages suggest at least seven of the notebooks in Charles's pre-London years originated from this bookseller, though they were likely purchased in different stages. The business was still in operation during the final year of Charles's pastorate at Waterbeach in 1853 (E. R. Kelly, ed., *The Post Office Directory of Cambridgeshire: With a Map Expressly Engraved for the Work* [2nd ed.; London: Kelly and Co., 1853], 111).

1   Ephes. 1. 5...   Adoption.   ✓   1

Meaning of the term.   Common among Romans.
2 Instances in Scripture ..   Moses & Esther ..
Adoption.. differs from Justification & Regeneration..

I. The sense in which believers are sons of God ..
     not as Jesus .. more so than of creatures.
— In some things spiritual adoption agrees with civil .
    1 In name & thing.   2 To an inheritance. 3. voluntary on
the part of the Adopter. 4. Taking the adopter's name
5. Taken into the Family. 6. Considered as children
food, protection, clothing, education, attendance provided
7. They are under the control of the Father ..
   —   In some things they disagree.
    1. Civil adoption requires the consent of the adopted.
    2. Civil adoption was intended to provide for childless persons
  3 & Civil adoption. the adopted had something to recommend him
    4. The nature of a son could not be given.
    5. The children did not inherit till their Father's death.
    6. The Pontifex might make it void.

II. The Cause.
  1. The Person.   God. Son. Spirit
  2. Motive ...   Free Grace not works ..

III. The objects of it .
    Elect sinners, not angels. — all believers
  Not all men but justified men.

April 13. 1851   Barton & Toft.
     " 20   "   Cherry Hinton
July 15.   "   Hythe.

1

✓[1]

ADOPTION[2]
Ephesians 1:5[3]

*"Having predestinated us unto the adoption of children by
Jesus Christ to himself, according to the good pleasure of his will."*

Meaning of the term.[4] Common among Romans. Two[5] instances in Scripture:
Moses[6] and Esther.[7] Adoption differs from Justification and Regeneration.

I. **THE SENSE IN WHICH BELIEVERS ARE SONS OF GOD.**[8]
Not as Jesus.[9] More so than of creatures.[10]

— [11] In some things spiritual adoption agrees with civil.
1. In name and thing. 2. To an inheritance. 3.[12] Voluntary on the part of
the Adopter. 4. Taking the adopter's name. 5. Taken into the Family. 6.
Considered as children. Food, protection, clothing, education, attendance
provided. 7. They are under the control of the Father.

— In some things they disagree.[13]
1. Civil adoption requires the consent of the adopted.
2. Civil adoption was intended to provide for childless persons.
3. In[14] civil adoption, the adopted had something to recommend him.
4. The nature of a son could not be given.
5. The children did not inherit 'till their Father's death.
6. The Pontifex[15] might make it void.

II. **THE CAUSE.**[16]
1. The Person. God. Son. Spirit.
2. Motive. Free Grace,[17] not works.[18]

III. **THE OBJECTS OF IT.**
Elect sinners, not angels.[19] All believers.
Not all men,[20] but Justified men.

April 13, 1851 . . . . .Barton and Toft.[21]
[April][22] 20, [1851] . . . . . . .Cherry Hinton[23]
July 15, [1851] . . . . .Hythe.

IV. Excellency of it.
1. It is an act of surprising grace. 1 John iii. 1. Consider the Persons.
2. It exceeds all others.
3. It makes men honourable.
4. Brings men into the highest relations.
5. Includes all things.
6. Immutable & Everlasting.

V. Effects of it.
1. Share in the love, pity, care of God.
2. Access with Boldness.
3. Conformity to the image of Jesus.
4. The Holy Spirit—
5. Heirship . . . . .

Encouragement. Appeal to saints & sinners.

Barton . . .	April. 13. 51.	11. 12, 13. 26.
Toft	April. 13. 51.	
Cherryhunton.	April. 20. 51.	
Hythe . . .	July 15. 51.	

IV. EXCELLENCY OF IT.

1. It is an act of surprising grace.[24] 1 John 3:1:[25] Consider the Persons.[26]
2. It exceeds all others.
3. It makes men honourable.
4. Brings men into the highest relations.
5. Includes all things.
6. Immutable[27] and Everlasting.[28]

V. EFFECTS OF IT.

1. Share in the love,[29] pity, care of God.
2. Access with Boldness.[30]
3. Conformity to the image of Jesus.[31]
4. The Holy Spirit.
5. Heirship.[32]

Encouragement. Appeal to saints and Sinners.[33]

---

[34]

Barton. . . . . April 13, [18]51   11. 12. 13. 26.[35]

Toft . . . . April 13, [18]51

Cherryhinton[36] . . . . April 20, [18]51

Hythe . . . . July 15, [18]51

1. The significance of the red check mark to the left of the number 1 is unclear; however, it may have been original to Susannah who transcribed this sermon for publication in her husband's *Autobiography*. If this is correct, the check mark in the following sermon, "Necessity of Purity for an Entrance to Heaven" (Sermon 2), could be explained given that she transcribed it also. However, there is no evidence of a check mark in the third sermon she transcribed, "Abraham Justified by Faith" (Sermon 3). It is also possible that Charles wrote these check marks to signify his preaching of the sermons.

2. Susannah transcribed this sermon outline in *Autobiography* 1:214. A comparison of her transcription with Charles's original words reveals the following alterations: The phrase "Taken into the Family" was changed to "Received into the Family." The phrase "They are under the control of the Father" was changed to "Under the control of the Father." The second Roman numeral, "The Cause," was changed to "The Cause of Adoption." The fourth Roman numeral, "Excellency of it," was changed to "The Excellency of it." The fifth Roman numeral, "Effects of it," was changed to "The Effects of it." Susannah's method is unclear; however, at times her literary liberties alter the text significantly. Having worked closely with her husband's publications, she may have adopted the editorial techniques he applied in the publication *My Sermon-Notes: A Selection from Outlines of Discourses Delivered at the Metropolitan Tabernacle by C. H. Spurgeon* (London: Passmore & Alabaster, 1889, The Spurgeon Library). If this is correct, Susannah's alterations may have reflected those Charles would have made if he had been successful in publishing his early sermons in 1857. See also Susannah's transcription of the following two sermons: "Necessity of Purity for an Entrance to Heaven" (Sermon 2) and "Abraham Justified by Faith" (Sermon 3).

3. This sermon outline is original to Baptist theologian, commentator, and London pastor John Gill (1697–1771). Charles lauded Gill as "the greatest scholar the church had yet chosen" (*Autobiography* 1:308) and relied heavily on his works in Notebook 1. On April 28, 1854, three years to the month after Charles first preached the sermon above, he accepted the pastorate of the New Park Street Chapel where Gill had pastored for fifty-one years (the congregation moved from the Baptist Meeting House on Carter Lane, St. Olave's Street, to New Park Street in 1833). Charles told the students at the Pastors' College that Gill's "method is admirable for a body of divinity, or a commentary, but not suitable for preaching" (*Lectures* 1:144). Yet in this sermon there is a significant amount of overlapping

content with the ninth chapter, "Of Adoption," of John Gill, *A Body of Doctrinal Divinity; or, A System of Evangelical Truths, Deduced from the Sacred Scriptures* ([3 vols.; London: printed for the author, and sold by George Keith, in Grace-church-street, 1769, The Spurgeon Library], 2:820–30). With regard to this work, Charles said, "As the fervent exposition of an entire and harmonious creed, it has no rival (*NPSP* 5:347). Almost the entirety of this outline is original to Gill, with the exception of the following words and phrases: "Meaning of the term;" "Adoption differs from Justification and Regeneration;" "education;" "not angels;" "encouragement;" and "Appeal to saints and Sinners." Charles would have known of John Rippon's standard biography of Gill, *A Brief Memoir of the Life and Writings of the Late Rev. John Gill* (London: John Bennett, 1838). For additional works on Gill, see George M. Ella, *John Gill: And the Cause of God and Truth* (Durham, England: Go Publications, 1995); Michael A. G. Haykin, ed., *The Life and Thought of John Gill (1697–1771): A Tercentennial Appreciation* (vol. 77 of Studies in the History of Christian Thought; ed. Robert J. Bast; Leiden, The Netherlands: Brill, 1997); Thomas J. Nettles, *By His Grace and for His Glory. A Historical, Theological, and Practical Study of the Doctrines of Grace in Baptist Life* ([Grand Rapids, MI: Baker, 1986], 73–107); and Timothy George and David S. Dockery, eds., *Theologians of the Baptist Tradition* ([rev. ed.; Nashville: B&H Academic, 2001], 11–33). In 1861, Charles preached an additional sermon on Eph 1:5 entitled "Adoption" (*MTP* 7, Sermon 360). The lack of structural similarities and overlapping content suggests Charles did not use the above outline in writing his later sermon. See also "The Orphan's Father" (*MTP* 28, Sermon 1695).

4.   "Adoption is that act of God, whereby men who were by nature the children of wrath, even as others, and were of the lost and ruined family of Adam, are from no reason in themselves, but entirely of the pure grace of God, translated out of the evil and black family of Satan, and brought actually and virtually into the family of God; so that they take his name, share the privileges of sons, and they are to all intents and purposes the actual offspring and children of God" (*MTP* 7:98).

5.   The location of the number 2 suggests Charles added it after he had written the phrase "Instances in Scripture."

6.   Cf. Exod 2.

7.   Cf. Esth 2:7. "[S]o Moses was adopted by *Pharaoh's* daughter; and among the *Hebrews*, so *Esther* by *Mordecai*" (Gill, *A Body of Doctrinal Divinity*, 2:821, italics in the original).

8. "I. Shall consider, in what sense believers are the sons of God; which is by adoption, and the nature of that: they are not the sons of God in so high a sense as Christ is, who is God's own Son, his proper Son, his only begotten Son; which cannot be said either of angels or men" (Gill, *A Body of Doctrinal Divinity*, 2:821).

9. Cf. 1 John 4:14.   10. Cf. Gen 1:27; Ps 8:6.

11. Charles used em dashes to signal subdivisions in this outline. For similar strokes, see "Beginning at Jerusalem" (Sermon 29) and "The Affliction of Ahaz" (Sermon 57). In this notebook, Charles occasionally used Roman numerals, cardinal numbers, English letters, and Greek letters to signal primary divisions and subdivisions.

12. Charles originally wrote the number 4. The number 3 was written in pencil in its place.

13. The following three lines follow Gill's wording closely: "*Secondly*, In some things civil and spiritual adoption differ. 1. Civil adoption could not be done without the consent of the adopted. . . . 2. Civil adoption was allowed of, and provided for the relief and comfort of such who had no children" (Gill, *A Body of Doctrinal Divinity*, 2:823–24, italics in the original).

14. Given the location of the word "in," Charles likely added it after he had written "Civil adoption."

15. The word "Pontifex" heralds to antiquity when the title "Pontifex Maximus" designated the high-priestly office of Caesar in the Roman Empire. Such authority allowed Caesar to marshal a "*comitia calata*, an assembly under the Presidency of the Pontifex Maximus called for religious purposes to witness ceremonies including adoptions" (Hugh Lindsay, *Adoption in the Roman World* [Cambridge: Cambridge University Press, 2009], 222). See also Josephus's comparison of Caesar to the Jewish high-priesthood in *Antiquity of the Jews* (Flavius Josephus, *The Works of Flavius Josephus: The Learned and Authentic Jewish Historian and Celebrated Warrior* [trans. William Whiston; London: William Allason and J. Maynard, 1818, The Spurgeon Library], 2:286–87). The reference to "Pontifex" in this sermon originated with Gill (see Gill, *A Body of Doctrinal Divinity*, 2:824); however, the Roman Catholic connotation likely did not escape Charles. His critiques of Roman Catholicism were often less subtle (see the 295-page essay he wrote in 1849, "Antichrist and

Her Brood; or, Popery Unmasked" (*Autobiography* 1:58); "Pleasure in the Stones of Zion" (Notebook 1, Sermon 53); "Self Deception" (Notebook 2, Sermon 78); "Justification by Imputed Righteousness" (Notebook 2, Sermon 117); and "Come Ye Out from Among Them" (Notebook 2, Sermon 119). In his dictionary Samuel Johnson defined the word "pontiff" with the words "The Pope" (Samuel Johnson, *A Dictionary of the English Language: In Which the Words Are Deduced from Their Originals, and Illustrated in Their Different Significations by Examples from the Best Writers, to Which Are Prefixed, a History of the Language, and an English Grammar* [6th ed.; 2 vols.; London: J. F. and C. Rivington et al., 1785, The Spurgeon Library], s.v. "pontiff").

16. The second and third Roman numerals were original to Gill (Gill, *A Body of Doctrinal Divinity*, 2:825 and 2:827).

17. Cf. "FREE GRACE" on the title page of this notebook. See also "The Treasure of Grace" (*NPSP* 6, Sermon 295).

18. Cf. Eph 2:9.   19. Cf. 2 Pet 2:4.   20. Cf. John 17:9.

21. On the following page Charles again listed the villages where he preached this sermon with their accompanying dates. The reason for this repetition is unclear; however, he may have originally concluded the sermon after the third Roman numeral and later expanded it onto the following page. Or, more likely, Charles sought more specificity and organization in the recording of this data. Whereas in the first list, the dates precede the villages, in the second, the villages precede the dates, separated by a vertical line from the numbers "11. 12. 13. 26."

22. Charles inserted ditto marks between the two dashes to signify the repetition of the word/number above.

23. On the following page, Charles spelled this village "Cherryhinton." See also his spelling in "Salvation" (Sermon 11).

24. The phrase "surprising grace" may have been inspired by Isaac Watts (1674–1748): "Just in the last distressing hour, / The Lord displays deliv'ring pow'r; / The mount of danger is the place / Where we shall see surprising grace" (Isaac Watts, *Psalms, Hymns, and Spiritual Songs* [London: T. Nelson and Sons, 1860, The Spurgeon Library], 432). For additional references to hymns by Watts, see *MTP* 17:371; 41:15; and 46:63. Charles used the phrase "surprising grace" throughout his later

ministry, e.g., "Nay, brethren, such is the surprising grace of God, that he has not only been pleased to save men who did not expect it, but he has even condescended to interpose for the salvation of men who were fighting with his grace and violently opposing his cause" (*ST* March 1872:111; see also *MTP* 20:72).

25. The Roman numeral iii was inserted above the line and indicated by a caret. First John 3:1, "Behold, what manner of love the Father hath bestowed upon us, that we should be called the sons of God: therefore the world knoweth us not, because it knew him not."

26. "1 *John* iii: 1. considering all things; and it will appear so, when the adopter and the adopted are put in a contrast " (Gill, *A Body of Doctrinal Divinity*, 2:827).

27. "6. All other inheritances are subject to corruption, and have pollution written upon them, are fading things, and liable to be lost, and often are; but this is an incorruptible crown, a crown of glory, that fadeth not away" (ibid., 2:829).

28. "Adoption is a blessing and privilege that always continues. The love of God, which is the source of it, always remains" (ibid.).

29. Charles added the word "love" to this list, likely exchanging it for Gill's word "compassion" in the sentence "V. The Effects of adoption.—1. A share in the pity, compassion, and care of God, their heavenly Father" (ibid.).

30. Cf. Eph 3:12; Heb 4:16.   31. Cf. Rom 8:29.

32. Cf. Rom 8:17; 2 Cor 6:18. Six dots appear after the word "Heirship." Charles likely intended them to signal the conclusion of his sermon and the beginning of his final remarks.

33. These remarks served as Charles's reminder as to how to conclude the sermon. For similar examples, see "Necessity of Purity for an Entrance to Heaven" (Sermon 2); "Beginning in Jerusalem" (Sermon 29); "Elijah's Faith and Prayer" (Sermon 44); and "Pleasure in the Stones of Zion" (Sermon 53).

34. The line that stretches across the page was a signal of the sermon's conclusion. The break in the line above the number 26 was unintentional. With the exceptions of "Regeneration" (Sermon 7), "Final Perseverance" (Sermon 8), and "Election"

(Sermon 10), Charles used similar lines to signal the conclusion of his sermons throughout the beginning of Notebook 1. Charles abandoned this tendency in the sermon "The Wrong Roads" (Sermon 32).

35. Numbers such as "11. 12. 13. 26." are found throughout the notebooks and correspond to the specific occasion on which Charles preached a particular sermon. For instance, on the eleventh, twelfth, thirteenth, and twenty-sixth times Charles preached, he did so using this sermon outline. This data is helpful in establishing not only a timeline of Charles's itinerate preaching ministry before his pastorate at Waterbeach Chapel but also patterns in his selection of biblical texts and topics. In this instance Charles preached from the same outline three times on two consecutive Sundays (twice on April 13 and once on April 20). After he became a pastor, he often preached two times each Sunday and five times during the week (*Autobiography* 1:38).

36. Charles separated the two words "Cherry" and "Hinton" on the previous page.

2

Rev. 21. 27. Necessity of Purity for an entrance to Heaven. 2

Enter in. Glory. joy. peace, happiness. Heaven. ✓

I. The Strictness of the Law... "anything"

   Satan cannot   what a matter of rejoicing to Xⁿ

   Sin cannot

Man cannot. He is defiled

? How can man enter? Not by ceremonies.

                        Not by Law

                        Not by Sincere Obedience in Part.

    The heart must be purified.

  All past sin forgiven. How?   By Free grace.

  All present sin crucified. How?   By the Holy Spirit

  All future sin avoided. How?   By the Spirit's help.

II. The Impossibility of entrance. "by no means"

God has said so. He will not allow it

  Nor angels. Nor the redeemed .. A wicked man would

not be happy in heaven....

No prayers. cries. groans. strife. can get a dead, unholy,

sinner into heaven ..   In no wise

III. If a man is not in he is out.

  for ever, no coming in, no change,

Call to enter in by faith in Jesus Christ.

Barton. Feb. 9. 51.   4.7.55.

Grantchester. Feb 23. 51.

Waterbeach Oct. 19. 51

2

✓[1]

NECESSITY *of* PURITY *for an* ENTRANCE *to* HEAVEN[2]
Revelation 21:27[3]

"And there shall in no wise enter into it any thing that defileth, neither whatsoever worketh abomination, or maketh a lie; but they which are written in the Lamb's book of life."

Enter in. Glory, joy, peace, happiness, Heaven.[4]

I. THE STRICTNESS OF THE LAW. *"anything."*

Satan cannot. ⎫
Sin cannot.   ⎬ What a matter of rejoicing to X^{n}.[5]

Man cannot. He is defiled.

? How can man enter?[6]

Not by ceremonies.
Not by Law.
Not by Sincere Obedience in Part.

The heart must be purified.

All past sin forgiven.	How?	By Free grace.[7]
All present sin crucified.	How?	By the Holy Spirit.
All future sin avoided.	How?	By the Spirit's help.

II. THE IMPOSSIBILITY OF ENTRANCE. *"by no means."*[8]
God has said so. He will not allow it. Nor angels. Nor the redeemed.
A wicked man would not be happy in heaven. No prayers,
cries, groans, strife can get a dead, unholy sinner into heaven. In no wise.[9]

III. IF A MAN IS NOT IN, HE IS OUT. FOREVER,
NO COMING IN, NO CHANGE.

— — — — — — — — — — — — — — — —[10]

Call to enter in by faith in Jesus Christ.[11]

Barton.	Feb. 9, [18]51	4. 7. 55.
Grantchester.	Feb 23, [18]51	
Waterbeach[12]	Oct. 19, [18]51	

1. As in the previous sermon, "Adoption" (Sermon 1), a red check mark appears in the top right corner of the page. Its significance is unclear.

2. Susannah included a transcription of this sermon outline in *Autobiography* 1:216. As in the previous sermon, "Adoption" (Sermon 1), Susannah altered Charles's wording and punctuation. The following changes were made: The word "'anything'" was changed to "any thing that defileth." The phrase "Man cannot. He is defiled" was deleted. The words "Not by Law" were changed to "Not by the law." The phrase "Free grace" was hyphenated. The phrase "by no means" was changed to "in no wise." The phrase "Nor angels" was changed to "nor will the angels." The underscore in the phrase "In no wise" was removed. And the line "If a man is not in he is out. Forever, no coming in, no change" was changed to "If a man is not in, he is out for ever, no coming in, no change." See also Susannah's transcription of "Adoption" (Sermon 1) and "Abraham Justified by Faith" (Sermon 3).

3. In 1881, Charles preached an additional sermon on Rev 21:27 entitled "The Barrier" (*MPT* 27, Sermon 1590). The overlapping context suggests Charles had in mind the above outline in writing his later sermon.

4. An alternative reading of this line is "Enter in[to] glory, joy, peace, happiness, [and] heaven."

5. Abbr., "Christian." For additional examples of this abbreviation throughout the notebooks, see "Jesus and His Acts" (Notebook 2, Sermon 84); "The Certain Judgment" (Notebook 3, Sermon 136); "Continue in Prayer" (Notebook 4, Sermon 220); "No Bone Broken" (Notebook 8, Sermon 370); and "Unsavoury Things" (Notebook 9, Sermon 398). An alternative reading of this line is "What a matter of rejoicing to [the] Christian!"

6. This is the only time in Notebook 1 that Charles preceded a sentence with a question mark.

7. This is the second occurrence of the phrase "free grace" in the sermons of Notebook 1 (the first occurrence is found in "Adoption" [Sermon 1]). See also "FREE GRACE" on the title page of this notebook.

8. Charles modified the KJV with the words "in no wise."

9. John 6:37, "All that the Father giveth me shall come to me; and him that cometh to me I will in no wise cast out." Charles preached on John 6:37 one additional time in his early notebooks (see "Nowise Cast Out," [Notebook 4, Sermon 212]). Later in his ministry he preached six additional sermons on John 6:37: "The Certainty and Freeness of Divine Grace" (*MTP* 10, Sermon 599); "High Doctrine and Broad Doctrine" (*MTP* 30, Sermon 1762); "All Comers to Christ Welcomed" (*MTP* 40, Sermon 2349); "The Big Gates Wide Open" (*MTP* 51, Sermon 2954); "No. 3000, Or, Come and Welcome" (*MTP* 52, Sermon 3000); and "The Last Message for the Year" (*MTP* 56, Sermon 3230).

10. Charles used dashes in this sermon to signal the beginning of his final remarks.

11. Charles wrote the phrase "Call to enter in by faith in Jesus Christ" to signal how he should conclude the sermon. These remarks suggest Charles extended publicly a call to repentance; however, altar calls were foreign to Charles's ministry. In the construction of the Metropolitan Tabernacle, Charles installed enquiry rooms for those who wished to seek spiritual counsel and respond to the sermon after the conclusion of the service (see *MTP* 30:456 and 46:583).

12. Charles had preached four sermons at Waterbeach Chapel before he preached from the above outline. His first sermon as pastor was "Salvation from Sin" (Sermon 33), on the fifty-first time Charles preached, and reveals that he incorporated previously written sermons into his ministry at Waterbeach. This tendency can be seen again after he accepted the pastorate at New Park Street Chapel in April 1854 and throughout his ministry at the Metropolitan Tabernacle. For instance, Charles likely had the above outline in mind for his sermon "The Barrier" (*MTP* 27:169).

3.

Genesis. 15. 6. Abraham justified by faith.

I. The Fact.. "believed God."

Leaving his Country. Life in Canaan. Sodom.
Isaac's birth. Promises to him. Isaac's Sacrifice.

2. Sorts of Faith. 1. Historical or Dead Faith.
2. Living Faith. producing works.

II. The Result.. "counted to him for righteousness".

1. Sins forgiven.

2. Righteousness imputed } by faith.

and by it.

He gained on earth. God's favour & love.
He gained Heaven & Eternal Life...

these bring. Peace. How easy lies the head that does will

Love. When we are pure we love God

Joy. The justified person has

Comfort. All things work together for good.

Security. None can condemn nor destroy.

III. As Abraham was saved so must we be.

Not by works or Abraham would have been.

Not by ceremonies Abram believed befor circumcis?

Reasons why we should believe God, both

sinner & Christian & exhortations to it.

ABRAHAM JUSTIFIED *by* FAITH[1]
Genesis 15:6[2]

"And he believed in the LORD; and he counted it to him for righteousness."

I. THE FACT. *"believed God."*[3]

Leaving his Country.[4] Life in Canaan. Sodom.[5] Isaac's birth.[6]
Promises to him.[7] Isaac's Sacrifice.[8]
Two[9] Sorts[10] of Faith: 1. Historical, or Dead Faith.[11]
                                  2. Living Faith, producing works.[12]

II. THE RESULT. *"counted to him for righteousness."*[13]

1. Sins forgiven.[14]
2. Righteousness imputed.[15]   } by faith

And by it:

He gained on earth God's favour and love.[16]
He gained Heaven and Eternal Life.

These bring:

Peace. How easy lies the head that does no ill.[17]
Love. When we are pure we love God.
Joy. The Justified person has.
Comfort. All things work together for good.[18]
Security. None can condemn nor destroy.[19]

III. AS ABRAHAM WAS SAVED, SO MUST WE BE.

Not by works, or Abraham would have been.
Not by ceremonies. Abram believed before[20] circumcision.[21]

Reasons why we should believe God, both[22] sinner and Christian, and exhortations to it.[23]

---

1. Susannah included a transcription of this sermon in *Autobiography* 1:216. Her alterations include the following changes: The words "believed God" in the first Roman numeral and "counted to him for righteousness" in the second were removed from Charles's original wording and aligned with the KJV's wording of Gen 15:6. The word "And" in the phrase "And by it" was deleted. The phrase "on earth" was deleted from the sentence "He gained on earth God's favour and love." An exclamation mark was added after the word "ill" in the sentence "How easy lies the head that does no ill." The line "Joy. The Justified person has" was changed to "Joy. The justified person has true joy." The final line, "Reasons why we should believe God, both sinner and Christian, and exhortations to it," was changed to "Reasons why sinners and Christians should believe God; exhortation to faith." See also Susannah's transcription of the previous two sermons, "Adoption" (Sermon 1) and "Necessity of Purity for an Entrance to Heaven" (Sermon 2).

2. In 1868, Charles preached an additional sermon on Gen 15:6 entitled "Justification by Faith—Illustrated by Abram's Righteousness" (*MTP* 14, Sermon 844). Overlapping content exists; however, the lack of structural similarities suggests Charles did not follow the general contours of the sermon above. The sermon that most resembles the outline above is "Abraham, a Pattern to Believers" (*MTP* 39, Sermon 2292). However, in this case also, there is not enough overlap to suggest Charles had the above outline in mind while writing his later sermon. For additional sermons on Abraham, see "The Call of Abraham" (Notebook 3, Sermon 152); "The Call of Abraham" (*NPSP* 5, Sermon 261); "Hearken and Look; or, Encouragement for Believers" (*MTP* 27, Sermon 1596); and "Sarah and Her Daughters" (*MTP* 27, Sermon 1633).

3. The phrase "believed God" does not come from Gen 15:6. Charles was quoting instead Rom 4:3, "For what saith the scripture? Abraham believed God, and it was counted unto him for righteousness."

4. Cf. Gen 12:1; Heb 11:8.   5. Cf. Gen 18:16–33.   6. Cf. Gen 21:5.

7. Cf. Gen 12:2–3; 13:14–17; 17:2–8; 22:17–18.   8. Cf. Gen 22:1–18.

9. Charles wrote the number 2 instead of the word "two." He may have originally intended this number to represent the second point in a list as seen beneath the second Roman numeral. However, for reasons that are unclear, he used the number 2 to represent the word "two" in the phrase "Two Sorts of Faith."

10. The letter "h" was added to the end of the word "Sort." Charles changed the "h" to "s."

11. Cf. Jas 2:17, 26.   12. Cf. Eph 2:10.

13. The phrase "counted to him for righteousness" does not come from Gen 15:6. Charles again quoted Rom 4:3, "For what saith the scripture? Abraham believed God, and it was counted unto him for righteousness." For an additional example, see "Necessity of Purity for an Entrance to Heaven" (Sermon 2).

14. "While the promise is still in his ears, while the ink is yet wet in the pen of the Holy Spirit, writing him down as justified, he must see a sacrifice, and see it, too, in emblems which comprehend all the revelation of sacrifice made to Aaron" (*MTP* 14:682).

15. Cf. "Jehova Tsidkenu—the Lord Our Righteousness" (*MTP* 7, Sermon 395).

16. Charles may have intended this line to read "He gained on earth" or "He gained on earth God's favour and love." Given the emphasis on "Heaven" in the line beneath, the former interpretation is more likely.

17. The phrase "How easy lies the head that does no ill" may have been influenced by William Shakespeare (1564–1616): "Uneasy lies the head that wears a crown" (William Shakespeare, *King Henry IV* [Arden ed.; ed. A. R. Humphreys; London: Thomson Learning, 2007; repr., London: Methuen & Co., Ltd, 1981], 2:91). Throughout his ministry Charles evidenced a familiarity with Shakespeare's works. His friend and biographer W. Williams reminisced, "We had several talks, on different occasions, about Shakespeare. He had read all his plays, and some of them many times" (*Autobiography* 4:284; see also W. Williams, *Personal Reminiscences of Charles Haddon Spurgeon* [2nd ed.; New York: Fleming H. Revell, 1895], 81). For Charles's personal copy of Shakespeare, see William Shakespeare, *The Poetical Works of William Shakespeare and the Earl of Surrey: With Memoirs, Critical Dissertations, and Explanatory Notes* (ed. George Gilfillan; Edinburgh: James Nichol, 1856, The Spurgeon Library).

18. Romans 8:28, "And we know that all things work together for good to them that love God, to them who are the called according to his purpose."

19. Cf. Rom 8:34.

20. Charles did not include the letter "e" in the word "before." He likely intended to abbreviate the entire phrase "before circumcision."

21. Abbr., "circumcision."

22. The letter "y" was written beneath "o" in the word "both." Charles may have originally written the word "by" before changing it to "both."

23. The phrase "and exhortations to it" was a reminder as to how to conclude the final remarks of this sermon. A similar phrase, "Call to enter in by faith in Jesus Christ," is found at the conclusion of the previous sermon, "Necessity of Purity for an Entrance to Heaven" (Sermon 2). See also Charles's use of the word "Directions" at the conclusion of "An Answer Required" (Sermon 19) and in "Making Light of Christ" (Sermon 21).

4.   Ephesians 5:4 .. 8 ... A Contrast.   4

Here we observe

I. The Past state of a Christian. "darkness"
  1. Ignorance . of God . of depravity , of Christ.
  2. Sin ... In heart, life
  3. Sorrow .. Indifference is smothered sorrow.

II. The Glorious Change . "now are ye light"
  1. Knowledge of God & spiritual things, as well as themselves
  2. Holiness — Purity. Love to God .
  3. Joy — Every Christian should rejoice

III. How effected "in the Lord."
Meritoriously.   By Jesus.
Actively ...   By the Holy Spirit.

IV. The Exhortation "walk as Children of light"
  1. Humbly, obediently. "as children".
  2. Trusting in their divine Father
  3. Cheerfully as children of light "or joy
  4. Holily. giving themselves to God ......
and in every way walking worthy of their dignity ..

Comberton. May 11/51

14.

A CONTRAST[1]
Ephesians[2] 5:8[3]

"For ye were sometimes darkness, but now are ye light in the Lord: walk as children of light."

Here we observe:

I.   THE PAST STATE OF A CHRISTIAN. *"darkness."*

    1. Ignorance of God, of depravity, of Christ.

    2. Sin. In heart, life.

    3. Sorrow. Indifference is smothered sorrow.[4]

II. THE GLORIOUS CHANGE. *"now are ye light."*

    1. Knowledge of God and spiritual things, as well as [of] themselves.

    2. Holiness. Purity.[5] Love to God.

    3. Joy. Every Christian should rejoice.

III. HOW EFFECTED. *"in the Lord."*

Meritoriously.   By Jesus.

Actively.   By the Holy Spirit.

IV. THE EXHORTATION. *"walk as Children of light."*

    1. Humbly, obediently, "as children."[6]

    2. Trusting in their divine Father.[7]

    3. Cheerfully, "as children of light," or joy[fully].

    4. Holily.[8] Giving themselves to God, and in every way walking worthy of their dignity.[9]

Comberton.   May 11/[18]51[10]

15[11]

1. This is the only time Charles preached a sermon on Eph 5:8. However, in 1887, he preached a similar sermon from Eph 5:11 entitled "The Child of Light and the Works of Darkness" (*MTP* 41, Sermon 2401). However, there is insufficient structural similarity to suggest Charles used the above outline in writing his later sermon.

2. The letter "h" was written in pencil between the letters "p" and "e" in the word "Ephesians." Charles may have sought to abbreviate the word as he did in the indices at the beginning and end of this notebook.

3. Charles originally wrote the number 4 in the Scripture reference. The correct Scripture reference for this sermon is Eph 5:8. The number 4 was struck through in pencil and replaced with the number 5. The correct Scripture reference was not listed in the beginning or ending indices in this notebook. If Charles intended to preach from Eph 4:8, the Scripture would have been "Wherefore he saith, When he ascended up on high, he led captivity captive, and gave gifts unto men." In 1871, Charles did preach a sermon on Eph 4:7–12 entitled "The Ascension of Christ" (*MTP* 17, Sermon 982).

4. The sentence "Indifference is smothered sorrow" was likely original to Charles; however, the phrase "smothered sorrow" was common to Victorian England. During the same year that Charles preached from the sermon outline above, the phrase was published in *The Baptist Magazine*: "Some were proud and elate as the cable jerked through the hawses, for they had left hunger and desolation far behind, and were now surely on the way to friends and hope and prosperity; some seemed drunk and dizzy with smothered sorrow; others sobbed passionately, rocking to and fro as the rough chant of the sailors swelled fitfully over their work" (*The Baptist Magazine for 1851*, vol. 43 [London: Houlston and Stoneman, 1851], 671).

5. Cf. "Necessity of Purity for an Entrance to Heaven" (Sermon 2).

6. Cf. Mic 6:8.

7. Cf. "In the Father . . . trustively" in "Salvation in God Only" (Sermon 24).

8. "Piously; with sanctity" (Johnson's *Dictionary*, s.v. "holily").

9. This line may have been inspired by English Puritan Thomas Manton (1620–1677): "Oh remember your dignity, and walk worthy of your high calling; walk as

having the world under your feet, with an holy scorn and contempt of sublunary enjoyments: And as you should walk worth of the *dignity* of your calling, so of the *purity* of it" (Thomas Manton, *A Practical Commentary; or, an Exposition with Notes on the Epistle of St. Jude, Delivered [for the most part] in Sundry Weekly Lectures, at Stoke-Newington in Middlesex* [2nd ed.; London: Luke Fawn, 1662, The Spurgeon Library], 24, italics in the original). The word "Sanctified," likely written by Charles, is found in the margin on the left side of this page.

10. Four days after Charles preached from the outline above, he wrote the following words in a letter to his father on May 15, 1851: "I am very comfortable and I may say, happy. Were it not for my vile heart, I might rejoice. I am the least of God's people. I am sure I am the worst. But yet, I am one, I believe, in Jesus and trust in him, and this I take it is the evidence of life. I can fall into his arms, though I cannot rest on my own merits, for I have none. Jesus and him alone is my defence. I know you pray for me. I think I have felt the answer to your earnest entreaties. Sometimes I pour my heart out sweetly, freely. At another time, I cannot hardly bring up a petition. What a contrast, mixture, paradox I am" (Angus Library and Archive, Regent's Park College, Oxford University, D/SPU 1, Letter 9).

11. Did Charles intend this number to be 14 or 15? The number 5 is darker than 4, which might evidence redaction; however, the number 15 is also found at the conclusion of his sermon in Comberton entitled "Future Judgment" (Sermon 6). This suggests Charles changed the number 15 to 14 in the sermon above.

5   2 Cor . 8 . 9 . Condescending Love of Jesus.

I . The glorious Person & his exalted state .

   a The son of God .. Ruler of the Universe — God .

   B. Rich in glory, authority, power, felicity.

Residence Heaven . Servants — angels . a crowned monarch

II. The gracious act .. "became poor".

   a . In the act of putting on humanity .

   B . He was poor all his life time .

   Y . He died a criminal . owed his burial to charity.

affliction . pain . hunger . temptation . fatigue. agony. death.

III . The persons for whom . "for our sake".

   1 . His own creatures .

   2 . Guilty . hell deserving sinners .

   3 . His own murderers . about to perish

The vilest of the vile . Mary . the thief . Saul .

IV . The purpose . "that ye through his poverty may be rich.

   a . We gain liberty

   b . Life is spared

   c . Deliverance from sin. Pardon.

   d . All things richly to enjoy . & heaven.

He gained our lost inheritance . more wealthy are we

than the possessor of India's golden mines .

     Of his own will . "he became."

Comberton . March 9. 51 & 9°

CONDESCENDING LOVE *of* JESUS
2 Corinthians 8:9[1]

"For ye know the grace of our Lord Jesus Christ, that, though he was rich,
yet for your sakes he became poor, that ye through his poverty might be rich."

I. THE GLORIOUS PERSON AND HIS EXALTED STATE.

α.[2] The son of God. Ruler of the Universe. God.

β. Rich in glory, authority, power, felicity. Residence: Heaven. Servants, angels. A crowned monarch.[3]

II. THE GRACIOUS ACT. *"became poor."*

α. In the act of putting on humanity.[4]

β. He was poor all his lifetime.[5]

γ. He died a criminal. Owed his burial to charity. Affliction.[6] Pain. Hunger. Temptation. Fatigue. Agony. Death.[7]

III. THE PERSONS FOR WHOM. *"for our sake."*

1. His own creatures.

2. Guilty, hell-deserving sinners.

3. His own murderers, about to perish.[8] The vilest of the vile. Mary.[9] The thief.[10] Saul.[11]

IV. THE PURPOSE. *"that ye through his poverty may be rich."*

a. We gain liberty.[12]

b. Life is spared.

c. Deliverance from sin. Pardon.[13]

d. All things richly to enjoy. And heaven.

He gained our lost inheritance. More wealthy are we[14] than the possessor of India's golden mines.[15]

. . . .[16]

Of his own will. "he became."

Comberton.   March 9, [18]51[17]

1. Charles preached six additional sermons on 2 Cor 8:9: "The Condescension of Christ" (*NPSP* 3, Sermon 151); "Christ's Motive and Ours" (*MTP* 37, Sermon 2232); "Poverty and Riches" (*MTP* 40, Sermon 2364); "Christ's Poverty, Our Riches" (*MTP* 47, Sermon 2716); "Knowing and Doing" (*MTP* 54, Sermon 3092); and "Our Lord's Voluntary Poverty" (*MTP* 59, Sermon 3380). The sermon that most resembles the above outline is "The Condescension of Christ." For Charles's later treatment of the doctrine of the incarnation, see C. H. Spurgeon, *"Good Tidings of Great Joy": Christ's Incarnation the Foundation of Christianity* ([London: Passmore & Alabaster, 1901, The Spurgeon Library], 43–46, 116–18, 131).

2. Charles incorporated four ordering techniques in this sermon: Greek letters (alpha, beta, gamma), Roman numerals, English letters, and cardinal numbers. See also "Christian Prosperity and Its Causes" (Sermon 51).

3. For later references to Christ's kingship, see *MTP* 11:700; 12:77; 19:57; 46:474; 49:134; and 62:591.

4. Cf. *MTP* 36:493.

5. A modernization of the words "life" and "time" is "lifetime."

6. "There are no scourgings for thee, believer, for the stripes have all fallen upon thy Substitute. God's sword of justice has been sheathed in the very heart of Christ" (*MTP* 47:102).

7. An alternative reading of this line is "Owed his burial to charity, affliction, pain, hunger, temptation, fatigue, agony, [and] death."

8. An alternative reading of this line is "His own murderers [who are] about to perish."

9. The context suggests Charles was referencing Mary Magdalene (see Luke 8:2).

10. Cf. Luke 23:32–43.

11. Cf. Acts 7:58–60; 8:1–3; 22:20.

12. "Christ's captivity has led your captivity captive" (*MTP* 47:101).

13. See "A Sense of Pardoned Sin" (*NPSP* 6, Sermon 316).

14. The location and size of the words "are we" suggests Charles wrote them after he had written "than the possessor of India's golden mines" in the line below.

15. In 1792, Britain discovered gold deposits in the Province of Malabar, India (Radhe Shyam Rungta, *Rise of Business Corporations in India: 1851–1900* [vol. 8 of Cambridge South Asian Studies, London: Cambridge University Press, 1970], 136). The ensuing gold rush resulted in the mining of 2.5 million sovereigns from 1851 to 1885 (Moreton Frewen, "The Great Drain of Gold to India," *The Nineteenth Century and After XIX–XX* [vol. 73 New York: Leonard Scott Publication Co., London: Spottiswoode & Co. Ltd., January–June 1913], 61). Charles later referenced the British occupation of India and the use of India's natural resources in his sermon "Independence of Christianity" (*NPSP* 3, Sermon 149; see also *MTP* 17:148). Similar statements can be seen throughout Charles's ministry. On April 27, 1877, Charles delivered an address at Exeter Hall before the Baptist Missionary Society and said, "Pray for men, brethren; a man is more precious than the gold of Ophir—a man who stands out with consecrated spirit. O God, if we had such men" (*Speeches by C. H. Spurgeon: At Home and Abroad* [London: Passmore & Alabaster, 1878, The Spurgeon Library], 132). In his sermons Charles also referenced the gold mines of California (*MTP* 21:662) and Peru (*MTP* 44:302).

16. Seven dots appear above the sentence "Of his own will. 'he became.'" Charles used these dots to signal the conclusion of the sermon.

17. The numbers 9 and 1 were written after "March 9.51" The significance of these numbers is not obvious, but they could suggest Charles also preached this sermon on March 1. Another interpretation is that Charles intended the stroke to serve as a vertical separator. The stippling around these numbers was smudged. Unlike the ellipses two lines above, the dots here could reflect a pause in his thinking as demonstrated in "Sinners Must Be Punished" (Sermon 9) and "The Men Possessed of the Devils" (Sermon 70).

6.

Colossians. 3. 25. Future Judgment. 6

I. There will be a future Judgment.

Arg 1. God's moral Government supposes it.

" 2. Reason gives assent to it.

" 3. There have been fearful judgments in <u>this</u> world.

" 4. The best suffer here & the evil prosper ∴ there is a judgment.

" 5. The fears of dying sinners do confirm it.

" 6. The death of Christ proves it.

" 7. God's word & oath cancels it —

II. It will be impartial.

Wealth. Learning. Professions will have no influence.

Arg 1. Because God is just

" 2. If any thing pleaded could be accepted, all would be acquitted

" 3. In the word of God rich are threatened as well as poor.

" 4. Christ the Judge was one of the most impartial of men.

Inf. 1. If wealth &c will be of no avail. how should the poor fear.

" 2. Sin is a fearful thing, since punishment follows it.

" 3. Sinners are in an awful condition.

" 4. No hope for a sinner but in Jesus.

_____

Comberton May 11. 51✳. 15. 49. 54.

FUTURE JUDGMENT
Colossians 3:25[1]

*"But he that doeth wrong shall receive for the wrong which
he hath done: and there is no respect of persons."*

I. THERE WILL BE[2] A FUTURE JUDGMENT.

Arg[3] 1. God's moral Government[4] supposes it.
" 2. Reason gives assent to it.
" 3. There have been fearful judgments in <u>this</u> world.
" 4. The best suffer here, and the evil prosper ∴[5] there is a judgment.
" 5. The fears of dying sinners do confirm it.
" 6. The death of Christ proves it.
" 7. God's word and oath[6] cancels it.

II. IT WILL BE IMPARTIAL.
Wealth, Learning, Professions will have no influence.

Arg. 1. Because God is just.
" 2. If anything pleaded could be accepted, all would be acquitted.
" 3. In the word of God, rich are threatened as well as poor.
" 4.[7] Christ the Judge was ~~one of~~[8] the most impartial of men.

Inf.[9] 1. If wealth and will be of no avail, how should the poor fear?
" 2. Sin is a fearful thing since punishment follows it.[10]
" 3. Sinners are in an awful[11] condition.
" 4. No hope for a sinner but in Jesus.[12]

Comberton.   May 11, [18]51[13]   15. 49. 54.

1. This is the only time Charles preached a sermon on Col 3:25. For additional sermons on judgment, see "Convince the World of Sin, Righteousness, and Judgment" (Notebook 4, Sermon 190); "The General Judgment" (Notebook 7, Sermon 323); "Jesus the Judge" (*MTP* 25, Sermon 1476); and "The Mediator, Judge, and Savior" (*MTP* 26, Sermon 1549).

2. Two diagonal pencil lines were written faintly beneath the words "be" and "moral" in the line below. Similar lines are found in "Final Perseverance" (Sermon 8) and "Christian and His Salvation" (Sermon 17).

3. Abbr., "Argument." This is the first time in Notebook 1 that Charles incorporated a form of argumentation of this kind. The structure of this outline is reminiscent of those of the Puritan sermons Charles was reading. See, for instance, Charles's personally signed copy of Charles Simeon, *Helps to Composition; or, Six Hundred Skeletons of Sermons, Several Being the Substance of Sermons Preached Before the University* ([3rd ed.; London: Luke Hansard & Sons, 1815, The Spurgeon Library], 4:454–57). For sermons in this notebook in which Charles borrowed from Simeon's outlines, see "The Son's Love to Us Compared with God's Love to Him" (Sermon 38) and "Regeneration, Its Causes and Effects" (Sermon 46). Charles inserted ditto marks throughout the sermon above to represent the repetition of the words "Argument" and "Inference."

4. Charles did not cite Jonathan Edwards directly, but he may have been influenced by Edwards's treatment of God's Moral Government: "I would again argue, that God must maintain a moral government over mankind, thus:—It is evident, that it was agreeable to the Creator's design, that there should be *some* moral government maintained amongst men; because, without any, either in nations, provinces, towns, or families, and also without any divine government over the whole, the world of mankind could not subsist, but would destroy itself. Men would be not only much more destructive to each other, than any kind of animals are to their own species, but a thousand times more than any kind of beasts are to those of any other species. . . . Therefore, it is doubtless the original design of the Creator, that there should be moral subordination amongst men, and that he designed there should be heads, princes, or governors, to whom honour, subjection, and obedience should be paid" (Jonathan Edwards et al., *The Works of Jonathan Edwards, A.M. With an Essay on His Genius and Writings* [2 vols.; London: Ball, Arnold, and Co., 1840, The Spurgeon Library], 2:512, italics in the original).

5. The three triangular dots form the symbol for the word "therefore." For similar uses of this symbol, see "Beginning at Jerusalem" (Sermon 29) and "Inventory and Title of Our Treasures" (Notebook 2, Sermon 92). The line reads "The best suffer here and the evil [ones] prosper. Therefore, there is a judgment."

6. The letter "t," likely written prematurely, appears beneath the letter "a" in the word "oath."

7. An illegible number, likely 3, was written beneath 4.

8. Charles struck through the words "one of" to highlight that Christ possessed the greatest degree of impartiality.

9. Abbr., "Inference." For an additional use of the word "inference," see "Can Two Walk Together Unless They Are Agreed?" (Sermon 76).

10. Cf. "Sinners Must Be Punished" (Sermon 9).

11. The letter "a" was smudged. The source of the smudge was likely the stippling in the line below.

12. A modernization of this line is "Jesus is the only hope for a sinner."

13. What appears to be an asterisk is found after the number 51. This symbol could also be the result of multidirectional strikethroughs of the number 1.

7   Regeneration.

I. Its character may be best understood from the terms
    denoting it as . "born again", "born from above"
 "new birth", "quickened", "Christ formed in us",
   "partakers of the divine nature" "grace", "spirit," "seed"
We may also learn that it is a work in which man
 is passive ,   it is 1 irresistable,
                            2. instantaneous.
                            3. perfect,
                            4. cannot be undone
                            5. Warfare in the soul accompanies it

II Cause.
        1 Efficient cause . A God not man
          a for man does not comprehend it.
          b. it is called Creation + Resurrection.
          c. Scripture denies it to be of man.
          B. God only . Father . Son . Spirit
      2. Impulsive .. Free Grace.
      3. Procuring . Christ's merits.
      4. Instrumental. Word of God .

III . Effects . 1 . Spirit of God is given.
                       2. Knowledge is imparted
                       3. Capacity for good works
                       4. Meetness for heaven .

REGENERATION[1]

I. ITS CHARACTER MAY BE BEST UNDERSTOOD FROM THE TERMS DENOTING IT AS:

"Born again,"[2] *"born from above," "new birth," "quickened," "Christ*[3] *formed in us,"*[4] *"partakers of the divine nature,"*[5] *"grace," "spirit,"*[6] *"seed."*[7]

We may also learn that it is a work in which man is passive.[8] It is:

1.[9] Irresistible.[10]

2. Instantaneous.

3. Perfect.

4. Cannot be undone.

5. Warfare[11] in the soul accompanies it.

II. CAUSE.

1. Efficient cause.
   A. God, not man.
     a. For man does not comprehend it.[12]
     b. It is called Creation and Resurrection.
     c. Scripture denies it to be of man.[13]
   B. God only. Father. Son. Spirit.[14]

2. Impulsive. Free Grace.[15]

3. Procuring.[16] Christ's merits.

4. Instrumental. Word of God.

III. EFFECTS.

1. Spirit of God is given.

2. Knowledge is imparted.

3. Capacity for good works.[17]

4. Meetness[18] for heaven.

Ques. Am I regenerate? See Look for the effects. —

Except a man be born again he cannot see the kingdom of God. —

2 Kings. 7. 3.4 — The Lepers.

77

The Lepers fit emblems of sinners as having a loathsome, incurable, and fatal malady. their conduct is a fit picture of the growth of grace — Here was.

I. Thoughtfulness — however produced this in an almost invariable antecedent of the new birth, yet not the new birth itself — Argument with the thoughtless &c —

II. A conviction of distress — in the sinner's case a conviction of sin and a shudder at the second death. this is not conversion — Arg with unconvinced men —

III. A setting about something — but in a wrong spirit going to the wrong quarter, a conviction that in works, ceremonies &c there is a grievous famine Some know this & yet perish — Arg with Pharisees &c

IV. A sight or slight recognition of the only help. Jes.

V. A going to him, entirely on the footing of grace with ropes on our necks &c — this is the final step &c &c —

102

Ques.[19] Am I regenerate?[20] See, Look for the effects.

Except a man be born again, he cannot see the Kingdom of God.[21]

77

THE LEPERS[22]
2 Kings 7:3–4[23]

"And there were four leprous men at the entering in of the gate: and they said one to another, 'Why sit we here until we die? If we say, We will enter into the city, then the famine is in the city, and we shall die there: and if we sit still here, we die also. Now therefore come, and let us fall unto the host of the Syrians: If they save us alive, we shall live; and if they kill us, we shall but die.'"

The Lepers fit emblems of sinners as having a loathsome, incurable, and fatal malady. Their conduct is a fit picture of the[24] growth of grace. Here was:

I.   THOUGHTFULNESS.
    However produced, this i[s][25] an almost invariable antecedent of the new birth,[26] yet not the new birth itself.[27] Argument with the thoughtless, etc.

II. A CONVICTION OF DISTRESS.
    In the sinner's case, a conviction of sin[28] and a shudder at the second death.[29] This is not conversion. Arg[30] with unconvinced men.

III. A SETTING ABOUT SOMETHING,
    BUT IN A WRONG SPIRIT.
    Going to the wrong quarter. A conviction that in works, ceremonies, etc., there is a grievous famine. Some know this and yet perish. Arg[31] with Pharisees, etc.

IV. A SIGHT OR SLIGHT RECOGNITION
    OF THE ONLY HELP. Jesus.

V.   A GOING TO HIM ENTIRELY ON THE FOOTING[32]
    OF GRACE WITH ROPES ON OUR NECKS,[33]
    etc. This is the final step, etc. etc.[34]

102

1.	This is one of four sermons in the early notebooks for which Charles did not provide a Scripture reference. See also "Creation of Man" (Notebook 8, Sermon 369); "Faith Before Baptism" (Notebook 9, Sermon 396); and "The Day of Vengeance, the Year of Acceptance" (Notebook 9, Sermon 397). In the latter two sermons, the context reveals that Charles preached from Genesis 1 and Acts 8:34. However, there is no evidence in the sermon above that Charles used a particular text of Scripture. For additional sermons on regeneration, see "Baptismal Regeneration" (*MTP* 10, Sermon 573) and "The Necessity of Regeneration" (*MTP* 54, Sermon 3121). As in the case of "Adoption" (Sermon 1), this outline is original to John Gill. Charles borrowed extensively from his chapter "Of Regeneration" (Gill, *A Body of Doctrinal Divinity*, 2:836–50). Given the significant amount of overlapping content, only the differences between Charles's outline and Gill's chapter are noted below.

2.	Cf. John 3:3.

3.	An illegible letter, likely "n," is found beneath the "C" in the word "Christ." Charles may have intended to write the word "new."

4.	Cf. Gal 4:19.	5.	Cf. 2 Pet 1:4.

6.	Cf. Titus 3:5.	7.	Cf. 1 Pet 1:23.

8.	For a contrast to the phrase "a work in which man is passive," see "Actively. By the Holy Spirit" in "A Contrast" (Sermon 4).

9.	The location of the number 1 suggests Charles may not have originally intended to begin a list and instead added the number after he had written "2. Instantaneous."

10.	Charles originally wrote the word "irresistable." The letter "i" was written in pencil over the "a" to correct his misspelling.

11.	A definition of spiritual warfare is found in Charles's personal copy of the 1611 publication *A Christian Dictionary*. The third meaning under "warfare" states, "The condition of the Ministers of God, in regard of the strong opposition and resistance made against them by Sathan [*sic*] and wicked" (Thomas Wilson, *A Christian Dictionary. Opening the Significations of the Chiefe Words Dispersed Generally Through Holy Scriptures of the Old and New Testament, Tending to Increase Christian Knowledge. Whereunto*

Is Annexed, a Particular Dictionary for the Revelation of S. John. For the Canticles or Song of Solomon. For the Epistle to the Hebrews. The Fourth Edition; Augmented by Addition of Divers Thousands of Words, Phrases, and Significations, and by Explication of Liviticall Rites: Also, of Most Difficult and Ambiguous Speeches, with Farre More Profitable Annotations Than Before. Whereunto Is Likewise Added a Large Edition, Both of Words and Phrases, by Mr. John Bagwell [4th ed.; London: Thomas Cotes, 1611, The Spurgeon Library]).

12. Cf. John 1:5.

13. Cf. Titus 3:5.

14. The directionality of the ink suggests the source of the smear was the word "Spirit." The smear extends for four lines toward the top of the page.

15. Cf. "FREE GRACE" on the title page of this notebook.

16. Samuel Johnson offered two meanings of the word "procure" that apply to the context in the sermon above: "1. To manage; to transact for another" and "2. To obtain; to acquire" (Johnson's *Dictionary*). For additional uses of this word in Charles's early notebooks, see "The Saints' Justification and Glory" (Sermon 68) and "Man's Weakness and God's Strength" (Notebook 2, Sermon 108).

17. Cf. Eph 2:10.

18. From "meet," which Samuel Johnson defined as "Fit; proper; qualified" (Johnson's *Dictionary*). See also "The Affliction of Ahaz" (Sermon 57).

19. Abbr., "Question."

20. The words "Ques. Am I regenerate?" constitute the only discernible difference between Charles's outline and Gill's chapter. Gill concludes his chapter with the following words: "[F]or *whatsoever is born of God, overcometh the world*, and sin and Satan, and every enemy, and is more than a conqueror over all, through Christ!" (Gill, *A Body of Doctrinal Divinity*, 2:850, italics in the original).

21. John 3:3, "Jesus answered and said unto him, Verily, verily, I say unto thee, Except a man be born again, he cannot see the kingdom of God." See also Charles's personal copy of Austin Phelps, *Born Again; or, The Soul's Renewal* (London: Hodder and Stoughton, 1873, The Spurgeon Library).

22. This outline constitutes the final sermon in Notebook 1. Evidently Charles ran out of space at the end of this notebook and inserted this sermon in the empty space after "Regeneration" (Sermon 7). In the textual index at the beginning of this notebook, Charles indicated the location of this final sermon with the words "77 after 7." Also, in the penultimate sermon of this notebook, "Can Two Walk Together Unless They Are Agreed?" (Sermon 76), Charles wrote, "For 77 see 7." The reason for selecting this particular page is unclear. Charles could have also used the empty space on the page separating "Final Perseverance" (Sermon 8) from "Sinners Must Be Punished" (Sermon 9), or the blank page separating "Election" (Sermon 10) from "Salvation" (Sermon 11).

23. This is the only time Charles preached a sermon on 2 Kgs 7:3–4 specifically. However, in 1886 he preached a sermon on 2 Kgs 7:3–7 entitled "Who Found It Out?" (*MTP* 32, Sermon 1903). In the winter of 1861/2, he preached a sermon on 2 Kgs 7:4 entitled "The Sinner's Only Alternative" (*MTP* 50, Sermon 2894). There is not enough overlapping content or structural similarity in either sermon to suggest Charles had the above outline in mind while writing these later sermons.

24. The letter "g" was written beneath the "t" in the word "the." Charles likely began writing the word "growth" prematurely.

25. Charles originally wrote the word "in" as follows: "however produced this in an almost invariable antecedent of the new birth." The context suggests Charles intended to write the word "is."

26. Cf. John 3:3.

27. An alternative reading of this line is "yet [it is] not the new birth itself."

28. "May God drive every unconverted sinner into a corner, and so compel him to yield to grace! May he bring you to act in earnest; may he drive you by the extreme necessities of your case to seek and to find, to search and to discover!" (*MTP* 32:311).

29. Cf. Rev 20:14.

30. Abbr., "Argument." For a similar use of this word, see "Future Judgment" (Sermon 6).

31. Abbr., "Argument."

32.   An ink smudge is found above the word "footing." The source of the smudge may have been the tail of the letter "y" in the word "only" in the line above.

33.   The phrase "On the footing of grace with ropes on our necks" was likely a reference to 1 Kgs 20:31, "And his servants said unto him, Behold now, we have heard that the kings of the house of Israel are merciful kings: let us, I pray thee, put sackcloth on our loins, and ropes upon our heads, and go out to the king of Israel: peradventure he will save thy life." The phrase is also reminiscent of one Jonathan Edwards offered in his sermon "Sinners in the Hands of an Angry God." Edwards said, "Your wickedness makes you as it were heavy as lead, and to tend downwards with great weight and pressure towards hell; and if God should let you go, you would immediately sink and swiftly descend and plunge into the bottomless gulf; and your healthy constitution, and your own care and prudence, and best contrivance, and all your righteousness, would have no more influence to uphold you and keep you out of hell, than a spider's web would have to stop a falling rock" (Jonathan Edwards, Henry Rogers, and Sereno E. Dwight, *The Works of Jonathan Edwards with an Essay on His Genius and Writings by Henry Rogers: and a Memoir by Sereno E. Dwight* [rev. ed.; ed. Edward Hickman; 2 vols.; London: Ball, Arnold, and Co., 1840, The Spurgeon Library], 2:9).

34.   The words "etc. etc." may have represented Charles's concluding remarks. At the end of his 1886 sermon on the lepers, Charles pleaded, "You poor lepers, you poor lost and ruined ones, come to my Lord Jesus! Believe it, the whole land is before you: the land that floweth with milk and honey is for you. This world is yours, and worlds to come. Christ is yours; yea, God himself is yours. Everything is to be had for nothing. Heaven and all its joys are to be had upon believing. God make you the discoverers this day of his wondrous grace, and to him shall be praise for ever and ever! Amen" (*MTP* 32:312).

8   Psalm 94 . 14.   Final Perseverance.

I The text teaches the saints final Perseverance
which may be argued.

1. From Scripture. Job XVII. 9. Psalm. 125. 1. 2. Jer. 32. 40
John 10 . 28. John 17. 12 . 1 Cor 1. 8. 9 .. 1 Pet . 1. 5

2. From the work of grace itself. Hope. Love . Faith .

3.   From the Promises.

4 .   From God's Perfections   1 Immutability
                                     2, Wisdom.
                                       3. Power
                                       4. Goodness & grace
                                       5. Justice
                                       6. Faithfulness

5 . From his Eternal Purposes.

6 . From Christ's love & actions. Purchase,
church is his fulness, his spouse, his portion, Hephzibah,
Intercession. Mansions in heaven.

7 . From his gracious acts to them. Adoption
Justification, pardon &c _

II. It teaches the manner or reason of it.
We forsake him , we are empty need supply.

16,

8

FINAL PERSEVERANCE[1]
Psalm 94:14[2]

"For the Lord *will not cast off his people, neither will he forsake his inheritance."*

I. THE TEXT TEACHES THE SAINTS' FINAL PERSEVERANCE, WHICH MAY BE ARGUED:

1. From Scripture.[3] Job XVII.9;[4] Psalm 125:1–2;[5] Jer. 32:40;[6] John 10:28;[7] John 17:12;[8] 1 Cor. 1:8–9;[9] 1 Pet. 1:5.[10]

2. From the work of grace itself. Hope. Love. Faith.[11]

3. From the Promises.[12]

4. From God's Perfections:[13]
   1.[14] Immutability.[15]
   2. Wisdom.
   3. Power.[16]
   4. Goodness and grace.[17]
   5. Justice.
   6. Faithfulness.

5. From his Eternal Purposes.[18]

6. From Christ's love[19] and actions. Purchase.[20] Church is his fulness,[21] his spouse,[22] his portion.[23] Hephzibah,[24] Intercession,[25] Mansions in heaven.[26]

7. From his gracious acts to them. Adoption,[27] Justification,[28] pardon,[29] etc.

II. IT TEACHES THE MANNER OR REASON OF IT.

We forsake him.[30] We are empty.[31] Need supply.

16.

1. As in the previous sermons "Adoption" (Sermon 1) and "Regeneration" (Sermon 7), the content of the sermon outline above is original to John Gill. With few exceptions Charles followed Gill's fifteenth chapter, "Of the Perseverance of the Saints," in his second volume of *A Body of Doctrinal Divinity*. The overlapping content is noted below. The doctrine of final perseverance played a significant role in Charles's conversion. In 1869, he said, "If anything in this world first led me to desire to be a Christian, it was the doctrine of final perseverance of the saints" (*MTP* 15:300). For additional sermons on the doctrine of final perseverance, see "Final Perseverance Certain" (Notebook 2, Sermon 82); "The Perseverance of the Saints" (*MTP* 15, Sermon 872); and "The Final Perseverance of the Saints" (*MTP* 23, Sermon 1361).

2. This is the only time Charles preached a sermon on Ps 94:14 specifically. However, on May 24, 1888, he preached a sermon on Ps 94:12–15 entitled "Blessed Discipline" (*MTP* 40, Sermon 2374). The lack of overlapping content and structural similarities suggests Charles did not have the outline above in mind during the writing of the later sermon. Charles's exposition of Ps 94:14 at the end of his 1888 sermon is noted.

3. With the exception of Ps 94:14, the following seven Scripture references follow identically those provided by Gill (Gill, *A Body of Doctrinal Divinity*, 2:883–91). Charles likely did not include Ps 94:14 in his list since he already cited it as the guiding Scripture reference of this sermon. In his sermon "The Perseverance of the Saints," Charles listed Rom 11:29 and Heb 6:9–10 as additional Scripture references to support the doctrine of final perseverance (*MTP* 15:294–95).

4. Job 17:9, "The righteous also shall hold on his way, and he that hath clean hands shall be stronger and stronger." Like Gill, Charles also used Roman numerals in the Scripture reference. His discontinuation of this practice in the following Scripture reference marks a point of departure from Gill.

5. Psalm 125:1–2, "They that trust in the LORD shall be as mount Zion, which cannot be removed, but abideth for ever. As the mountains are round about Jerusalem, so the LORD is round about his people from henceforth even for ever."

6. Jeremiah 32:40, "And I will make an everlasting covenant with them, that I will not turn away from them, to do them good; but I will put my fear in their hearts, that they shall not depart from me."

7. John 10:28, "And I give unto them eternal life; and they shall never perish, neither shall any pluck them out of my hand." A dark stain, likely due to the aging process of the manuscript, is found in the left margin beneath the word "John." The source of the stain was likely the tail of the letter "J." An imprint of this stain is found on the right side of the following page.

8. John 17:12, "While I was with them in the world, I kept them in thy name: those that thou gavest me I have kept, and none of them is lost, but the son of perdition; that the scripture might be fulfilled."

9. First Corinthians 1:8–9, "Who shall also confirm you unto the end, that ye may be blameless in the day of our Lord Jesus Christ. God is faithful, by whom ye were called unto the fellowship of his Son Jesus Christ our Lord."

10. First Peter 1:5, "Who are kept by the power of God, through faith unto salvation, ready to be revealed in the last time."

11. In his sixth point, Gill referenced "[T]he several particular graces of which the work consists, are abiding ones, as faith, hope, and love" (Gill, *A Body of Doctrinal Divinity*, 2:897). See also "Characteristics of Faith" (*NPSP* 6, Sermon 317). Cf. 1 Cor 13:13.

12. At the conclusion of his sermon "Blessed Discipline," Charles appended the following words to his exposition of Ps 94:14: "If any of you are deeply troubled, I counsel you to get a hold of this promise. Perhaps it seems to you as if two seas of sorrow had met around you, and that you were in a whirlpool of trouble; then I say again, lay hold of this text, and grip it firmly: 'Jehovah will not cast off his people, neither will he forsake his inheritance'" (*MTP* 40:395).

13. Charles altered Gill's wording slightly: "*First*, From the perfections of God" (Gill, *A Body of Doctrinal Divinity*, 2:891, italics in the original). Charles also adopted the following subpoints that were original to Gill: "1. The immutability of God" (2:891); "2. The wisdom of God" (2:892); "3. The power of God" (2:892); "4. The goodness, grace, and mercy of God" (2:892); "5. The justice of God" (2:893); and "6. The faithfulness of God" (2:893).

14. The location of the number 1 suggests Charles may not have originally intended to write a list and instead added the number afterward. A similar instance is found in a previous sermon, "Regeneration" (Sermon 7).

15. The first sermon Charles published in the *The New Park Street Pulpit* was entitled "The Immutability of God" (*NPSP* 1, Sermon 1). For similar sermons, see "The Immutability of Christ" (*NPSP* 4, Sermon 170) and "Jesus Christ Immutable" (*MTP* 15, Sermon 848). In 1868, Charles said, "There are no ups and downs in the love of Christ towards his people. On their highest Tabors he loves them, but equally as well in their Gethsemanes. When they wander like lost sheep his great love goes after them, and when they come back with broken hearts his great love restores them. By day, by night, in sickness, in sorrow, in poverty, in famine, in prison, in the hour of death, that silver stream of love ripples at their side, never stayed, never diminished. For ever is the sea of divine grace at its flood; this sun never sets; this fountain never pauses" (*MTP* 14:271).

16. "God is all powerful, his power is irresistible, nothing can withstand it, nor overcome it; nothing in earth and hell is a match for it" (Gill, *A Body of Doctrinal Divinity*, 2:892).

17. "The Spirit of God is the author of this work of grace; it is he who begins it, and will perform it, till the day of Christ, and finish what he has begun" (ibid., 2:897–98).

18. Charles altered Gill's wording: "*Secondly*, The final perseverance of the saints, may be concluded from the purposes and decrees of God" (ibid., 2:893, italics in the original). Cf. Eph 3:11.

19. Charles altered Gill's wording: "flowing from his everlasting and unchangeable love" (ibid., 2:894).

20. Cf. Heb 9:12.

21. Cf. Eph 1:23.

22. Cf. Eph 5:25–27.

23. Cf. Rom 12:5.

24. Gill did not mention Hephzibah, the mother of Manasseh (Cf. 2 Kgs 21:1; Isa 62:4) in *A Body of Doctrinal Divinity*. However, in his exposition, Gill noted that her name "signifies, *my delight is in her*" (John Gill, *An Exposition of the Books of the Prophets of the Old Testament, Both Larger and Lesser, in Two Volumes. In Which, It Is Attempted to Give an Account of the Several Books, and the Writers of Them; A Summary of Each Chapter, and the Genuine Sense of Every Verse: And Throughout the Whole, the Original Text, and Various Versions Are Inspected, and Compared; Interpreters of the Best Note, Both Jewish and Christian, Consulted; and the Prophecies Shewn Chiefly to Belong to the Times of the Gospel, and a Great*

Number of Them to Times Yet to Come. Vol. 1. Containing the Prophecies of Isaiah, Jeremiah, and the Book of the Lamentations [London: G. Keith and J. Robinson, 1757, The Spurgeon Library], 1:341, italics in the original).

25. Cf. Rom 8:34.   26. Cf. John 14:1–2.

27. "1. The adoption of the children of God into his family; by which he takes them for his sons and daughters; which is a wonderful instance of his love" (Gill, *A Body of Doctrinal Divinity*, 2:894). See also "Adoption" (Sermon 1). Cf. Eph 1:5.

28. Cf. Rom 5:1.

29. "3. Pardon of sin is another act of the riches of divine grace, and flows from unmerited and distinguishing love" (Gill, *A Body of Doctrinal Divinity*, 2:895). Cf. Mic 7:18.

30. "He chose them to be his inheritance, he has bought them as his inheritance, and he will never forsake them" (*MTP* 40:391).

31. Two diagonal pencil lines were written beneath the word "empty." Similar lines are found beneath the words "be" and "moral" in "Future Judgment" (Sermon 6).

Barton. May 18

BARTON. MAY 18[1]

1. The words "Barton. May 18" correspond to the sermon on the following page, "Sinners Must Be Punished" (Sermon 9). At the conclusion of "Sinners Must Be Punished," this information was recorded again. This page does not represent an example of an occasion when Charles intended to write a sermon but failed to finish it, as seen in the following instances: "Text for Boys and Girls" (Notebook 5, Sermon 239); "Text for Young Believers" (Notebook 5, Sermon 240); "Job, the Perfect Man" (Notebook 5, Sermon 263); "As the Rain Cometh Down and the Snow from Heaven" (Notebook 6, Sermon 291); "The Lord Be Gracious unto Us" (Notebook 6, Sermon 295); and "The Two Birds" (Notebook 8, Sermon 352). A smudge is found on the top right side of the page. The source of the smudge is the stain on the previous page beneath the word "John" in the sermon "Final Perseverance" (Sermon 8).

9   Psalm . 9. 17... Sinner's must be punished.

I. The Persons
  1. The wicked all who have broken God's com-
    mandments. Recapitulation of the law.—
      thought, imagination, word, act.
All men who are not converted.
  2 Forget.. not think, serve, seek, love him.
II. Doom." turned into hell". awful —

III. Reasons for this.—
         1. Because sin must be punished.
         2. Hell is the most fitting place for sinners
         3. No other place for them.
         4. Mercy has had its day.
         5. The sinner can bring no excuse
not. Ignorance, nor forgetfulness, want of heart,
nor want of time, nor part obedience,
   nor the hardness of the law.....

Barton. May 18/1851 | Mrs Spalding converted. 100 |
17. 100

9

SINNERS[1]
MUST BE PUNISHED
Psalm 9:17[2]

"The wicked shall be turned into hell, and all the nations that forget God."

I. THE PERSONS.

1. "The wicked."[3] All who have broken God's commandments.[4] Recapitulation[5] of the law. Thought, imagination, word, act. All men who are not converted.

2. "Forget." Not think, serve, seek, love him.[6]

II. DOOM. *"Turned into hell."* Awful.

III. REASONS FOR THIS:

1. Because sin must be punished.

2. Hell is the most fitting place for sinners.

3. No other place for them.

4. Mercy has had its day.

5. The sinner can bring no excuse. Not Ignorance, nor forgetfulness, want of heart, nor want of time, nor part obedience, nor the hardness of the law.

Barton.   May 18/1851[7]

Mrs. Spalding converted.[8] 100[9]

17. 100.[10]

1. Charles originally wrote the word "Sinner's" in the title of this sermon: "Sinner's Must Be Punished." However, the apostrophe before the letter "s" was struck through in pencil, thus converting the word from possessive to plural. Charles may have originally intended to write "Sinner's Punishment."

2. On November 4, 1860, Charles preached an additional sermon on Ps 9:17 entitled "Tender Words of Terrible Apprehension!" (*NPSP* 6, Sermon 344). The lack of overlapping content and structural similarities suggest Charles did not have the earlier outline in mind when writing the later sermon. Stippling is found above the number 17. For an additional example of his stippling, see the conclusion of the sermon "Condescending Love of Jesus" (Sermon 5).

3. For consistency with the quotation in the title of the second Roman numeral, "'Turned into hell,'" quotation marks have been inserted around the words "The wicked" in this line and the word "Forget" in the line below. The context suggests that in these three instances, Charles was quoting Ps 9:17.

4. Charles originally spelled the word "commadments." The letter "n" was inserted in pencil between the letters "a" and "d" and indicated by a caret beneath the word. The dark, yellow stain appearing beneath the letter "t" is likely the result of the aging process of the manuscript.

5. "Distinct repetition of the principle points" (Johnson's *Dictionary*, s.v. "recapitulation").

6. A modernized reading of this line is "[Those who] forget, [who do] not think, serve, seek, [or] love him."

7. The words "Barton. May 18" were also written on the previous page. In the sermon above, Charles added a slash and the year 1851 for specificity.

8. "Mrs. Spalding" was likely the same woman who Charles later identified as the first convert of his ministry (see also the conversion of "Mr. Charles" in "The Little Fire and Great Combustion" [Sermon 54]). "How my heart leaped for joy when I heard tidings of my first convert! I could never be satisfied with a full congregation, and the kind expressions of friends; I longed to hear that hearts had been broken, that tears had been seen streaming from the eyes of penitents. How I did rejoice, as one that findeth great spoil, one Sunday afternoon, when my good deacon said to me, 'God has set His seal on your ministry in this place, sir.' Oh, if anybody had said

to me, 'Someone has left you twenty thousand pounds,' I should not have given a snap of my fingers for it, compared with the joy which I felt when I was told that God had saved a soul through my ministry! 'Who is it?' I asked. 'Oh, it is a poor labouring man's wife over at such-and-such a place! She went home broken-hearted by your Sermon two or three Sundays ago, and she has been in great trouble of soul, but she has found peace, and she says she would like to speak to you.' I said, 'Will you drive me over there? I must go to see her;' and early on the Monday morning I was driving down to the village my deacon had mentioned, to see my first spiritual child. I have in my eye now the cottage in which she lived; believe me, it always appears picturesque. I felt like the boy who has earned his first guinea, or like a diver who has been down to the depths of the sea, and brought up a rare pearl. I prize each one whom God has given me, but I prize that woman most. Since then, my Lord has blessed me to many thousands of souls, who have found the Saviour by hearing or reading words which have come from my lips. I have had a great many spiritual children born of the preaching of the Word, but I still think that woman was the best of the lot. At least, she did not live long enough for me to find many faults in her. After a year or two of faithful witness-bearing, she went home, to lead the way for a goodly number who have followed her. I remember well her being received into the church, and dying, and going to Heaven. She was the first seal to my ministry, and a very precious one. No mother was ever more full of happiness at the sight of her first-born son. Then could I have sung the song of the Virgin Mary, for my soul did magnify the Lord for remembering my low estate, and giving me the great honour to do a work for which all generations should call me blessed, for so I counted and still count the conversion of one soul" (*Autobiography* 1:232–33. See also *Lectures* 1:94–95). The 1851 Census occurred on March 30, 1851, approximately ten months before the conversion of "Mrs. Spalding." Of all the female Spaldings living in Cambridgeshire at that time, the "Mrs. Spalding" to which Charles referred was likely forty-nine-year-old Hannah Spalding, the wife of Richard Spalding, who worked as an agricultural laborer. Born in Norfolk Upwell in 1802, Hannah resided at Outwell, Norfolk, by 1851, approximately twenty-nine miles from Waterbeach. This distance would explain why Charles, who often walked the six to seven miles from Cambridge to Waterbeach, needed to be driven to see her. Unlike fifty-four-year-old Sarah Spalding of Landbeach, forty-three-year-old Sarah Spalding of Bottisham, or twenty-three-year-old Mary Spalding of Waterbeach, Hannah Spalding did not register in the 1861 Census ten years later. In 1855, a certificate of death in Blything in Suffolk County registered one "Hannah

Spalding" as being deceased. This would corroborate Charles's account that "after a year or two of faithful witness-bearing, she went home." This sermon reveals that Charles preached 100 times before he recorded his first convert.

9.   The handwriting of the words "Mrs. Spalding converted. 100" within the box is noticeably different in size and characteristic from that of the body of this outline. For instance, when comparing the two Ms in the words "Mrs." and "May" on the same line, the contrast is even more noticeable. The letter "M" in the word "May" slants dynamically to the right and contains a well-defined bracket at its baseline, while the letter "M" in the former word contains no bracket and instead reveals an exaggerated looped ascender on the stem above the x-height. A similar disparity in handwriting can also be found in the sermon "Hew Down the Tree" (Notebook 4, Sermon 215) with the words "Cottenham. Young man brought out. 360." See also "I Have Found a Ransom" (Notebook 4, Sermon 224).

10. A cluster of dark ink smudges are on the lower left side of the page. They were likely the result of a malfunction of the writing instrument.

Eph 1 _ 4 _ Election ...

Doct 1 ... God has chosen some to Eternal life.
a countless number – but yet God has chosen them
which may be proved
   1. From Scripture _ Rom IX.
   2. From God's foreknowledge.
this doctrine is not opposed to justice since if God may with justice
damn all he may surely save whom he will – See where
Moses, Jacob, David were chosen & man while devils perished,

Doct II. Election is eternal and absolute,
Eternal since God is unchangeable – there is no time with
him – – .. Absolute. no merits in it – not on the
foresight of obedience since this is a fruit ... no obedience
deserves it ... nor can prayer or faith deserve it ...
If salvation be a gift there must be an election of receivers
& see how cross this runs – the base not the lofty – the thief
not Alexander, Publican not Pharisee, Jacob not Esau.
how humbling – no flesh here can glory ...

ELECTION[1]
Ephesians 1:4[2]

"According as he hath chosen us in him before the foundation of the world,
that we should be holy and without blame before him in love."

DOCT[3] I. GOD HAS CHOSEN SOME TO ETERNAL LIFE.[4]

A countless number, but yet God has chosen them. Which may be proved:

1. From Scripture. Rom IX.

2. From God's foreknowledge.[5] This doctrine is not opposed to justice since if
    God may with justice damn all, he may surely save whom he will. See where
    Moses,[6] Jacob,[7] David[8] were chosen, and man, while devils perished.[9]

DOCT[10] II. ELECTION IS ETERNAL AND ABSOLUTE.

Eternal since God is unchangeable.[11] There is no time with him.[12] Absolute.
No merits in it. Not on the foresight of obedience since this is a fruit.
No obedience deserves it. Nor can prayer or faith deserve it. If salvation be
a gift[13] there must be an election of receivers, and see how cross[14] this seems.
The base, not the lofty.[15] The thief,[16] not Alexander.[17] Publican,[18] not Pharisee.[19]
Jacob, not Esau.[20] How humbling. No flesh here can glory.[21]

1. Charles preached one additional sermon in his early notebooks with the word "election" in its title: "Calling and Election Sure" (Notebook 3, Sermon 135). For additional sermons on the doctrine of election, see "Election" (*NPSP* 1, Sermons 41–42); "Election and Holiness" (*NPSP* 6, Sermon 303); "Election No Discouragement to Seeking Souls" (*MTP* 10, Sermon 553); "How to Meet the Doctrine of Election" (*MTP* 30, Sermon 1797); "David Dancing Before the Ark Because of His Election" (*MTP* 34, Sermon 2031); and "Election: Its Defences and Evidences" (*MTP* 51, Sermon 2920). For academic treatments of the doctrine of election in Charles's theology, see Henry Franklin Colquitt, "The Soteriology of Charles Haddon Spurgeon Revealed in His Sermons and Controversial Writings" (PhD diss., University of Edinburgh, 1951); Jeremy F. Thornton, "The Soteriology of C. H. Spurgeon: Its Biblical and Historical Roots and Its Place in His Preaching" (PhD diss., Selwyn College, University of Cambridge, 1974); Douglas Rodney Earls, "The Evangelistic Strategy of Charles Haddon Spurgeon for the Multiplication of Churches and Implications for Modern Church Extension Theory" ([PhD diss., Southwestern Baptist Theological Seminary, 1989], 116–18); and Warren Dale Bullock, "The Influence of Puritanism on the Life and Preaching of Charles Haddon Spurgeon" ([master's thesis, Seattle Pacific College, 1969], 73–74).

2. This is the only time Charles preached a sermon on Eph 1:4 specifically. However, he preached two additional sermons on Eph 1:3–4: "Glory Be unto the Father" (*MTP* 29, Sermon 1738) and "Blessing for Blessing" (*MTP* 38, Sermon 2266). The lack of overlapping content and structural similarities suggests Charles did not have the outline above in mind when writing these later sermons.

3. Abbr., "Doctrine."

4. "I believe the doctrine of election, because I am quite certain that, if God had not chosen me, I should never have chosen Him; and I am sure He chose me before I was born, or else He never would have chosen me afterwards" (*Autobiography* 1:170; see also *Autobiography* 1:168–69 and *NPSP* 2:293). Charles did not use the word "predestination" here; however, in his 1869 sermon "A Sermon for the Most Miserable of Men" (*MTP* 15, Sermon 853), he addressed the more controversial elements of the doctrine of election and free agency: "They are two truths which stand together, and though it may not always be easy for us to reconcile them, it would be more difficult to make them disagree. . . . Fixed is everything, from the motion of a grain of dust in the summer's wind to the revolution of a planet in its

orbit, and yet man is as free as if there was no God, as independent an actor as if everything were left to chance. I see indelible marks both of predestination and free agency everywhere in God's universe. . . . Come, and you are ordained to come; stay away, and you deserve to perish" (*MTP* 15:70). Charles also wrote, "That God predestines, and yet that man is responsible, are two facts that few can see clearly. They are believed to be inconsistent and contradictory; but they are not. The fault is in our weak judgment. Two truths cannot be contradictory to each other. If, then, I find taught in one part of the Bible that everything is fore-ordained, *that is true*; and if I find, in another Scripture, that man is responsible for all his actions, *that is true*; and it is only my folly that leads me to imagine that these two truths can ever contradict each other. I do not believe they can ever be welded into one upon any earthly anvil, but they certainly shall be one in eternity. They are two lines that are so nearly parallel, that the human mind which pursues them farthest will never discover that they converge; but they do converge, and they will meet somewhere in eternity, close to the throne of God, whence all truth doth spring" (*Autobiography* 1:177, italics in the original). For a treatment of Charles's attitude toward Arminianism, see "Pleasure in the Stones of Zion" (Sermon 53).

5. Cf. Rom 8:29.

6. Cf. Exod 3:10.

7. Cf. Mal 1:2; Rom 9:13.

8. Cf. 1 Sam 16:1.

9. "On my principle, the deed is just enough; men and devils have both sinned and have both deserved to be damned for their sins; God, if he shall so resolve, can justly destroy them all, or he may save them all, if he can do it with justice; or, he may save one of them if he pleases, and let the others perish; and if as he has done, he chooses to save a remnant, and that remnant shall be men, and if he allows all the fallen angels to sink to hell, all that we can answer is, that God is just, and he has a right to do as he pleases with his creatures" (*NPSP* 2:293). An alternative reading of this line is "See where Moses, Jacob, David, and man were chosen while devils perished."

10. The swash of the letter "D" is exaggerated and noticeably different from that in the "D" of "Doct 1." For an additional example of Charles's versatile penmanship, see the letter "D" in the phrase "Devils and men" in the sermon "The Children Cast Out" (Notebook 2, Sermon 104).

11.   Cf. Mal 3:6.   12.   Cf. 2 Pet 3:8.   13.   Cf. Eph 2:8.

14.   The word "cross" had numerous meanings. In the phrase "and see how cross this seems," Charles likely used the word to mean "perverse; untractable" or "contrary" (see Johnson's *Dictionary*, s.v. "cross"). To contextualize the word, Johnson quoted English preacher Robert South (1634–1716): "The mind brings all the ends of a long and varied hypothesis together; sees how one part coheres with, and depends upon, another; and so clears off all the appearing contrarieties and contradictions, that seemed to lie *cross* and uncouth, and to make the whole unintelligible" (italics in the original). For Charles's personal copy of South's quotation, see Robert South, *Sermons Preached upon Several Occasions: A New Edition* ([4 vols.; London: Thomas Tegg, 1843, The Spurgeon Library], 1:99).

15.   Cf. 1 Cor 1:27.   16.   Cf. Luke 23:32–43.   17.   Cf. 2 Tim 4:14.

18.   A publican was a tax collector (Matt 9:9–13; Luke 18:13; 19:1–10). For an additional reference in this notebook, see "The Physician and His Patients" (Sermon 74).

19.   Cf. Matt 23:13–35.   20.   Cf. Mal 3:6.   21.   Cf. 1 Cor 1:29.

[blank page][1]

1. For reasons unknown Charles did not write a sermon outline on this page. Three faint discolorations, likely fingerprints, are found on the lower right side of the page. The yellowed splotches on the left side are likely the result of the aging process of the manuscript. The only other remarkable feature on this page is an imprint at the top left corner. The origin of the imprint is the number 11 on the opposite page in the sermon "Salvation" (Sermon 11).

Heb 7. 25. Salvation — *Doddridge*

Paul does not mention his name in this epistle.
The words imply that Man is in danger.
I "able to save unto the uttermost"
1. Completely... He justifies from all sin, sanctifies
the heart, delivers from Satan, gives final persever.
help in death, and glorious resurrection.
2. Always.. He has .. he does .. he will always.

This may be argued. 1. From his dignity, God.
                               2. From his offices.
                               3. From his character
                               4 from his suffering.
                               5 From numerous instances.
II. "them that come unto God by him".
     Here is implied. 1. Sense of need.
                         2. Persuasion of Jesus Power.
                         3. Belief in his willingness
                         4. Agreement to the way of salvation
                         5. Full surrender.
                         6. Dependance on him.

Cherryhinton. June 1. 51

19.

SALVATION[3]
Hebrews 7:25[4]

*"Wherefore he is able also to save them to the uttermost
that come unto God by him, seeing he ever liveth to make intercession for them."*

Paul does not mention his name in this epistle.
The words imply that Man is in danger.

I. "ABLE TO SAVE UNTO THE UTTERMOST."[5]

1. Completely.[6] He justifies from all sin, sanctifies the heart,[7] delivers from Satan, gives final perseverance,[8] help in death, and glorious resurrection.[9]

2. Always. He has, he does, he will always.
   This[10] may be argued:

   1. From his dignity.[11] God.
   2. From his offices.[12]
   3. From his character.
   4. From his suffering.[13]
   5. From numerous instances.

II. "THEM THAT COME UNTO GOD BY HIM."

Here is implied:[14]

   1. Sense of Need.
   2. Persuasion of Jesus['s] Power.[15]
   3. Belief in his willingness.
   4. Agreement to the way of salvation.[16]
   5. Full surrender.
   6. Dependance[17] on him.

Cherryhinton.   June 1, [18]51
19.[18]

1. The imprint of the ink from the number 11 can be seen in the top left corner on the previous blank page.

2. Philip Doddridge (1702–1751) was an English nonconformist preacher, author, and hymnist. By the time Charles began his itinerate preaching ministry in the villages surrounding Cambridge, he had already familiarized himself with Doddridge's writings. Charles wrote, "I remember, when I was seeking Christ, how I read through Doddridge's 'Rise and Progress of Religion' with an avidity such as I showed when as a boy I read some merry tale" (*MTP* 25:203; see also *Autobiography* 1:104). Nearly one year before he preached the sermon above at Cherryhinton, Charles wrote the following words in a letter to his father on August 22, 1850: "I am studying through Romans in the Greek, with Barnes, Doddridge and Chalmers, for my commentaries" (Angus Library and Archive, Regent's Park College, Oxford University, D/SPU 1, Letter 6). In his personal library Charles placed Doddridge's *Lectures on Preaching* between John Gill and Adam Clarke because, as he said, "I have no desire to have my rest broken by wars among the authors" (Charles Spurgeon, *Commenting and Commentaries: Two Lectures Addressed to the Students of the Pastors' College, Metropolitan Tabernacle, Together with a Catalogue of Biblical Commentaries and Expositions* [London: Passmore & Alabaster, 1876], 9). For Charles's additional comments about Doddridge, see *NPSP* 5:475 and *MTP* 20:111. The above outline is a distillation of Doddridge's sermon on Heb 7:25 entitled "Power and Grace of Christ: The Ability of Christ to Save to the Uttermost" (Phillip Doddridge, *The Works of Phillip Doddridge in Ten Volumes* [Leeds: Edward Baines, 1803, The Spurgeon Library], 2:213–27). Charles appropriated Doddridge's sermon more heavily in the first Roman numeral than in the second. Overlapping content is noted below.

3. On June 2, 1851, the day after Charles preached from the above outline, he delivered an essay entitled "An Essay Read June 2, 1851." Charles had already written two essays before this date: "Depravity" and "Antichrist and Her Brood; or, Popery Unmasked" (see *Autobiography* 1:57–58). There does not appear to be any correlation between the above outline and Charles's essays.

4. On June 8, 1856, Charles preached an additional sermon on Heb 7:25 entitled "Salvation to the Uttermost" (*NPSP* 2, Sermon 84). On August 22, 1886, he preached a sermon on Heb 7:23–25 entitled "The Ever-Living Priest" (*MTP* 32, Sermon 1915). There is not enough overlapping content or structural similarity to suggest Charles had the above outline in mind when writing these later sermons.

5.   "First, I am to consider what we are to understand by Christ's being *able to save to the uttermost*" (Doddridge, 216, italics in the original).

6.   "The Lord Jesus Christ will also save us *entirely*: he will work out the salvation of the whole man, body, soul, and spirit. He ever lives to save his people to the utmost, that is to say, all his people, and all of every one of his people. Nothing essential to manhood shall be left to perish in the case of those whom he redeems. . . . God's deliverances are always complete" (*MTP* 32:455, italics in the original).

7.   "The almighty power of Christ, as a Saviour, extends to the 'sanctification of our natures,' as well as to the justification of our persons before God" (Doddridge, 220).

8.   The final letters "ance" in the word "perseverance" trail into the margin. For additional words that trail into margins in this notebook, see the word "persevere" in "Free Grace" (Sermon 13) and the words "famine" and "Jesus" in "The Lepers" (Sermon 77). Doddridge wrote, "And it shall appear, to the everlasting disappointment and shame of all the host of hell, that it was not a vain boast, but the words of eternal wisdom, as well as invariable faithfulness, when he said, *I will give unto my sheep eternal life, and they shall never perish, neither shall any pluck them out of my hand*" (Doddridge, 221, italics in the original).

9.   "The Lord Jesus Christ is *able to save* his people *to the uttermost*, as 'he can raise their bodies from the dissolution of the grave, and conduct their complete persons to the regions of eternal felicity.' He is *The resurrection and the life*" (Doddridge, 221–22, italics in the original).

10.   Charles originally wrote Roman numeral II beneath the word "This." Either he intended to write the phrase "This may be argued" at the beginning of the second Roman numeral and he intended the Roman numeral II below to be Roman numeral III, or, more likely, Charles decided to include this information beneath the first Roman numeral.

11.   "Still he mingled the dignity" (Doddridge, 223).

12.   Jesus Christ is "the *Head-stone of the corner,* on whom was fixed all the stress of man's eternal interests; and as that awful judge, before whose tribunal the greatest of the children of men should stand, and from whom all should receive the decisive

sentence, which should fix them in final happiness, or despair" (Doddridge, 224, italics in the original). Doddridge also wrote, "But how much more prevalent is the atonement of Jesus, our great high-priest" (Doddridge, 226).

13. "Nay, even in his deepest humiliation, on the cursed tree, a ray of divine glory broke through that dark cloud of infamy, with which he was then surrounded; and amidst all the scorn and rage of insulting enemies, who were reproaching him as a wretch abandoned by God and man, he speaks from the cross as from the throne; and, as the King of heaven, takes upon him to dispose of seats in paradise, and to promise life and glory to one who was then sharing with him in the agonies of death, and the ignominy of crucifixion; *Verily I say unto thee, to-day shalt thou be with me in paradise*" (Doddridge, 224, italics in the original).

14. Charles did not rely on Doddridge's sermon for this section of the outline. These six points were original to him.

15. An alternative reading of this line is "Persuasion of Jesus. Power."

16. "This is no subject for gaudy eloquence, and for high-flying attempts at oratory; this is a matter to be put to you plainly and simply. Sinners—you must either be cursed of God, or else you must accept Christ, as bearing the curse instead of you" (*MTP* 15:311).

17. Throughout this notebook, Charles spells the word "dependance."

18. Three discolorations, likely fingerprints, appear beneath and to the right of the number 19. The source of the ink was likely the Roman numeral II that was smudged beneath the word "This" in the middle of the page. See also the fingerprint on the final page of this notebook to the right of the word "Ghost."

12   Ezek. 18. 4 —   Death the Consequence of Sin.

I. That Part which has already taken place. "Death"

1 Spiritual .. Loss of Purity, Company of angels & God.
Loss of love to holiness, no longer a part of God's family.
    Loss of Happiness. — —
            We see a sinner whole soul is dead —
                his feet run not in God's ways,
                his hands are not lifted up to pray or work good,
                his ears hear not spiritually,
                his eyes see not, weep not
                his mouth sings, nor prays,
                his heart melts not though grace is preached
    Loss of Power to do good.

2. Death Legal.   Loss of all claim for merit.
                Loss of his inheritance
                His rights of citizenship.
                He is under sentence of death.

II That Part which shall take place here "death"

III. That Part threatened hereafter "death".
    Agonizing, unmingled, perpetual, eternal death.

Coton. May 25
18.

12

DEATH, *the* CONSEQUENCE *of* SIN
Ezekiel 18:4[1]

"Behold, all souls are mine; as the soul of the father,
so also the soul of the son is mine: the soul that sinneth, it shall die."

I. THAT PART WHICH HAS ALREADY TAKEN PLACE. *"Death."*

1. Spiritual.[2] Loss of Purity, Company of angels and God. Loss of love to holiness. No longer a part of God's family.[3] Loss of happiness. We see a sinner's[4] whole soul is dead.

> His feet run not in God's ways.[5]
> His hands are not lifted up to pray or work good.[6]
> His ears hear not spiritually.[7]
> His eyes see not, weep not.
> His mouth neither[8] sings nor prays.
> His heart melts not, though grace is preached.[9]

   Loss of Power to do good.[10]

2. Death Legal.

> Loss of all claim for merit.
> Loss of his inheritance.
> His rights of citizenship.
> He is under sentence of death.

II. THAT PART WHICH SHALL TAKE PLACE HERE. *"Death."*

III. THAT PART THREATENED HEREAFTER. *"Death."*

Agonizing, unmingled, perpetual, eternal death.[11]

Coton.   May 25
18.

1. This is the only time Charles preached a sermon on Ezek 18:4. For additional sermons on death, see "Death and Life: the Wage and the Gift" (*MTP* 31, Sermon 1868); "His Own Funeral Sermon" (*MTP* 38, Sermon 2234); and "Death, a Sleep" (*MTP* 54, Sermon 3077). These sermons do not contain enough overlapping content to suggest Charles had in mind the outline above in their writing.

2. Cf. Eph 2:1.

3. The phrases "Loss of Purity" and "Company of angels and God" should not be interpreted to mean Charles upheld a belief in the loss of salvation after regeneration. In his sermon "Election" (Sermon 10), Charles argued, "Election is eternal and absolute." Likewise, in Philip Doddridge's outline in the previous sermon, "Salvation" (Sermon 11), Charles noted that Christ "gives final perseverance," and in the following sermon, "Free Grace" (Sermon 13), he noted that Jesus is the one "enabling us to persevere." Charles's adherence to the doctrine of final perseverance is consistent throughout both his Cambridgeshire and London ministries. To him, final perseverance is the basis of the doctrine of assurance and one of "those deep and mysterious truths on which the entire gospel system must rest" (*NPSP* 1:269). For a treatment of this doctrine in Charles's theology, see Nettles, *Living by Revealed Truth*, 219–23. See also "Peculiar Sleep of the Beloved" (*NPSP* 1, Sermon 12) and "The Final Perseverance of the Saints" (*MTP* 23, Sermon 1361).

4. Charles did not insert an apostrophe between the letters "r" and "s" at the end of the word "sinners." The context suggests, however, that he intended the word to be possessive, not plural.

5. Cf. Prov 3:23.   6. Cf. 1 Tim 2:8.   7. Cf. Matt 11:15.

8. Charles inserted the word "neither" above the line and indicated it with a caret.

9. Cf. "The Stony Heart Removed" (*MTP* 8, Sermon 456).

10. Cf. Eph 2:10.   11. Cf. Matt 25:41; Mark 9:43; Rev 21:8.

13   13

Revelation . 21. 6 —   Free Grace.

Jesus is the beginning & ending

I. In Creation.

II. In Providence.

III. In Salvation.

1. As to provision – in covenant & redemption.

2. Operatively in calling, regeneration & conversion.

He is first in all our soul matters.

3. In supporting us and enabling us to persevere.

4. In all our duties which are holy.

5. In death he will be the Omega.

Inf 1. Jesus is the only Saviour.

Inf 2. All God's people are safe.

In the second part of the text.

1st There is plenty. fountain of the water of life.

2nd There is freeness.   "give" "freely"

3rd There is mercy.   not to the great.

4. The Character is "athirst." feel their need.

_____

Milton. June 15 | 20. 21. 213.
Tollesbury. June 23 |

138

13

FREE GRACE[2]
Revelation 21:6[3]

*"And he said unto me, It is done. I am Alpha and Omega, the beginning and the end.
I will give unto him that is athirst of the fountain of the water of life freely."*

Jesus is the beginning and ending.[4]

I.   IN CREATION.[5]

II. IN PROVIDENCE.

III. IN SALVATION.

    1. As to provision, in covenant and redemption.

    2. Operatively in calling,[6] regeneration, and Conversion. He is first in all our soul matters.[7]

    3. In supporting us and enabling us to persevere.[8]

    4. In all our duties which are holy.

    5. In death he will be the Omega.[9]

Inf.[10] 1. Jesus is the only Saviour.[11]

Inf. 2. All God's people are safe.[12]

    In the second part of the text.

    1st There is plenty. Fountain of the water of life.[13]

    2nd There is freeness. "Give" "freely."

    3rd There is mercy. Not to the great.[14]

    4.[15] The Character is "athirst." Feel their need.

Milton.   June 15[16]   20. 21. 213.

Tollesbury.   June 29

1. The number 13 is smudged.

2. In the index at the end of this notebook, Charles entitled this sermon "Alpha and Omega." There is no evidence to suggest he attempted to correct the mistake in the index.

3. In 1880, Charles preached an additional sermon on Rev 21:6 entitled "Good News for Thirsty Souls" (*MTP* 26, Sermon 1549). Overlapping content exists in the second Roman numeral of the above outline and *MTP* 26:414. However, there is not enough overlapping content to suggest Charles had the above outline in mind when he wrote the later sermon. See also "Free Grace a Motive for Free Giving" (*MTP* 26, Sermon 1542) and "A Free Grace Promise" (*MTP* 35, Sermon 2082).

4. "You are not on the right way unless Christ is first and last with you. His precious blood to put away your sin, his glorious resurrection to be your justification, his ascension to heaven to take possession of a place for you, his second coming to receive you to himself—all these are the way. Christ is all in all to the man who is on the right road" (*MTP* 36:368).

5. Cf. John 1:1; Col 1:15.   6. Cf. Luke 5:32.

7. "My Christ is first, My Christ is last / My Christ is All in all" (*MTP* 30:215). See also Hymn XIII, "A Song of Praise for Christ" in *Spiritual Songs, or Songs of Praise to Almighty God, upon Several Occasions, by the Rev. John Mason, M.A., Rector of Water-Stratford, Buckingham. And Penitential Cries, by the Rev. Thomas Shepherd, M.A., Minister of Braintree, Essex* ([London: D. Sedgwick and Hamilton, Adams, and Co., 1859, The Spurgeon Library], 21).

8. Cf. Phil 1:6. The final letters of the word "persevere" trail into the margin. For an additional example, see "Salvation" (Sermon 11).

9. Cf. "Alpha and Omega" (*MTP* 9, Sermon 546).

10. Charles abbreviated the word "Inference" in this line and also in the line below. This is the second time in Notebook 1 that Charles used the word "inference." See also "Future Judgment" (Sermon 6) and "Can Two Walk Together Unless They Are Agreed?" (Sermon 76).

11. Cf. John 14:6. For sermons on the exclusivity of Jesus Christ, see "The Way to God" (*NPSP* 5, Sermon 245); "The Way" (*MTP* 16, Sermon 942); "Jesus the Way" (*MTP* 51, Sermon 2938); and "The Only Road" (*MTP* 62, Sermon 3544).

12. Cf. John 6:39.   13. Cf. John 4:14.

14. Cf. Ps 138:6; Prov 3:34; Jas 4:6.

15. Charles departed from his ordering technique by writing only the number 4 and not 4th.

16. Charles preached the above sermon in the village of Milton four days before his seventeenth birthday. Exactly one year later, on June 19, he completed his final sermon in the second notebook (see Charles's inscription on the inside front cover of Notebook 2). A vertical line separates "June 15" and "June 29" from the numbers "20. 21. 213." For an additional example of a vertical line used in this way, see the conclusion of "Adoption" (Sermon 1).

14   1. Cor. 15. 10   God's Grace given to us.

I. How all may say this "by the grace of God &c."
Birth – Bodies – Minds – Temporal Mercies –
Means of Grace & Liberty –

II. The grace given to Saints alone
In Election – Redemption – Conversion – Pardon –
Justification – Adoption – Support – Spirit
    Perseverance.

III. The Grace given to the sinner –
Longsuffering – sparing – delivering grace.
Restraining Grace & striving grace.

1. Think much on grace Christian
2. Live showing gratitude.
3. Be humble. tis all grace

1. Sinner be thankful.
2. Repent
3. Remember Judgment comes on apace.

_____

Hythe. July 1/51
22.   336.

GOD'S GRACE GIVEN *to* US[1]
1 Corinthians 15:10[2]

*"But by the grace of God I am what I am: and his grace which
was bestowed upon me was not in vain; but I laboured more abundantly
than they all: yet not I, but the grace of God which was with me."*

I. HOW ALL MAY SAY THIS?
"By the grace of God I am," etc. Birth, Bodies, Minds, Temporal Mercies,
Means of Grace,[3] and Liberty.

II. THE GRACE GIVEN TO SAINTS ALONE.[4]
In Election,[5] Redemption,[6] Conversion,[7] Pardon,[8] Justification,[9] Adoption,[10]
Support,[11] Spirit,[12] Perseverance.[13]

III. THE GRACE GIVEN TO THE SINNER.
Longsuffering,[14] sparing, delivering grace. Restraining Grace,[15] and
shining grace.[16]

1. Think much on grace, Christian.
2. Live showing gratitude.[17]
3. Be humble.[18] 'Tis all grace.

1. Sinner, be thankful.
2. Repent.
3. Remember, Judgment comes on apace.[19]

Hythe.   July 1/[18]51[20]
22. 336.

1. The doctrine of grace played a significant role in Charles's theology. He said, "Of the things which I have spoken unto you these many years, this is the sum. Within the circle of these words my theology is contained, so far as it refers to the salvation of men. I rejoice also to remember that those of my family who were ministers of Christ before me preached this doctrine, and none other. My father, who is still able to bear his personal testimony for his Lord, knows no other doctrine, neither did his father before him" (*MTP* 61:469). For additional treatments of the doctrine of grace, see "The Certainty and Freeness of Divine Grace" (*MTP* 10, Sermon 599); C. H. Spurgeon, *All of Grace* (New York: Robert Carter and Brothers, 1886, The Spurgeon Library); and John B. Hall, "The Application of the Doctrine of Grace in the Life and Ministry of Charles Haddon Spurgeon" (master's thesis, Covenant Theological Seminary, 1982).

2. Charles preached two additional sermons on 1 Cor 15:10: "Lessons on Divine Grace" (*MTP* 49, Sermon 2833) and "Paul's Parenthesis" (*MTP* 54, Sermon 3084). Neither sermon contains enough overlapping content or structural similarity to suggest Charles had the above outline in mind when writing these later sermons.

3. For Charles, the concept "means of grace" included the following practices: observing the Sabbath, baptism, partaking in the Lord's Supper, preaching, prayer, and the study of Scripture (see *MTP* 30:204 and 35:438). Charles believed that "sickness is also a means of grace: those who have much grace may be called to endure much disease" (*MTP* 35:199). In his sermon "By the Fountain," Charles said, "Every means of grace may be denied the believer, but the grace of the means will still come to him" (*MTP* 35:608). Additional uses of the phrase "means of grace" are found in "Satan and His Devices" (Notebook 2, Sermon 122), "Continue in Prayer" (Notebook 4, Sermon 220), and "The Lord Reigneth" (Notebook 8, Sermon 371).

4. "The very marrow of the gospel lies in special, discriminating, distinguishing grace. As for your universal grace, let those have it who care for such meatless bones; but the special gospel of electing love, of distinguishing grace, this is the gospel which is like butter in a lordly dish to a child of God, and he that has once fed on it will take no meaner fare" (*MTP* 13:429). See also "Distinguishing Grace" (*NPSP* 5, Sermon 262).

5. Cf. Rom 11:5. See also "Election" (Sermon 10).

6. Cf. Eph 1:7.

7. Cf. Rom 10:9. See also "The Dying Thief in a New Light" (*MTP* 32, Sermon 1881).

8. Cf. 1 John 1:9.

9. Cf. Rom 5:1. See also "Abraham Justified by Faith" (Sermon 3).

10. Cf. Rom 8:17. See also "Adoption" (Sermon 1); "Love Manifest in Adoption" (Sermon 16); and "Offending God's Little Ones" (Sermon 67).

11. Cf. Rom 8:26.

12. Cf. Acts 1:8. See Charles's inscription "And only skeletons without the Holy Ghost" on the title page of this notebook, and also the final stanza of the Doxology on the final page.

13. Cf. Phil 1:6. See also "Final Perseverance" (Sermon 8).

14. Cf. Rom 2:4.

15. "We now see that the Lord held us back from plunging into the deepest abysses of sin. He would not let us commit crimes by which we might have ended our lives before conversion. He kept us back from sins which might have linked us in sad connections, and led us into such circumstances that we never might have been brought to hear his word, or seek his face at all" (*MTP* 32:438). In his autobiography, Charles revealed the significance of the doctrine of restraining grace in his own spiritual development: "Through the Lord's restraining grace, and the holy influence of my early home-life, both at my father's and my grandfather's, I was kept from certain outward forms of sin in which others indulged" (*Autobiography* 1:81). In his sermon "Amazing Grace," Charles added, "I know that, if I was not permitted to indulge in grosser vices, yet I went as far as I could, and should have gone infinitely farther if it had not been for his restraining grace" (*MTP* 22:102).

16. The reference to "shining grace" may have been inspired by Isaac Watts: "From the third heaven where God resides, / That holy happy place, / The New Jerusalem comes down, / Adorn'd with shining grace" (Hymn 21 in *The Works of the Reverend and Learned Isaac Watts, D.D. Containing, Besides His Sermons, and Essays on Miscellaneous*

Subjects, Several Additional Pieces, Selected from his Manuscripts by the Rev. Dr. Jennings, and the Rev. Dr. Doddridge, in 1753: To Which Are Prefixed, Memoirs of the Life of the Author [6 vols.; comp., George Burder; London: John Barfield, 1810, The Spurgeon Library], 4:263). See also *MTP* 37:353.

17. Cf. 1 Thess 5:8.   18. Cf. Eph 4:2.

19. "Quick; speedily; used of things in motion" (Johnson's *Dictionary*, s.v. "apace"). A modernized reading of this line is "Remember, judgment comes quickly." Charles used the word "apace" throughout his ministry, e.g., "kings of armies flee apace" (*MTP* 23:227); "his legions fly apace" (*MTP* 40:610); and the Day of Reckoning "cometh on apace" (*ST* August 1875:359). Susannah also used the word "apace" to describe her bourgeoning relationship with Charles: "From that time our friendship grew apace" (*Autobiography* 2:8). Of her children, Susannah wrote that they "grew apace in the sweet country air" (*Autobiography* 2:291).

20. The number 2 was written beneath the bolded number 1.

Luke. II. 49.   Christ about his Father's business.   12

1. How Jesus did his "Father's business."

a. By coming to earth & assuming human nature.

b. By his Perfect life distinguished for   filial duty
                                            benevolence
                                            patience

which Answered two purposes.   self denial
                                              humility

    1. as justifying righteousness for the elect.   boldness

    2. As a Perfect Pattern for imitation.   spirituality
                                              & Prayerfulness

c. By his works, sufferings & death as a Redeemer.

2. How Jesus now does his "Father's business."

    α. As a Priest. blessing the People intercedig for them

    β. As a Mediator. the way of access.

    γ. As a Counsellor & Advocate.

    δ. As the Captain of our Salvation.

    ε. As he who appears to help his people by the Spirit

3. How Jesus shall do his "Father's business"

    By conquering Satan & leading captivity captive.

    By Judging the world in righteousness —

    1. The People of God should be about their Father's busi.

Hythe. July 8. /51

23. 190.

15

CHRIST[1] *about* HIS FATHER'S BUSINESS
Luke 2:49[2]

"And he said unto them, How is it that ye sought me? wist ye not that I must be about my Father's business?"

1. HOW JESUS <u>DID</u> HIS "FATHER'S BUSINESS."

   a. By coming to earth[3] and assuming human nature.[4]

   b. By his Perfect life, distinguished for:
   Filial duty,[5] Benevolence, Patience, Self-denial,
   Humility, Boldness, Spirituality, and Prayerfulness.
   Which Answered two purposes:
   1. As a[6] Justifying righteousness for the elect.
   2. As a Perfect Pattern for imitation.

   c. By his works, sufferings, and death as a Redeemer.

2. HOW JESUS NOW DOES HIS "FATHER'S BUSINESS."

   α.[7] As a Priest.[8] Blessing the People. Interceding for them.[9]

   β. As a Mediator.[10] The way of access.[11]

   γ. As a Counsellor[12] and Advocate.[13]

   δ. As the Captain of our Salvation.[14]

   ε. As he who appears to[15] help his people by the Spirit.[16]

3. HOW JESUS SHALL DO HIS "FATHER'S BUSINESS."
   By conquering Satan[17] and leading captivity Captive.[18]
   By Judging the world in righteousness.[19]
   1. The People of God should be about their Father's business.[20]

Hythe.   July 8/[18]51

23. 190.[21]

1. Charles inserted an apostrophe after the letter "t" in the word "Christ." It is possible that he originally intended this word to be in the possessive. An illegible letter, possibly an "s" or "i," follows the apostrophe. If the letter were an "i," Charles may have started to write the word "Christian" in the title of this sermon.

2. On March 15, 1857, Charles preached an additional sermon on Luke 2:49 entitled "Christ About His Father's Business" (*NPSP* 3, Sermon 122). Similarities in structure exist and suggest Charles likely had this outline in mind when writing his later sermon. Charles also preached a sermon on Luke 2:48–49 entitled "The First Recorded Words of Jesus" (*MTP* 28, Sermon 1666). However, in this sermon, Charles focused more on verse 48 than verse 49.

3. Cf. John 1:9.   4. Cf. Phil 2:7.   5. Cf. John 17:4; 1 John 4:14.

6. The letter "a" was likely added for consistency after Charles had written the words "As a Perfect Pattern for imitation" in the line below.

7. Charles used three ordering techniques in this sermon: English letters, cardinal numbers, and Greek letters (alpha, beta, gamma, delta, and epsilon). For similar ordering techniques, see "Condescending Love of Jesus" (Sermon 5), "Christian Prosperity and Its Causes" (Sermon 51), and "Satan and His Devices" (Notebook 2, Sermon 122).

8. Cf. Heb 4:14–15.   9. Cf. Rom 8:34.   10. Cf. 1 Tim 2:5.

11. Cf. Rom 5:2.   12. Cf. Isa 9:6.   13. Cf. 1 John 2:1.

14. Hebrews 2:10, "For it became him, for whom are all things, and by whom are all things, in bringing many sons unto glory, to make the captain of their salvation perfect through sufferings." For similar references, see "The Fight" (Sermon 37b); "An Exhortation to Bravery" (Sermon 72); "David in the Cave of Adullam" (Notebook 2, Sermon 116); "In the World Ye Shall Have Tribulation" (Notebook 3, Sermon 167); "Following Jesus with a Cross on Our Back (Notebook 3, Sermon 187); "The Ark of the Covenant" (Notebook 4, Sermon 197); "All Fulness in Jesus" (Notebook 5, Sermon 254); "The Mind of Christ" (Notebook 7, Sermon 330); and "Christ in You" (Notebook 8, Sermon 359). For references to Christ as a captain in his later ministry, see "Recruits for King Jesus" (*MTP* 30, Sermon 1770); "David's Spoil" (*MTP* 34, Sermon 2017); and "The Prince of Life" (*MTP* 36, Sermon 2139). The

sermon in which Charles addressed this title specifically is "The Captain of Our Salvation" (*MTP* 45, Sermon 2619). Approximately forty years after he preached from the above outline, Charles offered the following words in the final sermon he preached at the Metropolitan Tabernacle on June 7, 1891: "Young men, if you could see our Captain, you would [fall] down on your knees and beg him to let you enter the ranks of those who follow him" (*MTP* 37:323). On New Year's Day 1892 in Mentone, France, only four weeks before his death, Charles also said, "What a joy to see Jehovah himself as our banner, and God himself with us as our Captain!" (*ST* February 1891:55)

15. Charles wrote the words "his people[']s eyes" above the line. Either he intended the line to read, "As he who appears to help his people's eyes by the Spirit," or less likely, "As he who appears to his people's eyes by the Spirit." If the latter interpretation is correct, it is unclear why Charles did not strike through the phrase "help his people."

16. On this point Charles may have been influenced by nonconformist minister and commentator Matthew Henry (1662–1714): "Christ has many ways of making himself known to his people; usually in his ordinances, but sometimes by his Spirit he visits them when they are employed in common business" (Matthew Henry, *An Exposition of the New Testament: Wherein Each Chapter Is Summed Up in Its Contents: The Sacred Text Inserted at Large in Distinct Paragraphs: Each Paragraph Reduced to Its Proper Heads: The Sense Given, and Largely Illustrated: With Practical Remarks and Observations. By Matthew Henry, Late Minister of the Gospel. With Preface by the Rev. C. H. Spurgeon. Vol. V. John, Chaps. IX–XXI* [London: Thomas C. Jack, 1886–1888, The Spurgeon Library], 5:339). By the time the above sermon was written, Charles possessed such a familiarity with Henry's commentaries that he recognized them in the sermon of Cornelius Elvin (*Autobiography* 1:250).

17. Cf. Rom 16:20; Rev 20:1–3.   18. Cf. Eph 4:8.   19. Cf. Acts 17:31.

20. The final letter of the word "business" is a long "s" that trails into the margin.

21. The dot above the number 1 does not appear to bear significance on the text. The cluster of dots and lines on the right side of the page are imprints of the date "July 1" on the opposite page. See "God's Grace Given to Us" (Sermon 14).

16

1 John III. 1   Love manifest in Adoption

1st In the Blessing itself — this love may be seen.
It is an Exalted Blessing
          Special Blessing
          Unpurchasable Blessing
          Superlative Blessing
          Everlasting Blessing
and a precious blessing in its concomitants.
to Love + favour.   Right to enter his house &c &c.

II. In the Person conferring it ... "the Father"
God .. most excellent in dignity by the fact of his
     giving makes us say "Behold.

III In the object of it. "on us" "that we"
          Insignificant.
          Worthless.
          Rebellious.
          Depraved ..

IV. The way + manner of conferring it.
     1. By Jesus Christ's death here is wonder —
     2. The Spirits power
     3. The Father's decree.

16

LOVE MANIFEST
in ADOPTION
1 John 3:1[1]

*"Behold, what manner of love the Father hath bestowed upon us, that we should be called
the sons of God! therefore the world knoweth us not, because it knew him not."*

1ST IN THE BLESSING ITSELF THIS LOVE MAY BE SEEN.

It is an: Exalted Blessing.

Special Blessing.

Unpurchasable Blessing.

Superlative Blessing.

Everlasting Blessing.

And a precious blessing in its concomitants.[2] God's[3] Love and favour.

Right to enter his hous[e],[4] etc., etc.

II.[5] IN THE PERSON CONFERRING IT.

"the Father." God. Most excellent in dignity by the fact of his giving.
Makes us say, "Behold."[6]

III. IN THE OBJECT OF IT. *"on us," "that we."*

Insignificant.

Worthless.

Rebellious.

Depraved.

IV. THE WAY AND MANNER OF CONFERRING IT.

1. By Jesus Christ's death. Here is wonder.

2. The Spirit's power.

3. The Father's decree.

1.   Charles originally wrote "John 3:1" which reads, "There was a man of the Pharisees, named Nicodemus, a ruler of the Jews." The number 1 was written in pencil before the word "John" to construct the correct Scripture verse for this sermon, 1 John 3:1. In the index at the front of this notebook, Charles wrote the correct reference; however, in the concluding index, Charles incorrectly wrote "John 3:1." On July 19, 1885, Charles preached an additional sermon on 1 John 3:1 entitled "'And We Are:' A Jewel from the Revised Version" (*MTP* 32, Sermon 1934). The lack of overlapping content suggests Charles did not use the outline above when writing his later sermon. For additional sermons on adoption, see "Adoption" (Sermon 1); "Offending God's Little Ones" (Sermon 67); "The Spirits of Bondage and Adoption" (Notebook 5, Sermon 262); "Adoption" (*MTP* 7, Sermon 360); and "Adoption—the Spirit and the Cry" (*MTP* 24, Sermon 1435).

2.   "Companion; person or thing collaterally connected" (Johnson's *Dictionary*, s.v. "concomitant").

3.   The close proximity of the word "God" to "Love" suggests Charles likely added the word "God" afterward.

4.   The letter "e" was written in pencil at the end of the word "hous."

5.   It is unclear why Charles changed his numbering technique from ordinal numbers to Roman numerals.

6.   An alternative reading of this line is "God [is] most excellent in dignity by the fact of his giving. [It] makes us say, 'Behold.'"

17

Isaiah 45 .. 17 .. Christian & his Salvation.

We notice

I. The Character described "Israel".

Look at it as it refers to Jacob. men of God must be.

Sons of Abraham — by faith so was Jacob.

Elect of God — Jacob have I loved.

Men preferring heaven to earth — giving the pottage for birthright

Men of Prayer. wrestling men.

Or as Israelites —

Such as have been in Bondage

have groaned under it.

have eaten the Paschal lamb

have been delivered out of Egypt.

men yet in the wilderness, perhaps in captivity, —

distinct from all other men in their habits.

II. The Promise — "shall be saved" — everlasting salvation.

From a condemning law for ever.

From temptations of their own hearts

From Sin — from Satan — from hell —

Sweet Promise for us to trust in.

III. "In the Lord". Here is the way.

In him as a Refuge.

1 In him as a Surety   2 meritoriously by him.

In him as an Atoner.   Effectively by him.

Layer Breton. July 13/51.   Wratting Sepr 6/51.   24. 33. 39. 41. 43
Coton. Augst 3/51.   Waterbeach Octr 12/51   52. 109
Dunmow. Aug 31/51.   Trumpington Mar 5/52
Tatt. Septr 20/51.

17

CHRISTIAN *and* HIS SALVATION[1]
Isaiah 45:17[2]

"But Israel shall be saved in the LORD *with an everlasting salvation;*
ye shall not be ashamed nor confounded world without end."

We notice:

I. THE CHARACTER DESCRIBED. *"Israel."*

Look at it as[3] it refers to Jacob. Men of God must be:

> Sons of Abraham. By faith, so was Jacob.
> Elect of God. Jacob have I loved.[4]
> Men preferring heaven to earth. Giving the pottage[5] for birthright.[6]
> Men of Prayer. Wrestling men.[7]

Or as Israelites:

> Such as have been in Bondage.[8] Have groaned under it.
> Have eaten the Paschal lamb.[9] Have been delivered out of Egypt.[10]

Men yet in the wilderness,[11] perhaps in captivity, distinct from all other men in their habits.[12]

II. THE PROMISE. *"shall be saved," "everlasting salvation."*

> From a condemning law for ever.[13]
> From temptations[14] of their own hearts.[15]
> From Sin,[16] from Satan,[17] from hell.[18]
> Sweet Promise for us to trust in.

III. *"In the Lord."* HERE IS THE WAY.

> In him as a Refuge.[19]

1. In him as a Surety.[20]	2. Meritoriously[21] by him.[22]
In him as an Atoner.[23]	Effectively.

Layer Breton.	July 13/[18]51	Wratting[24] Sept[r25] 6 / [18]51	24. 33. 39. 41. 43.
Coton.	Augst[26] 3/[18]51	Waterbeach Oct 12 / [18]51	52. 109.[27]
Dunmow.	Aug 31/[18]51	Trumpington Mar 5 / [18]52	
Toft.	Sept[t] 13 /[18]51		

1. Charles preached the above sermon seven recorded times in this notebook. The next most-frequently preached sermons in this notebook were "The Plant of Renown" (Sermon 20) and "Heaven's Preparations" (Sermon 28), each of which was preached on five occasions, and "Adoption" (Sermon 1) and "The Wrong Roads" (Sermon 32), each of which was preached on four occasions.

2. This is the only time Charles preached a sermon on Isa 45:17. For additional sermons on salvation, see "Salvation to the Uttermost" (*NPSP* 2, Sermon 84); "Salvation of the Lord" (*NPSP* 3, Sermon 131); "Salvation Altogether of Grace" (*MTP* 12, Sermon 703); "Salvation All of Grace" (*MTP* 18, Sermon 1064); "Salvation by Faith and the Work of the Spirit" (*MTP* 21, Sermon 1228); "Salvation by Knowing the Truth" (*MTP* 26, Sermon 1516); "Salvation by Works, a Criminal Doctrine" (*MTP* 26, Sermon 1534); "Salvation by Grace" (*MTP* 47, Sermon 2741); and "Salvation as It Is Now Received" (*MTP* 56, Sermon 3223).

3. A vertical pencil line appears above the word "as." For similar lines, see "Future Judgment" (Sermon 6).

4. Cf. Mal 1:3; Rom 9:13.

5. Samuel Johnson defined the word "pottage," which is similar to "porridge," as "anything boiled or decocted for food" (Johnson's *Dictionary*).

6. Cf. Gen 25:29–34.

7. Cf. Gen 32:22–32.

8. Cf. Exodus 1.

9. Cf. Exodus 12.

10. Cf. Exod 6:6.

11. Cf. Num 32:13.

12. Cf. Deut 7:6.

13. Cf. Rom 3:20; 8:3; Gal 3:11–12.

14. It is unclear why Charles wrote the letter "y" before the word "temptations."

15. Cf. Matt 6:13.

16. Cf. Eph 2:1–5.

17. Cf. Luke 22:31–32; Rev 20:10.

18. Cf. Ps 10:16; Matt 25:46; John 3:16.

19. Cf. Pss 18:2; 91:2.

20. Cf. Heb 7:22.

21. Cf. Phil 3:9.

22. Charles's use of "In him" at the beginning of this line suggests he intended the words "by him" to apply to both "Meritoriously" and "Effectively," that is, "by him Meritoriously" and "by him Effectively."

23. Cf. Rom 3:23.

24. A superscript "W" was written above the larger "W" in the word "Wratting." It was likely the abbreviation "West" to represent the name of the village of West Wratting.

25. Abbr., "September."

26. Abbr., "August."

27. The imprint of the smudged number 109 is found directly below the number.

18   Ps. 10. 16.   Gods sovereignty.

I   God has right to be king   1 as Creator
                                       2. as Sustainer
                                       3. from his own nature.

II. As a king he has dominions and subjects.
   In heaven. Angels. redeemed Spirits.
   In hell. Vengeance is executed. Devils restrained
On earth. Inanimate objects are under his power
        All events are under his control.
        He putteth down one & setteth up another.
    2. As a king he has regalia. crown, sceptre. throne.
       he has decrees. and these are absolute.
           laws. and a right to obedience
          power of life and death. election just.

C. 1. Christians are safe.
   2. Christians are Princes.
   3. Should submit to all his appointments

S. 1 All ought to obey this king.
   2. Charge them with high treason.
   3. Sinners in danger from so great a king

Sayer Breton. July 13/51.   25

GOD'S SOVEREIGNTY[1]
Psalm 10:16[2]

*"The L*ORD *is King for ever and ever: the heathen are perished out of his land."*

I.[3] GOD HAS RIGHT TO BE KING:[4]

1. As Creator.[5]
2. As Sustainer.[6]
3. From his own nature.[7]

II. AS A KING HE HAS DOMINIONS AND SUBJECTS:

In heaven. Angels.[8] Redeemed Spirits.[9]

In hell.[10] Vengeance is executed.[11] Devils restrained.

On earth. Inanimate objects are under his power.[12]

 All events are under his control.

 He putteth down one and setteth up another.[13]

2.[14] AS A KING HE HAS REGALIA, CROWN, SCEPTRE, THRONE.[15]

He has: Decrees,[16] and these are absolute

 Laws.[17] And a right to obedience.

 Power of life and death.[18] Election, just.[19]

c.[20] 1. Christians are safe.[21]

 2. Christians are Princes.[22]

 3. Should submit to all his appointments.[23]

d. 1. All ought to obey this king.

 2. Charge them with high treason.[24]

 3. Sinners in danger from so great a king.[25]

Layer Breton. July 13/[18]51. 25

1. In 1866, Charles said, "No doctrine in the whole word of God has more excited the hatred of mankind than the truth of the absolute sovereignty of God" (*MTP* 58:13). A definition of God's sovereignty may be borrowed from James Smith of Cheltenham who gave an address at the Metropolitan Tabernacle on April 11, 1861. Charles published Smith's address, which was entitled "Effectual Calling," in *The Metropolitan Tabernacle Pulpit*: "The way we put it is—God is the Creator, he has a right to do as he wills; he is Sovereign, there is no law above him, he has a right to make and to unmake, and when man hath sinned, he has a right to save or to destroy. If he can save, and yet not impair his justice, heaven shall ring with songs; if he destroy, and yet his goodness be not marred, then hell itself with its deep bass of misery, shall swell the mighty rollings of his glorious praise" (*MTP* 7:322). The doctrine of God's sovereignty played a significant role in Charles's theology, so much so that he reprinted Elisha Cole's *A Practical Discourse of God's Sovereignty* and recommended it "to the attention of our friends" (*MTP* 13:vii).

2. This is the only time Charles preached a sermon on Ps 10:16. For additional sermons on God's sovereignty, see "Absolute Sovereignty" (Notebook 3, Sermon 177); "Divine Sovereignty" (*NPSP* 2, Sermon 77); "Testimony to Free and Sovereign Grace" (*MTP* 33, Sermon 1953); and "The Sequel to Divine Sovereignty" (*MTP* 58, Sermon 3284). See also C. H. Spurgeon, *The Treasury of David: Containing an Original Exposition of the Book of Psalms; A Collection of Illustrative Extracts from the Whole Range of Literature; A Series of Homiletical Hints upon Almost Every Verse; and Lists of Writers upon Each Psalm*, vol. 1: Psalm 1 to 26 ([3rd ed.; London: Passmore & Alabaster, 1872, The Spurgeon Library], 1:141, 144).

3. Charles used Roman numerals, English letters, and cardinal numbers in the ordering of this outline.

4. An alternative reading of this line is "God has [the] right to be king."

5. Cf. Gen 1:1; Col 1:16.   6. Cf. Pss 54:4; 55:22.   7. Cf. 1 Tim 6:15.

8. Cf. Rev 7:11–12.   9. Cf. 1 Tim 5:21.   10. Cf. Ps 139:8.

11. Cf. Deut 32:35; Rom 12:19.   12. Cf. John 13:13; 1 Cor 15:27; Eph 1:22.

13. Cf. Ps 75:7.

14. The context suggests Charles intended the number 2 to be Roman numeral III instead. There does not appear to be corresponding content in the paragraph above to necessitate the number 1.

15. In his "Explanatory Notes and Quaint Sayings" on Ps 89:14 in *The Treasury of David*, Charles included the following quotation from George Swinnock: "Now, saith the Psalmist, justice and judgment are the pillars upon which God's throne standeth, as Calvin expoundeth it, the robe and diadem, the purple and sceptre, the regalia with which God's throne is adorned" (George Swinnock, quoted in C. H. Spurgeon, *Treasury of David* [London: Passmore & Alabaster, 1875, The Spurgeon Library], 4:178).

16. Cf. Job 22:28.

17. An alternative reading of this line is "He has decrees, and these are absolute laws."

18. Cf. John 17:2.

19. Charles may have abbreviated the word "justification." If so, the line would read "Election, justification." Cf. Rom 9:20–23.

20. The presence of letters "c" and "d" is problematic given the ordering techniques in this sermon. Charles may have intended them to be primary divisions IV and V.

21. Cf. Isa 54:17; 2 Thess 3:3; 1 John 5:18.   22. Cf. 1 Pet 2:9.

23. Cf. Jas 4:7. An alternative reading of this line is "[Christians] should submit to all his appointments."

24. "Every sinner is guilty of high treason against the majesty of heaven, for he does, as far as he can, snatch from God's hand the scepter of sovereignty, and pluck from his brow the crown of universal dominion" (*MTP* 55:280).

25. The letter "a" is flattened and appears to be a hyphen. The context suggests, however, that Charles intended to include the article between the words "great" and "king."

2 Samuel. 24. 13. An answer required.

The Characters in which a Preacher comes, thus illustrating his question.

As Ambassador.   Are you willing to be at peace?
As Messenger of Good news —   Will you receive the Gospel?
As Inviter to a Feast.   Will you come?
As Servant of the Great Physician.   Take his medicine
As Life Boatsman.   Come in to his free grace boat

The question   Are you willing to be saved — God's way.
It is a Way that will not admit of boasting.
    a way of holiness. Sanctification
    a way requiring, self-denial, repentance, submission
self dedication,   love to God & obedience to him.
But a way of peace, joy, safety, blessedness.
    Account of myself — with remarks.

2 Answer.   I desire to be saved but not his way.
1. I see no need of salvation
3. I intend soon . when I am older & better.
4. I am afraid to trust. he will not receive one
5. I accept it. Direction .... What some may say to amen

28   Balsham. July 2//51.   31, 40

An ANSWER REQUIRED
2 Samuel 24:13[1]

"So Gad came to David, and told him, and said unto him, Shall seven years
of famine come unto thee in thy land? or wilt thou flee three months before
thine enemies, while they pursue thee? or that there be three days' pestilence in thy land?
now advise, and see what answer I shall return to him that sent me."

THE CHARACTERS IN WHICH A PREACHER COMES, THUS ILLUSTRATING HIS QUESTION:

As Ambassador.	Are you willing to be at peace?[2]
As Messenger of Good News.	Will you receive the gospel?[3]
As Inviter to a Feast.	Will you come?[4]
As Servant of the Great Physician.	Take his medicine.[5]
As Life Boat'sman.[6]	Come in to this freegrace boat.[7]

[1.][8]THE[9] QUESTION: ARE YOU WILLING TO BE SAVED IN GOD'S WAY?

It is a way that will not admit of boasting. A way of holiness, Sanctification. A way requiring self-denial, repentance, submission, self dedication, love to God, and obedience to him. But a way of peace, joy, safety, blessedness.

Account of myself, with remarks.[10]

2. ANSWER: I DESIRE TO BE SAVED, BUT NOT THIS WAY.

1.[11] I see no need of salvation.

3.[12] I intend soon when I am older and better.

4. I am afraid to trust. He[13] will not receive me.

5. I accept it. Directions.[14] O that some may say so. Amen.

28[15]

1. This is the only time Charles preached a sermon on 2 Sam 24:13.

2. Cf. Rom 12:18.   3. Cf. John 1:12.   4. Cf. Luke 14:15–24.

5. Cf. Ps 103:3; Jer 30:17; Matt 9:12. See also the words "From the cures effected by its medicines" in the following sermon, "The Plant of Renown" (Sermon 20).

6. In Victorian England a "boat'sman," or "boatman," was the captain of a water-going vessel who transported travelers across a body of water. An example is found in an 1812 complaint in *The Liverpool Mercury* by "A Man of Business" with regard to the removal of the "Old Dock Bridge": "When we consider what a great thorough-fare this part of the town is, and how many passengers, and heavily laden porters must be *daily* impeded on their way, and compelled either to wait for a considerable time, or to go more than a quarter of a mile out of their way, unless they choose to pay a boatman for ferrying them over . . . we must feel astonished that so serious a nuisance should have been tolerated so long" ("To the Editor of the Liverpool Mercury," *The Liverpool Mercury* [July 31, 1812] italics in the original). In the sermon outline above, Charles drew an analogy between the boat'sman and the preacher.

7. "Thou hast fallen off the main deck, thou art in the sea, the floods surround thee, thou seemest to have no hope, thou catchest at straws, what shalt thou do now? Do? why lie upon the sea of trouble, and float upon it, be still, and know that God is God, and thou wilt never perish. All thy kicking and struggling will sink thee deeper; but lie still, for behold the life-boat cometh; Christ is coming to thy help; soon he will deliver thee, and fetch thee out of all thy perplexities" (*NPSP* 1:100). Charles made similar statements throughout his ministry. In 1881, he said, "We are first of all saved by grace like drowning mariners snatched from the deep, but afterwards we are taught to man the life-boat ourselves for the rescue of others from destruction" (*MTP* 27:106). Ten years later he said, "[G]et into Christ's Word as a sinking sailor would get into a life-boat, and once there, keep inside the boat: do not throw yourself out into the stormy waves through despair, but continue in the place of hope" (*MTP* 37:114).

8. Charles did not include the number 1 before the words "The question." For consistency with the second cardinal number corresponding to "Answer," the number 1 has been added.

9. The bowl of an illegible letter, likely an "A," was written beneath the letter "T" in the word "The." Charles may have prematurely begun writing "Are." This occurrence also can be found in the following sermon, "The Plant of Renown" (Sermon 20).

10. This is the only time in a sermon of Notebook 1 that Charles reminded himself to include a personal experience from his life. He did not specify what "account" he had in mind; however, confessional remarks were common throughout his later ministry, e.g., "My heart was fallow, and covered with weeds; but, on a certain day, the great Husbandman came, and began to plough my soul. Ten black horses were His team, and it was a sharp ploughshare that he used, and the ploughers made deep furrows. The ten commandments were those black horses, and the justice of God, like a ploughshare, tore my spirit. I was condemned, undone, destroyed,—lost, helpless, hopeless, I thought hell was before me" (*Autobiography* 1:75). The context suggests Charles may have shared an account of his own salvation or of his love for God. In a letter to his father on January 30, 1850, Charles wrote, "How sweet is prayer. I would be always engaged in it. How beautiful is the Bible. I never loved it so before. It seems to me as necessary as food. I feel that I have not one particle of spiritual life in me but what the Spirit placed there. I feel that I cannot live if he depart. I tremble and fear lest I should grieve him. I dread lest sloth or pride should overcome me and I should dishonour the gospel by neglect of prayer or the scriptures or by sinning against God" (Angus Library and Archive, Regent's Park College, Oxford University, D/SPU 1, Letter 3; see also the transcription of this letter in *Autobiography* 1:117).

11. Charles originally wrote the number 2 beneath 1.

12. If Charles intended to begin his list with the number 1 in the line above, then the number 3 in this line is out of sequence.

13. The letter "G" was written over the "h" in the word "he." Charles may have begun writing the word "God." If this interpretation is correct, the line would have read "God will not receive me."

14. The word "Directions" was written in superscript above the line and between the words "it" and "O that." The word likely signaled Charles's final remarks. See also the conclusion of "Abraham Justified by Faith" (Sermon 3).

15. For reasons unknown the bottom portion of the page containing the dates and villages where Charles preached this sermon has been removed. The texture of the edge suggests the page was cut with a blade and not torn by hand. Evidently the cut was applied along the line of ink that stretched across the page. Similar lines are found in "Adoption" (Sermon 1), "Necessity of Purity for an Entrance to Heaven" (Sermon 2), and "Abraham Justified by Faith" (Sermon 3). A remaining section of this line can be seen on the left beneath the number 28. The words "Balsham. July 2/51" and the numbers "31. 46" belong to the sermon "Making Light of Christ" (Sermon 21). The dates and villages in the following sermon, "The Plant of Renown" (Sermon 20), are also missing.

26

Ezekiel 34 . 29 . The Plant of Renown.

Enumeration of various plants of renown.
Lily . Rose . wheat . vine . oak.
Palm tree . Cow tree . Sandal wood.

Tree of Life . Olive Branch . Palm Trees of Elim
Tree at Marah . Grapes of Eschol . Jonathan's wood.
Balm of Gilead . Jonah's gourd.
Jesus is a Plant of Renown .

1 . From his Planter .
2 . From the ancient date of his plantity.
3 . From the place of planting .
4 . From remembrances which it brings up.
5 . From its beauty . height,
6 . For his productions . bread . fruit . wine . clothing.
   Spices . ornamental flowers.
7 . From the cures effected by its . medecines.
   cordials, revivals,
8 . From the variety of his products.
9 . From his perpetual fruitfulness
10 . From the abundance of his fruit .   27

11 . His freeness to all .   184

The PLANT *of* RENOWN
Ezekiel 34:29[1]

"And I will raise up for them a plant of renown, and they shall be no more consumed with hunger in the land, neither bear the shame of the heathen any more."

Enumeration of various plants of renown.[2] Lily. Rose. Wheat. Vine. Oak. Palm tree. Cow tree.[3] Sandalwood.[4]

Tree[5] of Life.[6] Olive Branch.[7] Palm Trees of Elim.[8] Tree at Marah.[9] Grapes of Eschol.[10] Jonathan's wood.[11] Balm of Gilead.[12] Jonah's gourd.[13]

JESUS IS A PLANT OF RENOWN:

1. From his Planter.[14]
2. From the ancient date of his planting.[15]
3. From the place of planting.[16]
4. From remembrances which it brings up.
5. From its beauty, height.
6. For his productions: bread, fruit, wine, clothing, spices, ornamental flowers.[17]
7. From the cures effected by its medicines,[18] cordials,[19] revivals.[20]
8. From the variety of his products.
9. From his perpetual fruitfulness.[21]

27^{22}

10. From the abundance of his fruit.[23]
11. His freeness to all.

184

[24]

1. In 1879, Charles preached a sermon at the Metropolitan Tabernacle with a similar title, "A Plant of Renown." However, this sermon was not published in the *Metropolitan Tabernacle Pulpit*, likely because Charles preached it during the week instead of on Sunday. Instead, the sermon is found in *The Baptist Messenger: An Evangelical Treasury and Chronicle of the Churches for the Year 1879* ([London: Paternoster Row, 1879, The Spurgeon Library], 169–78). The lack of structural similarities and overlapping content suggests Charles did not have the above outline in mind while writing his later sermon. However, it is likely that Charles used this outline in his exposition of Ezek 34:29 at the conclusion of his 1856 sermon "Zion's Prosperity" (*MTP* 44, Sermon 2576): "Jesus is 'a plant of renown,' because you may go to him at all times, and you will always find fruit on him. That is more than you can say of any other plant. You may go to him, and you will always find the sort of fruit you want; is he not 'a plant of renown?' You will find healing virtue in his leaves, and satisfying fruits hanging in clusters upon him. He is 'a plant of renown,' because his Father planted him; because he has food enough for all his saints, and a gracious variety for all their tastes; because he will blossom through eternity; because of the multitude who sit under his shadow, and rejoice therein. He is 'a plant of renown' to his people, for under his shadow they are begotten and brought forth; the greatest transactions of their lives have taken place beneath the shadow of that old tree, 'the plant of renown'" (*MTP* 44:312). See also Charles Spurgeon, *Evening by Evening; or, Readings at Eventide for the Family or the Closet* ([New York: Sheldon and Company, 1869, The Spurgeon Library], June 1).

2. As a child, Charles's interest in the natural world manifested in the trees and animals he illustrated (*Autobiography* 1:42). At the Stockwell School in Colchester, he favored Gilbert White's *Natural History of Selborne* (*Autobiography* 1:41), a book he kept in his personal library (see Gilbert White, *The Natural History of Selborne and The Naturalist's Calendar* [London: Blackie & Son, Ltd., 1895, The Spurgeon Library]). Charles's artistic ability advanced during his studies at the Agricultural College in Maidstone and also during his education in Newmarket, as can be seen in his 1849 notebook of bird sketches entitled "Notes on the Vertebrate Animals Class Aries." After moving to Cambridge, Charles posted a personal advertisement in a local newspaper in which he offered to tutor students in a wide range of subjects, including "Natural history" and "drawing" (*Autobiography* 1:341). For Charles's spiritualization of nature, see C. H. Spurgeon, *Teachings of Nature in the Kingdom of Grace* (London: Passmore & Alabaster, 1896). Charles's personal library was well stocked

with books on the natural world and included J. H. Balfour, *Botany and Religion; or, Illustrations of the Works of God in the Structure, Functions, Arrangement, and General Distribution of Plants* (4th ed.; Edinburgh: Oliphant, Anderson, and Ferrier, 1882, The Spurgeon Library); Francis George Heath, *Our Woodland Trees* (London: Sampson Low, Marston, Searle, and Rivington, 1878, The Spurgeon Library); and Mrs. Dyson, *The Stories of the Trees* (London: Thomas Nelson and Sons, 1890, The Spurgeon Library).

3. The "Cow tree" (*brosimum galactodendron*) is native to South America and has sap that resembles the texture and taste of cow's milk. It is commonly used to make chewing gum and candle wax. The bark is also useful in making clothes, blankets, and sails (Alfred Bircher, *Encyclopedia of Fruit Trees and Edible Flowering Plants in Egypt and the Subtropics* [Cairo: American University of Cairo Press, 2000], 67). The Victorians were fascinated by the medicinal properties of "lactescent" trees, as noted in an article in *The Glasgow Herald*, published during the same year in which Charles wrote the sermon above (see "The Cow Tree of South America," *The Glasgow Herald*, October 14, 1851). A story is found in Charles's personal copy of William Edwards's *A Voyage of the River Amazon* in which Edwards encountered a cow tree in his travels through Brazil. He noted that when the tree was cut, the milk "resembled cream in appearance and taste, and might be used as a substitute for milk in coffee; or, diluted with water, as a drink. It is, however, little used, except as a medicine, or for the adulteration of rubber" (William H. Edwards, *A Voyage of the River Amazon, Including a Residence at Pará* [London: John Murray, 1847, The Spurgeon Library], 44).

4. Commonly used to make chests and wardrobes, "sandalwood" (*santalaceae*) is an Eastern Asian and South Pacific tree in which the wood constitutes an insect repellent (William Nielson, *Webster's New International Dictionary of the English Language* [2nd ed.; Springfield, MA: G&C Merriam, 1958], 2211). It is not clear as to how Charles referenced this tree in the above sermon; however, a chapter is found in his personal copy of Elizabeth Twining's work that reveals its religious uses among the Hindus of India: "The Brahmins consider it one of their sacred trees, and employ the dust of the wood in compounding the pigment with which they paint the mysterious mark on the forehead of their god Vishnoo. The oil used in religious ceremonies and at funerals is extracted from the wood or its shavings" (Elizabeth Twining, *Illustrations of the Natural Orders of Plants with Groups and Descriptions, Reduced from the Original Folio Edition* [London: Sampson Low, Son, and Marston, 1868, The Spurgeon

Library], 2:120). In 1875, Charles said that Jesus Christ "was the sandal-wood tree, and yours was the hand that held the axe that wounded him, yet he perfumed the axe, and also the hand that wielded it, and healed that hand of all its leprosies; yea, healed your whole being of whatsoever disease it had. Thank God for love like that" (*MTP* 52:224). In the sermon above, Charles may have spiritualized the tree as he did in 1889: "Be like the sandalwood tree, which perfumes the axe that fells it. Be all gentleness, and kindness, and love; and be this your prayer, 'Father, forgive them'" (*MTP* 39:266).

5. The bowl of the letter "O" was written beneath the letter "t" in the word "Tree." Charles likely began writing the word "Olive" prematurely. This tendency also can be found in the previous sermon, "An Answer Required" (Sermon 19).

6. Cf. Gen 2:16–17; Rev 22:14.   7. Cf. Gen 8:11.

8. Cf. Exod 15:27.   9. Cf. Exod 15:25.

10. Cf. Num 13:23; Charles misspelled the word "Eshcol" by inserting the letter "c" before the "h." The letter "c" was circled in pencil and indicated by a line and a caret.

11. Cf. 1 Sam 14:29.   12. Cf. Jer 8:22.

13. Cf. Jonah 4:6.   14. Cf. John 20:31.

15. Cf. John 1:2. "[T]he Plant of Renown produces many lovely flowers with rich perfume, and a multitude of choice fruits of dainty taste" (*MTP* 59:169).

16. Cf. John 16:10.

17. "Christ is that plant of renown. If he be sown in the soil of your soul, he will gradually eat out the roots of all ill weeds and poisonous plants, till over all your nature there shall be Christ in you" (*MTP* 29:273).

18. "Whether it is true or not, you and I have been bitten by the old serpent Satan, and there is 'the Plant of Renown,' the Lord Jesus Christ; and if we go and feed upon him, all the wounds that sin can make will soon be healed" (*MTP* 57:487–88). Charles also wrote, "There is but one cure for the nations—the leaves of the tree. There grows no healing herb but the one plant of renown" (Spurgeon, *Teachings of*

Nature in the Kingdom of Grace, 316–17). See also the words "Take his medicine" in the previous sermon, "An Answer Required" (Sermon 19).

19. "Some plants may be a good medicine, but not a good cordial; the plant of renown is good every way" (*MTP* 17:465).

20. "Though it seems to you that you must be stunted by the chill blast and the cruel soil which environ you, yet the great husbandman can so foster you that you shall become a plant of renown. God can turn disadvantageous circumstances into means of growth" (*MTP* 36:622).

21. Cf. John 15:5.

22. A vertical dotted line connects the number 27 to the number 184. The numbers in the margin on this page correspond to those to their right in the margin of the following sermon, "Making Light of Christ" (Sermon 21). Charles may have included them here because the bottom portion of the page was removed. These numbers likely represent the specific occasion on which Charles preached the sermon (the twenty-seventh, twenty-ninth, thirty-seventh, and 186th times that he preached). The numbers 28 and 11 were struck through on the following page, likely because Charles realized he had already preached two sermons on those occasions: "Adoption" (Sermon 1) and "An Answer Required" (Sermon 19).

23. "The botanist must find his flowers in their seasons, but our plant of renown blooms in our souls all the year round" (*MTP* 12:472). Cf. Rom 10:13.

24. As in the previous sermon, "An Answer Required" (Sermon 19), it is unclear why the bottom portion of this page was removed (see notes in the previous sermon). The upper part of the words "Tollesbury" and "Cherryhinton" are visible beneath the line. The month on the right side of the page is not evident, but the date may have been July 21, 1851.

Matt 22. 5 ~ Making Light of Christ. Baxter 21

I. What men make light of.

1. Jesus as Reconciler. Mediator, Redeemer, Sustainer Saviour, Intercessor, Priest. Lover.

2. Gospel & its blessings. Salvation, Forgiveness. Justification. God's love & favour, Promises, Adoption, Heaven

II. How they do it.

1. By hearing without attention.

2. By attending without feeling.

3. By refusing to love God supremely.

4. Non-compliance with Gospel terms.

5. Profession without Possession.

III. The Causes of this sin.

1 Ignorance, 2 Foolishness. 3. Self Conceit. 4. Unbelief.

5. Hardness of heart. 6. Carnality. 7. Thoughtlessness.

8. Presumption 9. Commoness of the Gospel.

IV. Enquiries whether some here are not guilty of it.

1 Those who think not much. 2 nor talk much. 3 nor strive much

4 Such as will not give up sin. 5. Love God supremely. 6. wicked friends.

Exhortations and directions

29
30
37

Balsham. July 27/51.   31. 46

(21)   <u>Baxter</u>[1]

MAKING LIGHT *of* CHRIST
Matthew 22:5[2]

"But they made light of it, and went their ways, one to his farm, another to his merchandise."

I. WHAT MEN MAKE LIGHT OF:

1. Jesus as Reconciler, Mediator, Redeemer, Sustainer, Saviour, Intercessor, Priest, Lover.

2. Gospel and its blessings. Salvation, Forgiveness, Justification, God's love and favour, Promises, Adoption, Heaven.

II. HOW THEY DO IT:

1. By[3] hearing without attention.

2. By attending without feeling.[4]

3. By refusing to love God supremely.

4. Non-compliance with Gospel terms.

5. Profession without Possession.[5]

III. THE CAUSES OF THIS SIN:

1. Ignorance. 2. Foolishness. 3. Self Conceit. 4. Unbelief.[6]
5. Hardness of heart.[7] 6. Carnality.[8] 7. Thoughtlessness.
8. Presumption.[9] 9. Commonness[10] of the Gospel.[11]

IV. ENQUIRIES WHETHER SOME HERE ARE NOT GUILTY OF IT:

1. Those who think not much.[12] 2. Nor talk much.[13] 3. Nor strive much.[14]
4. Such as will not give up sin. 5. Love God supremely.[15] 6. Wish friends.[16]

Exhortations and directions.[17]

~~28~~[18]

29
30
37
~~31~~

Balsham.   July 27/[18]51[19]   31. 46

1. This outline is original to English Puritan and minister at Kidderminster, Richard Baxter (1615–1691). From a young age Charles had become familiar with Baxter's writings. On Sunday evenings his mother, Eliza, read *Call to the Unconverted* to him and to his siblings around the dinner table (*Autobiography* 1:68, 80, 104). Charles admired Baxter's productivity, saying that he was "a man whose vigorous sermons were supplemented by such voluminous writings that his works are a prodigy of toil" (*MTP* 15:465), and "to be like Baxter is seraphic" (C. H. Spurgeon, *An All Round Ministry: Addresses to Ministers and Students*, [2nd ed.; London: The Banner of Truth Trust, 1965], 177). Charles also admired Baxter's piety and, in comparing it to his own, he noted, "I blush at my cold heart" (*MTP* 8:81). On January 4, 1859, Charles offered the following words to the Young Men's Christian Association at Exeter Hall: "Oh, that I could have the Spirit of God in me, till I was filled with it to the brim, that I might always feel as Baxter did when he said, —'I preached as never sure to preach again, And as a dying man to dying men'" (*Autobiography* 3:43). For additional references to Baxter, see *NPSP* 2:417 and *Lectures* 1:6–7, 1:11, 1:181. In the outline above, Charles borrowed heavily from Baxter's sermon on Matt 22:5 entitled "Making Light of Christ and Salvation" (Richard Baxter, *Making Light of Christ and Salvation. Too Oft the Issue of Gospel Invitations: A Call to the Unconverted to Turn and Live: The Last Work of a Believer; His Passing Prayer, Recommending His Departing Spirit to Christ, to Be Received by Him: Of the Shedding Abroad of God's Love on the Heart by the Holy Ghost* [London: Thomas Nelson, 1846]). The overlapping content is noted below. See also Charles's personal copy of Richard Baxter, *The Reformed Pastor; A Discourse on the Pastoral Office. Designed Principally to Explain and Recommend the Duty of Personal Instruction and Catechising. To Which Is Added an Appendix, Containing Some Hints of Advice to Students for the Ministry, and to Tutors. Abridged and Reduced to a New Method by Samuel Palmer* [ed. Samuel Palmer; London: J. Buckland, 1766, The Spurgeon Library]). A recent treatment of Baxter is found in Tim Cooper, *John Owen, Richard Baxter, and the Formation of Nonconformity* (Farnham, England: Ashgate, 2011).

2. On August 17, 1856, Charles preached an expanded version of this sermon at Exeter Hall (see "Making Light of Christ" [*NPSP* 2, Sermon 98]). Both sermons share an almost identical outline with one exception: in the later sermon, Charles did not include the content in Baxter's fourth Roman numeral. Also, only in the above outline did Charles credit Baxter with writing this outline.

3. A cluster of dots appears beneath the word "By." The significance of these dots is not obvious, but they do share similarities with the triangular cluster of dots that

Charles used to represent the word "therefore" in "Future Judgment" (Sermon 6) and "Beginning at Jerusalem" (Sermon 29).

4.   Charles wrote the word "fealing" but corrected the misspelling by writing the letter "e" over the "a."

5.   When comparing the use of the long "s" in the words "Possession" and "Profession" in this line, Charles's inconsistency in using this letter becomes noticeable.

6.   "The main cause of the slighting of Christ and salvation is, a secret root of unbelief in men's hearts. Whatsoever they may pretend, they do not soundly and thoroughly believe the word of God" (Baxter, *Making Light of Christ and Salvation*, 10).

7.   "The heart is hard naturally, and by custom in sinning made more hard, especially by long abuse of mercy, and neglect of the means of grace, and resisting the Spirit of God" (ibid., 11).

8.   "A carnal man apprehendeth not a suitableness in these spiritual and heavenly things to his mind, and therefore he sets light by them, and hath no mind of them. When you tell him of everlasting glory, he heareth you as if you were persuading him to go play with the sun: they are matters of another world, and out of his element" (ibid., 10).

9.   An illegible letter, possibly "C," is found beneath the letter "P" in the word "Presumption." Charles may have intended to write the word "Commonness" here.

10. Charles spelled the word "Commonness" with one "n" instead of with two. The superscript number 2 was inserted above the word to signal the inclusion of an additional "n."

11. "Men take occasion to make light of Christ by the commonness of the gospel; because they do hear of it every day, the frequency is an occasion to dull their affections; I say, an occasion, for it is no just cause. Were it a rarity it might take more with them; but now, if they hear a minister preach nothing but these saving truths, they say, 'We have these every day'" (Baxter, *Making Light of Christ and Salvation*, 15).

12. "Things that men highly value will be remembered, they will be matter of their freest and sweetest thoughts" (ibid., 21).

13. "Things that we highly value will be matter of our discourse; the judgment and heart will command the tongue. Freely and delightfully will our speech run after them" (ibid., 22).

14. "That which we highliest value, we shall think no pains too great to obtain" (ibid., 23).

15. "Christ and salvation are freely given, and yet the most of men go without them, because they cannot enjoy the world and them together" (ibid., 24).

16. "That which men highly esteem, they would help their friends to as well as themselves" (ibid.).

17. Baxter offered the following exhortation at the end of his sermon: "I have delivered my message, the Lord open your hearts to receive it. I have persuaded you with the word of truth and soberness; the Lord persuade you more effectually, or else all this is lost. Amen" (Baxter, *Making Light of Christ and Salvation*, 39). Charles did not specify the content of "Exhortations and directions" (see also "Abraham Justified by Faith" [Sermon 3]). However, at the conclusion of his 1856 sermon, he offered the following exhortation: "Mark this man's word to-night; go away and laugh at it; but remember, I say to you again, it will be a solemn thing for you when Christ shall come to judgment, if you have made light of him, and worse than all, if you should ever be locked up in the caverns of despair, if you should ever hear it said, 'Depart ye cursed,' if you should ever mingle your awful shrieks with the doleful howls of lost myriads, if you should see the pit that is bottomless, and the gulf that has walls of fire. It will be a fearful thing to find thyself in there, and to know that thou canst ne'er get out again! Sinner, this night I preach the gospel to thee. E'er thou goest, hear it, and believe it; may God grant thee grace to receive it, so thou shalt be saved" (*NPSP* 2:360).

18. For an explanation of these marginal numbers, see the notes in the previous sermon, "The Plant of Renown" (Sermon 20).

19. This was likely the first sermon Charles preached after he returned from his visit to London in 1851 to see the Great Exhibition at the Crystal Palace in Hyde Park. Upon the opening of the Exhibition in May, Charles wrote a let-

ter to his father in which he asked permission to attend the event: "I hope very much you will be so kind as to let me go to the Exhibition" (May 15, 1851, Angus Library and Archive, Regent's Park College, Oxford University, D/SPU 1, Letter 9). When Charles returned to Cambridge, he reflected on his visit in a letter to his aunt on June 25, 1851: "I have much enjoyed my three days in London, and am now happy at home" (*Autobiography* 1:211). Traveling to London for the Great Exhibition was a common practice in 1851, especially for those living in Cambridgeshire. *The Cambridge Chronicle* reported that during one weekend in June, "every line running into London brought monster trains filled with visitors. . . . Trains from Colchester, Peterborough, Ely, Norwich, and Yarmouth brought several thousands to the metropolis" ("The Great Exhibition," *The Cambridge Chronicle and University Journal, Isle of Ely Herald, and Huntingdonshire Gazette*, June 14, 1851). Charles Darwin visited the Exhibition only one month after Spurgeon. See the account of Josiah Chater, a contemporary of Charles, who also lived in Cambridge and traveled to the Exhibition in June (Enid Porter, *Victorian Cambridge: Josiah Chater's Diaries, 1844–1884* [London: Phillimore & Co., 1975], 76–78). See also Charles's reference to the Exhibition in a letter to his mother on May 3, 1851 (*Autobiography* 1:197) and his later spiritualization of the event (*MTP* 21:619). For a recent treatment of the Great Exhibition's effect on nineteenth-century religion, see Geoffrey Cantor, *Religion and the Great Exhibition of 1851* (Oxford: Oxford University Press, 2011).

22 Colossians 3. 11 Christ is all. See 292

1. He is all in our Redemption.
2. In our pardon. nothing but Christ can procure pardon for us. In atonement.
3. In a Saint's Justification.
4. All as an argument for our prayers being heard
5. All as our dependance & supply.
6. He is all our comfort
7. He will be all in our acceptance.
8. He shall be all in our estimation.

Inf. 1. He is all in all.
" 2. He is all or nothing.
" 3. This suits not pride.
" 4. How we ought to love Christ.

Coton. Augst 3/51.   32. 370.

22

See 292[1]

CHRIST IS ALL
Colossians 3:11[2]

"Where there is neither Greek nor Jew, circumcision nor uncircumcision,
barbarian, Scythian, bond nor free: but Christ is all, and in all."

1. He is all in our Redemption.[3]

2. In our pardon. Nothing but Christ can procure[4] pardon for us.[5]
   In atonement.[6]

3. In a Saint's Justification.[7]

4. All as an argument for our prayers being heard.

5. All as our dependance and supply.[8]

6. He is all our comfort.

7. He will be all in our acceptance.[9]

8. He should[10] be all in our estimation.

Inf.[11] 1. He is all in all.

"   2. He is all or nothing.

"   3. This suits not pride.

"   4. How we ought to love Christ.[12]

Coton.   Augst[13] 3/[18]51   32. 370.

1. The words "See 292" were a cross-reference to Charles's 292nd sermon, "Christ Is All" (Notebook 6, Sermon 292). The two sermons share a common Scripture reference but contain little structural resemblance or overlapping content.

2. In addition to the above sermon and "Christ Is All" (Notebook 6, Sermon 292), Charles preached four additional sermons later in his ministry on Col 3:11: "Christ Is All" (*MTP* 17, Sermon 1006); "All and All in All" (*MTP* 43, Sermon 2501); "Christ Is All" (*MTP* 50, Sermon 2888); and "Christ Is All" (*MTP* 61, Sermon 3446). The four sermons differ in emphases and do not contain enough overlapping content to suggest Charles had the above outline in mind when writing these later sermons.

3. Cf. Gal 3:13; Eph 1:7.

4. See "Salvation in God Only" (Sermon 24).

5. The phrase "procure a pardon" was common in Puritan England, as seen in the writing of Thomas Watson (1620–1586): "Christ *himself* could not procure a Pardon but by *Dying*" (Thomas Watson, *A Body of Practical Divinity: Consisting of Above One Hundred Seventy Six Sermons on the Lesser Catechism Composed by the Reverend Assembly of Divines at Westminster: With a Supplement of Some Sermons on Several Texts of Scripture* [London: Thomas Parkhurst, 1692], 813, italics in the original). John Gill also wrote, "There is nothing a man has, or can do, by which he can procure the pardon of sin, either for himself, or for others" (Gill, *A Body of Doctrinal Divinity*, 2:786).

6. Cf. 1 John 2:2.

7. Cf. Rom 4:5; 5:1; Gal 2:16.

8. Cf. Phil 4:19.

9. Cf. Eph 1:6.

10. Charles originally wrote the word "shall" here before changing it to "should." The line can read, "He shall be all in our estimation" or "He should be all in our estimation." Given the phrasing in the line above, "He *will* be all in our acceptance" (emphasis added), the former interpretation is more likely. However, Charles may have sought to change the direction of his reasoning from observation to persuasion through the use of the word "should," as seen in his final remarks, "A Christian should be as well known and as peculiar as the ancient Israelite or Jew," in his sermon "The Peculiar People" (Sermon 25).

11.   Abbr., "Inference." For an additional instance in which Charles used this word, see "Can Two Walk Together Unless They Are Agreed?" (Sermon 76).

12.   "I commend to you Christians that you give your whole selves to Christ, that from this day forward ye serve him, spirit, soul and body, for after all there is nothing worth living for, nothing worth even giving a single tear for if you lose it, nor worth a smile if you gain it, save only that which comes from Christ, and can be used for Christ, and is found in Christ. Christ is all. May he be so to you. Amen" (*MTP* 23:324).

13.   Abbr., "August." See also Charles's abbreviation of this word at the conclusion of "Christian and His Salvation" (Sermon 17).

2 Peter. 1. 1 — Faith precious.

1. Precious in its appropriations.
It appropriates God — in all his persons & attributes.
Father — might — wisdom — truth — justice, eternity. Godhead
Son — Blood — righteousness — mediation — intercession — love &c —
Spirit. Influence — guiding — teaching — helping.

2. Precious in its discoveries ... as an eye. ear. wings.
Past regions. election. redemption. infinite love
Present things. Sin. Jesus. security. Spirit's influence
Future realities. Support. Death. Heaven.

3. Precious in its accompanying benefits.
Justification. Adoption. Love and favour of God.
Regeneration — access with boldness. Promises
    all salvation —

4. Precious in its influences.
It gives life. animation. vigour.
Freedom. security. happiness. support —
Meetness for heaven by holiness.

5. Precious in its own nature.
As the work & gift of God. The evidence of glory.
For its eternity.. and its unfailingness in time
    of necessity.

Barton. Aug 19/51   35

23

FAITH PRECIOUS[1]
2 Peter 1:1[2]

"Simon Peter, a servant and an apostle of Jesus Christ,
to them that have obtained like precious faith with us through the
righteousness of God and our Saviour Jesus Christ."

1. **PRECIOUS IN ITS APPROPRIATIONS.**
   It appropriates God in all his persons and attributes.
   Father: might,[3] wisdom,[4] truth,[5] justice,[6] eternity,[7] Godhead.[8]
   Son: Blood,[9] righteousness,[10] mediation,[11] intercession,[12] love,[13] etc.
   Spirit: Influence,[14] guiding,[15] teaching,[16] helping.[17]

2. **PRECIOUS IN ITS DISCOVERIES.**
   As an eye, ear, wings.
   Past regions: election,[18] redemption,[19] infinite love.[20]
   Present things: Sin, Jesus, security,[21] Spirit's influences.
   Future realities: Support, Death, Heaven.

3. **PRECIOUS IN ITS ACCOMPANYING BENEFITS.**
   [1.][22] Justification,[23] Adoption,[24] Love and favour of God.[25]
   2. Regeneration,[26] access with boldness,[27] Promises, All salvation.

4. **PRECIOUS IN ITS INFLUENCES.**
   It gives life,[28] animation,[29] vigour, Freedom,[30] security, happiness, support,
   meetness for heaven by holiness.[31]

5. **PRECIOUS IN ITS OWN NATURE.**
   As the work and gift of God.[32] The evidence of glory.[33] For its eternity
   and its unfailingness in time of necessity.

Barton. Aug. 10[34]/[18]51   35

1. In the index at the conclusion of this notebook, Charles reversed the order of these two words by writing "Precious Faith" instead of "Faith Precious."

2. On May 8, 1870, Charles preached a sermon on three scriptural references, including 2 Pet 1:1, entitled "Three Precious Things" (*MTP* 16, Sermon 931). On January 24, 1864, he also preached a sermon on 2 Pet 1:1–4 entitled "Faith and Life" (*MTP* 10, Sermon 551). The lack of structural similarity and overlapping content in these sermons suggests Charles did not have in mind the above outline when writing his later sermons. For additional sermons on faith, see "Faith the Substance of Things Hoped For" (Notebook 6, Sermon 297); "The Necessity of Faith" (Notebook 8, Sermon 376); "Faith before Baptism" (Notebook 9, Sermon 396); "Characteristics of Faith" (*NPSP* 6, Sermon 317); "The Centurion's Faith and Humility" (*MTP* 14, Sermon 800); "The Hold-Fasts of Faith" (*MTP* 36, Sermon 2159); and "Growth in Faith" (*MTP* 59, Sermon 3384).

3. Cf. John 9:3.

4. Cf. Eph 4:17.

5. Cf. John 1:14.

6. Cf. Deut 10:18.

7. Cf. 1 Tim 1:17.

8. Cf. 1 Cor 11:3.

9. Cf. John 6:53; 1 John 1:7.

10. Cf. Rom 10:14.

11. Cf. 1 Tim 2:5.

12. Cf. Rom 8:34.

13. Cf. 1 John 3:16.

14. Cf. John 3:8; 15:26; Acts 4:31.

15. Cf. Luke 24:32.

16. Cf. Luke 12:12; John 14:6.

17. Cf. Acts 2:4; Rom 8:11.

18. "He tells us too, that faith is '*precious*;' and is it not precious? for it deals with precious things, with precious promises, with precious blood, with a precious redemption, with all the preciousness of the person of our Lord and Saviour Jesus Christ. Well may that be a precious faith which supplies our greatest want, delivers us from our greatest danger, and admits us to the greatest glory. Well may that be called 'precious faith,' which is the symbol of our election, the evidence of our calling, the root of all our graces, the channel of communion, the weapon of prevalence, the shield

of safety, the substance of hope, the evidence of eternity, the guerdon [reward] of immortality, and the passport of glory. O for more of this inestimably precious faith. Precious faith, indeed it is" (*MTP* 10:54, italics in the original). Cf. 1 Thess 1:4.

19. Cf. Eph 1:7.

20. Cf. John 3:16. The imprint of a yellow discoloration is found after the word "love." The source is the number 3 in the previous sermon, "Salvation in God Only" (Sermon 24).

21. Cf. John 6:37; 10:29.

22. Charles wrote the number 1 above the word "Adoption." However, the context suggests he intended the number to apply to the entirety of the line. The number has been inserted before the word "Justification" to reflect this intention.

23. Cf. Rom 5:1; Gal 3:24; Titus 3:7.

24. Cf. 2 Cor 6:18; Eph 1:5.

25. Cf. Gen 39:3–4; Job 10:12; Ps 30:5.

26. Cf. 2 Cor 5:17; Titus 3:5.

27. Cf. Eph 3:12; Heb 4:16.

28. Cf. Gal 2:20.

29. A series of ink dots is found above the letter "n" in the word "animation." The source of these dots is not evident.

30. Cf. Eph 3:12.

31. Cf. 2 Cor 7:1; 1 Pet 1:15–16.

32. Cf. Eph 2:8-9.

33. Cf. Heb 11:1.

34. The bowl of an illegible number, likely 0, was written beneath the number 10.

Jer. 3. 23 ..   Salvation in God only –

The All important question "How can I be saved.

Mountains & Hills the natural strongholds of the

country – but this tells us.

<u>I</u> .. That salvation cannot come from them.

   these mountains are .

1. Mount Rome .. penance, merit, money, pilgrimage

2. Mount Pusey .. Bapt. Conf. Lord's supper. church. &c.

3. Mount Pharisee . morality .. honesty. decency –

4. Mount Amendment – promises of better conduct. procrastned

5. Mount Presumption – on God's absolute mercy.

6. The Hill Infidelity – or doubt of God's truth ..

   Besides multitudes of other mountains –

<u>II</u>. But "truly in the Lord. our God is the salvₙ of Israel –

1. In him only .   In the Father .. donatively

2. In him surely.   In the Son .. procuratively

3. In him perpetually   In the Spirit ... effectively

4. In him only ..

To a Christian here is strong consolation

    Every unconverted man is a fool –

Barton. Aug. 10/51   34 . 119.

SALVATION *in* GOD ONLY
Jeremiah 3:23[1]

"Truly in vain is salvation hoped for from the hills, and from the multitude of mountains: truly in the LORD *our God is the salvation of Israel."*

The All important question: "How can I be saved?"[2] Mountains and Hills, the natural strongholds of the country.[3] But this tells us:

I. THAT SALVATION CANNOT COME FROM THEM.
    These mountains are:

    1. Mount Rome:[4] penance, merit, money, pilgrimage.[5]

    2. Mount Pusey:[6] Bapt.[7] Conf.,[8] Lord's supper, church, etc.

    3. Mount Pharisee: morality, honesty, decency.[9]

    4. Mount Amendment: promises of better conduct, procrastination.[10]

    5. Mount Presumption:[11] on God's absolute mercy.

    6. The Hill Infidelity:[12] or doubt of God's truth.

    Besides multitudes of other mountains.[13]

II. BUT "TRULY IN THE LORD OUR GOD
    IS THE SALV[14] OF ISRAEL.["]

    1. In him only.   In the Father: trustively.[15]

    2. In him surely.   In the Son: procuratively.

    3. In him perpetually.   In the Spirit: effectively.

    4. In him only.

To a Christian, here is strong consolation. Every unconverted man is a fool.

Barton.   Aug. 10/[18]51[16]   34. 119.

1. This is the only time Charles preached a sermon on Jer 3:23 specifically. However, on February 14, 1886, he preached a sermon on Jer 3:22–23 entitled "Hope for the Worst Backsliders" (*MTP* 42, Sermon 2452). The emphasis of this sermon is on verse 22, not 23; however, there is enough overlapping content to suggest Charles may have had the above outline in mind when writing the content of *MTP* 42:80–81. See also "Christian and His Salvation" (Sermon 17).

2. Cf. Acts 16:30.

3. An alternative reading of this line is "Mountains and hills [are] the natural strongholds of the country."

4. Charles's early critique of Roman Catholicism and Anglicanism is best understood against the backdrop of his nonconformist upbringing. For at least 200 years, dissenting sentiment had existed in Charles's family. His father, John Spurgeon, and also his grandfather, James Spurgeon, were both Independent Congregational ministers. Charles's great-grandfather's grandfather, Job Spurgeon—a Quaker from Dedham—was imprisoned for almost four months for not paying a fine for attending a nonconformist meeting (*Autobiography* 1:8). As a young child who often stayed with his grandfather in Stambourne, Charles was exposed to anti-Catholic literature such as *The Evangelical Magazine* (see *Autobiography* 1:16) and Puritan tomes (*Autobiography* 1:22–23). Charles's first substantial literary endeavor was a 295-page essay entitled "Antichrist and Her Brood; or, Popery Unmasked" (*Autobiography* 1:57). Anti-Catholic propaganda was also common in Cambridge in 1851. In January of that year, about two months after this sermon was first preached, the following words were published in a local Cambridge newspaper: "In these days of Popish resuscitation, every Protestant ought to be prepared with arguments to refute the errors of Popery, in whatever form or place they may appear" (A Protestant, "Controversial Sermons on Popery," *The Cambridge Chronicle and University Journal, Isle of Ely Herald, and Huntingdonshire Gazette* [January 11, 1851]).

5. Charles was not referring to the biblical theme of pilgrimage but instead to the Roman Catholic *abuses* of this practice. Peter Morden is correct to suggest that for Charles, the allegory of pilgrimage was a "framework for understanding the Christian life" (Morden, *"Communion with Christ and His People,"* 29). Charles lauded the metaphor of pilgrimage and incorporated it often into his sermons (see "The Fight and the Weapons" [Sermon 37a]; "The Pilgrim's Grateful Recollec-

tions" [*MTP* 16, Sermon 939]; "The Pilgrim's Longings" [*MTP* 18, Sermon 1030]; "The Valley of the Shadow of Death" [*MTP* 27, Sermon 1595]; "Singing in the Ways of the Lord" [*MTP* 27, Sermon 1615]; "The Holy Road" [*MTP* 32, Sermon 1912]; "Crossing the Jordan" [*MTP* 34, Sermon 2039]; and "Entangled in the Land" [*MTP* 37, Sermon 2188]). Charles encountered the metaphor of pilgrimage in the Puritan authors he read in his grandfather's attic in Stambourne. Charles Hambrick-Stowe has noted that the metaphor of pilgrimage was the "principle metaphor running through Puritan spirituality and devotional practice" (Charles Hambrick-Stowe, *The Practice of Piety: Puritan Devotional Disciplines in Seventeenth-Century New England* [Chapel Hill: University of North Carolina Press, 1982], 54). The metaphor of pilgrimage appears throughout Puritan sermons as N. H. Keeble posited (see "'To be a pilgrim': Constructing the Protestant Life in Early Modern England" in Colin Morris and Peter Roberts, eds., *Pilgrimage: The English Experience from Becket to Bunyan* [Cambridge: Cambridge University Press, 2002], 110). In the December 1858 preface to the fourth volume of *NPSP*, Charles wrote that even Roman Catholics were reading his sermons as they traveled on pilgrimage (see *NPSP* 4:v–vi).

6.   Edward Bouverie Pusey (1800–1882) was a prominent Anglican who gave leadership to the Oxford Movement, which was a resurgence of conservative Anglicanism at Oxford University sparked by John Keble's 1833 sermon "National Apostasy" (see R. W. Church, *The Oxford Movement: Twelve Years 1833–1845*, vol. 6 [London: MacMillan, 1897]). Pusey championed the doctrine of baptismal regeneration, as seen in his *Tract for the Times by Members of the University of Oxford*, no. 67: Scriptural Views of Holy Baptism, part I ([2nd ed.; London: J. G. F. & J. Rivington; Oxford: J. H. Parker, 1840], 4). Charles's opposition to this doctrine resulted in his highly controversial sermon in 1864, "Baptismal Regeneration" (*MTP* 10, Sermon 573). For a recent work on Pusey, see Rowan Strong and Carol Engelhardt Herringer, eds., *Edward Bouverie Pusey and the Oxford Movement* (Anthem Nineteenth-Century Series; London: Anthem Press, 2012). On one occasion Charles remembered hearing "Mr. Jay, of Bath" preach sermons against Puseyism, saying, "You do need a Mediator between yourselves and God, but you do not need a Mediator between yourselves and Christ" (*Autobiography* 1:208). He also said, "Puseyism is a lie" (*MTP* 26:386–87).

7.   Abbr., "Baptism." See also "An Exhortation to Bravery" (Sermon 72).

8.   Abbr., "Confirmation."

9.   Charles originally spelled this word "decensy." The letter "c" was written in pencil above the "s" to correct this misspelling.

10. The final letters of the word "procrastination" trail into the margin.

11. "Presumption says, 'I am a child of God, and I may live as like. I know I am saved, I need not therefore seek to have present communion with Christ'" (*NPSP* 4:252).

12. "Once infidelity was philosophical and thoughtful, and great names were to be found upon her roll; but now her noisiest advocates are bullies after the manner of Tom Paine, men who seem to delight in wounding the feelings of the godly and crushing every sacred thing under their feet. These are the true followers of the men whose mouths were full of 'Crucify him! Crucify him!'" (*MTP* 28:135).

13. Charles did not elaborate on what the "multitudes of other mountains" might have been. However, additional uses of this metaphor are found in "Oh That Thou Wouldest, Etc." (Notebook 3, Sermon 171); "Light at Eventide" (Notebook 3, Sermon 176); and "Christian Citizenship" (Notebook 7, Sermon 384).

14. Abbr., "salvation."

15. This is the only time Charles used the word "trustively" in his early notebooks. Samuel Johnson did not offer a definition of the adverbial modification of the word "trust." The context suggests Joseph Worcester's 1859 definition of the word "trustingly" may be used: "In a trustful manner; with trust or confidence" (Worcester's *Dictionary*). To confirm the first letter of this word, note the characteristics of the letter "t" in the word "Trusting" in the sermon "A Contrast" (Sermon 4).

16. The date of August 10 was also written in the previous sermon, "Faith Precious" (Sermon 23). Since both sermons were delivered at Barton on the thirty-fourth and thirty-fifth times Charles preached, the previous sermon was likely preached in the morning service and this one in the evening.

Deut 14. 2 — The Peculiar People

25

The Israelites a type of God's own spiritual people.

1. They were made peculiar by God's dealings to them.
Chosen from among men — loved with a peculiar love — as his
delivering them from Egypt — His patience with them & his
oft repeated pardons testify — as do also his peculiar discoveries
of himself to them — his teachings & chastisements of them —
the gift of Canaan and help at Jordan —

2. They were peculiar in their habits.
Sojourn in tents — feast of Passover — peculiar garments,
— food even manna — nothing unclean — their conflicts —
their conquests — their pursuits — the country they might.

3. Peculiar in their actions.
worship — priests — temple — sacrifice — prayer — God —
conduct — obedience to law — Study of Scripture

A Christian should be as well known & as
peculiar as the ancient Israelite or Jew.

Milton. Aug. 17/51.   36.

25

The PECULIAR PEOPLE
Deuteronomy 14:2[1]

"For thou art an holy people unto the LORD thy God, and the LORD hath chosen thee to be a peculiar people unto himself, above all the nations that are upon the earth."

The Israelites: a type[2] of God's own spiritual people.[3]

1. THEY WERE MADE PECULIAR BY GOD'S DEALINGS TO THEM.
    Chosen from among men.[4] Loved with a peculiar love.[5] As his delivering them from Egypt.[6] His patience with them[7] and his oft-repeated pardons testify, as do also his peculiar discoveries[8] of himself to them. His teachings and chastisements of them.[9] The gift of Canaan[10] and help at Jordan.[11]

2. THEY WERE PECULIAR IN THEIR HABITS.
    Sojourn in tents.[12] Feast of Passover.[13] Peculiar garments.[14] Food, even manna.[15] Nothing unclean.[16] Their conflicts, their conquests,[17] their pursuits, the country[18] they sought.

3. PECULIAR IN THEIR ACTIONS.
    Worship,[19] priests,[20] temple,[21] sacrifice,[22] prayer,[23] God,[24] conduct,[25] obedience to law,[26] study of Scripture.[27]

A Christian should be as well known and as peculiar as the ancient Israelite or Jew.

Milton.   Aug. 17/[18]51.   36.

1. This is the only time Charles preached a sermon on Deut 14:2. On April 6, 1884, Charles preached a sermon on Ps 4:3 entitled "A Peculiar People" (*MTP* 43, Sermon 2530); however, this sermon shares no overlapping content or structural similarity with the outline above.

2. Samuel Johnson defined the word "type" as an "emblem; mark of something" and "that by which something future is prefigured" (Johnson's *Dictionary*). Typology played a significant role in Charles's hermeneutic. For instance, in his sermon "The Day of Atonement" (*NPSP* 2, Sermon 95), Charles interpreted the sacrificial goat in Lev 16:5 as a type of Jesus Christ whose blood was shed as a sin offering for the people. In "The Love of Jonathan and the Love of Jesus" (*MTP* 39, Sermon 2336), Jonathan's love for David was a type of love that Christ possessed for his people. Abel, too, "was a type of the Saviour in that, being a shepherd, *he sanctified his work to the glory of God, and he offered sacrifice of blood upon the altar of the Lord*" (*MTP* 11:542, italics in the original). In a lecture entitled "On Spiritualizing," Charles said to his students at the Pastors' College, "The largest capacity for typical interpretation will find abundant employment in the undoubted symbols of the Word of God, and it will be safe to enter upon such an exercise, because the symbols are of divine appointment" (*Lectures* 1:109). Sidney Greidanus critiqued Charles's typological hermeneutic, saying that his "single-minded concern to preach Jesus Christ often leads him to reading Christ back into the Old Testament text. He generally uses the life of Jesus as a grid for interpreting the Old Testament. In other words, he frequently fails to do justice to the literal sense and the historical context of the Old Testament passages" (Sidney Greidanus, *Preaching Christ from the Old Testament: A Contemporary Hermeneutical Method* [Grand Rapids, MI: Eerdmans, 1999], 160).

3. An alternative reading of this line is "The Israelites [were] a type of God's own spiritual people."

4. Cf. Exod 6:7; Deut 7:7.   5. Cf. Jer 31:3.

6. Cf. Exod 6:6. Charles may have intended these two sentences to be more closely connected. The line could read, "Loved with a peculiar love as [seen in] his delivering them from Egypt."

7. Cf. Num 14:18.

8.   The final letters of the word "discoveries" trail into the margin.

9.   Cf. Prov 3:12; Heb 12:6.   10.   Cf. Gen 17:8.

11. Cf. Joshua 3; 4:23.   12.   Cf. Num 1:22; Heb 11:9.

13. Cf. Exod 12:1–29.   14.   Cf. Lev 21:10.

15. Cf. Exodus 16.   16.   Cf. Leviticus 12–13.

17. Cf. Num 21:1–3; Joshua 6; 8:1–24.

18. The ink beneath the descender line of the letter "y" was smeared toward the bottom of the page.

19. Cf. Deuteronomy 12.   20.   Cf. Leviticus 8–10.

21. Cf. 1 Kgs 6; 1 Chron 29:1–20.   22.   Cf. Leviticus 7.

23. Cf. Dan 6:10.   24.   Cf. Exod 20:3.

25. Cf. Deut 7:6.   26.   Cf. Exod 19:5; Deut 11:1; Ps 119:44.

27. Cf. Ezra 7:10.

26

Prov. 29.1.   Despisers Warned.

Solomon - the wise - the inspired man. —

1. How we are reproved.

By parents, friends, teachers - ministers

By the Bible, by conscience, by God's judgments

By affliction in their persons & sudden death of others

2. Of what we are reproved.

Of sin in general - lying, sabbath breaking, disobedience

thoughtlessness - unbelief - love of the world, hardness of heart

procrastination.

3. How we harden our necks.

By inattention to warnings - light thoughts of sin -

Sloth in amendment - obstinacy in going on in sin.

pride or rejection of appeals - Stifling conscience

4. How they shall be destroyed -

1 By some punishment - suddenly "the wicked are taken

2. By death which is always sudden to an unbeliever

cannot be put off "without remedy"

3. By hell - which will come unlooked for - dreadfully

no remedy for Jesus is the only Saviour -

Turn or die - Repent or Perish -

Cherry Hinton. Aug 24/41.

26

DESPISERS WARNED
Proverbs 29:1[1]

*"He, that being often reproved hardeneth his neck,
shall suddenly be destroyed, and that without remedy."*

Solomon, the wise,[2] the inspired man.[3]

1. HOW WE ARE REPROVED:
   By parents, friends, teachers,[4] ministers. By the Bible,[5] by conscience,[6] by God's judgments. By affliction[7] in their[8] persons, and sudden death of others.[9]

2. OF WHAT WE ARE REPROVED:
   Of sin in general: lying,[10] sabbath breaking,[11] disobedience, thoughtlessness, unbelief, love of the world,[12] hardness of [13] heart, procrastination.

3. HOW WE HARDEN OUR NECKS:
   By inattention to warnings, light thoughts of sin,[14] sloth in amendment, obstinacy in going on in sin, pride or rejection of appeals, shifting conscience.

4. HOW THEY SHALL BE DESTROYED:
   1.[15] By some punishment. "Suddenly" the wicked are taken.[16]
   2. By death, which is always sudden to an unbeliever. Cannot be put off "without remedy."
   3. By hell,[17] which will come unwished[18] for, dreadfully. No remedy. For Jesus is the only Saviour.[19] Turn or die. Repent or Perish.

~~Cherryhinton. Aug. 24/51.~~[20]

1. This is the only time Charles preached a sermon on Prov 29:1.

2. Cf. 1 Kings 3.

3. A line was written above and to the right of the period. The significance of this line is not evident, except to divide the opening line from the rest of the outline. An alternative reading of this line is "Solomon—the wise [and] inspired man."

4. Charles was often reproved by his parents and teachers. On one occasion Charles went into debt for a pencil. He reflected, "How my father came to hear of this little stroke of business, I never knew, but some little bird or other whistled it to him, and he was very soon down upon me in right earnest. God bless him for it; he was a sensible man, and none of your children-spoilers; he did not intend to bring up his children to speculate, and play at what big rogues call financing, and therefore he knocked my getting into debt on the head at once, and no mistake. He gave me a very powerful lecture upon getting into debt, and how like it was to stealing, and upon the way in which people were ruined by it; and how a boy who would owe a farthing, might one day owe a hundred pounds, and get into prison, and bring his family into disgrace. It was a lecture, indeed; I think I can hear it now, and can feel my ears tingling at the recollection of it. Then I was marched off to the shop, like a deserter marched into barracks, crying bitterly all down the street" (*Autobiography* 1:40; see also 1:51 and *Lectures* 1:189).

5. Cf. 2 Tim 3:16–17.

6. In a letter to his father on May 15, 1851, Charles wrote, "Were it not for my vile heart, I might rejoice. I am the least of God's people. I am sure I am the worst" (Angus Library and Archive, Regent's Park College, Oxford University, D/SPU 1, Letter 9). Cf. John 16:8.

7. Cf. 2 Cor 12:7.

8. Charles originally wrote the word "others." He struck through the letter "o" and changed the "s" to "r" to construct the word "their." The reason for this change is not evident; however, given that Charles wrote the word "others" at the end of the sentence, his changes were likely made to avoid repetition.

9. An alternative reading of this line is "By affliction in other persons and [in their] sudden death[s]."

10. Cf. Lev 19:11.

11. Cf. Exod 31:14.

12. Cf. 1 John 2:15.

13. The word "of" can be found between the words "hardness" and "heart."

14. "Light thoughts of sin breed light thoughts of the Saviour. . . . Repentance and faith are like Siamese twins. If one is sick, the other cannot be well, for they live but one life. If you are ever asked which comes first, repentance or faith, you may answer, by another question, 'Which spoke of a wheel moves first when the wheel begins to revolve?' You know that they are all set in motion at the same time" (*MTP* 53:352; see also "Making Light of Christ" [Sermon 21]). Charles also said, "That false peace which results from light thoughts of sin is the work of Satan; get rid of it at once if he has wrought it in you. Do not be afraid to look at your sins, do not shut your eyes to them; for you to hide your face from them may be your ruin, but for God to hide his face from them will be your salvation" (*MTP* 57:567; see also *NPSP* 1:166–67).

15. Given the location and size of the number 1, it was likely added after Charles had written the sentence following it. For an additional example, see "God's Sovereignty" (Sermon 18) in which Charles did not insert the number 1 under the Roman numeral II. See also the placement of the word "Repentance" in his sermon "Beginning at Jerusalem" (Sermon 29).

16. Cf. Prov 6:14–15.

17. Cf. Rev 21:8.

18. The letters "un" are flattened but detectable in the word "unwished."

19. Cf. Acts 4:12.

20. It is unclear why Charles struck through "Cherryhinton. Aug. 24/51." This redaction was not the result of a duplicated date. It is possible that Charles planned to preach this sermon in Cherry Hinton on August 24 but for reasons unknown did not succeed.

Philippians. 3. 9. Paul's renunciation.

<u>I.</u> What Paul gave up.

1. His ceremonial righteousness. His circumcision, washings, his descent from Abram.

2. His Pharisaic righteousness. Education, forms, ceremonies, exactness, obedience to the law - morality.

3. His sincere obedience. Paul a most sincere man.

4. His zealous supererogation - if the term may be allowed. Stephen - persecution.

5. His sanctification - prayers, repentance, zeal, his sufferings, trials, perseverance, courage, visions.

<u>II.</u> When we see what he renounced we cannot see but that - he took up —

1. A Superior Righteousness to his own.

2. A Sufficient Righteousness.

3. A Perfect Righteousness.

4. A Divine Righteousness. & it must have been.

5. The Righteousness of Jesus imputed. He could mean no other. Answer to objections. 1 Imputation not absurd.

<u>III.</u> If Paul did so how much more we.

Dunmow. Aug. 31/51.   38.

PAUL'S RENUNCIATION[1]
Philippians[2] 3:9[3]

"And be found in him, not having mine own righteousness, which is of the law, but that which is through the faith of Christ, the righteousness which is of God by faith."

I. WHAT PAUL GAVE UP:[4]

1. His ceremonial righteousness. His circumcision,[5] washings, his descent from Abram.[6]

2. His Pharisaic[7] righteousness.[8] Education, forms, ceremonies, exactness, obedience to the law, morality.

3. His sincere obedience. Paul, a most sincere man.[9]

4. His zealous supererogation,[10] if the term may be allowed. Stephen.[11] Persecution.[12]

5. His sanctification. Prayers, repentance, zeal, his sufferings, trials, perseverance, courage, visions.

II. WHEN WE SEE WHAT HE RENOUNCED, WE CANNOT SEE BUT THAT HE TOOK UP:

1. A Superior Righteousness to his own.

2. A Sufficient Righteousness.[13]

3. A Perfect Righteousness.

4. A Divine Righteousness, and it must have been.[14]

5. The Righteousness of Jesus imputed.[15] He could mean no other. Answer to objections.

1. Imputation not absurd.[16]

2. ~~2.~~

III. IF PAUL DID SO, HOW MUCH MORE WE?[17]

Dunmow.   Aug. 31/[18]51   38.

1. In the sermon above, Charles borrowed from John Gill's *A Body of Divinity* (2:794–820) and Gill's exposition of Phil 3:9 in John Gill, *An Exposition of the New Testament, in Three Volumes, in Which the Sense of the Sacred Text Is Given; Doctrinal and Practical Truths Are Set in a Plain and Easy Light, Difficult Places Explained, Seeming Contradictions Reconciled; and Whatever Is Material in the Various Readings, and the Several Oriental Versions, Is Observed. The Whole Illustrated with Notes Taken from the Most Ancient Jewish Writings* ([3 vols.; London: printed for the author, and sold by Aaron Ward, 1746, The Spurgeon Library] 3:140–41).

2. Charles spelled this word "Phillippians"; however, the second letter "l" was struck through in pencil to construct the correct spelling.

3. This is the only time Charles preached on Phil 3:9 specifically. However, on June 3, 1877, he preached a sermon on Phil 3:7–9 entitled "A Business-Like Account" (*MTP* 23, Sermon 1357). Structural similarities and overlapping content exist in the first and third Roman numerals in the above outline and the first and second Roman numerals in the later sermon (Cf. *MTP* 23:314, 322). Charles likely had the above outline in mind during the writing of the 1877 sermon.

4. "Let us enter the prison and put a personal question to the good man. Paul, your faith has brought you to absolute penury and friendlessness: what is your estimate of it now? Theory is one thing, but does practice bear it out? . . . 'Well,' saith he, 'I confess I have suffered the loss of all things.' And do you deeply regret it, Paul? 'Regret it,' saith he, 'regret the loss of my Phariseeism, my circumcision, my Israel-itish dignity? Regret it! No,' he says, 'I am glad that all these are gone, for I count it to be a deliverance to be rid of them'" (*MTP* 23:320).

5. Charles originally spelled this word "circucision." The letter "m" was added between the "u" and "c," and its location was indicated by a caret.

6. Cf. Phil 3:5.

7. Charles originally spelled this word "Pharasaic." The letter "i" was written in pencil over the "a" to construct the correct spelling of the word.

8. "He was a Jesuit among the Catholics, one who went to the extreme among extremists, one of those initiated into the innermost secrets of the faith. . . . [H]e himself was as to every detail of the law, every little point of ritual, and every particular rubric, altogether blameless" (*MTP* 23:315).

9. An alternative reading of this line is "Paul [was] a most sincere man."

10. "Performance of more than duty requires" (Johnson's *Dictionary*, s.v. "supererogation"). For additional instances in which Charles used the word "supererogation," see *MTP* 8:557 and 11:140.

11. Cf. Acts 22:20.   12. Cf. 1 Cor 15:9.

13. See "Self-Sufficiency Slain" (*NPSP* 6, Sermon 345) and "All-Sufficiency Magnified" (*NPSP* 6, Sermon 346).

14. An alternative reading of this line is "A divine righteousness—and it must have been [divine]."

15. Cf. 2 Cor 5:21.

16. An alternative reading of this line is "Imputation [is] not absurd."

17. An alternative reading of this line is "If Paul did so, how much more [should] we?"

28

John. 14.2   Heaven's preparations.

I. What are provided : "Mansions"

The word Mansions conveys the idea of

1. plenty, wealth, riches, abundance,

2. Rest, ease, retirement.

3. Rank, Splendour, Honour.

4. Convenience, content, satisfaction, happiness.

5. The word also means "enduring, remaining."

We may notice that these are golden, silken, royal,
       heavenly. everlasting mansions . —

II. How many are prepared – "many"

As many as the elect, beloved, redeemed, believing,
sanctified people of God – and they shall all arrive
there for thy "are" "not" shall be prepared already

III. Where? "in my Father's house." On Zion Hill
apartments in one house
1. Communion & fellowship with him & with one another
2. Divine providence, love &c in ... ... Heaven. fine situation this

IV. Who prepares them? "Jesus."

He bought them by his death & now he prepares
them — and therefore nothing will be wanting.
     For you – for all his people – —

Dunmow. Aug 31/51 .   40. 128. 151. 346. 409.

28

HEAVEN'S PREPARATIONS
John 14:2[1]

"In my Father's house are many mansions: if it were not so,
I would have told you. I go to prepare a place for you."

I. WHAT ARE PROVIDED. *"Mansions."*

The word Mansions conveys the idea of:

1. Plenty, wealth, riches, abundance.

2. Rest, ease, retirement.

3. Rank, Splendour, Honour.

4. Convenience, content, satisfaction, happiness.

5. The word also means "enduring, remaining."[2]

We may notice that these are golden, silken, royal, heavenly, everlasting mansions.

II. HOW MANY ARE PREPARED. *"Many."*

As many as the elect, beloved, redeemed, believing, sanctified people of God.[3]
And they shall all arrive there, for they[4] "are"—not "shall be"—prepared already.

III. WHERE? *"In my Father's house."* <u>On Zion</u> Hill.[5]

Apartments in one house.[6]

1. Communion and fellowship with him and with one another.[7]

2. Divine providence, love, etc. In one house.[8] Heaven. Fine situation this.

IV. WHO PREPARES THEM? *"Jesus."*[9]

He bought them by his death,[10] and now he prepares them.[11]
And therefore, nothing will be wanting.[12] For <u>you</u>, for all his people.

Du[n]mow.[13]   Aug 31/[18]51   40.[14] 128. 151. 346. 409.

1. On May 25, 1879, Charles preached a sermon on two Scripture references, including John 14:2 entitled "A Prepared Place for a Prepared People" (*MTP* 47, Sermon 2751). On September 23, 1883, Charles preached a sermon on John 14:1–2 entitled "Let Not Your Heart Be Troubled" (*MTP* 29, Sermon 1741). The lack of structural similarities suggests Charles did not have the above outline in mind when writing these later sermons. A similar title is found in Charles's sermon on 2 Cor 5:5, "Preparation for Heaven" (*MTP* 62, Sermon 3538).

2. Charles did not supply the source for his quotation of "enduring, remaining." It is unlikely that the quote was original to Samuel Johnson, who defined the word "mansion" as "a dwelling-house; a house of residence; a dwelling; a seat; particularly a house of some magnitude" (Johnson's *Dictionary*). Johnson's definition fails to capture the permanence of the word as Charles used it. Charles was likely quoting not a dictionary but a commentary. As in the previous sermon, "Paul's Renunciation" (Sermon 27), it appears Charles relied on John Gill, and in this case, his exposition of John 14:2: "*mansions* of love, peace, joy, and rest, which always remain" (Gill, *An Exposition of the New Testament*, 2:53, italics in the original). Additional traces of Gill's influence in this sermon are noted.

3. "[I]t denotes fulness and sufficiency of room for all [Christ's] people; for the many ordained to eternal life, for whom Christ gave his life a ransom, and whose blood is shed for the remission of their sins, whose sins he bore, and whom he justifies by his knowledge; who receive him by faith, and are the many sons he'll bring to glory" (Gill, *An Exposition of the New Testament*, 2:53). Cf. 1 Pet 2:9–12.

4. The size and location of the word "they" suggest Charles wrote it afterward. The script resembles the words "On Zion Hill" and "Apartments in one house" one and two lines below.

5. Cf. Rev 14:1.

6. The size and spacing of the words "apartments in one house" suggest Charles may have written the phrase afterward. He may have gleaned this information from Gill, who mentioned the multiplicity of mansions within one residence: "[Christ's] Father had a house, and in it were many mansions" (Gill, *An Exposition of the New Testament*, 2:53).

7. Cf. "Can Two Walk Together Unless They Are Agreed?" (Sermon 76).

8. The size and location of the phrase "in one house" suggest Charles may have written it afterward. The writing of this phrase resembles the words "apartments in one house" two lines above.

9. "By being in heaven our Lord occupies a vantage-ground for the sure accomplishing of his purposes of love. As Joseph went down into Egypt to store the granaries, to prepare for Israel a home in Goshen, and to sit upon the throne for their protection, so hath our Lord gone away into the glory for our good, and he is doing for us upon his throne what could not so advantageously have been done for us here" (*MTP* 29:525).

10. Cf. 1 Cor 6:20.

11. An alternative reading of this line is "He bought them by his death, and now he prepares [a place for] them." The em dash after the word "them" was smudged toward the right side of the page and was likely the source of the discoloration surrounding the word "Divine" three lines above. In 1879, Charles said, "[Jesus] used to stand still here on earth, and work miracles; but this was a miracle that he could not perform while he was here. He had to go back to his home above in order to prepare a place for his people. What sort of place, then, must it be that needs Christ himself to prepare it?" (*MTP* 47:519).

12. Cf. Phil 4:19.

13. Charles spelled this word "Dumow." A diagonal pencil stroke was written over the letter "m," likely to signal the need of the letter "n" to construct the correct spelling of the village name, "Dunmow."

14. A dot was written above the 0 but appears to have no significance to the number 40.

Luke. 24. 47. Beginning at Jerusalem. 29.

I. The Gospel. "Repentance & Remission of sins."

1. Repentance. Unfeigned sorrow for sin, abhorrence of self.
— Forsaking of all sin in future. --

2. Remission. Full, Free, Entire, Perpetual Forgiveness.
the one procures not the other - yet is a necessary accompaniment.

II. The characters to whom "all nations, beginning at Jerusalem",
The Jew and Gentile, bond & free, rich & poor. --
Jerusalem the very sink of sin, murder, hypocrisy,
death of Jesus, against light, love & privilege.
' The vilest sinner repenting can be saved.
1. Because they had most need.
2. Their Conversion would bring glory to Jesus.
3. It is to encourage others.
4. And that men may have no excuse.

III. Use -- Exhortation to the vilest to come.
———————— to little sinners to come.

Comfort to the desponding.
Warning to Presuming souls. --
A Solemn address to all men in Christ's name.

Balsham. Sept. 6/57.   42. 232.

29

BEGINNING *at* JERUSALEM[1]
Luke 24:47[2]

"And that repentance and remission of sins should be preached
in his name among all nations, beginning at Jerusalem."

I. THE GOSPEL. *"Repentance and Remission of sins."*

1. Repentance:[3] Unfeigned sorrow for sin,[4] abhorrence of self.
Forsaking of all sin in future.

2. Remission:[5] Full,[6] Free, Entire, Perpetual[7] Forgiveness.[8] The one procures
not the other yet is a necessary accompaniment.[9]

II. THE CHARACTERS TO WHOM.[10] *"all nations, beginning at Jerusalem."*

The Jew and Gentile,[11] bond and free, rich and poor.[12] Jerusalem,[13] the very sink
of sin,[14] murder,[15] hypocrisy, death of Jesus,[16] against light,[17] love, and privilege.

The Vilest sinner repenting can be saved.[18]

1. Because they had most need.[19]
2. Their Conversion would bring glory to Jesus.[20]
3. It is to encourage others.[21]
4. And that men may have no excuse.[22]

III. USE.

Exhortation to the vilest to come.[23]

[Exhortation][24] to little sinners to come.[25]

Comfort to the desponding.[26]

Warning to Presuming[27] souls.

A solemn address to all men in Christ's name.

Balsham   Sept[r28] 6/[18]51   42. 232.[29]

1. This outline is original to the Puritan preacher and author John Bunyan (1628–1688). Charles first discovered Bunyan's works in his grandfather's attic in Stambourne (see *Autobiography* 1:23). He said, "Read anything of his, and you will see that it is almost like reading the Bible itself. . . . 'Why, the man is a living Bible! Prick him anywhere; and you will find that his blood is Bibline, the very essence of the Bible flows from him. He cannot speak without quoting a text, for his soul is full of the Word of God'" (*Autobiography* 4:268). Charles owned at least thirteen of Bunyan's books in his personal library and quoted him extensively throughout his sermons (see "The Comforter" [*NPSP* 1, Sermon 5]; "Christ Crucified" [*NPSP* 1, Sermons 7–8]; "Final Perseverance" [*NPSP* 2, Sermon 75]; "Christ's First and Last Subject" [*NPSP* 6, Sermon 329]; "Christ the End of the Law" [*MTP* 22, Sermon 1325]; and "Encouragement for the Depressed" [*MTP* 61, Sermon 3489]. In the outline above, Charles borrowed heavily from Bunyan's treatment of Luke 24:47 in *The Jerusalem Sinner Saved*. For Charles's copy, see *The Jerusalem Sinner Saved; or, Good News for the Vilest of Men: Being a Help for Despairing Souls, Showing That Jesus Christ Would Have Mercy in the First Place Offered to the Biggest Sinners. The Third Edition, in Which Is Added, an Answer to Those Grand Objections That Lie in the Way of Them That Would Believe: For the Comfort of Them That Fear They Have Sinned Against the Holy Ghost* [London: printed for Elizabeth Smith, at the Hand and Bible, on London Bridge, 1691] in George Offor, ed., *The Works of John Bunyan: With an Introduction to Each Treatise, Notes, and a Sketch of His Life, Times, and Contemporaries*, vol. 1 [3rd ed.; London: Blackie and Son, 1856, The Spurgeon Library], 67–103). For Charles's copy of Bunyan's autobiography, see John Bunyan, *Grace Abounding to the Chief of Sinners; or, A Brief and Faithful Relation of the Exceeding Mercy of God in Christ to His Poor Servant, John Bunyan; Wherein Is Particularly Showed the Manner of His Conversion, His Sight and Trouble for Sin, His Dreadful Temptations, Also How He Despaired of God's Mercy, and How the Lord at Length Through Christ Did Deliver Him from All the Guilt and Terror That Lay upon Him. Whereunto Is Added a Brief Relation of His Call to the Work of the Ministry, of His Temptations Therein, As Also What He Hath Met with in Prison. All Which Was Written by His Own Hand There, and Now Published for the Support of the Weak and Tempted People of God* ([London: printed by George Larkin, 1666], 1:1–49). For recent treatments of Bunyan, see John Stachniewsk and Anita Pacheco, eds., *John Bunyan, Grace Abounding with Other Spiritual Autobiographies* (Oxford: Oxford University Press, 2008) and Richard Greaves, *John Bunyan and English Nonconformity* (London: The Hambledon Press, 1992).

2. Charles preached three additional sermons on Luke 24:47: "Christ's First and Last Subject" (*NPSP* 6, Sermon 329); "Beginning at Jerusalem" (*MTP* 29, Sermon

1729); and "Repentance and Remission" (*MTP* 56, Sermon 3224). A section of "Beginning at Jerusalem" is an expansion of the outline above (Cf. *MTP* 29:373–75). In this sermon Charles said, "And, lastly, to come to the meaning which Mr. John Bunyan has put upon the text in his famous book called 'The Jerusalem Sinner Saved,' I have no doubt that the Saviour bade them begin at Jerusalem, *because the biggest sinners lived there*" (*MTP* 29:384, italics in the original). In "Repentance and Remission," Charles also borrowed from Bunyan, saying, "John Bunyan has a masterly treatise upon this text, entitled 'The Jerusalem sinner saved; or, good news for the vilest of men: being a help for despairing souls, showing that Jesus Christ would have mercy in the first place offered to the biggest sinners.' Those of you who have his works will find the whole treatise well worth reading; but I am going to borrow some of his divisions, and speak upon them after my own fashion" (*MTP* 56:560–61). Overlapping content and structural similarities are also found in "Christ's First and Last Subject" and suggest Charles likely had the above outline in mind when writing this later sermon.

3.   "Gospel repentance is a change of mind of the most radical sort—such a change as never was wrought in any man except by the Spirit of God" (*MTP* 29:374).

4.   "Wherever there is real sorrow for sin, wherever there is an honest determination, by God's grace, to cease from sin, wherever there is a complete change of mind with regard to sin,—for that is what repentance means,—that repentance has been produced by the Spirit, of God, and it is as much a gift of the covenant of grace as even the pardon which comes with it is" (*MTP* 56:555).

5.   "Let every man understand that he will never have remission of sin while he is in love with sin; and that if he abides in sin he cannot obtain the pardon of sin. There must be a hatred of sin, a loathing of it, and a turning from it, or it is not blotted out" (*MTP* 29:374).

6.   "But the pardon of God once given stands for ever. If he has cast our sin into the depths of the sea it will never be washed up again. If he has removed our transgressions from us as far as the east is from the west, how can they return to condemn us? Once washed in the blood of the Lamb we are clean. The deed is done: the one offering has put away for ever all the guilt of believers" (*MTP* 29:375).

7.   "We are to preach *repentance in its perpetuity*. Repentance is not a grace which is only to be exercised by us for a week or so at the beginning of our Christian career: it is

to attend us all the way to heaven. Faith and repentance are to be inseparable companions throughout our pilgrimage to glory" (*MTP* 29:374, italics in the original).

8. "This pardon makes a clean sweep of the accumulated heaps of defilement that have resulted from years of iniquity" (*MTP* 56:557).

9. The final letters in the word "accompaniment" trail into the margin.

10. Charles may have intended to convey "The characters to whom [the gospel was intended]."

11. Cf. Eph 3:6.   12.   Cf. Gal 3:28.

13. Charles reinforced the letters "u" and "s" in the word "Jerusalem." It is possible that he originally misspelled the word.

14. "Jerusalem was therefore now greatly backslidden, and become the place where the truth and true religion were much defaced. It was also now become the very sink of sin" (Bunyan, *The Jerusalem Sinner Saved*, 69).

15. "And it is to be observed, namely, that the first sermon which they preached after the ascension of Christ, it was preached to the very worst of these Jerusalem sinners, even to those that were the murderers of Jesus Christ" (ibid., 71).

16. Cf. Matt 27:32–56.

17. "Two sins are not so many as three; nor are three that are done in ignorance so big as one that is done against light, against knowledge and conscience" (Bunyan, *The Jerusalem Sinner Saved*, 94).

18. An alternative reading of this line is "The vilest sinner [who repents] can be saved."

19. "First, Because *the biggest sinners have most need thereof.* He that has most need, reason says, should be helped first" (Bunyan, *The Jerusalem Sinner Saved*, 73, italics in the original).

20. "*Second,* Christ Jesus would have mercy offered, in the first place, to the biggest sinners, because *when they, any of them, receive it, it redounds most to the fame of his name*" (ibid., 75, italics in the original).

21. "*Third*, Christ Jesus would have mercy offered, in the first place, to the biggest sinners, because, *by their forgiveness and salvation, others, hearing of it, will be encouraged the more to come to him for life*" (ibid., 76, italics in the original).

22. Charles departed from Bunyan's outline on this point: "*Eighth*, and lastly, Christ Jesus will have mercy to be offered, in the first place, to the biggest sinners, *for that by that means the impenitent that are left behind will be, at the judgment, the more left without excuse*" (ibid., 84, italics in the original).

23. In his later sermon on Luke 24:47, Charles extended a similar exhortation: "Will you not come to Christ at once? Oh that you would believe in him! Oh that you would believe in him to-night" (*MTP* 29:384).

24. This line served as a repetition device for the word "Exhortation." For similar instances in which Charles used a blank line for repetition, see "Future Judgment" (Sermon 6) and "The Lepers" (Sermon 77).

25. "Alas! Christ Jesus has but little thanks for the saving of little sinners" (Bunyan, *The Jerusalem Sinner Saved*, 82).

26. "There are four sorts of despair. There is the despair of devils; there is the despair of souls in hell; there is the despair that is grounded upon men's deficiency; and there is the despair that they are perplexed with that are willing to be saved, but are too strongly borne down with the burden of their sins" (ibid., 91).

27. "Presumption, then, is that which severeth faith and repentance; concluding that the soul shall be saved by grace, though the man was never made sorry for his sins, nor the love of the heart turned therefrom" (ibid., 93). For additional references to presumption, see "Making Light of Christ" (Sermon 21) and "The Fight and the Weapons" (Sermon 37a).

28. For an additional abbreviation of the word "September," see "Christian and His Salvation" (Sermon 17).

29. The ink of the period at the end of the number 42, and the ink of the number 232, were smeared toward the bottom of the page. The three dots beneath the numbers resemble the triangular cluster of dots representing the word "therefore" in the sermon "Future Judgment" (Sermon 6).

30

Proverbs 10 – 3. Salvation from Starvation

"Jonah &c"

1. As to things temporal. "Elijah"; woman fed by her enemy

2. As to things spiritual. Eunuch. ~~All~~ the glorified saints

ground for strong faith

1. God has said it. It should be a Proverb among us.

2. "He is able also to perform."

3. "He feeds the ravens" & all creatures.

4. He always has supplied his people.

5. "His love in time past" argues this

6. He is "our Father" & cannot let us die.

circumstances in which this promise
is peculiarly sweet and cheering

1. To those who are just beginning to hunger & thirst.

2. To the Poor in this world.

3. To those who cannot live on anything but Jesus

4. "When all created streams are dry"

44

4

SALVATION *from* STARVATION
Proverbs 10:3[1]

"The Lord *will not suffer the soul of the righteous to famish: but he casteth away the substance of the wicked."*

1. ## AS TO THINGS TEMPORAL:

"Elijah,"[2] "Woman fed by her enemy,"[3] "Jonathan," etc.[4]

2. ## AS TO THINGS SPIRITUAL:

Eunuch,[5] All[6] the glorified saints.[7]

Ground for strong faith.

1. God has said it. It should be a Proverb among us.
2. "He is able also to perform."[8]
3. "He feeds the ravens"[9] and all creatures.
4. He always has supplied his people.
5. "His love in time past"[10] argues this.
6. He is "our Father"[11] and cannot let us die.

Circumstances in which this promise is peculiarly sweet and cheering:

1. To those who are just beginning to hunger and thirst.
2. To the[12] Poor in this world.
3. To those who cannot live on anything but Jesus.
4. "When all created streams are dry."[13]

44[14]

1. This is the only time Charles preached a sermon on Prov 10:3. See also "Bread for the Hungry" (*MTP* 7, Sermon 418) and "The Hungry Filled, the Rich Emptied" (*MTP* 52, Sermon 3019).

2. First Kings 17:13, "And Elijah said unto her, Fear not; go and do as thou hast said: but make me thereof a little cake first, and bring it unto me, and after make for thee and thy son."

3. Revelation 12:6, "And the woman fled into the wilderness, where she hath a place prepared of God, that they should feed her there a thousand two hundred and threescore days."

4. First Samuel 14:29, "Then said Jonathan, My Father troubled the land: see, I pray you, how mine eyes have been enlightened, because I tasted a little of this honey."

5. Cf. Matt 19:10–12.

6. The letter "m" was written in bold over the "a." The reason for this inclusion is not evident; however, Charles may have originally intended to write the word "many" before changing it to "all." Given the size and location of the phrase "the glorified saints," it is possible that the line originally read, "As to things spiritual: Eunuch, all ground for strong faith."

7. Cf. 2 Thess 1:10.

8. Romans 4:21, "And being fully persuaded, that what he had promised, he was able also to perform."

9. Luke 12:24, "Consider the ravens: for they neither sow nor reap; which neither have storehouse nor barn; and God feedeth them: how much more are ye better than the fowls?" See also "The Raven's Cry" (*MTP* 12, Sermon 672).

10. This is a reference to Isa 12:2, "Behold, God is my salvation: I will trust, and not be afraid; for the Lord Jehovah is my strength and my song; he also is become my salvation." This line may have been inspired by John Newton (1725–1807): "His love in time past / Forbids me to think / He'll leave me at last / In trouble to sink" (*The Works of the Rev. John Newton, Late Rector of the United Parishes of St. Mary Woolnoth & St. Mary Woolchurch Haw* [6 vols.; 2nd ed.; London: printed for author's

nephew, sold by T. Hamilton; L. B. Seeley; and J. Hatchard, 1816, The Spurgeon Library], 3:609). For additional references to Newton's hymn, see *NPSP* 5:394 and *MTP* 12:117.

11.   Cf. Matt 6:9.

12.   A dark stain can be seen above the letter "e" in the word "the," and also above the letter "T" in the word "To" in the line above. These stains are likely the result of the aging process of the manuscript and are also found on the back of the page (see "Beginning at Jerusalem" [Sermon 29]).

13.   This is a reference to a hymn by John Ryland (1753–1825): "When all created streams are dried, / Thy fulness is the same; / May I with this be satisfied, / And glory in thy name!" (*Hymns and Verses on Sacred Subjects by the Late Rev. John Ryland, D.D., Of Bristol, The Greater Part of Which Are Now Published for the First Time from the Originals. With a Biographical Sketch* [London: Daniel Sedgwick; Hamilton, Adams, & Co., 1862], 29). For additional references to Ryland's hymns, see *NPSP* 2:103 and *MTP* 12:58.

14.   The smudged number 4 at the lower left corner of the page may have been Charles's second attempt at numbering this sermon (see also "Adoption" [Sermon 1]). The stroke after the number could be the number 1. If this is correct, then Charles may have intentionally smudged the number since he had already preached a sermon on the forty-first occasion of his ministry (see "Christian and His Salvation" [Sermon 17]).

Proverbs. 19 – 2 .   Ignorance its evils .

I. Ignorance of God.
  1. His being . Idolatry. Polytheism . Atheism . Deism .
  2. His attributes. 1. mercy. Ig of leads to despair despondency
              2 justice . leads to presumption .
Ig of his designs .   3. Spirituality – wrong modes of worship .
              4. Power . Doubt. groundless Fear .
              5. Unchangeableness . slavish fear .

II. Ignorance of Christ . the evils of ignorance of
his deity . his atonement, his death, his righteousness
his love to us . the way of salvation by himself . his intercession

III. Ignorance of the Spirit.
  necessity of his instruction . support , comfort &c .

IV. Ignorance of ourselves.
  leads to pride , self trusting , Phariseeism .
  rings us into sin , confusion , pain .
  Ig of self destroys the souls of men by blinding their
  eyes to their own depravity .

  The necessity of a study of the Scriptures .
earnest prayer and the teaching of the Spirit.

50

IGNORANCE, ITS EVILS
Proverbs 19:2[1]

"Also, that the soul be without knowledge, it is not good;
and he that hasteth with his feet sinneth."

I. IGNORANCE OF GOD.
1. His being: Idolatry. Polytheism. Atheism. Deism.
2. His attributes:

    Ig[norance] of his designs.
    1. Mercy.[2] Ig.[3] of leads to despair, despondency.[4]
    2. Justice.[5] Leads to presumption.
    3. Spirituality.[6] Wrong modes of worship.
    4. Power.[7] Doubt, groundless Fear.
    5. Unchangeableness.[8] Slavish fear.

II. IGNORANCE OF CHRIST.
The evils of ignorance of his deity,[9] his atonement,[10] his death,[11] his righteousness, his love to us,[12] the way of salvation by himself,[13] his intercession.[14]

III. IGNORANCE OF THE SPIRIT.
Necessity of his instruction,[15] support,[16] comfort,[17] etc.

IV. IGNORANCE OF OURSELVES.
sinners and saints[18]
Leads to pride,[19] self-trusting,[20] Phariseeism.[21] Brings us into sin, confusion, pain. Ig[norance] of self destroys the souls of men by blinding their eyes to their own depravity.
The necessity of a study of the Scriptures,[22] earnest prayer,[23] and the teaching of the Spirit.[24]

50

1. This is the only time Charles preached a sermon on Prov 19:2. See also "Sins of Ignorance" (*MTP* 23, Sermon 1386); *NPSP* 2:335; and 3:225.

2. Cf. Eph 2:4.

3. Charles abbreviated the word "Ignorance" throughout this outline. For consistency and clarity, the missing letters of this word have been inserted within brackets throughout the remainder of this sermon.

4. An alternative reading of this line is "Ignorance of mercy leads to despair, despondency."

5. Cf. Isa 61:8.

6. Cf. John 16:13.

7. Cf. 1 Cor 6:14.

8. Cf. Mal 3:6.

9. Cf. Col 2:9; 1 John 5:20.

10. Cf. 1 John 2:2.

11. Cf. Matt 27:32–56.

12. Cf. Rom 5:8; Eph 2:4–5.

13. Cf. Acts 4:12.

14. Cf. Rom 8:34; Heb 7:25.

15. Cf. John 14:26.

16. Cf. Rom 8:26.

17. Cf. John 14:26.

18. The words "sinners and saints" were written vertically in the left margin beside Roman numeral IV. The handwriting in these three words differs from that found throughout the outline. For additional examples of this script, see the following two sermons: "The Wrong Roads" (Sermon 32) and "Salvation from Sin" (Sermon 33).

19. Cf. Prov 11:2; Gal 6:3; Jas 4:6.

20. In a letter to his mother dated June 11, 1850, Charles wrote, "I trust the Lord is weaning me daily from all self-dependence and teaching me to look at myself as less than nothing" (Angus Library and Archive, Regent's Park College, Oxford University, D/SPU 1, Letter 4; see also *Autobiography* 1:125). Cf. Prov 3:5–6; 16:9; 28:26.

21. Cf. Matt 23.

22. Cf. Josh 1:8; Ps 119:11; 2 Tim 3:14–17.

23. Cf. 2 Chron 7:14; 1 Thess 5:17.

24. "You must, first of all, be taught by *the Holy Spirit*. He is willing and able to come into your mind, and to influence it in a very extraordinary but very effectual way. He can teach your reason, reason; and cause your understanding to understand aright" (*MTP* 39:355, italics in the original). See also "The Holy Ghost—the Great Teacher" (*NPSP* 1, Sermon 50). Cf. John 16:23.

32

Prov. 14 - 12.   The Wrong Roads.

Man chooses that which seems good but he is often mistaken. the way seems to lead to happiness, peace and heaven but it leads to hell. seems right but leads to death. spiritual & eternal.

1 Way of vice is called the way of pleasure, the way of sin is called harmless mirth. many young ones are lost herein.

2. Way of business & covetousness is called the way of prudence love of the world is called "business". carnality – forethought. conformity – politeness. Laxity – Gentility

3. Way of Profession – Hypocrites deceive themselves Formalists shall perish. nothing but vital Christianity will do.

4. Way of Ostentation. pride in duties, love of men's praise, unholy motives.

5. Way of Justification by works. looks fair but is false – "by the works of the law" &c

How is it men are deceived.   6. The way by (faith without works) may be mentioned here.

1. By their natural depravity, 2. evil habits, 3. custom of this world. 4. Ignorance of Scripture. 5. The Devil.

Means for choosing the right way –
trial by Scripture, prayer, self examination watchfulness. distrust of self. desire to be right 45. 47. 67. 262. faith in Jesus guidance.

The WRONG ROADS
Proverbs 14:12[1]

"There is a way which seemeth right unto a man; but the end thereof are the ways of death."

MAN CHOOSES THAT WHICH SEEMS GOOD, BUT HE IS OFTEN MISTAKEN.

The way seems to lead to happiness, peace and heaven, but it leads to hell. Seems right, but leads to death. Spiritual and eternal.[2]

1.[3] Way of vice is called the way of pleasure. The way of sin is called harmless mirth.[4] Many young ones are lost herein.
2. Way of business and covetousness[5] is called the way of prudence. Love of the world is called "business." Carnality. Forethought. Conformity.[6] Politeness.[7] Laxity. Gentility.
3. Way of Profession. Hypocrites[8] deceive themselves. Formalists[9] shall perish. Nothing but vital Christianity[10] will do.
4. Way of Ostentation. Pride in duties, love of men's praise, unholy motives.
5. Way of Justification by works.[11] Looks fair but is false. "By the works of the law,"[12] etc.
6.[13] The way by (faith without works) may be mentioned here.[14]

HOW IS IT MEN ARE DECEIVED:

1. By their natural depravity.[15] 2. Evil habits. 3. Custom of this world.
4. Ignorance of Scripture.[16] 5. The Devil.[17]

Means for choosing the right way: trial by Scripture, prayer, self examination, watchfulness,[18] distrust of self, desire to be right,[19] faith in Jesus['s] guidance.

45. 47. 67. 262.

1. This is the only time Charles preached a sermon on Prov 14:12.

2. An alternative reading of these sentences is "[It] seems right, but leads to spiritual and eternal death."

3. It is unclear why Charles inserted quotation marks before the number 1.

4. "Harmless Mirth" was the name by which Lord Lasciviousness identified himself in John Bunyan's *The Holy War* (John Bunyan, *The Holy War, Made by Shaddai upon Diabolus, for the Regaining of the Metropolis of the World; or, The Losing and Taking Again of the Town of Mansoul* [London: Dorman Newman and Benjamin Alsop, 1682] in George Offor, ed., *The Works of John Bunyan: With a Sketch of His Life, Times, and Contemporaries*, vol. 3 [London: Blackie and Son, 1856, The Spurgeon Library], 3:333). For additional references to "Harmless Mirth," see *MTP* 12:65 and 36:100.

5. "Oh! how tight those fingers are when they are once closed! How pleased they are when money accumulates!" (*MTP* 15:640)

6. Cf. Rom 12:2.   7.   Cf. *MTP* 62:507.

8. The letter "q" was written beneath the "t" and "e" in the word "hypocrites."

9. For additional uses of the word "Formalist," see *NPSP* 1:379; *MTP* 15:713–14; 36:6. See also Helmut Thielicke's reference to Charles's opposition to formalism in Helmut Thielicke, *Encounter with Spurgeon* ([trans. John W. Doberstein; Stuttgart, Germany: Quell-Verlag, 196], 39).

10. This is the only time in his early notebooks that Charles used the phrase "vital Christianity." The phrase is often associated with the revivals of George Whitefield and Jonathan Edwards in the eighteenth century. With reference to Edwards, J. I. Packer wrote that "true and vital Christianity is a religion of the heart as well as of the head" (J. I. Packer, *A Quest for Godliness: The Puritan Vision of the Church Life* [Wheaton, IL: Crossway, 1990], 312). A definition of "vital Christianity" is found in Charles's personal copy of Alexander Vinet's *Vital Christianity* (see Alexander Vinet, *Vital Christianity: Essays and Discourses on the Religions of Man and the Religion of God* [trans. Robert Turnbull; Glasgow; Paternoster Row, n.d., The Spurgeon Library], 38). In this work the Swiss theologian wrote that vital Christianity is "a religion of sentiment. Without doubt this sentiment is love, and a love which has God for its object." Charles often used the phrase

"vital godliness" synonymously with vital Christianity. He described vital godliness as "not a religious Sunday, it is a religious Monday; it is not a pious church, it is a pious closet; it is not a sacred place to kneel, it is a holy place to stand in all day long" (*NPSP* 1:108; see also 6:122; *MTP* 7:413; 16:223; 49:457; and *ST* December 1866:532).

11. "I become more and more convinced that, to attempt to be saved by a mixed covenant of works and faith is, in the words of Berridge, 'To yoke a snail with an elephant'" (*Autobiography* 1:192; see also "Salvation from Sin" [Sermon 33]).

12. Galatians 2:16, "Knowing that a man is not justified by the works of the law, but by the faith of Jesus Christ, even we have believed in Jesus Christ, that we might be justified by the faith of Christ, and not by the works of the law: for by the works of the law shall no flesh be justified."

13. The sentence "The way by (faith without works) may be mentioned here" was written in the empty space beneath the phrase "'by the works of the law,' etc." The handwriting of these words suggests Charles added this sixth point after he had written "How is it men are deceived." The handwriting is consistent with the words written vertically in the margins of the previous sermon, "Ignorance, Its Evils" (Sermon 31).

14. James 2:17, "Even so faith, if it hath not works, is dead, being alone." A dot appears above the word "be." Its inclusion does not seem to be significant to the text.

15. Cf. Ps 51:5; Rom 3:23; 5:12.   16. Cf. Matt 22:29.

17. Cf. John 8:44; 1 Pet 5:8.   18. Cf. Matt 24:42; 1 Cor 16:13.

19. A cluster of dots appears above the letters "r" and "i."

Matthew 1 - 21 - Salvation from sin.

The two parts of this Salvation are Justification & Sanctification

I. Justification including pardon & imputation of righteousness

1. Pardon. free, perfect, instantaneous, irreversible bringing
with it deliverance from the consequences of sin which are
1 God's just displeasure 2 The curse of the Law. 3. Incapacity for heaven
4. Liability yea certain destination to eternal punishment

2. Imputation of righteousness - causing a man to be
regarded as holy, sinless, worthy of commendation & reward
its accompaniments are 1 Gods love. 2 Blessing of the law
3 Capacity for heaven. 4 A right & title yea certain possession of heaven

This Jesus effected. as to the first by his death & sufferings
as to the second by his holy obedience to the law

II Sanctification including deliverance from sin & positive holiness
1 victory over, of our natural depravity. 2. the habits of sin
3 the temptations 4 backslidings -

2. Working in us all holy affections. 1. Holy nature. 2 Holy habits -

3. Desire for holiness 4. progress in divine grace
this is unlike Justification in that it is gradual
imperfect, progressional, never consummated but in
heaven.

This he does. 1. By showing us his example. 2 By the spirit
& command

Deliverance from the guilt, consequences & effects
of sin - this is the beauteous salvation Jesus gives.

51

SALVATION *from* SIN[1]
Matthew 1:21[2]

"And she shall bring forth a son, and thou shalt call his name Jesus:
for he shall save his people from their sins."

The two parts of this Salvation are Justification and Sanctification.

I. JUSTIFICATION,[3] INCLUDING PARDON AND
    IMPUTATION OF RIGHTEOUSNESS.
    1. Pardon. Free, perfect, instantaneous, irreversible. Bringing with[4] it deliverance
        from the consequences of sin, which are: 1.[5] God's just displeasure.
        2. The Curse of the Law.[6] 3. Incapacity for heaven. 4. Liability. Yea, certain[7]
        destination to eternal punishment.[8]
    2. Imputation of righteousness. Causing a man to be regarded as holy,[9]
        sinless, worthy of commendation and reward. Its accompaniments are:
        1. God's love. 2. Blessing of the law 3. Capacity for heaven.
        4. A right and title. Yea, certain possession of heaven.[10]
    { This, Jesus effected. As to the first, by his death and sufferings.[11]
    { As to the second, by his holy obedience to the law.[12]

II. SANCTIFICATION INCLUDING DELIVERANCE
    FROM SIN AND POSITIVE HOLINESS.[13]
    1. Victory over: 1.[14] Our natural depravity.[15] 2. The habits of sin.
        3. The temptations.[16] 4. Backslidings.
    2. Working in us all holy affections. 1.[17] Holy nature. 2. Holy habits.
        3.[18] Desire for holiness. 4. Progress in divine grace.

    { This is unlike Justification in that it is gradual, imperfect,
    { progressional, never consummated but in heaven.[19]
    { This he does: 1. By showing us his example[20] and commands.[21]
    { 2. By the Spirit.

Deliverance from the guilt, consequences and effects of sin.[22] This is the beauteous
salvation[23] Jesus gives.

51[24]

1. This was the first sermon Charles preached as pastor of Waterbeach Chapel. According to a letter to his father on October 16, 1851, Charles agreed to supply the pulpit of Waterbeach Chapel through the end of October 1851 (Angus Library and Archive, Regent's Park College, Oxford University, D/SPU 1, Letter 10; the dating of this letter is inaccurate in *Autobiography* 1:228). Charles also preached on Matt 1:21 for his final sermon as pastor of Waterbeach Chapel, and for his first sermon as pastor of the New Park Street Chapel. Charles recounted, "As this was my first text in Waterbeach so by the help of God it shall be the one with which I would close my stated ministry among you" (Notebook 8, Sermon 365). Susannah noted, "It is delightful to notice that JESUS was the keynote of his ministry both in Waterbeach and in London, and that not one of his many thousands of Sermons was out of harmony with that opening note" (*Autobiography* 1:229). Susannah also transcribed the above outline (*Autobiography* 1:229–30). Her alterations are as follows: The beginning of the sentence "This is unlike Justification" was changed to "Sanctification is unlike Justification." The phrase "This he does" was changed to "This is the work of Jesus." The sentence "Deliverance from the guilt, consequences and effects of sin—this is the beauteous salvation Jesus gives" was changed to "This is the beauteous salvation Jesus gives, complete deliverance from the guilt, consequences, and effects of sin."

2. In 1878, Charles preached an additional sermon on Matt 1:21 entitled "Jesus" (*MTP* 24, Sermon 1434). The lack of structural similarities and overlapping content suggests Charles did not use the above outline in writing his later sermon.

3. See "Abraham Justified by Faith" (Sermon 3).

4. A dark, yellow stain, likely the result of the aging process of the manuscript, appears to the left of the word "with." Its imprint can be found above the word "way" in the previous sermon, "The Wrong Roads" (Sermon 32).

5. Both the location of the number 1 and the absence of the period suggest Charles did not originally intend this line to begin his list.

6. Cf. Gal 3:13.

7. Charles originally spelled this word "sertain." He corrected the misspelling by writing the letter "c" over "s."

8. Cf. Matt 25:46.   9. Cf. 1 Pet 2:9.

10. The final letters of the word "heaven" trail into the margin. For additional examples of this tendency, see "The Church and Its Boast" (Sermon 75).

11. Cf. Matt 27:32–56.   12. Cf. Gal 2:16.

13. For an additional use of the phrase "positive holiness," see *MTP* 32:146. On this point Charles may have been influenced by John Bunyan's *A Discourse on the Pharisee and the Publican* in which the concepts of positive and negative holiness were explained with regard to the righteousness of the Pharisee: "The Pharisee's definition of righteousness; the which standeth in two things: 1. In negatives. 2. In positives. *In negatives*; to wit, what a man that is righteous must not be: I am no extortioner, no unjust man, no adulterer, nor yet as this publican. *In positives*; to wit, what a man that is righteous must be: I fast twice a week, I give tithes of all that I possess, &c" (George Offor, ed., *The Works of John Bunyan*, 2:222, italics in the original).

14. An illegible letter appears beneath the bolded number 1.

15. In a letter to his father on September 19, 1850, Charles wrote, "I feel persuaded that I shall never fathom the depths of my own natural depravity, nor climb to the tops of the mountains of God's eternal love" (Angus Library and Archive, Regent's Park College, Oxford University, D/SPU 1, Letter 7). Cf. Ps 51:5; Rom 3:23; 5:12.

16. Cf. 1 Cor 10:13.

17. The curve at the top of the number suggests Charles may have first written 2 instead of 1.

18. Charles originally wrote the number 2 beneath 3.

19. Cf. 1 John 3:2.   20. Cf. 1 Pet 2:21.

21. The words "and commands" were written above the word "example." The handwriting in these words differs from that of the outline and is consistent with the notations found in the two previous sermons, "Ignorance, Its Evils" (Sermon 31) and "The Wrong Roads" (Sermon 32).

22. Cf. Rom 6:18.

23. "Salvation is not a natural production from within: it is brought from a foreign zone, and planted within the heart by heavenly hands" (*MTP* 61:475).

24. An ink stain appears in the lower right side of the page. It was likely an imprint of the number 45 from the previous sermon, "The Wrong Roads" (Sermon 32).

34   Rev. 5 . 5. 6.   The Lamb & Lion conjoined

Jesus is compared to a Lamb – as he was a Man God.
1. Humility. 2. Gentleness 3. Weakness. 4. Submission
5. His sweetness to his friends
     were eminently concentred in him.
   He is a Lion in his 1. Dignity. 2 Boldness 3. Strength
4. Invincibility .5 His fury to his enemies.

He was a Lamb when first he became incarnate.
  When he submitted to his parents, suffered the despite
of men, was pained, when he took little children to
him – when he died the just for the unjust
   In his Condescension, Incarnation. Life. Death. Atonement.
He was a Lion when in Glory he reigned – when he conquered
Satan in the wilderness, in his miracles & sometimes reproofs.
In his resisting unto blood, victory on the tree and
    triumphant resurrection

He is a Lamb now in intercession, pleading, continual
offering. bearing with the sons of men,
He is a Lion in protecting his people against Satan
an invincible Lion in never suffering their destruction
    At Last when every Saint is saved the
mighty Lion shall show himself so to be
  in the judgment and damnation of his foes
and in that grandest scene – his triumphant
entrance into heaven "leading captivity captive"

48.

34

The LAMB *and* LION CONJOINED[1]
Revelation 5:5–6[2]

"And one of the elders saith unto me . . . Weep not: behold, the Lion of the tribe of Judah, the Root of David, hath prevailed to open the book, and to loose the seven seals thereof. And I beheld, and, lo, in the midst of the throne and of the four beasts, and in the midst of the elders, stood a Lamb as it had been slain, having seven horns and seven eyes, which are the seven Spirits of God sent forth into all the earth."

Jesus is compared to a Lamb, as he was a Man God.[3]

1. Humility.[4] 2. Gentleness.[5] 3. Weakness. 4. Submission.[6] 5. His sweetness to his friends. Were eminently concentred[7] in him.[8]

He is a Lion in his 1. Dignity. 2. Boldness. 3. Strength. 4. Invincibility. 5. His fury to his enemies.[9]

· [10]

He was a Lamb when first he became incarnate.[11] When he submitted to his parents,[12] suffered the despite of men, was pained, when he took little Children to him,[13] when he died, the just for the unjust.[14] In his Condescension,[15] Incarnation,[16] Life, Death, Atonement.

x x x x x x x x x x x x x x x x x x x x x x x x x x x x x x x x x x x x x x x[17]

He was a Lion when in glory he reigned,[18] when he conquered Satan in the wilderness,[19] in his miracles and sometimes reproofs, in his resisting unto blood,[20] victory on the tree,[21] and triumphant resurrection.[22]

· ·

He is a Lamb now in intercession,[23] pleading, continual offering, bearing with the sons of men.

· ·

He is a Lion in protecting his people against Satan.[24] An invincible Lion in never suffering their destruction. At Last, when every Saint is saved, the mighty Lion shall show himself so to be in the judgment and damnation of his foes, and in that grandest scene: his triumphant entrance into heaven, "leading captivity captive."[25]

48.

1.   An 1855 illustration, housed in the Heritage Room Archives of Spurgeon's College (B2.02.1), portrays Charles preaching from the sermon above. The following description is found in the Heritage Room catalogue: "[Charles Spurgeon] standing at lectern with open handwritten book, right hand pointing upwards." The visual characteristics of this sermon corroborate the sermon above, especially the horizontal line of dots and Xs that stretch across the page. It is likely the handwritten book in the illustration is a depiction of Notebook 1. If this is correct, this illustration constitutes the only known historical depiction of Charles's early notebooks. Also, if the dating of 1855 is correct in the Heritage Room catalogue, it would suggest Charles preached from his Waterbeach sermons at the New Park Street Chapel in London and further explains his promise to publish his early sermons in 1857 (see preface to *NPSP* 3). The correct date also may be 1854.

2.   This is the only time Charles preached a sermon on Rev 5:5–6. However, on July 4, 1889, he preached a sermon on Rev 5:6–7 entitled "The Lamb in Glory" (*MTP* 35, Sermon 2095). Similarities between the above outline and the later sermon exist, particularly in the metaphorical contrast between Jesus as lamb and lion (*MTP* 35:387–88). Charles likely had the above outline in mind during the writing of his later sermon.

3.   An alternative reading of this phrase is "Man of God."

4.   Cf. Phil 2:7.   5.   Cf. Matt 11:29.

6.   Cf. John 6:38; 14:31.

7.   From "concentre," which Samuel Johnson defined as "to tend to one common centre; to have the same centre as something else" (Johnson's *Dictionary*). See also *MTP* 35:389–92.

8.   An alternative reading of this sentence is "His sweetness to his friends [who] were eminently concentred in him."

9.   Cf. Rev 19:5.

10. Charles drew this line of dots to signal the separation in his sermon between Jesus as represented as a lamb and Jesus as represented as a lion.

11. Cf. Heb 2:14.

12. Cf. Luke 2:51.

13. Cf. Matt 19:14.

14. Cf. 1 Pet 3:18.

15. Cf. "The Condescension of Christ" (*NPSP* 3, Sermon 151).

16. Cf. John 1:14.

17. To be consistent, Charles should have written a horizontal line of Xs to represent the change in his topic from Jesus as represented as a lamb to Jesus as represented as a lion.

18. Cf. Matt 19:28; John 16:28; Acts 2:33; Rom 8:17.

19. Cf. Matt 4:1–11.

20. Cf. Heb 12:4.

21. Cf. John 19:30.

22. Luke 24:1–7; 1 Cor 15:20–22.

23. Cf. Rom 8:34; Heb 7:25.

24. Cf. Luke 22:31–32.

25. Cf. Eph 4:8. An alternative reading of this sentence is "and in that grandest scene: his triumphant entrance into heaven [when he led] 'captivity captive.'"

Prov. 4..18.   The Path of the Just   35

In the text there is plainly –

I. The Excellency of Christian Character . "shining light"
1. Beauty dwells in the character of the Just –
2. Usefulness to all in causing the well being of the world
   in preserving the earth from destruction.
3. Purity like as the sun is pure so is real Christian character
4. Sublimity the sun dwells not on earth, he is heavenly

II   The Progress of Christian character "shineth more &"
the figures used in Scripture imply this – such as.
new birth & growth to manhood … Growth as a plant..
teaching some more learned than others. A race.
there is
         1. Increase of Knowledge of God. his works, dispensations
                              duty. temptation. self..
         2. Increase of Graces. Love, Patience, Humility. Faith.
         3. Increase of Purity.
This is the effect of the Spirit – —
Depravity disturbs & obstructs the course.

III   The Certain Perfection of Xⁿ Character "perfect day"
Realized only in heaven.   this is proved –
   1. By Gods past acts in them.
   2. By their election to holiness.
   3. By the Intercession of Jesus.
   4. By the text & other Scriptures.

№ 72.549.

The PATH *of the* JUST
Proverbs 4:18[1]

"But the path of the just is as the shining light, that shineth more and more unto the perfect day."

In the text there is plainly:

I. THE EXCELLENCY OF CHRISTIAN CHARACTER. *"shining light."*

1. Beauty dwells in the character of the Just.[2]
2. Usefulness to all in causing the well being of the world in preserving the earth from destruction.[3]
3. Purity. Like as the sun is pure, so is real Christian character.
4. Sublimity. The sun dwells not on earth. He is heavenly.

II. THE PROGRESS OF CHRISTIAN CHARACTER *"shineth more" than*

The figures used in Scripture imply this, such as: New birth[4] and growth to manhood.[5] Growth as a plant.[6] Teaching some[7] more learned than others. A race. There is:

1. Increase of Knowledge of God. His works, dispensation,[8] duty, temptation, self.
2. Increase of Graces. Love, Patience, Humility, Faith.[9]
3. Increase of Purity.

This is the effect of the Spirit. Depravity disturbs and obstructs the course.[10]

III. THE CERTAIN PERFECTION OF XN[11] CHARACTER,[12] *"perfect day."*

Realized only in heaven. This is proved:

1. By God's past acts in them.[13] 2. By their election to holiness.[14]
3. By the Intercession of Jesus.[15] 4. By the text and other Scriptures.[16]

35[17] 72. 549.[18]

1. This is the only time Charles preached a sermon on Prov 4:18. See also "The Sun of Righteousness" (*MTP* 17, Sermon 1020) and "The Rising Sun" (*MTP* 25, Sermon 1463b).

2. Cf. Prov 28:6; Rom 5:3–5.

3. "In us instrumentally lies the hope of the world" (Notebook 3, Sermon 173).

4. Cf. John 3:3; 2 Cor 5:17.   5.   Cf. 1 Cor 13:11.

6. Cf. "The Plant of Renown" (Sermon 20).

7. A vertical ink smear appears over the letter "e" in the word "some." The source of the smear was likely the letter "e."

8. For Charles's critique of John Nelson Darby (1800–1882), the father of dispensationalism, see *ST* February 1867:32 and July 1869:326.

9. Cf. Gal 5:22–23.   10.   Cf. Rom 7:14–25.

11. Abbr., "Christian."

12. "This is true Christian perfection, when every gracious quality is present, and present in perfection" (*MTP* 43:478). Given the phrase "realized only in heaven," it is likely Charles did not have in mind the Christian perfectionism often associated with the theology of John Wesley (see John Wesley, *A Plain Account of Christian Perfection* [New York: G. Lane & P. P. Sandford, 1844]. See also William J. Abraham, James E. Kirby, eds., *The Oxford Handbook of Methodist Studies* [Oxford: Oxford University Press, 2009], 587–601). Charles addressed Wesley's perfectionism more directly in his sermon "Our Position and Our Purpose" (*MTP* 57, Sermon 3245). For a further critique of John and Charles Wesley, see Charles's 1861 lecture entitled "The Two Wesleys: On John and Charles Wesley" [orig. pub. London: Alabaster, Passmore, & Sons, 1861; reprint Eugene, OR: Wipf & Stock, 2014]). See also notes on Arminianism in "Pleasure in the Stones of Zion" (Sermon 53).

13. Cf. Jer 31:3.   14.   Cf. Eph 4:24.

15. Cf. Rom 8:34; Heb 7:25.   16.   Cf. Rom 8:30; 1 John 3:2–4; Rev 21:1–8.

17. The number 35 was struck through three times, likely because Charles had already preached the sermon "Faith Precious" (Sermon 23) on his thirty-fifth time to preach.

18. Two ink dots are seen at the bottom left side of the page. The source of the ink was the number 48 in the previous sermon, "The Lamb and Lion Conjoined" (Sermon 34).

36

Joshua 21. 45. Certain fulfilment of promises.

God's promises will be fulfilled for.

I. This verse affirms the fulfilment of some.

Promises to Abraham, Isaac & Jacob of a numerous seed & of the land of Canaan for possession.

Promise to them in Egypt to Moses. & then to Joshua. Land flowing with milk & honey — All the land. Enemies conquered — Lands allotted. — . . . . . Zebulon dwelt by the sea. Judah had praise. Issachar had an agricultural district. Asher dipped his foot in oil. Naphtali had the sea east.

II. There were peculiar difficulties in the way. Abraham & Sarah old & childless. Isaac offered. Rebeckah barren. Jacob threatened by Esau. . Grievous famine — Anger of the neighbours excited Bondage in Egypt. murder of all males. Red sea — want of water & bread — war with Amalek Sin in the camp — Difficulties in conquest — Anakims giants, walled town, chariots of iron, vast numbers

III. God has fulfilled many others to his Israel. The gift of Jesus. No destruction by flood. to Gideon, David. the apostles. He promised to hear prayer, to comfort, to bless, instruct strengthen. support, provide for thee & he has done it. Believe then his promise 1. That Jesus shall be satisfied. 2 That thou shalt be heard. 3. That thou shalt persevere. 4. That thou shalt inherit glory

CERTAIN FULFILMENT[1]
of PROMISES
Joshua 21:45[2]

"There failed not ought of any good thing which the LORD had spoken unto the house of Israel; all came to pass."

GOD'S PROMISES WILL BE FULFILLED, for:

I.   This verse affirms the fulfilment of some: Promises to Abraham, Isaac, and Jacob of a numerous seed,[3] and of the land of Canaan for possessions.[4] Promises to them in Egypt, to Moses,[5] and then to Joshua.[6] Land flowing with milk and honey.[7] All the land. Enemies conquered.[8] Lands allotted.[9] Zebulon dwelt by the sea.[10] Judah had praise.[11] Issachar had an agricultural district.[12] Asher dipped his foot in oil.[13] Naphtali had the sea and coast.[14]

II. There were peculiar difficulties in the way. Abraham and Sarah, old and childless.[15] Isaac offered.[16] Rebeckah[17] barren.[18] Jacob threatened by Esau.[19] Grevious famine.[20] Anger of the neighbours excited.[21] Bondage in Egypt.[22] Murder of all males.[23] Red sea.[24] Want of water and bread.[25] War with Amalek.[26] Sin in the camp.[27] Difficulties in conquest. Anakims[28] giants. Walled town.[29] Chariots of iron.[30] Vast numbe[r].[31]

III. God has fulfilled many others to his Israel:[32] The Gift of Jesus. No destruction by flood.[33] To Gideon,[34] David,[35] the apostles.[36] He promised[37] to hear prayer,[38] to comfort,[39] to bless,[40] instruct,[41] strengthen,[42] support,[43] provide for thee,[44] and he has done it.

BELIEVE, THEN, HIS PROMISE:
1. That Jesus shall be satisfied.
2. That thou shalt be heard.
3. That thou shalt persevere.[45]
4. That thou shalt inherit glory.

1. Charles used the British spelling of "Fulfilment" throughout this sermon.

2. This is the only time Charles preached a sermon on Josh 21:45. See also "Obtaining Promises" (*MTP* 8, Sermon 435); "A Promise for Us and Our Children" (*MTP* 10, Sermon 564); "The Covenant Promises of the Spirit" (*MTP* 37, Sermon 2200); "All the Promises" (*MTP* 46, Sermon 2657); "A Promise and Precedent" (*MTP* 55, Sermon 3127); "A Promise for the Blind" (*MTP* 55, Sermon 3139); and "A Promise and a Providence" (*MTP* 62, Sermon 3528).

3. Cf. Gen 28:13–14.   4. Cf. Exod 6:4, 8.   5. Cf. Exod 6:1.

6. Cf. Josh 1:9; 21:45.   7. Cf. Exod 3:8; 33:3.   8. Cf. Josh 6; 8:1–2; 10:10.

9. Cf. Joshua 18. The ellipses after the word "allotted" likely served as a signal to Charles to include more examples of God's promises.

10. Cf. Gen 49:13; Deut 33:19; Josh 19:10–17.

11. By using the phrase "Judah had praise," Charles was referencing the meaning of the Hebrew name "Judah" (יְהוּדָה), which was translated as "celebrated" in his personal copy of a Hebrew lexicon (see Wilhelm Gesenius, *A Hebrew and English Lexicon of the Old Testament Including the Biblical Chaldee* [trans., Edward Robinson; Boston: Crocker and Brewster, 1836, The Spurgeon Library], 407, italics in the original). In another Hebrew lexicon Charles owned, the Hebrew name is translated "praised" (Benjamin Davies, ed., *Student's Hebrew Lexicon: A Compendious and Complete Hebrew and Chaldee Lexicon to the Old Testament; Chiefly Founded on the Works of Gesenius and Fürst, with Improvements from Dietrich and Other Sources* [2nd ed.; London: Albert Cohn, 1876], 255). Cf. Gen 49:8.

12. Cf. Josh 19:17–23.   13. Cf. Deut 33:24; Josh 19:24–31.

14. Cf. Josh 19:32–39. The words "and coast" trail into the margin.

15. Cf. Gen 15:2.   16. Cf. Gen 22:1–18.

17. This is the only time in the early notebooks Charles spelled the name "Rebeckah." In the KJV the Hebrew word Ribqah (רִבְקָה) is spelled "Rebekah" and "Rebecca" (Cf. Gen 22:23; 25:20–28; 28:5; Rom 9:6–19). However, the name "Rebeckah"

was commonly given in the mid-nineteenth century. In a newspaper article printed only months before Charles preached the above sermon, the marriage of "Rebeckah Henrietta" was announced (see "Married," *London Morning Chronicle*, October 7, 1850).

18. Cf. Gen 25:21.　　19. Cf. Gen 27:41–42.　　20. Cf. Gen 26:1.

21. Cf. Gen 26:16.　　22. Cf. Exod 1:1–14.　　23. Cf. Exod 1:22.

24. Cf. Exodus 14.　　25. Cf. Exod 16:13; 17:3.

26. Cf. Exod 17:8.　　27. Cf. Joshua 7–9.

28. Cf. Deut 1:28; 2:10; Josh 11:21; 15:13. Charles did not include an apostrophe at the end of the word "Anakims." Either he intended the word to be plural ("Anakims, giants") or singular possessive ("Anakim[']s giants"). The latter interpretation is more likely.

29. Cf. Josh 5:13–6:27　　30. Cf. Josh 17:18.

31. The word "number" trails into the margin. Though likely intended, Charles did not originally include the letter "r" in the word "number" due to lack of space.

32. An alternative reading of this line is "God has fulfilled many other [promises] to his Israel."

33. Cf. Gen 9:11.　　34. Cf. Judg 6:16.

35. Cf. 2 Sam 7:1–16.　　36. Cf. Heb 13:15.

37. The size and location of the letter "d" suggest Charles likely added it afterward.

38. Cf. Jer 29:12; 1 John 5:14.　39. Cf. 2 Cor 1:4.　　40. Cf. Eph 1:3.

41. Cf. John 14:26.　　42. Cf. Phil 4:13.　　43. Cf. Rom 8:26; Phil 1:6.

44. Cf. Phil 4:19.

45. See "Final Perseverance" (Sermon 8); "Salvation" (Sermon 11); "Free Grace" (Sermon 13); and "God's Grace Given to Us" (Sermon 14).

2 Corinthians 10-4.   The Fight & the weapons.   37

I. The warfare — not carnal for we are all peacemen.
there has been a spiritual warfare in all times.
  our enemies are
    1. The world.   2 The Devil 3. The Flesh.
  each possessing their own fortifications. —
  1. The world entrenching itself with False Systems of
  Religion, Romanism, Puseyism &c — . . . . — —
  Formality, Hypocrisy, Profession, Infidelity
  Cares of this life, love of money, discontent, covetous,
  Pride, Pomp, False morality, trade tricks.
  Sin, temptations in it — Persecution - Favour.
  2. The Devil. Instances in Pilgrim's Progress.
      False Terrors. False hopes. Evil Insinuations.
  3. Our selves. Instances in Pilgrim's Progress.
  Pride, sloth, drowsiness, forgetfulness.
  Carnality. Lusts of the flesh — Presumption
II. The weapons "not carnal." "but mighty"
To Falsehood oppose truth, to sin oppose righteousness.
To Persecution Kindness, to Favour watchfulness.
To Satans. Insinuation oppose the word of God,
prayer & supplication, resisting & looking for him

To Self oppose Habits of devotion, Holy Fear, Faith,
Love to God, activity in his service,   Holy Spirit
— . . . . . . — . . . . . . — . . . — —
Mighty are the weapons and if we conquer not
it is our own fault.

The FIGHT *and the* WEAPONS
2 Corinthians 10:4[2]

"(For the weapons of our warfare are not carnal, but mighty
through God to the pulling down of strong holds)."

I. THE WARFARE. Not carnal, for we are all peacemen.[3]
There has been a spiritual warfare in all times. Our enemies[4] are:

   1. The world.[5] 2. The Devil.[6] 3. The Flesh.[7] Each possessing their
own fortifications.

     1. The world. Entrenching itself with False Systems of Religion:
Romanism, Puseyism,[8] etc. Formality,[9] Hypocrisy,[10] Profession,
Infidelity,[11] Cares of this life, love of money,[12] discontent,[13]
covetousness,[14] Pride,[15] Pomp, False morality,[16] trade tricks,
Sin, temptations in it,[17] Persecution, Favour.

     2. The Devil. Instances in Pilgrim's Progress.[18] False Terrors.[19]
False hopes. Evil Insinuations.[20]

     3. Our selves. Instances in Pilgrim's Progress: Pride,[21] sloth,[22]
drowsiness,[23] forgetfulness,[24] Carnality, Lusts of the flesh,[25]
Presumption.[26]

II. THE WEAPONS. *"Not carnal," "but mighty."*
To Falsehood, oppose truth. To sin, oppose righteousness. To Persecution, Kindness. To Favour, watchfulness. To Satan's Insinuation, oppose the word of God, prayer, and supplication,[27] resisting and looking for him. To Self, oppose Habits of devotion, Holy Fear, Faith, Love to God, activity in his service, Holy Spirit.

- [28]

Mighty are the weapons, and if we conquer not it is our own fault.[29]

1. This sermon is numbered "37a."

2. Charles preached an additional sermon on 2 Cor 10:4 in the following sermon, "The Fight" (Sermon 37b). Both sermons are numbered 37. In his index at the end of this notebook, Charles did not include the above sermon and instead listed the following sermon, which may suggest his preference of the two. The similarities between the two sermons are substantial, particularly under the second primary divisions: "II. The weapons" and "II. Our army, our allies, our weapons." A similar two-sermon set is also found in "Christ the Power and Wisdom of God" (Notebook 3, Sermon 169a) and "Christ the Power of God" (Sermon 169b). Charles did not preach on 1 Cor 10:4 in his later ministry.

3. Cf. Matt 5:9; Rom 12:18; Heb 14:12.

4. Cf. Eph 2:1–3; 1 John 2:6. Cf. "The Allied armies of the World, flesh, Devil, with whom we will never sign a truce or treaty" ("The Fight" [Sermon 37b]). See also "The Children Cast Out" (Notebook 2, Sermon 104).

5. Cf. Rom 12:2.   6. Cf. 1 Pet 5:8.   7. Cf. Gal 5:17.

8. See Charles's reference to "Mount Rome" and "Mount Pusey" in his earlier sermon "Salvation in God Only" (Sermon 24).

9. Charles wrote the vertical word "defence" in the left margin before "Religion." The word "Offence" was also written beneath. The characteristics of this handwriting differ from that found in the body of his outline. For additional examples of this handwriting, see "Ignorance, Its Evils" (Sermon 31), "The Wrong Roads" (Sermon 32), and "Salvation from Sin" (Sermon 33).

10. Charles may have had in mind Formalist and Hypocrisy, two characters in John Bunyan's *The Pilgrim's Progress* who abandoned Christian at the foot of Hill Difficulty (Bunyan, *The Pilgrim's Progress*, 41). See also "The Wrong Roads" (Sermon 32).

11. Cf. "The Hill Infidelity" in "Salvation in God Only" (Sermon 24).

12. Cf. 1 Tim 6:10.   13. Cf. Phil 4:11.   14. Cf. Luke 12:15.

15. Cf. Prov 16:15; Jas 4:6; 1 John 2:16. Charles wrote the vertical word "Offence" in the left margin before "Pride."

16. "To do evil that good may come is false morality, and wicked policy" (*MTP* 15:245).

17. Jas 1:14–15.

18. Charles first discovered John Bunyan's *The Pilgrim's Progress* as a child in his grandfather's attic in Stambourne (see *Autobiography* 1:22–23). Bunyan's allegory became Charles's favorite book. During his courtship with Susannah, he gave her a copy of this book with the inscription "Miss Thompson[,] with desires for her progress in the blessed pilgrimage. From C. H. Spurgeon. April 20, 1854" (*Autobiography* 2:7). With regard to Bunyan's use of allegory, Charles said, "Mr. Bunyan is the chief, and head, and lord of all allegorists, and is not to be followed by us into the deep places of typical and symbolical utterance. He was a swimmer, we are but mere waders, and must not go beyond our depth" (*Lectures* 1:114). In his final early-sermon notebook, Charles wrote, "No Book has been more honoured of God than the Pilgrim's Progress" ("Deaf Cured" [Notebook 9, Sermon 368]). For additional references to Bunyan in this notebook, see "Beginning at Jerusalem" (Sermon 29) and "The Wrong Roads" (Sermon 32).

19. Charles may have had in mind the two lions that guarded the Palace Beautiful and had caused Mistrust and Timorous to turn back. Bunyan wrote, "Then [Christian] was afraid, and thought also himself to go back after them, for he thought nothing but death was before him: But the *Porter* at the Lodge, whose Name is *Watchful*, perceiving that *Christian* made a halt, as if he would go back, cried unto him, saying, Is thy strength so small? fear not the Lions, for they are Chained: and are placed there for trial of faith where it is; and for discovery of those that have none: keep in the midst of the Path, and no hurt shall come unto thee" (Bunyan, *The Pilgrim's Progress*, 49, italics in the original).

20. See Christian's encounter with Apollyon in the Valley of Humiliation (ibid., 64–69). For additional references to Apollyon, see *MTP* 19:19; 36:605; 43:485; and 55:186. It is also possible Charles had in mind the "wicked one" that Christian encountered in the Valley of the Shadow of Death who "got behind him, and stept up softly to him, and whisperingly suggested many grievous blasphemies to him, which he verily thought had proceeded from his own mind" (Bunyan, *The Pilgrim's Progress*, 74).

21. See *"Adam the first"* whom Faithful met at the foot of Hill Difficulty. The third daughter of Adam the First was named *"[P]ride of life"* (Bunyan, *The Pilgrim's Progress*, 80, 81, italics in the original).

22. Christian encountered the character *"Sloth,"* who was one of "three Men asleep with Fetters upon their heels," after having departed from the Interpreter's House. The other two characters were *"Simple"* and *"Presumption."* Upon being wakened by Christian, Sloth said, *"Yet a little more sleep"* (ibid., 40, italics in the original). See also "The Improvement of Our Talents" (Sermon 61).

23. See Christian's slumber before descending the Hill Difficulty (Bunyan, *The Pilgrim's Progress*, 46).

24. *"Do you not remember that one of the Shepherds bid us beware of the Inchanted ground? He meant by that, that we should beware of sleeping; wherefore let us not sleep as do others, but let us watch and be sober"* (ibid., 163, italics in the original).

25. "Once I, like Mazeppa, lashed to the wild horse of my lust, bound hand and foot, incapable of resistance, was galloping on with hell's wolves behind me, howling for my body and my soul as their just and lawful prey. There came a mighty hand which stopped that wild horse, cut my bands, set me down, and brought me into liberty" (*Autobiography* 1:101). See also *The Works of Lord Byron Complete in Five Volumes* ([2nd ed.; Leipzig: Bernhard Tauchnitz, 1866, The Spurgeon Library], 2:469–94).

26. See "Making Light of Christ" (Sermon 21) and "Beginning at Jerusalem" (Sermon 29).

27. An alternative reading of this line is "To Satan's insinuations [and] opposition to the word of God, prayer and supplication."

28. In this sermon Charles departed from his usual inclusion of an unbroken line at the bottom of the page. The dashes here served the same function, which was to signal the conclusion of his sermon. For an additional example of his use of dashes, see "Necessity of Purity for an Entrance to Heaven" (Sermon 2).

29. A large smudge appears at the bottom of the page. The source of the ink is unknown. Its imprint is not detected in the previous sermon.

37.   2 Cor. 10 - 4 .   The Fight.

In war men use castles for defence, sword & spear for
offence, so do our enemies, and so we also have
weapons nor "carnal, but mighty through God to pull them down

I   Our enemies and the defences & weapons.

The Allied armies of the world, flesh. Devil with
whom we will never sign a truce or treaty.

1 The world. Castles are False religions, Formalism,
Self righteousness —

It has troops of cares. Captain Careful. Showy troops Capt Pride.
Captain Pleasure leads a host of sins. Captain Custom. also.
Captain Blood - persecutors. Capt. Deceit. favourers
Captain Conformity heads an ambuscade.

2. The Devil. needs no castle against us but gains Christ
attacks us, with Black terrors, white hopes, Filth Insinuation

3. Self dwells in "natural depravity." "sloth". forgetfulness.
fight us with pride, carnality, dagger of lust, presumption

II Our army, our allies, our weapons

To the worlds castle of False Religion we bring the ram of truth
To Sin the gun of righteousness & holy conduct.
To Persecution. the hot coals of love & kindness.
The scaling ladder of Zeal — the siege of perseverance

To Satan. prayer, resistance. watchfulness, courage.

To Self. Energy, faith the wall of Jericho, activity for God.
watchfulness, habits of devotion. meditation —

The Spirit our Strength.
Jesus Christ our Captain.

53. 214.

The FIGHT
2 Corinthians 10:4[2]

"(For the weapons of our warfare are not carnal, but mighty
through God to the pulling down of strong holds)."

In war, men use castles for defence, sword and spears for offence.[3] So do our enemies. And so, we also have weapons. Nor[4] "carnal, but mightily through God to pull them down."[5]

I. OUR ENEMIES AND THE DEFENCES AND WEAPONS.
The Allied armies[6] of the world,[7] flesh, Devil with whom we will never sign a truce or treaty.

1.[8] The world. Castles are False religions. Formalism.[9] Self righteousness.[10] It has troops of cares: Captain Careful,[11] Showy troops, Capt[12] Pride, Captain Pleasure[13] leads a host of sins. Captain Custom, also. Captain Blood-persecutors, Cap[tain] Deceit, Favourers. Captain Conformity[14] heads an ambuscade.[15]

2. The Devil needs no castle against us but against Christ. Attacks us with Black terrors, white hopes, Filth, Insinuation.[16]

3. Self dwells in "natural depravity," "sloth,"[17] forgetfulness. Fight us with pride,[18] carnality, dagger of lust, presumption.

II. OUR ARMY, OUR ALLIES, OUR WEAPONS.
To the world[']s castle of False Religion we bring the <u>ram</u> of truth.
To Sin, the gun of righteousness and holy conduct.
To Persecution, the hot coals of love and kindness.[19]
The scaling ladder of zeal,[20] the siege of perseverance.[21]
To Satan: prayer, resistance,[22] watchfulness, courage.[23]
To Self: Energy, faith. The wall of Jericho,[24] activity for God, watchfulness, habits of devotion. Meditation.[25]

The Spirit our Strength.
Jesus Christ our Captain.[26]

53. 214.[27]

1.   This sermon is numbered "37b."

2.   Charles also preached on 2 Cor 10:4 in the previous sermon, "The Fight and the Weapons" (Sermon 37a). Both sermons are numbered 37. In the index at the end of this notebook, Charles listed only the above sermon, which may suggest preference. Given that Charles did not list specific dates or villages in the previous sermon, it may have served as a first draft of the sermon. Charles used the above sermon when he preached on his fifty-third and 214th times. A similar two-sermon set is found in "Christ the Power and Wisdom of God" (Notebook 3, Sermon 169a) and "Christ the Power of God" (Notebook 3, Sermon 169b). Charles did not preach on 1 Cor 10:4 in his later ministry.

3.   There may be a correlation between this sentence and the words "defence" and "Offence" that are found in the left margin of his previous sermon, "The Fight and the Weapons" (Sermon 37a).

4.   Charles may have intended to use the word "not" instead of "nor." If this is correct, the sentence would read, "And so we also have weapons [that are not] 'carnal but [mighty] through God to pull them down.'"

5.   Charles altered the wording of the KJV for 2 Cor 10:4. For additional alterations, see the title page of this notebook.

6.   Charles wrote the letter "i" in the word "armies" prematurely. He corrected his mistake by including a tittle over the original letter "e."

7.   It is possible Charles originally misspelled the word "world," or he may have smeared the letters "o" and "r." The former interpretation is more likely.

8.   The size and location of the number 1, and also the absence of punctuation, suggest Charles did not originally intend to begin a list on this line. He likely added the number afterward.

9.   See "The Wrong Roads" (Sermon 32).

10.   Cf. Luke 18:9; Rom 10:3.

11.   These names are original to Charles and may have been inspired by references in his previous sermon to John Bunyan's *The Pilgrim's Progress* (see "The Fight and the Weapons" [Sermon 37a]).

12. Abbr., "Captain."

13. An illegible letter appears beneath the letter "u" in the word "Pleasure." Charles may have misspelled this word originally.

14. Cf. Rom 12:12.

15. "A private station in which men lie to surprise others; a snare laid for an enemy; an ambush" (Johnson's *Dictionary*, s.v. "ambuscade").

16. Charles may have intended to connect these two words as such: "filth[y] Insinuation."

17. Compare "sloth," "forgetfulness," "pride," and "carnality" with the instances from Bunyan's *The Pilgrim's Progress* in the previous sermon, "The Fight and the Weapons" (Sermon 37a).

18. The letter "i" in the word "pride" was slightly underscored in pencil. Charles may have intended to underscore the whole word. A similar stroke is found beneath the word "threatenings" in the sermon "God's Estimation of Men" (Sermon 41).

19. Cf. Prov 25:21–22.   20. Cf. Rom 12:11.

21. Cf. Gal 6:9; 2 Thess 3:13.   22. Cf. Jas 4:7.

23. Cf. Deut 1:6–8; 1 Cor 16:13; 2 Tim 1:7.   24. Cf. Josh 6:20.

25. Cf. Josh 1:8; Pss 1:2; 19:14; 119:148.

26. Heb 2:10, "For it became him, for whom *are* all things, and by whom *are* all things, in bringing many sons unto glory, to make the Captain of their salvation perfect through sufferings." For additional references to Jesus Christ as captain, see "Christ About His Father's Business" (Sermon 15); "An Exhortation to Bravery" (Sermon 72); "David in the Cave of Adullam" (Notebook 2, Sermon 116); "Bring My Soul out of Prison" (Notebook 3, Sermon 164); "The Captain of Our Salvation" (*MTP* 45, Sermon 2619); and "Jesus Our Lord" (*MTP* 48, Sermon 2806).

27. A cluster of dots is found at the bottom right side of the page. The source of their ink is the numbers 56 and 58 in the following sermon, "The Son's Love to Us Compared with God's Love to Him" (Sermon 38).

Simeon 54

John. 15. 9. The Son's love to us compared with God's love to his 38

Neither reason, nor the law of God. have sufficient power over men to make them love God and hate sin.

This the gospel does do by declaring the love of Jesus to us.

I. The Comparison – the nature of Christ's love to us.

Not equality but resemblance. the love of Jesus the Father was 1. Without beginning, eternal love – as Matt. 3.17. John 1. 18. Isa 42. 1. John 17. 24. declare.

Even so the love of Xt to his people was without beginning as Election, the eternal council, & everlasting covenant tion.

2. Without measure, paternal love, only son, dutiful son oneness, loved even as he loved himself. this he showed by the great honour given and promised to him –

Even so Christ's love to his people has no bounds, as his acts of kindness – prove – surpasses knowledge of men & angels

3. Without variation. He loved him in trial, pain & death.

Even so Christ's love knows no change, chastisements, troubles only prove his love. for what son is there unchastised.

4. Without end. He will never cease to love him

Even so Jesus loves us with an everlasting love.

II. The Duty resulting from it "continue ye in my love"

1. To love Christ. Our duty from creation, much more here Let him be precious and other things despised

2. To continue in love to him. Avoid declensions either open or secret.. let us not be faint

3. To abound in acts of love. In secret and public.

Was his love so unmerited, unbounded, invariable and lasting – and shall ours be weak and transient

Let us live alone for him.

56. 58

Simeon <u>54</u>[1]

38

THE SON'S LOVE *to* US COMPARED *with* GOD'S LOVE *to* HIM
John 15:9[2]

"As the Father hath loved me, so have I loved you: continue ye in my love."

Neither reason[3] nor the law of God[4] have sufficient power over men to make them love God and hate sin. This the gospel does do by declaring[5] the love of Jesus to us.[6]

I. THE COMPARISON. The nature of Christ's love to us. Not equality, but resemblance.[7] The love of ~~Jesus~~[8] the Father was:
1. Without beginning, eternal love, as Matt. 3:17,[9] John 1:18,[10] Isa. 42:1,[11] John 17:24[12] declare. Even so, the love of Xt[13] to his people was without beginning[14] as Election, the eternal council, and everlasting covenant prom[ises].[15]
2. Without measure. Paternal love, only son, dutiful son, oneness,[16] loved even as he loved himself. This he showed by the great honour given[17] and promised to him. Even so, Christ's love to his people has no bounds as his acts of kindness prove.[18] Surpasses knowledge of men and angels.
3. Without variation.[19] He loved him in trial, pain and death. Even so, Christ's love knows no change. Chastisements, troubles only prove his love.[20] For what son is there unchastised?
4. Without end. He will never cease to love him.[21] Even so, Jesus loves us with an everlasting love.[22]

II. THE DUTY RESULTING FROM IT.
"continue ye in my love."[23]
1. To love Christ. Our duty from creation, much more here.[24] Let him be precious[25] and other things despised.[26]
2. To continue in love to him. Avoid declensions,[27] either open or secret. Let us not be faint.[28]
3. To abound in acts of love. In secret and public.[29] Was his love so unmerited, unbounded, invariable, and lasting? And shall our[s][30] be weak and transient?[31]

Let us[32] live alone for him.

56. 58

1. This outline is original to Charles Simeon (1759–1836), "the famous English clergyman of Cambridge" (*MTP* 30:179) whom Charles often cited throughout his ministry and even called "St. Simeon" (*MTP* 16:628; see also 9:299; 16:628; and 42:451). The number 54 refers to Simeon's fifty-fourth sermon skeleton, entitled "A Comparison Between the Father's Love to Christ, and Christ's to Us" (Simeon, *Helps to Composition*, 1:400–403). See also Charles's use of Simeon in "Regeneration, Its Causes and Effects" (Sermon 46). The overlapping content is noted below. When quoted, the excessive em dashes and brackets Simeon included have been minimized. With regard to Simeon's outlines, Charles wrote, "Not commentaries, but we could not exclude them. They have been called 'a valley of dry bones': be a prophet and they will live" (Spurgeon, *Commenting and Commentaries*, 42). For more information about Simeon, see Charles Smyth, *Simeon & Church Order: A Study of the Origins of the Evangelical Revival in Cambridge in the Eighteenth-Century* [Cambridge: Cambridge University Press, 1940; repr., 2015]) and Hugh Evans Hopkins, *Charles Simeon of Cambridge* [Eugene, OR: Wipf & Stock, 1977]).

2. Charles preached an expanded version of this outline again in his sermon at Waterbeach Chapel entitled "Love of Christ to Us Compared with the Father's Love to Him" (Notebook 8, Sermon 378). In it Charles again relied heavily on Simeon's work, particularly in the first Roman numeral. In his later ministry Charles preached two additional sermons on John 15:9: "Love at Its Utmost" (*MTP* 33, Sermon 1982) and "Cheering Words" (*MTP* 41, Sermon 2444). The former sermon most resembles the above outline in structure and substance and may have been inspired by Simeon's outline (Cf. "1. The Comparison" and *MTP* 33:512–13).

3. "REASON could never suggest motives sufficient to counteract the passions" (Simeon, *Helps to Composition*, 1:400).

4. "The law of God itself, with all its sanctions, could not change the heart" (ibid.).

5. Charles wrote the word "declaring" instead of borrowing Simeon's word "revealing." Simeon added, "Hence our Lord reminds us of his love in order to confirm our love to him" (ibid., 1:401).

6. Cf. John 17:16; Rom 5:1; 2 Cor 5:14.

7. "The comparison in the text denotes not equality, but resemblance" (Simeon, *Helps to Composition*, 1:401).

8. "The love of Christ to us, like that of his Father to him, is 1. Without beginning" (ibid.). Charles departed from Simeon's outline by striking through the word "Jesus" and instead writing the words "the Father."

9. Charles copied this Scripture reference and the following references in this line from the footnotes to Simeon's outline. Matt 3:17, "And lo a voice from heaven, saying, This is my beloved Son, in whom I am well pleased" (see Scripture reference in Simeon, *Helps to Composition*, 1:401, footnote).

10. John 1:18, "No man hath seen God at any time: the only begotten Son, which is in the bosom of the Father, he hath declared him" (see Scripture reference in Simeon, *Helps to Composition*, 1:401, footnote).

11. Isa 42:1, "Behold my servant, whom I uphold; mine elect, in whom I delighteth: I have put my spirit upon him; he shall bring forth judgment to the Gentiles" (see Scripture reference in Simeon, *Helps to Composition*, 1:401, footnote).

12. John 17:24, "Father, I will that they also whom thou hast given me be with me where I am; that they may behold my glory, which thou hast given me: for thou lovedst me before the foundation of the world" (see Scripture reference in Simeon, *Helps to Composition*, 1:401, footnote).

13. Abbr., "Christ."

14. "There never was a period when Christ first began to love us—His love is first *manifested* when we believe in him—But our faith in him is the effect, not the cause, of his love to us" (Simeon, *Helps to Composition*, 1:401, italics in the original).

15. The final letters of this word trail into the margin. The letters "p" and "i" are evident, which suggests Charles may have intended to write the word "promises." It is also possible, though less likely, that he intended to write the word "prior." There is no evidence in Simeon's outline to suggest which interpretation is correct.

16. "He is one with Christ in nature, and therefore in affection—He has shewn the greatness of his love to him, in the gifts bestowed upon him, and in his constant co-operation with him" (Simeon, *Helps to Composition*, 1:401).

17. Cf. John 5:23.

18. "Christ's love to us is also unbounded. It produces most astonishing acts of kindness toward us" (Simeon, *Helps to Composition*, 1:401).

19. "The Father's love to Christ was unchangeable" (ibid., 1:402).

20. "Christ's love to us also is unchangeable[.] There are seasons when he *seems* to withdraw his love—But his chastisements are tokens of his love" (ibid., italics in the original).

21. "The Father's love to Christ shall endure for ever—He has given him a pledge of this in his exaltation to heaven" (ibid.).

22. "Christ's love to us shall also be everlasting—He knows no change of mind with respect to what he has bestowed—Whomsoever he loves he continues to love—This truth is a just ground of joy and confidence" (ibid.). Cf. Jer 31:3.

23. "II. The duty resulting from it[.] This part of the text requires application rather than discussion—It sets before us, not merely *our privilege* (which is, to continue in a sense of Christ's love to us) but *our duty*" (Simeon, *Helps to Composition*, 1:402, italics in the original).

24. An alternative reading of this line is "Our duty from creation is to love Christ. How much more here?"

25. Charles's first sermon in Teversham was preached on the subject of the preciousness of Jesus Christ from 1 Pet 2:7, "Unto you therefore which believe he is precious" (see *Autobiography* 1:200–201 and "Christ Is Precious" [Notebook 8, Sermon 311]).

26. "1. To love Christ[.] This would have been our duty, though he had not so loved us—But the obligation to it is greatly increased by his love—Let him then be exceeding precious to us—Let us despise every thing in comparison of him" (Simeon, *Helps to Composition*, 1:402).

27. "Tendency from a greater to a lesser degree of excellence" (Johnson's *Dictionary*, s.v. "declension").

28. "2. To continue in love to him[.] We are too apt to decline in our love—But declen-

sions, however secret, are very offensive—They will, if continued in, disqualify us for heaven—They will reduce us to a worse situation than ever—Let us therefore cleave to the Lord with full purpose of heart" (Simeon, *Helps to Composition*, 1:402–3).

29. An alternative reading of this line is "To abound in acts of love in secret and public."

30. Charles originally wrote the word "our."

31. "3. To abound in all acts and office of love to him[.] In secret, let us contemplate, admire, and adore his excellences—In public, let us confess, honour, and obey him—It commends to us that duty as resulting from the declaration that precedes it[.] The love of Christ towards us is the strongest of all motives to the love of him—Was Christ's love to us so unmerited, unbounded, invariable, and lasting? and shall ours to him be weak and transient?" (Simeon, *Helps to Composition*, 1:403).

32. Simeon's concluding words, "*Let us* not rest satisfied with what we have attained" (ibid., italics added), likely inspired the phrasing of Charles's final remarks, "*Let us* live alone for him" (italics added).

39 Matt. 3. 7. Pharisees & Sadducees reproved.

1. The Occasion. After prophets had ceased the Jews became divided into sects. Pharisees, Sadducees Essenes. John Baptist, singular man, draws crowds around him, he babtizes in the Jordan, the P & S come to his babtism he refuses it and addresses them thus before all the people.

2. The Characters. "Sadducees", Infidel, denying resurrection, spirit, reward, or punishment. Corrupt in life. False in doctrine.
"Pharisees". Fond of ceremonies, punctilious in small matters. proud & ostentatious. selfrighteous Secret Sinners, corrupt in heart, plunderers.
Search for such Characters here.

3. The name he gave them "broods of vipers". Deceitful, crafty, hypocritical, serpent like. Detestable, hated by God & Christian men. Worthy of Death, seed of the devil.

4. His exhortation "repentance.
Sadducee. amend his errors & life.
Pharisee. turn from his own righteousness. and see to the purity of his heart.
This disappointed them. hurt their pride excited their enmity.
The Publican the Hopeful one.

57

39

PHARISEES *and* SADDUCEES REPROVED
Matthew 3:7[1]

"But when he saw many of the Pharisees and Sadducees come to his baptism, he said unto them, O generation of vipers, who hath warned you to flee from the wrath to come?"

1. THE OCCASION. After prophets had ceased, the Jews became divided into sects. Pharisees, Sadducees, Essenes. John Baptist, singular man, draws crowds around him.[2] He baptizes in the Jordan.[3] The P[4] and S[5] come[6] to his baptism. He refuses it and addresses them thus before all the people.

2. THE CHARACTERS. *"Sadducees:"[7]*
Infidel.[8] Denying resurrection,[9] spirit,[10] reward, or punishment.[11] Corrupt in life. False in doctrine. "Pharisees:"[12] Fond of ceremonies. Punctilious[13] in small matters. Proud and ostentatious.[14] Self righteous.[15] Secret Sinners.[16] Corrupt in heart.[17] Plunderers. Search for such Characters here.[18]

3. THE NAME HE GAVE THEM, *"broods of vipers."*
Deceitful,[19] crafty,[20] hypocritical,[21] serpent-like, Detestable. Hated by God and Christian[22] men. Worthy of Death. Seed of the devil.

4. HIS EXHORTATION, *"repentance."[23]*
Sadducee: amend his errors and life.
Pharisee: turn from his own righteousness[24] and see to the purity of his heart.

This disappointed them, hurt their pride, excited their enmity.

The Publican,[25] the Hopeful one.

57[26]

1. On October 23, 1881, Charles preached an additional sermon on Matt 3:7 entitled "Flee from the Wrath to Come" (*MTP* 46, Sermon 2704). There is not enough structural similarity or overlapping content to suggest he used the above outline in writing his later sermon. For additional sermons on Pharisees, see "A Righteousness Better Than the Pharisees" (Notebook 5, Sermon 268); "Hypocrisy" (*NPSP* 5, Sermon 237); "The Woman Which Was a Sinner" (*MTP* 14, Sermons 801–802); and "A Sermon for the Worst Man on Earth" (*MTP* 33, Sermon 1949).

2. Cf. Mark 1:5.

3. Cf. Matt 13:3; Mark 1:5, 9.

4. Abbr., "Pharisees."

5. Abbr., "Sadducees."

6. The letters "re" were written beneath the letters "co" in the word "come." It is likely Charles intended to write the word "refuses," as he does later in the line.

7. "He observed the law of Moses, but he clung rather to the letter of it than to its spirit, and he did not accept all that was revealed, for he denied that there was such a thing as an angel or a spirit" (*MTP* 46:578).

8. Cf. Luke 12:1. It is not obvious why Charles bolded the letters "In" in the word "Infidel." The boldness was likely the result of a malfunction of the writing instrument and not an intention to draw attention to the word.

9. Cf. Matt 22:23; Mark 12:18; Luke 20:27; Acts 23:8.

10. Charles was likely referring to the Holy Spirit, not to angels or spirits.

11. Cf. Matt 12:39.

12. "There came to him a Pharisee, a very religious man, one who observed all the details of external worship, and was very careful even about trifles, a firm believer in the resurrection, and in angels and spirits, and in all that was written in the Book of the law, and also in all the traditions of his fathers, a man who was overdone with external righteousness, a Ritualist of the first order, who felt that, if there was a righteous man in the world, he certainly was that one" (*MTP* 46:577).

13. "Nice; very exact; precise; scrupulous; punctual or exact to excess" (Johnson's *Dictionary*, s.v. "punctilious").

14. Cf. Matt 23:6; Luke 11:43; 20:46.

15. Cf. Luke 18:11. Charles joined the words "self" and "righteous" in this line. He usually separated these two words, as demonstrated in his sermon "The Fight" (Sermon 37b).

16. Cf. Matt 5:20.

17. Cf. Matt 23:25–26; Luke 11:39.

18. Cf. Acts 4:1; 5:17.

19. Cf. Luke 11:52.

20. Cf. Luke 20:47.

21. Cf. Matt 15:23; 23:13.

22. Charles prematurely wrote the letter "a" after the "t" in the word "Christian." He corrected the misspelling by inserting the letter "i" and adding a tittle above the "a."

23. Matt 3:8, "Bring forth therefore fruits meet for repentance."

24. At the end of Charles's 1881 sermon "Flee from the Wrath to Come" (*MTP* 46, Sermon 2704), he preached, "I pray you, brethren and sisters, wherever you are, you who think you are so good, be anxious to get rid of all that fancied goodness of yours. I beseech you, if you have any self-righteousness about you, to ask God to strip it off you at once. . . . You will be as surely damned by your righteousness, if you trust in it, as you will by your unrighteousness" (*MTP* 46:584–85).

25. An illegible letter is found beneath the "a" in the word "Publican." Charles may have misspelled this word by first writing the letter "o." Cf. Luke 18:13.

26. The inversion of the number 57 is found on the opposite side of this page beneath the word "one." This is the first and only example in this notebook of an imprint caused by the folding of a single page in half before the ink was dry. More common is the closing of the notebook such that the excess ink either bleeds through the page or imprints onto the sermon on the page opposite. See also the ink smudging in "God's Grace Given to Us" (Sermon 14) and "Christ About His Father's Business" (Sermon 15).

Phil. 4. 4 .   Christian Joy —   40

All men seek joy the Christian is herein told to take
his full of it , and constantly to rejoice .

I The Matter & Manner of Joy " in the Lord."

I. In his attributes. 1 Power . all exercised on our behalf

2. Wisdom & Knowledge. He knows Satan, our evils, our wants &c

3. Mercy . the captive in the dungeon loves the sound of mercy

4. Love . with all its qualities and degrees —

5. Righteousness. A source of joy to all believers —
        Omnipresence. Eternity, Immutability

II. In his acts. Creation, Election, Redemption, Conversion.
        Adoption — his putting himself into relations with us

This is a hallowed holy Joy (in the Trinity) of which none
can take too much .

II. The Time mentioned "always".

In Prosperity we should not rejoice in self but in him.

In Adversity we must still rejoice for God changes not.

Some reasons for the Apostles advice .

1. This is a most excellent way of rejoicing

2. This pleases God the giver of our mercies.

3. This exercises faith & Love.

4. This eases the roughness of the way.

5. This recommends religion & is most consonant
        with its doctrines & objects . — —

59

CHRISTIAN JOY
Philippians 4:4[1]

"Rejoice in the Lord alway: and again I say, Rejoice."

All men seek joy.[2] The Christian is herein told to take his full of it and constantly to rejoice.[3]

I.[4] THE MATTER AND MANNER OF JOY. *"in the Lord"*

 I.[5] In his attributes:

  1.[6] Power.[7] All exercised on our behalf.

  2. Wisdom and Knowledge.[8] He knows Satan, our evils, our wants,[9] etc.

  3. Mercy.[10] The captive in the dungeon loves the sound of mercy.

  4. Love. With all its qualities and degrees.[11]

  5. Righteousness.[12] A source of joy to all believers. Omnipresence,[13] Eternity,[14] Immutability.[15]

 II. In his acts: Creation,[16] Election,[17] Redemption,[18] Conversion,[19] Adoption,[20] his putting himself into relations with us.[21] This is a hallowed, holy Joy[22] (in the Trinity) of which none can take too much.

II. THE TIME MENTIONED. *"always."*

In Prosperity, we should not rejoice in self but in him.[23]

In Adversity, we must still rejoice[24] for God changes not.[25]

Some reasons for the Apostle[']s advice:

 1. This is a most excellent way of rejoicing.

 2. This pleases God, the giver of our mercies.[26]

 3. This exercises faith and Love.

 4. This eases the roughness of the way.

 5. This recommends religion and is most consonant with its doctrines and objects.

59

1. On March 20, 1887, Charles preached an additional sermon on Phil 4:14 entitled "Joy, a Duty" (*MTP* 41, Sermon 2405). The following similarities are found: "The Time mentioned 'always'" (Roman numeral II in the outline above) and "Thirdly, let us think of the Time Appointed for this rejoicing: 'Rejoice in the Lord *alway*'" (*MTP* 41:138, italics in the original). For additional sermons on joy, see: "The Fruit of the Spirit: Joy" (*MTP* 27, Sermon 1582); "All Joy in All Trials" (*MTP* 29, Sermon 1704); "Jubilee Joy; or, Believers Joyful in Their King" (*MTP* 33, Sermon 1968); "The Pastor's Joy and Confidence" (*MTP* 36, Sermon 2154); "The Believer's Heritage of Joy" (*MTP* 41, Sermon 2415); "Joy in Place of Sorrow" (*MTP* 43, Sermon 2525); "Joy in God" (*MTP* 44, Sermon 2550); "Christ's Joy and Ours" (*MTP* 51, Sermon 2935); "How to Become Full of Joy" (*MTP* 57, Sermon 3272); "The Oil of Joy for Mourning" (*MTP* 59, Sermon 3341); and "Fulness of Joy Our Privilege" (*MTP* 60, Sermon 3406).

2. "Does the world satisfy thee? Then thou hast thy reward and thy portion in this life; make much of it, for thou shalt know no other joy" (*ST* January 1867:29).

3. "You know *re* usually signifies the re-duplication of a thing, the taking it over again. We are to joy, and then we are to re-joy. We are to chew the cud of delight; we are to roll the dainty morsel under our tongue till we get the very essence out of it" (*MTP* 41:134, italics in the original).

4. By writing two identical sets of Roman numerals, Charles's technique for ordering is inconsistent in this sermon. He likely bolded the first Roman numeral to distinguish it from the second.

5. Charles may have originally written the number 1 before changing it to Roman numeral I.

6. The size and location of the number 1 suggest Charles originally did not intend to begin a list before the word "Power." The number was likely added afterward.

7. Cf. Ps 62:11; 1 Cor 6:14; 2 Cor 13:4.

8. Cf. 1 Cor 1:25, 30; Col 2:3; Jas 3:17.

9. Cf. Matt 6:8; Phil 4:19.

10. Cf. Eph 2:4–7; Titus 3:4–5; Heb 4:16; 1 Pet 1:3–4.

11. Cf. Ps 86:15; Rom 5:8; 1 John 3:1; 4:9–11.

12. Cf. Deut 32:4; Pss 97:2; 119:137; 142; 145:17; Jer 12:1; Phil 3:9.

13. Cf. Ps 139:7–10; Jer 23:24.

14. Cf. John 8:58; 1 Tim 1:17; Rev 1:8.

15. Cf. Mal 3:6; Heb 13:8; Jas 1:17.

16. Cf. Gen 1:1; Rom 1:20; Col 1:16.

17. Cf. Rom 8:29; Eph 1:3–5; 1 Pet 1:2.

18. Cf. Gal 3:13; Eph 1:7; Col 1:14.

19. Cf. Acts 2:38; Rom 15:13.

20. Cf. Rom 8:4, 17; Gal 4:7; Eph 1:5.

21. Cf. 2 Cor 5:19. The word "us" trails into the margin.

22. Charles struck through the letter "l" in the word "Joly" to construct the correct spelling, "Joy."

23. Cf. Deut 30:9.

24. Cf. Isa 29:19; 2 Cor 4:16–18. See also "The Immutability of Christ" (*NPSP* 4, Sermon 170).

25. Cf. Mal 3:6; Heb 13:8; Jas 1:17.

26. Cf. 1 Cor 1:3.

41.　　Ex. 11. 7 –　God's estimation of men.

There have ever been two different parties in this world from the time of Adam as History proves. Cain & Seth – Noah & Ham. Abraham & the Sodomites. Egyptians & Jews.　Some on the Lord's side in the desert. Time of Saul. Samuel. Elijah's complaint. Daniel in captivity. The three youths. Maccabees. Jesus. Apostles. Martyrs in all time. Now –

　　God regards these two sorts in different lights.
　　He regards them now & will eternally do so.

1. For it is reasonable that he should do so for they are radically different – Scoffer & man of Prayer – Lover of self – Proud. Presumptuous, despisers, sinners –　Honest men. Fearing – Godloving, holy –

2. His ordinances show it.
　　Baptism & the Lord's supper for believers only –

3. His past actions.　In his saints in his showing of himself to them – in Adoption – Justification &c.

4. His preparations in eternity "Heaven and Hell are builded. preparations are made.

5. His solemn oath – his rewards & threatenings all proclaim it –

　　Exhortation to searching of heart. –

60.

GOD'S ESTIMATION *of* MEN
Exodus 11:7[1]

"But against any of the children of Israel shall not a dog move his tongue, against man or beast: that ye may know how that the LORD *doth put a difference between the Egyptians and Israel."*

There have ever been two different parties in this world from the time of Adam as History proves. Cain and Seth,[2] Noah and Ham,[3] Abraham and the Sodomites,[4] Egyptians and Jews.[5] Some on the Lord's side in the desert,[6] Time of Saul,[7] Samuel,[8] Elijah's complaint,[9] Daniel in captivity,[10] The three youths,[11] Maccabees, Jesus, Apostles. Martyrs in all time.[12] How God regards these two sorts in different lights. He regards them now and will eternally do so.

1. For it is reasonable that he should do so, for they are radically different. Scoffer[13] and man of Prayer,[14] Lover of self,[15] Proud,[16] Presumptuous,[17] despisers,[18] sinners.[19] Honest men,[20] Fearing,[21] Godloving,[22] holy.[23]

2. His ordinances show it. Baptism and the Lord's supper[24] for believers[25] only.[26]

3. His past[27] actions. To his saints in his showing of himself to them in Adoption,[28] Justification,[29] etc.

4. His preparations in eternity. Heaven[30] and Hell are builded. Preparations are made.[31]

5. His solemn oath. His rewards and threatenings[32] all proclaim it.

Exhortation to searching of heart.[33]

60

1. On March 25, 1860, Charles preached an additional sermon on Exod 11:7 entitled "Separating the Precious and the Vile" (*NPSP* 6, Sermon 305). Although overlapping content is found in the first paragraph of the above outline and *NPSP* 6:150–52, Charles likely did not use the above outline in writing the other sections.

2. Cf. Genesis 4.

3. Cf. Gen 9:18–24.

4. Cf. Genesis 19.

5. "Before the starry sky was spread, or the foundations of the earth were digged, the Lord had made a difference between Israel and Egypt. This, however, is a mighty secret, and though we are to tell it as we find it in the Word, yet we are not intrusively to pry into it" (*NPSP* 6:150). Cf. Exodus 1; 20:2.

6. Cf. Numbers 26.

7. Cf. 1 Sam 13:13–14; 2 Sam 7:15.

8. Cf. 1 Samuel 3.

9. Cf. 1 Kgs 19:10.

10. Cf. Daniel 1.

11. Cf. Dan 3:23.

12. Cf. Matt 16:24–25; 29:4; Rev 18:24.

13. Cf. 2 Pet 3:3–4; Jude 18.

14. Cf. Ps 109:4.

15. Cf. 2 Tim 3:2.

16. Cf. Prov 16:18; Jas 4:6.

17. See "The Fight and the Weapons" (Sermon 37a).

18. Cf. 2 Pet 2:10.

19. Cf. Rom 3:23.

20. Cf. Matt 5:37; Col 3:9; 1 Pet 3:10–12.

21. Cf. Gen 22:12; Job 1:1; Prov 9:10; Acts 10:2.

22. Cf. Ps 18:1.

23. Cf. 1 Pet 1:26; 2:9. A dark spot, likely the result of the aging process, appears on the right side of the page. The imprint of this spot is found beneath the word "in" in the following sermon, "King of Righteousness and Peace" (Sermon 42).

24. "The saints of God gather at the communion table, and the spreading of that table is not intended to be a means of grace to the unconverted: on the contrary, it is fenced and guarded, and reserved for believers only, and none have any right there but those who are in Christ. The object of the Lord's supper is not conversion, but edification: it is intended that as many as are alive unto God should there be fed, that those emblems should remind them of the body and blood of Jesus Christ, which are the food of their spiritual life" (*MTP* 27:583). See also "Slavery Destroyed" (Sermon 73); "The Blood Shed for Many" (*MTP* 33, Sermon 1971); "The Lord's Supper: a Remembrance of Jesus" (*MTP* 34, Sermon 2038); "Communion with Christ and His People" (*MTP* 58, Sermon 3295); and Nettles, *Living by Revealed Truth*, 593.

25. Charles originally inserted an apostrophe after the letter "r" in the word "believers." However, the context suggests he intended the word to be plural, not possessive.

26. "If you are saved, God's ordinances will be blessed things to you, but if you are not a believer you have no right to them; and with regard to Baptism and the Supper, every time you touch them you increase your guilt. Whether it be Baptism or the Lord's Supper, you have no right to either, except you be saved already, for they are both ordinances for believers, and for believers only. These ordinances are blessed means of grace to living, quickened, saved souls; but to unsaved souls, to souls dead in trespasses and sins, these outward ordinances can have no avail for good, but may increase their sin, because they touch unworthily the holy things of God" (*MTP* 8:29). In his diary entry for May 25, 1850, Charles wrote: "I fear Mr. T. is doing much harm by telling people that the Lord's Supper will save them. Work, Lord, work! Thou hast encouraged me; may I not be disappointed! 'Bless the Lord, O my soul.' The Covenant is my trust, the agreement signed between my Elder Brother and the Almighty standeth sure. 'None shall pluck them out of My hand'" (*Autobiography* 1:140).

27. An illegible letter, likely "t," was written beneath the "s" in the word "past." Charles may have prematurely written the letter "t" before inserting the "s."

28. See "Adoption" (Sermon 1).

29. Cf. Rom 5:1. See also "The Saints' Justification and Glory" (Sermon 68).

30. Charles inserted opening quotation marks before the word "Heaven." He likely intended to add closing quotation marks after the word "hell."

31. Cf. John 14:3; Heb 11:16. See also "Heaven's Preparations" (Sermon 28).

32. The letter "n" was underscored in pencil. A similar stroke is found beneath the word "Pride" in the sermon "The Fight" (Sermon 37b). A dark, yellow smear—likely the result of the aging process of the manuscript—is found beneath the word.

33. In his 1860 sermon on Exod 11:7, Charles offered the following exhortation: "Remember, the way to heaven is open. 'He that believeth in the Lord Jesus shall be saved.' Believe on him, believe on him, and live. Trust him, and you are saved. Cast your soul's confidence on Jesus, and you are *now* delivered. God help you to do that now, and there shall be no difference any more between you and the righteous, but you shall be of them, and with them, in the day when Jesus cometh to sit upon the throne of his father David, and to reign among men" (*NPSP* 6:156).

King of Righteousness & Peace. Heb. 7-2. 42

Various opinions as to Melchizedek, some supposing him to have been Christ incarnate — chiefly on the ground of his superiority to Abram, his being "without father or mother &c. Most however agree that he was a king of a town in this country and that the sense of the passage is that he had no predecessor in the priestly office and that as no time of birth or death is mentioned he is thus a type of our Lord. And that his superiority arose out of his priestly office.

His name & title are here referred typically to Christ

1 Not to his nature. Jesus is righteous & peaceful.
We are apt to conceive of him as all love and the Father as all justice but they are both infinite in each.
Jesus has every attribute in infinite perfection.

2. In the plan of salvation. He had due regard to justice the wisdom of the plan is its wise provision both for the justice of God and the happiness of man.

3. In the execution of the plan. Jesus satisfied law both by his life and sufferings, he remitted not one farthing of the debt but paid it all = and also worked out peace by reconciling men to God.

4. In his application of salvation — He first pardons justifies and purifies before he plants peace. purity, piety. peace all go together.

5. In his general dealing with the world to the wicked he will display his justice but to his saints his peace. in heaven's profound peace.

61

42

KING *of* RIGHTEOUSNESS *and* PEACE
Hebrews 7:2 [1]

"To whom also Abraham gave a tenth part of all; first being by interpretation
King of righteousness, and after that also King of Salem, which is, King of peace."

Various opinions as to Melchizedek.[2] Some supposing him to have been Christ incarnate chiefly on the ground of his superiority to Abram, his being "without father or mother,"[3] etc. Most, however, agree that he was a king of a town in this country, and that the sense of the passage is that he had no predecessor in the priestly office. And that, as no time of birth or death is mentioned, he is thus a type of our Lord. And that his superiority arose out of his priestly office.

His name and title are here referred typically[4] to Christ.[5]

1.[6] As to his nature. Jesus is righteous[7] and peaceful.[8] We are apt to conceive of him as all love and the Father as all Justice, but they are both infinite in each. Jesus has every attribute in infinite perfection.[9]

2. In[10] the plan of salvation. He had due regard to justice. The wisdom of the plan is its wise provision both for the justice of God and the happiness of man.

3. In the execution of the plan. Jesus satisfied law[11] both by his life and sufferings. He remitted not one farthing[12] of the debt, but paid it all and also worked out peace by reconciling[13] men to God.[14]

4. In his application of salvation. He first pardons,[15] justifies,[16] and purifies[17] before he plants peace. Purity, piety, peace[18] all go together.

5. In his general dealing with the world. To the wicked he will display his justice,[19] but to his saints, his peace in heaven's profound peace.[20]

61

1. On February 8, 1884, Charles preached an additional sermon on Heb 7:2 entitled "First King of Righteousness, and After That King of Peace" (*MTP* 30, Sermon 1768). Structural similarities exist in the first paragraph of the outline above and in Charles's treatment of Melchizedek as the "king of righteousness" in *MTP* 30:121–24. It is possible Charles had the above outline in mind while writing that section in his later sermon.

2. In his 1884 sermon, Charles did not begin his sermon with Christophanical theories about Melchizedek (Cf. *MTP* 30:121).

3. Heb 7:3, "Without father, without mother, without descent."

4. Charles prematurely wrote the letter "i" after the "t" in the word "typically." He corrected the misspelling by converting the "i" into a "y."

5. In a later sermon Charles compared Melchizedek to Paul: "[I]n his breaking of bread, he was dimly like Melchizedek, blessing men, and refreshing them with bread and wine" (*MTP* 55:242; see also 47:52).

6. The size, location, and lack of punctuation after the number 1 suggest Charles did not originally intend to begin his list with the phrase "As to his nature." He likely added the number afterward.

7. Cf. 1 Cor 1:30.

8. "This Melchizedek, whom we exhibit as a type, is *such a king as God is*. He is according to divine model. He is priest of the Most High God, and he is like the Most High God, for the Lord Jehovah himself is, first, King of righteousness, and after that also King of peace" (*MTP* 30:123, italics in the original).

9. For a discussion of *communicatio idiomatum* in Charles's Christology, see George, "Jesus Christ, The 'Prince of Pilgrims,'" 74–78. For a broader treatment of *communicatio idiomatum*, see T. F. Torrance, *Incarnation: The Person and Life of Christ* ([ed., Robert T. Walker; Milton Keynes, England: Paternoster, 2008], 210), and Timothy Larsen and Daniel J. Treier, eds., *The Cambridge Companion to Evangelical Theology* ([Cambridge: Cambridge University Press, 2007], 51).

10. A dark spot, likely the result of the aging process of the manuscript, appears beneath the word "in." The imprint of this spot is found after the word "holy" in the previous sermon, "God's Estimation of Men" (Sermon 41).

11. Cf. Matt 5:17.

12. A "farthing" was a British coin worth one-fourth of a penny. Samuel Johnson called it "the smallest English coin" (Johnson's *Dictionary*). The farthing was officially phased out as legal tender on December 31, 1960. For additional references to this coin, see "Inventory and Title of Our Treasures" (Notebook 2, Sermon 92); "David in the Cave Adullam" (Notebook 2, Sermon 116); *NPSP* 3:154; 5:203; *MTP* 18:198; 28:198; 29:504; 41:593; and 63:112.

13. Charles originally spelled this word "reconcling." He corrected the misspelling by inserting the letter "i" between the "c" and the "l."

14. Cf. Rom 5:1; 2 Cor 5:8.

15. "'Why,' says one, 'I have not been a believer more than a week.' I do not care if you have not been a believer more than ten minutes: he that believeth hath everlasting life and everlasting love" (*MTP* 30:129). Cf. 1 John 1:9.

16. Cf. Rom 3:24; 5:1; Gal 2:16.   17.   Cf. 1 John 1:7.

18. "Remember that our Lord Jesus has not come to make us live at peace with sin. . . . We must have 'war to the knife' with that which would rob God of his glory and men of their salvation. Our peace is on the footing of righteousness, and on no other ground" (*MTP* 30:129).

19. Cf. 2 Thess 2:8; Rev 19:15.

20. Cf. Rev 21:14. An alternative reading of this line is "but to his saints [he will display] his peace in heaven's profound peace."

43   Psalm. 72. 6.   Jesus the Shower from heaven

This Psalm was written like some others as prophetic of Messiah. The figure refers perhaps to the heavy dews as well as to the Showers _____

I Jesus is like to rain — Jesus in his gracious operations

1. Pure, as the rain is pure so the grace of Jesus is pure and holy, unadulterated, purifying.

2. Life giving. the parched and arid plains put on life at the coming of the rain — so does the soul.

3. Restoring — it makes the drooping revive and put on life afresh so Jesus revives the dying soul.

4. It is necessary both to beauty and existence.

II. Jesus is like rain in the manner of his descent.

1. It comes from heaven so must true grace.

2. It comes sovereignly at God's appointment not under man's governance but Gods.

3. It enters, penetrates, dwells in the man.

4. It sometimes comes gently, imperceptibly & but sometimes in a Storm & tempest.

5. It falls not every where, men cover themselves from it: it is on the Bible, in the Sanctuary and at prayer it comes. We should keep ourselves where this rain falls although we cannot control it.

62. 73.

JESUS, *the* SHOWER *from* HEAVEN
Psalm 72:6[1]

"He shall come down like rain upon the mown grass; as showers that water the earth."

This Psalm was written like some others as prophetic of Messiah. The figure refers perhaps to the heavy dews as well as to the showers.

I. JESUS IS LIKE[2] TO RAIN. JESUS IN HIS GRACIOUS OPERATION:

1. Pure. As the rain is pure so the grace of Jesus is pure and holy,[3] unadulterated, purifying.

2. Life giving.[4] The parched and arid plains put on life at the coming of the rain. So does the soul.

3. Restoring.[5] It makes the drooping revive and put on life afresh. So Jesus revives the dying soul.

4. It is necessary both to beauty and existence.

II. JESUS IS LIKE RAIN IN THE MANNER OF HIS DESCENT.

1. It comes from heaven.[6] So must true grace.[7]

2. It comes sovereignly at God's appointment.[8] Not under man's governance but God's.

3. It enters, penetrates, dwells in the man.[9]

4. It sometimes comes gently,[10] imperceptibly,

5. but sometimes in a storm and tempest.[11]

5. It falls not every where.[12] Men cover themselves from it. It is on the Bible, in the sanctuary, and at prayer it comes.[13]

We should keep ourselves where this rain falls although we cannot control it.

62. 73.

1. This is the only time Charles preached a sermon on Ps 72:6. However, similar themes are found in his sermon on Deut 32:2 entitled "Small Rain for Tender Herbs" (*MTP* 33, Sermon 1999). In his exposition of Ps 72:6 in *The Treasury of David*, Charles placed more emphasis on the "mown grass" than he did on the "showers that water the earth." Overlapping content is found in his sentence "We need to preach him more, for no shower can so refresh the nations" (*TD* 3:318). In Notebook 6, Charles began writing the outline of a sermon entitled "As the Rain Cometh Down and the Snow from Heaven" (Notebook 6, Sermon 291). However, for reasons unknown, the content of the sermon is missing.

2. Charles may also have intended to use the word "likened" here.

3. Cf. 1 Corinthians 3.   4. Cf. Luke 20:38; John 3:16; 5:21, 26.

5. Cf. Joel 2:25; 1 Pet 5:10.

6. "The reign of Christ even now is to the poor dispirited sons of men like rain upon the mown grass; and when he shall come in his glory, as he will shortly come, his coming shall be as blessed to this world as the gentle showers are to the grass that is newly mown" (*MTP* 42:70). Cf. John 3:13; 6:38, 51; 1 Thess 4:16.

7. A dark, yellow spot—likely the result of the aging process of the manuscript—is found beneath the word "grace." The spot can also be seen above the word "worthy" in the following sermon, "Elijah's Faith and Prayer" (Sermon 44).

8. Cf. 1 Cor 4:5; Phil 2:6–8.   9. Cf. Eph 3:17; Col 3:16.

10. Cf. Matt 11:29.

11. "I do not doubt that servants of God in times of danger at sea, when the huge billows have roared and the tempest has raged, and the vessel seemed likely to go to pieces, have often cheered their hearts with such a thought as this—'Now, he that holdeth the waters in the hollow of his hand, will take care of us, and cover us with his feathers, and under his wings may we trust.' Perhaps at this very moment, down in some cabin, or amidst the noise and tumult, and the raging of the ocean, when many are alarmed, there are Christians with calm faces, patiently waiting their Father's will, whether it shall be to reach the port of heaven, or to be spared to come again to land, into the midst of life's trials and struggles once more. They

feel that they are well-cared for, they know that the storm has a bit in its mouth, and that God holds it in, and nothing can hurt them; nothing can happen to them but what God permits" (*MTP* 15:650). Charles struck through the number 5 at the beginning of this line. He likely sought to include the content of this line beneath his fourth point. Cf. Mark 4:35–41.

12. Cf. John 17:9.

13. Cf. 1 Kgs 18:41–45. Elijah's faith and prayer for rain may have inspired the topic of Charles's following sermon.

1 Kings. 18. 43. Elijah's faith & prayer.   44

The Land of Israel was in drought at Elijah's own request; he has now been in prayer for its removal. His faith is strong that the answer shall come & he sends his servant to look — even seven times, while he himself wrestles with God at length the answer comes
This teaches us ⏋ the power of prayer.
It was for a temporal mercy for the glory of God, it was one man who prayed, and a whole nation is blessed.
We have friends to pray for. Some special mercy to seek. Some distress to be removed — let us remember this — God hears prayer and has often heard it.
II. Let us learn "importunity" go again 7 times there may have been some fault in our asking, or the time was not proper, or God is trying our faith, if it be a worthy object let us persevere for. 1 The thing is worth it. 2. Christ loves importunity, 3 The answer is certain.
III. Let us during prayer exercise faith.
No prayer can be acceptable without it — Faith in God, in Jesus our High Priest, in the promises.
The Prayer of faith glorifies God. —
IV. Let us look for the answer of our prayers. —
We pray & then we have done, now we ought to be expecting the answer to our prayers, and looking for it
The prophet believed even when it was only a cloud as large as a man's hand.
Exhortation to these Christian duties.

63

44

ELIJAH'S FAITH
and PRAYER
1 Kings 18:43[1]

*"And said to his servant, Go up now, look toward the sea. And he went up,
and looked, and said, There is nothing. And he said, Go again seven times."*

The land of Israel was in drought at[2] Elijah's own request.[3] He has now been in
prayer for its removal. His faith is strong that the answer shall come, and he sends
his servant to look even seven times while he himself wrestles with God at length.
The answer comes.[4] This[5] teaches us:

I. THE POWER OF PRAYER.[6] It was for a temporal mercy, for the
   glory of God. It was one man who prayed and a whole nation is blessed.
   We have friends to pray for. Some special mercy to seek. Some distress to
   be removed. Let us remember this: God hears prayer and has often heard it.[7]

II. LET US LEARN "IMPORTUNITY."[8] Go again 7 times.
   There may have been some fault in our asking,[9] or the time was not proper,
   or God is trying our faith.[10] If it be a worthy object let us persevere,[11] for

   1. The thing is worth it.

   2. Christ loves importunity.

   3. The answer is certain.

III. LET US DURING PRAYER EXERCISE FAITH. No
   prayer can be acceptable without it. Faith in God, in Jesus our High
   Priest,[12] in the promises. The Prayer of faith glorifies God.[13]

IV. LET US LOOK FOR THE ANSWER OF OUR
   PRAYERS. We pray and then we <u>have done</u>.[14] Now we ought to be
   expecting the answer to our prayers[15] and looking for it.[16] The prophet
   believed even when it was only a cloud as large as a man's hand.

Exhortation to these Christian duties.[17]

63

1. This is the only time Charles preached a sermon on 1 Kgs 18:43. On July 2, 1868, he preached a similar sermon on 1 Kgs 18:41 entitled "God's Answer to Persistent Prayer" (*MTP* 59, Sermon 3376). The similarities are found at the beginning of both sermons (cf. "I. The power of prayer" in the outline above with *MTP* 59:494–96). For additional sermons on Elijah, see "Elijah's Plea" (*MTP* 31, Sermon 1832); "Where Is the God of Elijah?" (*MTP* 44, Sermon 2596); "Elijah Fainting" (*MTP* 47, Sermon 2725); and "God's Care of Elijah" (*MTP* 57, Sermon 3264).

2. Charles originally wrote the letters "an" beneath the word "at." He may have intended to write the word "and."

3. Cf. 1 Kgs 17:1.

4. The word "comes" was written above and to the right of "answer." An alternative reading of this sentence is "While he himself wrestles with God at length, the answer comes."

5. The capital letter "H" was written beneath the "t" in the word "This." Cf. "His faith" three lines above. Charles likely intended to write the word "His."

6. "Prayer is an aspect of Spurgeon's life and ministry that has rarely been examined or given its due weight" (Morden, *Communion with Christ and His People*, 137). One of Charles's most popular sermons on prayer was "The Golden Key of Prayer" (*MTP* 11, Sermon 619). See also "The Secret of Power in Prayer" (*MTP* 34, Sermon 2002). For academic treatments of prayer in Charles's theology and ministry, see John D. Mashek, "Charles H. Spurgeon: A Study of His Theology and Practice of Prayer" (master's thesis, Concordia Theological Seminary, 1980) and Kevin W. Regal, "Charles H. Spurgeon's Theology of Prayer" (master's thesis, The Southern Baptist Theological Seminary, 2000). In 1905, Passmore & Alabaster published a collection of Charles's prayers entitled *C. H. Spurgeon's Prayers* (London: Passmore & Alabaster, 1905, The Spurgeon Library). Charles possessed numerous books on prayer in his personal library, including: T. Teignmouth Shore, *Prayer* (London: Cassell & Company, 1886, The Spurgeon Library) and Thomas Cobbet, *A Practical Discourse of Prayer. Wherein Is Handled, the Nature, the Duty, the Qualifications of Prayer; the Several Sorts of Prayer; viz. Ejaculatory, Publick, Private, and Secret Prayer. With Necessity of, and Ingagements unto Prayer. Together, with Sundry Cases of Conscience About It* (London: Thomas Newberry, 1657, The Spurgeon Library).

7. "Though unuttered and unexpressed by any sounds which could reach a human ear, yet God hears the breathing of his servant's soul, and hides not his ear from it" (*MTP* 54:122). Cf. 1 John 5:14–15.

8. "Incessant solicitation" (Johnson's *Dictionary*, s.v. "importunity").

9. "How much, alas, is there of *impurity of motive* to mar our prayers! We ask for revival, but we want our own church to get the blessing, that we may have the credit of it. We pray God to bless our work, and it is because we wish to hear men say what good workers we are. The prayer is good in itself, but our smutty fingers spoil it" (*MTP* 54:125, italics in the original). Cf. Jas 4:3.

10. Cf. Ps 66:10–12; Isa 48:10; Zech 13:9; Heb 11:17–19.

11. Cf. Ps 40:1; Luke 11:5–10; Eph 6:18.

12. "If he cannot go with us through all the rough places of our pilgrim-way, how can he be our guide? If he has never travelled in the night himself, how can he whisper consolation to us in our darkest hours? We have a fully qualified High Priest in our Lord Jesus Christ: he is perfect in that capacity" (*MTP* 32:590).

13. Cf. John 14:13.

14. It is not evident whether Charles intended to strike through or underscore the words "have done." The latter interpretation is more likely.

15. Cf. "Constant, Instant, Expectant" (*MTP* 25, Sermon 1480).

16. The word "it" trails into the margin.

17. Charles did not offer a final exhortation in this sermon. However, at the conclusion of his 1868 sermon on Elijah, he said, "Fall flat upon the promise which he gives you in his dear Son, and surely so doing you shall feel that great rain for which your thirsty soul is longing, for the very invitation is a sound of abundance of rain" (*MTP* 59:501).

45   Hos. 13 – 9   The Author's of Damnation & Salvation

The Subject may be easily divided into.

I   The Sinner's destruction. –

1. Sinner's are destroyed now. Man is not what he was. His passions, his heart is depraved. His judgement his whole soul is depraved

2. Sinners destroy themselves. God does not do it. Satan cannot. Man acts freely when he sins. The provisions of salvation cut off all reply.

3. Sinners shall suffer themselves. Friends, our county the world suffer by sin. But man suffers most himself. He shall bear his sin, —

II. A Sinner's Salvation

1. There is hope even for souls thus destroyed, But 2. This is in God alone. Not in our righteousness – not in our own strength. It is all of God both 1 in planning salvation

2 In providing salvation. Jesus did it all. no help is needed by Jesus, no penance.

3. All of him in the application. The Gospel provisions will be of no avail unless applied by the Spirit. The will is averse to good. none but a divine power can turn the heart. —

This teaches the duty of Submission. Penitence Shows us our dependance on God alone.

64. 66. 587.

The AUTHORS[1] *of*
DAMNATION *and* SALVATION
Hosea 13:9[2]

"O Israel, thou hast destroyed thyself; but in me is thine help."

The Subject may be easily divided into:

I. THE SINNER'S DESTRUCTION.

1. Sinners[3] <u>are</u> destroyed now. Man is not what he was.[4] His passions, his heart is depraved.[5] His judgment,[6] his whole soul is depraved.[7]

2. <u>Sinners</u> destroy themselves. God does not do it. Satan cannot. Man acts freely when he sins.[8] The provisions of salvation cut off all reply.

3. Sinners shall suffer <u>themselves</u>. Friends, our country, the world suffer by sin. But man suffers most himself. He shall bear his sin.[9]

II. A SINNER'S SALVATION.

1. There is hope even for souls thus destroyed. But

2. This is in God alone. Not in our righteousness.[10] Not in our own strength.[11] It is all of God, both

   1. In planning salvation.[12]

   2. In providing salvation.[13] Jesus did it all. No help is needed by Jesus.[14] No penance.

   3. All of <u>him</u> in the application. The Gospel provisions will be of no avail unless applied by the Spirit.[15] The will is averse to good.[16] None but a divine power can turn the heart.[17] This teaches the duty of Submission.[18] Penitence shows us our dependence on God alone.

64. 66. 587.

1. Charles inserted an apostrophe between the letters "r" and "s" in the word "Authors." He may have intended the title of this sermon to read "The Author's Damnation and Salvation." Charles's use of apostrophes throughout this sermon is inconsistent (cf. "The Sinner's Destruction" in the first Roman numeral with the word "Sinners" beneath it). Charles likely intended the word "Authors" in the title to be plural, not possessive.

2. On August 11, 1887, Charles preached an additional sermon on Hos 13:9 entitled "Self-Destroyed, yet Saved" (*MTP* 41, Sermon 2425). Structural similarities exist in the first and second Roman numerals in the outline above. Cf. "The Sinner's destruction" with "First, then, here is a Sad Fact: 'O Israel, thou hast destroyed thyself'" (*MTP* 41:374). Cf. also "A Sinner's salvation" with "Here is, secondly, A Hopeful Assurance: 'But in me is thine help'" (*MTP* 41:378). Charles added a third Roman numeral in the later sermon: "An Instructive Warning: 'It is thy destruction, O Israel, that thou art against me, against thy help'" (*MTP* 41:380). These commonalities suggest Charles had the above outline in mind when writing his 1887 sermon.

3. Charles originally inserted an apostrophe between the "r" and "s" in the word "Sinners." The context suggests Charles intended this word to be plural, not possessive. See also the word "Authors" in the title of the sermon "The Authors of Damnation and Salvation."

4. Cf. Genesis 3; Rom 3:12, 23.   5. Cf. Jer 17:9.

6. Cf. Rom 8:7; Col 1:21.   7. Cf. Ps 51:5; Rom 5:12.

8. See "Sovereign Grace and Man's Responsibility" (*NPSP* 4, Sermon 207).

9. Cf. Ezek 18; Gal 6:5.   10. Cf. Phil 3:9.

11. Cf. 2 Tim 1:9.   12. Cf. Eph 1:4; 1 Pet 1:20.

13. Cf. Eph 1:7.

14. An alternative reading of this line is "No help is needed [in addition to] Jesus."

15. Cf. Rom 5:5; 1 Cor 6:11; Eph 1:13. See Charles's pneumatological comments on the title page of this notebook and also in his sermon "The Eloquence of Jesus" (Sermon 49).

16. Cf. Rom 7:15.   17. Cf. 2 Pet 1:3.

18. Cf. Jas 4:7.

Simeon 42. 1. Pet. 1. 3-5. Regeneration its causes and effects. 46

The Ungodly may be patient, but seldom joyful in affliction

Their happiness depends on outward circumstances but the regenerate have always reason to rejoice — Those to whom the apostle wrote were scattered by persecution, yet he begins his epistle, not in terms of pity but of praise & thanksgiving —

I. The Causes of regeneration

1. The efficient cause "God" — It can be no one else. He was under the law the God of Abraham but now "of our Lord Jesus Christ" He is our father by Creation and regeneration.

2. The final cause — "our eternal happiness" — A lively hope now not a carnal hope — and an inheritance hereafter.
   Not corruptible as "earthly treasure which moth & rust corrupt".
   Not defiled like the Canaan of old. —
   Not fading by use, age, or enjoyment like the pleasures of sense

3. The instrumental cause Jesus Christ. By his resurrection. by his death as witnessed to be accepted by his resurrection.

4. The moving cause "mercy". Mercy not merit. the conversion of a soul is a marvellous miracle of mercy yea abundant mercy.

II. The security of the regenerate

Some of God's people doubt whether God will give them the inheritance
Others fear they shall fall short through sin.

But. The inheritance is "reserved for them" earthly crowns can boast no security but this is out of danger.

they are "kept" "garrisoned" surrounded by a fort. when they commit themselves by faith to God.

Infer. 1. How happy God's people are here. Their change, their prospects, their security must ever be a source of happiness under all distress.

2. How happy the regenerate will be. The very hope of it now fills them with joy, how much will the full fruition

This is only for those who are "born again"

65

Simeon, 42.[1]

46

REGENERATION, ITS CAUSES *and* EFFECTS
1 Peter 1:3–5[2]

"Blessed be the God and Father of our Lord Jesus Christ, which, according to his abundant mercy, hath begotten us again unto a lively hope, by the resurrection of Jesus Christ from the dead, To an inheritance incorruptible, and undefiled, and that fadeth not away, reserved in heaven for you. Who are kept by the power of God, through faith unto salvation, ready to be revealed in the last time."

The Ungodly may be patient but seldom joyful in affliction. Their happiness depends on outward circumstances, but the regenerate have always reason to rejoice. Those to whom the apostle wrote were scattered by persecution.[3] Yet he begins his epistle, not in terms of pity, but of praise[4] and thanksgiving.[5]

I. THE CAUSES OF REGENERATION.

1.   The efficient cause: "God."[6] It can be no one else. He was under the law, the God of Abraham.[7] But now, "of our Lord Jesus Christ." He is our father by Creation and regeneration.[8]

2. The final cause: "our eternal happiness."[9] <u>A lively</u> hope now, not a carnal hope.[10] And an inheritance hereafter. Not corruptible as "earthly treasure which moth and rust corrupt."[11] Not defiled like the Canaan of old.[12] Not fading by use, age, or enjoyment like the pleasures of sense.

3. The instrumental cause: Jesus Christ.[13] By his resurrection, by his death as witnessed to be accepted by his resurrection.[14]

4. The moving cause: "mercy." Mercy, not merit.[15] The conversion of a soul is a marvellous miracle of mercy,[16] yea, abundant mercy.

II. THE SECURITY OF THE REGENERATE.

Some of God's people doubt whether God will give them the inherita[nce].[17] Others fear they shall fall short through sin,[18] but the inheritance is "reserved for them."[19] Earthly crowns can boast no security,[20] but this is out of danger. They are "Kept," "garrisoned,[21] surrounded by a fort[22] when they commit themselves by faith to God.[23] Infer.[24]

1. How happy God's people are here. Their change, their prospects, their security must ever be a source of happiness under all distress.[25]

2. How happy the regenerate will be. The very hope of it now fills them with joy. How much will the ful[l][26] fruition.[27] This is only for those who are "born again."[28]

65[29]

1.   This is the second outline Charles borrowed from Charles Simeon in this notebook (see also "The Son's Love to Us Compared with God's Love to Him" [Sermon 38]). This is also the second sermon on the subject of regeneration in which Charles relied heavily on the works of an author (see Charles's use of John Gill in "Regeneration" [Sermon 7]). In the sermon above, Charles borrowed from Simeon's forty-second sermon outline entitled "Regeneration Considered in Its Causes and Benefits" (Simeon, *Helps to Composition*, 1:364–67). At times Charles used Simeon's words verbatim. The overlapping content is noted below. When quoted, the excessive em dashes and brackets that Simeon included have been minimized.

2.   On August 28, 1870, Charles preached an additional sermon on 1 Pet 1:3–5 entitled "A String of Pearls" (*MTP* 16, Sermon 948). There is not enough overlapping content or structural similarity to suggest Charles had the outline above in mind during the writing of his 1870 sermon.

3.   Cf. 1 Pet 1:1.   4.   Cf. 1 Pet 1:3.

5.   "The ungodly may be patient, but are seldom joyful, in affliction—Their happiness almost entirely depends on outward circumstances—But the regenerate have sources of joy peculiar to themselves—Nor can they be in any state wherein they have not abundant cause to bless God—The persons to whom St. Peter wrote, were scattered abroad, and in a state of persecution—Yet he begins his epistle to them, not in terms of pity and condolence, but of praise and thanksgiving" (Simeon, *Helps to Composition*, 1:364–65).

6.   A smudge, likely the result of a malfunction of the writing instrument, appears after the letter "d" in the word "God."

7.   An alternative reading of this line is, "He was under the law [of] the God of Abraham."

8.   "And he certainly is the Father of our spirits, both in their first formation, and in their subsequent renovation" (Simeon, *Helps to Composition*, 1:365).

9.   Here Charles altered the wording of the KJV. The original wording reads "to an inheritance incorruptible."

10. A lack of punctuation after the word "now" makes compelling the alternative reading, "Now, not a carnal hope."

11. Matt 6:19, "Lay not up for yourselves treasures upon earth, where moth and rust doth corrupt, and where thieves break through and steal."

12. "Not defiled, like the earthly Canaan, by wicked inhabitants" (Simeon, *Helps to Composition*, 1:365).

13. "Christ is the medium of every blessing, whether of grace or glory" (ibid.).

14. "His resurrection assured to us the acceptance of his sacrifice—It is also a pledge and earnest of the resurrection of all his members—Besides, it enables him both to intercede for us, and to send the Spirit to us" (ibid., 1:366).

15. "God has not respect to any goodness or merit in the creature—He is actuated only by his own grace and 'mercy'" (ibid.).

16. Charles departed from Simeon's wording: "Of this the conversion of a soul is a marvellous display" (ibid.). Charles later said, "[I]n the deepest sense, it is indeed a work to convert a soul. If Niagara could suddenly be made to leap upward instead of for ever dashing downward from its rocky height, it were not such a miracle as to change the perverse will and the raging passions of men" (*MTP* 15:290).

17. The final letters of the word "inheritance" trail into the margin.

18. Charles replaced Simeon's word "frailty" with "sin."

19. Here Charles altered the words of the KJV. The original reads "reserved in heaven for you."

20. "Earthly inheritances may be taken away by fraud and violence—Not even crowns or kingdoms can boast of any stability" (Simeon, *Helps to Composition*, 1:366).

21. Charles inserted quotation marks around the words "kept" and "garrisoned." The phrase "kept garrisoned" is not found in 1 Pet 1:3–5 but is similar to Simeon's wording, "God keeps them as in an impregnable garrison" (Simeon, *Helps to Composition*, 1:367). It is possible Charles used quotation marks to cite Simeon in this instance.

"Garrisoned" is from "garrison," or "to secure by fortresses" (Johnson's *Dictionary*, s.v. "garrison").

22. Charles may have been influenced by Simeon's line, "They are surrounded also with hosts of enemies" (Simeon, *Helps to Composition*, 1:366).

23. "God keeps them according to his promise—God keeps them as in an impregnable garrison—God keeps them unto their full and final salvation" (ibid., 1:366–67).

24. Abbr., "Inference." For additional examples in this notebook of Charles's use of this word, see "Future Judgment" (Sermon 6), "Gethsemane's Sorrow" (Sermon 63), and "Can Two Walk Together Unless They Are Agreed?" (Sermon 76).

25. "How happy are God's people here! The change they have experienced in regeneration is truly blessed—The prospects they enjoy are bright and glorious—Their security enhances these blessings—What then need they regard in this world?—Surely they should rejoice, though in the midst of tribulations—Let every one then, when encompassed with troubles of whatever kind, say, 'Blessed be God, who hath begotten me again'" (Simeon, *Helps to Composition*, 1:367).

26. Charles departed from Simeon's spelling of the word "full" (ibid.) by not adding an additional letter "l." See also Charles's spelling of the word "full" in his sermon "The Eloquence of Jesus" (Sermon 49).

27. "What sensations then will the full enjoyment of this inheritance excite!—What joy will that be when it is without any alloy of sin or sorrow!" (Simeon, *Helps to Composition*, 1:367) An alternative reading of this line is "How much will the ful[l] fruition [be]?"

28. "But let us remember, that 'we must be born again' in order to have any title to this inheritance—If we continue unregenerate, we shall inherit a far different portion—But if we have really experienced the new birth, we are heirs of glory—And the salvation reserved for us is 'ready to be revealed'—Let us then labour to secure this glorious inheritance—And look for it with holy ardour and eager expectation" (ibid.).

29. A cluster of dots appear on the lower right side of the page. The source of these dots is not found in previous or following sermons.

47   2 Sam. 7. 14 -- The Father and the Children.

God's promise to David will apply to every believing soul.

I. What is meant by "I will be his Father"

1. Love of the highest order. eternal, irreversible.

2. Provision for every present and future want. cleansing, clothing, healing, food, drink, attendance

3. Protection. From their numerous enemies. This God's children always need, because they always are children.

4 Instruction we are all by nature ignorant, our Father will teach us by his Holy Spirit.

5. Correction. Sin needs to be whipped out of us. God's people shall have it according to his wisdom.

6. An Inheritance is provided.

II. What is meant by " he shall be my son".

There are certain tempers. which are necessary marks of Son Ship -- as

1 Love. absolutely necessary, all other marks vain.

2. Obedience, a holy life cannot be dispensed with God will make his children obey him.

3. Trust faith in his promises of protection

4. Teachableness -- sitting at his feet to learn of him.

5. Submission to his correction, sons have this.

6. Preparation for glory, the business of our lives. _ _ _ _

69

The FATHER *and the* CHILDREN
2 Samuel 7:14[1]

"I will be his father, and he shall be my son. If he commit iniquity,
I will chasten him with the rod of men, and with the stripes of the children of men."

God's promise to David will apply to every believing soul.

I. WHAT IS MEANT BY "I WILL BE HIS[2] FATHER."

1. Love of the highest order. Eternal,[3] irreversible.

2. Provision for every present and future want: cleansing,[4] clothing,[5] healing,[6] food,[7] drink,[8] attendance.[9]

3. Protection. From their numerous enemies.[10] This God's children always need because they always are children.[11]

4. Instruction. We are all by nature ignorant.[12] Our Father will teach us by his Holy Spirit.[13]

5. Correction. Sin needs to be whipped out of us.[14] God's people shall have it according to his wisdom.

6. An Inheritance is provided.

II. WHAT IS MEANT BY "HE SHALL BE MY SON."

There are certain tempers which are necessary marks of Sonship,[15] as:

1. Love. Absolutely necessary.[16] All other marks vain.[17]

2. Obedience. A holy life cannot be dispensed with.[18] God will make his children obey him.

3. Trust. Faith in his promises of protection.

4. Teachableness. Sitting at his feet to learn of him.[19]

5. Submission to his correction.[20] Sons have this.

6. Preparation for glory,[21] the business of our lives.[22]

69

1. This is the only time Charles preached a sermon on 2 Sam 7:14. For additional sermons on Paterology, see "God, the Father of a Family" (Notebook 2, Sermon 129); "The Fatherhood of God" (*NPSP* 4, Sermon 213); "Special Thanksgiving to the Father" (*NPSP* 6, Sermon 319); "His Name—the Everlasting Father" (*MTP* 12, Sermon 724); "The Righteous Father Known and Loved" (*MTP* 23, Sermon 1378); "The Son Glorified by the Father and the Father Glorified by the Son" (*MTP* 25, Sermon 1465); "The Orphan's Father" (*MTP* 28, Sermon 1695); and "Our Heavenly Father's Pity" (*MTP* 45, Sermon 2639). The best academic treatment of Charles's Paterology to date is by German scholar Peter Spangenberg in his section "Die Unvergleichlichkeit Gottes in Sein, Attributen, Werken und Wort" (Peter Spangenberg, *Theologie und Glaube bei Spurgeon* [Gütersloh, Germany: Gütersloher Verlaghaus Gerd Mohn, 1969], 78).

2. Charles wrote the word "my" beneath "his." An alternative reading of this line is "[He] will be my Father."

3. Cf. Psalm 136. 4. Cf. Ps 51:10; Heb 10:22.

5. Cf. Gen 3:21; Isa 61:10; Matt 6:28–30; Luke 12:28.

6. Cf. Ps 103:3; Jer 30:17. 7. Cf. Prov 22:9; John 6:35.

8. Cf. Isa 44:3; Matt 6:25; John 4:13–14. 9. Cf. Ps 61:1; Phil 4:19.

10. Cf. 2 Sam 22:3–4; Ps 91:1–3; 2 Thess 3:3.

11. Cf. Luke 11:11–13. 12. Cf. Eph 4:18.

13. Cf. John 14:26; 1 John 2:27. 14. Cf. Heb 12:6, 11.

15. Charles separated the words "Son" and "Ship." He combined these two words in the following sermons: "The Spirit Crying 'Abba Father'" (Notebook 2, Sermon 91); "The Second Psalm" (Notebook 2, Sermon 101); and "Enduring Temptation" (Notebook 2, Sermon 123).

16. Cf. 1 Cor 13:13.

17. An alternative reading of this line is "Love [is] absolutely necessary. All other marks [are] vain."

18. Cf. I Pet 1:16.   19. Cf. Luke 10:39.

20. "Should not the creature be submissive to the Creator, to whom it owes its existence, without whom it had never been, and without whose continuous good pleasure it would at once cease to be?" (*MTP* 22:61). Cf. Prov 12:1.

21. Cf. Rom 9:23; I Pet 5:10.

22. An alternative reading of this line is "Preparation for glory [is] the business of our lives."

1 Tim 2.1   Intercession of the Saints.   148

No man can be a Christian who does not pray, yet some good men pray for themselves yet not for others. Now the apostle Paul corrects this — we should pray for

1. all men, universally, since God is good to all — pray that all nations may be converted and blessed in every way

2. For kings & governors, remembering the superiority of our government, and the responsibility of governors.

3. For ministers. Paul requested it much more common ministers, it will promote usefulness & mutual comfort.

4. For friends, in their particular cases, rich or poor, Moses prayed for Miriam, we should not speak ill of them.

5. For enemies. Thus shall we be like Jesus, this is one of the ways of killing enemies. plead for their salvation

6. For the oppressed, sick, poor, afflicted. Specially for the saints of God in their spiritual troubles.

Give some reasons why this should be done.

1. Because common humanity, not to say philanthropy and patriotism requires this of us

2. The universal love of the Gospel demands it.

3. Love to Christ and desire of the extension of his Kingdom should lead us to strive for it.

4. There are so many benefits to ourselves resulting from this, and so much to others that we should as for instance. enmity & hatred will soon die in our hearts.

5. The examples of the great and holy.
Abraham for Ishmael, Abimelech, & Sodom.
Moses for the transgressing Israelites.
Hezekiah for the land in danger
and our great Jesus prayed on earth & now intercedes in heaven. —

68. 282. 287.

INTERCESSION *of the* SAINTS
1 Timothy 2:1[1]

*"I exhort therefore, that, first of all, supplications, prayers, intercessions,
and giving of thanks, be made for all men."*

No man can be a Christian who does not pray. Yet some good men pray for themselves, yet not for others. Now, the apostle Paul corrects this. We should pray for:

1. All men universally since God is good to all.[2] Pray that all nations[3] may be converted and blessed in every way.

2. For kings and governors,[4] remembering the superiority of our government[5] and the responsibility of governors.

3. For ministers.[6] Paul requested it much more [for] common ministers.[7] It will promote usefulness and mutual comfort.

4. For friends in their particular cases, rich or poor.[8] Moses prayed for Miriam.[9] We should not speak ill of them.

5. For enemies.[10] Thus shall we be like Jesus.[11] This is one of the ways of killing enemies. Plead for their salvation.[12]

6. For the oppressed, sick, poor, afflicted.[13] Specially for the saints of God in their spiritual troubles.

Give some reasons why this should be done.

1. Because[14] common humanity, not to say philantropy[15] and patriotism requires this of us.

2. The universal love of the Gospel[16] demands it.

3. Love to Christ and desire of the extension of his Kingdom should lead us to strive for it.

4. There are so many benefits to ourselves resulting from this and so much to others that we should do it. As for instance, enmity and hatred will soon die in our hearts.[17]

5. The examples of the great and holy: Abraham for Ishmael,[18] Abimelech,[19] and Sodom;[20] Moses for the transgressing Israelites;[21] Hezekiah for the land in danger;[22] and our great Jesus prayed on earth[23] and now intercedes in heaven.[24]

68. 282. 287.

1. This is the only time Charles preached a sermon on 1 Tim 2:1. For additional sermons on intercession, see "Intercessory Prayer" (*MTP* 7, Sermon 404); "Intercessory Prayer" (*MTP* 18, Sermon 1049); "Samuel, an Example of Intercession" (*MTP* 26, Sermon 1537); and "Intercession and Supplication" (*MTP* 47, Sermon 2745).

2. Cf. Matt 5:45.

3. "We pray for all nations also. O Lord, bless and remember the lands that sit in darkness, and let them see a great light, and may missionary enterprise be abundantly successful. And let the favoured nations where our God is known, especially this land and the land across the mighty ocean that love the same Saviour and speak the same tongue, be always favoured with the Divine presence and with abundant prosperity and blessing" (C. H. Spurgeon and Dinsdale T. Young, *C. H. Spurgeon's Prayers* [London: Passmore & Alabaster, 1905, The Spurgeon Library], 151). See also *MTP* 41:390 and 61:31.

4. "Remember our dear country. Bless the Sovereign. Remember all those that lead our legislature. Be gracious unto all ranks and conditions of men" (*C. H. Spurgeon's Prayers*, 59). See also "Fast-Day Service" (*NPSP* 3, Sermons 154–155; for the context of this sermon, see *Autobiography* 2:239). Cf. 1 Tim 2:2.

5. By 1851, Britain had become "by far the richest country in the world" (Geoffrey Best, *Mid-Victorian Britain 1851–75* [London: Fontana Press, 1971; repr., 1988], 21). Pronational sentiment, patriotism, and British superiority were common attitudes throughout the British Empire in the 1850s, as seen in numerous newspaper articles (see *The Cambridge Chronicle and University Journal, Isle of Ely Herald, and Huntingdonshire Gazette* [October 31, 1857]). For Charles, patriotism was "one of the highest of worldly virtues" (*MTP* 13:284). For additional references to patriotism, see *MTP* 8:597; 17:315; and 30:182.

6. "We pray for Thy ministers everywhere; for Thy missionary servants. Remember brethren that are making great sacrifice out in the hot sun or in the cold and frozen north. Everywhere preserve those who for Christ's sake carry their lives in their hands" (*C. H. Spurgeon's Prayers*, 49). See also *Autobiography* 1:343; *MTP* 7:452; and 62:538.

7. A less likely alternative reading of this line is "Paul requested it much more [than] common ministers."

8. "England needs many who shall shake her and waken her out of her sleep. . . . She needs men who will preach the truth, and tell it to her poor men, ay, and to her rich men, too, and if ever we are to get these, it must be in answer to prayer" (*MTP* 60:413; see also *Autobiography* 4:128).

9. Cf. Num 12:13.

10. "We would all pray for the conversion of our worst enemy, and David would have done the same" (*TD* 5:157).

11. Cf. Matt 5:44; Luke 6:28.

12. The final letters of the word "salvation" trail into the margin.

13. "The sick bed is soft when Thou art there. The furnace of affliction grows cool when Thou art there, and the house of prayer when Thou art present is none other than the house of God, and it is the very gate of heaven" (*C. H. Spurgeon's Prayers*, 2). Cf. Jas 5:14.

14. An illegible letter was written beneath the letter "B" in the word "Because." It is possible Charles did not originally capitalize the word.

15. "Love of mankind; good nature" (Johnson's *Dictionary*, s.v. "philantropy").

16. Cf. Ezek 18:23; John 3:16.

17. Charles likely penned the final "s" beneath the line in the word "hearts" because he ran out of space in the margin.

18. Cf. Gen 17:18.

19. Cf. Gen 20:17.

20. Cf. Gen 18:20–32.

21. Cf. Exod 32:12–14.

22. Cf. 2 Kgs 20:2–5.

23. Cf. John 17.

24. Cf. Rom 8:34; Heb 7:25.

49.   John. 7. 46.   The Eloquence of Jesus

This testimony is the more valuable as coming from enemies

It relates both to his eloquent manner and sacred matter.

I. As to his manner. there are two things to be noticed.

1. The qualities of the speaker.   Incorruptible Truth.

Fidelity. — to the young man. to the rich. to his followers.

Boldness. to the people at Nazareth. Capernaum. High Priest.

Zeal. He came to do his father's work and he did it.

Prudence. Could not be entrapped. — No premature disclosure.

Wisdom. Confounding his enemies. Suited his discourses to his hearers

Humility. Woman of Samaria, Conversation with Children.

Love. Jerusalem. "Weep not for me". "Father forgive them"

2. The Characteristics of his style.

Simplicity. His discourses. Parables. Figures, to the Poor.

Seriousness. No smile or joke. Rich man and Lazarus.

Earnestness. His whole heart and soul was in it.

Directness. Vineyard & Samaritan woman. Address. Scribe & Pharisees

II. As to the matter. "never man spake like this man"

1. Important. Soul. Sin. God. Holiness. Hell. Heaven.

2. Joyful. Pardon. Redemption. Restoration. Liberty

If we compare Jesus with others he excels.

Moses. could preach law not gospel. terror not love,

Noah. preacher of righteousness not full gospel.

Nathan's personality. He excelled him in other things

Elijah needed a little gentleness & love

Jeremiah. was all pathetic. Jesus sometimes rejoiced.

    Jesus concentrated the marrow of

      all styles, the jewels of language and

      the solemnities of eternity.

Ect. 1. His small success sets forth our dependance on the Spirit

while his character is the model of a minister.

70

49

The ELOQUENCE *of* JESUS
John 7:46[1]

"The officers answered, Never man spake like this man."

This testimony is the more valuable as coming from enemies. It relates both to his eloquent manner and sacred matter.

I. AS TO HIS MANNER. There are two things to be noticed:

1. The qualities of the speaker:[2]
    Incorruptible Truth.[3]
    Fidelity: To the young man, to the rich,[4] to his followers.
    Boldness: To the people at Nazareth,[5] Capernaum,[6] High Priest.[7]
    Zeal: He came to do his father's work,[8] and he did it.
    Prudence: Could not be entrapped.[9] No premature disclosures.[10]
    Wisdom: Confounding his enemies.[11] Suited his discourses to his learner.[12]
    Humility: Woman of Samaria.[13] Conversation with Children.[14]
    Love: Jerusalem,[15] "Weep not for me,"[16] "Father, forgive them."[17]

2. The Characteristics of his style.
    Simplicity:[18] His discourses, Parables, Figures, to the Poor.
    Seriousness: No smile or joke.[19] Rich man and Lazarus.[20]
    Earnestness:[21] His whole heart and soul was in it.[22]
    Directness:[23] Vineyard,[24] Samaritan woman,[25] Adultress,[26]
        Scribe[s] and Pharisees.[27]

II. AS TO THE MATTER, "Never man spake like this man."

    1. Important: Soul, Sin, God, Holiness, Hell, Heaven.

    2. Joyful: Pardon, Redemption, Restoration, Liberty.

    If we compare Jesus with others, he excels.
        Moses could preach law,[28] not gospel; terror, not love.[29]
        Noah, preacher of righteousness,[30] not full gospel.[31]
        Nathan's personality.[32] He excelled him in other things.
        Elijah needed a little gentleness and love.[33]
        Jeremiah was all pathetic.[34] Jesus sometimes rejoiced.[35]

Jesus concentrated the marrow of all styles, the jewels of language, and the solemnities of eternity.

Yet. 1.[36] His small success sets forth our dependance[37] on the Spirit,[38] while his character is the model of a minister.

70.

1. After accepting the pastorate of New Park Street Chapel in London, Charles preached a sermon on John 7:46 entitled "The Eloquence of Jesus" [Notebook 9, Sermon 394]). This sermon was a thirteen-page expansion of the outline above. On September 18, 1870, Charles preached a third sermon on John 7:46 entitled "The Unrivalled Eloquence of Jesus" (*MTP* 16, Sermon 951). There is a significant amount of overlapping content between the above outline and the 1870 sermon; however, in his 1870 sermon Charles offered the following primary divisions instead: "The Peculiar Qualities of our Lord's eloquence;" "Some Personal Recollections of the Savior's eloquence;" and "Prophetic Anticipations which lodge in our souls with regard to that eloquence in the future" (*MTP* 16:519, 523, 526).

2. Cf. Lecture 8, "On the Voice" (*Lectures* 1:117–35).

3. Cf. John 14:6.

4. Cf. Matt 19:16–22.

5. Cf. Luke 4:16–20.

6. Cf. Mark 1:21.

7. Cf. Mark 14:53.

8. Cf. Luke 2:49; John 4:34; 6:38.

9. Cf. Luke 20:19–26.

10. The letter "s" at the end of the word "disclosures" may be a period. If this is correct, the word should be read as singular instead of plural.

11. Cf. Mark 12:13–17.

12. Like the word "disclosures" in the line above, the word "learner" trails into the margin. Charles may have intended the word to be plural, not singular.

13. Cf. John 4:1–42.

14. Cf. Luke 18:15–17.

15. Cf. Luke 13:34.

16. Cf. Luke 23:28.

17. Cf. Luke 23:34.

18. "The preacher must also mind that he preaches Christ *very simply*. He must break up his big words and long sentences, and pray against the temptation to use them. It is usually the short, dagger-like sentence that does the work best. A true servant of Christ must never try to let the people see how well he can preach; he must never go out of his way to drag a pretty piece of poetry into his sermon, nor to introduce

some fine quotations from the classics. He must employ a simple, homely style, or such a style as God has given him; and he must preach Christ so plainly that his hearers can not only understand him, but that they cannot misunderstand him even if they try to do so" (*MTP* 56:489, italics in the original). Charles also said, "[W]herever the gospel has been preached simply, not with enticing words of man's wisdom, but with the plain words of the common tongue . . . it has never failed in any place, or in any time, to draw attention to itself, to excite enquiry, and to compel men to take sides about it one way or the other" (*MTP* 60:90–91).

19. "We must be serious as death in this solemn work. There are boys and girls who are always giggling, but who never laugh; and they are the very image of certain ever-jesting preachers. I like an honest laugh; true humour can be sanctified, and those who can stir men to smile can also move them to weep. But even this has limits, which the foolish soon exceed" (*MTP* 59:189–90). The Irish actor and tutor of elocution at Stepney College, Sheridan Knowles, told his students that Charles "can do anything he pleases with his audience! He can make them laugh, and cry, and laugh again, in five minutes" (*Autobiography* 1:354; see also 2:115; 4:277). For a more thorough treatment of Charles's wit, see Richard Briscoe Cook, *The Wit and Wisdom of Rev. Charles H. Spurgeon: Containing Selections from His Writings, and a Sketch of His Life and Work* (Baltimore, MD: RH Woodward and Company, 1892).

20. Cf. Luke 16:19–31.

21. See "Earnest Expostulation" (*MTP* 29, Sermon 1714).

22. "That is what you must do with your sermons, make them red-hot; never mind if men do say you are too enthusiastic, or even too fanatical, give them a red-hot shot. . . . We do not go out snow-balling on Sundays, we go fire-balling; we ought to hurl grenades into the enemy's ranks" (C. H. Spurgeon, *The Soul-Winner; or, How to Lead Sinners to the Saviour* [New York: Fleming H. Revell, 1895], 69). Charles also said, "A pulpit may be a refrigerator, but it ought to be a furnace, or rather it should be the fire-place in the house to which all the family turn for warmth" (*ST* February 1880:58).

23. "I will give nothing for that indirect, essay-like preaching which is as the sheet lightning of summer, dazzling for the moment, and flaming over a broad expanse, but altogether harmless, since no bolt is launched from it, and its ineffectual fires leave no trace behind" (*MTP* 29:193).

24. Cf. Matt 20:1–16. It is unclear why Charles struck through the comma after the word "Vineyard." A similar redaction is found in the comma after the word "Adultress" in the same line.

25. Cf. John 4:1–42.

26. Cf. John 8:1–11. Charles originally spelled this word "Addltress." He corrected the misspelling by adding the letter "u" between the "d" and "l." The modern spelling of this word is "Adulteress."

27. See "Pharisees and Sadducees Reproved" (Sermon 39).

28. Cf. Acts 15:21.

29. An alternative reading of this line is "Moses could preach law, [but] not gospel. [He could preach] terror, [but] not love."

30. Cf. 2 Pet 2:5.

31. An alternative reading of this line is "Noah [was the] preacher of righteousness, [but he could] not [preach the] full gospel."

32. Cf. 2 Sam 12:1–13; 1 Kgs 1:10–12.   33. Cf. 1 Kgs 18:25–29.

34. Samuel Johnson defined the word "pathetik" as "affecting the passions; passionate; moving" (Johnson's *Dictionary*). Cf. Jer 4:19–21.

35. Cf. Luke 10:21.

36. By inserting the number 1, Charles may have intended to begin a list.

37. The bolded letter "c" suggests Charles wrote the final letter "e" in the word "dependance" prematurely.

38. See the phrase "And only skeletons without the Holy Ghost" on the title page of this notebook.

Isaiah 55.7.   Repentance and Salvation.   30

Isaiah the evangelical prophet. herein exhorts men to repent.
Repentance is sorrow for sin. and hatred of it.
  it is also a turning from sin, leaving even wrong thoughts
  it is a returning to God and seeking forgiveness.
I. But repentance does not deserve salvation for.
  1. This is always ascribed to the mercy of God.   — innocent
  2. It does not agree with divine justice to treat the guilty
  3. Human governments do not do so.
  4. God's providential dealings do not act thus.
  5. Repentance is imperfect
  6. Such a doctrine would open the floodgates of sin
II. But yet sin cannot be pardoned without it
  1. God never has done so. pardon & holiness go together.
  2. The threatnings imply this. God says he will punish sin
III. God will forgive those who turn. for.
  1. Many Scriptures affirm. it
  2. This was the purpose of Jesus death.
  3. The innumerable multitude of instances.
a call to repentance on this account.
Abundant pardon for abundant sin.
      1. The necessity of atonement.
      2. The folly of impenitence.
      3. The great mercy of God.

71

50

REPENTANCE *and* SALVATION
Isaiah 55:7[1]

"Let the wicked forsake his way, and the unrighteous man his thoughts: and let him return unto the Lord, *and he will have mercy upon him; and to our God, for he will abundantly pardon."*

Isaiah, the evangelical prophet, herein exhort[s] men to repent. Repentance is sorrow for sin and hatred of it. It is also a turning from sin, leaving even wrong thoughts. It is a returning to God[2] and seeking[3] forgiveness.

I. BUT REPENTANCE DOES NOT DESERVE SALVATION, for
   1. This is always ascribed to the mercy of God.[4]
   2. It does not agree with divine justice to treat the guilty as innocent.[5]
   3. Human governments do not do so.
   4. God's providential dealings do not act thus.
   5. Repentance is imperfect.
   6. Such a doctrine would open the floodgates of sin.

II. BUT YET, SIN CANNOT BE PARDONED WITHOUT IT.
   1. God never has done so. Pardon and holiness go together.[6]
   2. The threat[e]nings[7] imply this. God says he will punish sin.[8]

III. GOD WILL FORGIVE THOSE WHO TURN, for
   1. Many Scriptures affirm it.[9]
   2. This was the purpose of Jesus['s] death.[10]
   3. The innumerable multitudes of instances.[11]

A call to repentance on this account.[12] Abundant pardon for abundant sin.
   1. The necessity of atonement.[13]
   2. The folly of impenitence.
   3. The great mercy of God.

71

1. Charles preached two additional sermons on Isa 55:7: "Abundant Pardon" (*MTP* 20, Sermon 1195) and "The Need and Nature of Conversion" (*MTP* 48, Sermon 2797). He also preached a sermon on Isa 55:7–9 entitled "God Forgiving Sin" (*MTP* 36, Sermon 2181). These three sermons share common subjects; however, there is not enough overlapping content or structural similarity among them to suggest Charles used the outline above in their composition. For additional sermons on repentance, see "Repentance Unto Life" (*NPSP* 1, Sermon 44); "Judgments and No Repentance: Repentance and No Salvation" (*MTP* 34, Sermon 2054); "Repentance after Conversion" (*MTP* 41, Sermon 2419); "Mistaken Notions about Repentance" (*MTP* 47, Sermon 2743); "God's Goodness Leading to Repentance" (*MTP* 49, Sermon 2857); and "Repentance and Remission" (*MTP* 56, Sermon 3224).

2. Cf. Joel 2:12.

3. A cluster of dots surround the letter "s" in the word "seeking." The source of the dots is not evident.

4. Cf. Titus 3:5.

5. Charles wrote the word "innocent" above the line, likely to avoid having to roll it onto the next line and thereby misaligning the structure of his list.

6. Cf. 1 John 1:9.

7. Charles originally spelled this word "threatnings." When compared to other uses of the word such as "his rewards and threatenings" in the sermon "God's Estimation of Men" (Sermon 41), it becomes evident the correct spelling is "threatenings."

8. Cf. Rom 2:6–10; 2 Cor 5:10; Rev 20:12.

9. Cf. 2 Chron 7:14; Jonah 3:4; Acts 3:19; 5:31; 2 Pet 3:9; 1 John 1:9.

10. Cf. Luke 19:10; John 10:10; 18:37; 1 Tim 1:15.

11. Cf. Ps 103:12; Isa 43:25; Dan 9:9; Mic 7:18–19; Matt 26:28; Col 1:13–14; Heb 8:12.

12. See "Necessity of Purity for an Entrance to Heaven" (Sermon 2).

13. Cf. Heb 9:12.

51   Psalm. 1-2-3. Christian Prosperity and its causes.
Christian prosperity one of the aims of a Gospel ministry.
The Psalmist describes a prosperous Christian & gives advice as to
I . The Character here described . here is   the arriving at the same

1 . Fatness, absence of want, food convenient & sufficient, to such
a man, the word, prayer, the ordinances will be rivers of water
his soul will be satisfied enjoying Divine manifestation & communion
2 . Healthful-growth. upward in love, downward in humility
he is increasing in all graces and in spiritual strength.
3 . Stability, he is "setfast", trees are sometimes carried down
rivers, he is stedfast. – neither adversity no prosperity can move
him. he is stedfast in principle, doctrine, and action.
4 . Fruitfulness - to God' glory he brings forth good works and
these are "in season", when required, meekness under scorn,
faith under trial, patience in endurance.
5 . Happiness – marked contrast near water courses,
a flourishing Christian will be happy
II . The means for arriving at this state

1 . Avoiding evil.
   α . Not holding the principles of ungodly men, men without God.
   β . Not acting in the same way as sinners, or open transgressors.
   γ . Not favouring, association with scorners, or contemners of religion
      gradation "walk", "stand", "sit" — "ungodly", "sinners", "scorners"
2 . Cleaving to good .
   α . Delight in God's law, it may include the moral law,
but it means the whole Christian dispensation.
   a delight and love to the truth, necessary to prosperity
   β . meditation on divine things is like ruminating it
by day it is good to take some passage and think on
by night, to think on him when we may –
Exhortation to a diligent use of these means in
order that the end may be attained ——

74 .

(51)

CHRISTIAN PROSPERITY
and ITS CAUSES
Psalm 1:1–3[1]

"Blessed is the man that walketh not in the counsel of the ungodly,
nor standeth in the way of sinners, nor sitteth in the seat of the scornful:
But his delight is in the law of the LORD; *and in his law doth he meditate day and night.*
And he shall be like a tree planted by the rivers of water, that bringeth forth his fruit
in his season; his leaf also shall not wither; and whatsoever he doeth shall prosper."

Christian prosperity, one of the aims of a Gospel ministry.[2] The Psalmist describes a prosperous Christian, and give[s][3] advice as to the arriving at the same.[4]

I. THE CHARACTER HERE DESCRIBED. Here is:

1. Fatness, absence of want. Food convenient and sufficient.[5] To such a man, the word, prayer, the ordinances[6] will be rivers of water. His soul will be satisfied enjoying Divine manifestation and communion.[7]

2. Healthful growth. Upward in love,[8] downward in humility.[9] He is increasing in all graces and in spiritual strength.

3. Stability. He is "set fast."[10] Trees are sometimes carried down rivers.[11] He is ste[a]dfast.[12] Neither adversity nor prosperity can move him. He is ste[a]dfast in principle, doctrine, and action.

4. Fruitfulness. To God's glory he brings forth good works,[13] and these are "in season." When required: meekness under scorn,[14] faith under trial,[15] patience in endurance.[16]

5. Happiness. Marked contrast near water courses.[17] A flourishing Christian will be happy.

II. THE MEANS FOR ARRIVING AT THIS STATE:

1. Avoiding evil.[18]

   α.[19]Not holding the principles of ungodly men, men without God.

   β. Not acting in[20] the same way as sinners[21] or open transgressors.

   γ. Not favouring, associating with scorners[22] or contemners[23] of religion.[24] Grad[u]ation:[25] "walk," "stand," "sit," "ungodly," "sinners," "scorners."[26]

2. Cleaving to good.

   1.[27]Delight in God's law. It may include the moral law,[28] but it means the whole Christian dispensation.

   a. Delight and love to the truth. Necessary to prosperity.[29]

   b. Meditation on divine things is like ruminating it.[30] By day,[31] it is good to take some passage and think on. By night, to think on him when we may.[32]

Exhortation to a diligent use of these means in order[33] that the end may be attained.

74.

1. On November 14, 1864, Charles preached an additional sermon on Ps 1:1–3 entitled "The Truly Blessed Man" (*MTP* 57, Sermon 3270). The overlapping content suggests the later sermon was an expanded version of the outline above. The most noticeable similarities are found in "I. Who the 'Blessed Man' Is" (*MTP* 57:469); "II. What the 'Blessed Man' Avoids" (*MTP* 57:471); and "III. Wherein the 'Blessed Man' Delights" (*MTP* 57:472). For additional sermons on Christian prosperity, see "Peace at Home, and Prosperity Abroad" (*NPSP* 6, Sermon 314); "Prosperity Under Persecution" (*MTP* 17, Sermon 997); "Zion's Prosperity" (*MTP* 44, Sermon 2576); and "Unmitigated Prosperity" (*MTP* 51, Sermon 2963).

2. "It is not outward prosperity which the Christian most desires and values; it is soul prosperity which he longs for" (*TD* 1:2). An alternative reading of this line is "Christian prosperity [is] one of the aims of a gospel ministry."

3. An illegible letter is written beneath the "g" in the word "give."

4. The phrase "give[s] advice as to the arriving at the same" was written in a smaller script, which suggests Charles likely either ran out of space or added it afterward. The former interpretation is more likely.

5. An alternative reading of this sentence is "Food [is] convenient and sufficient."

6. See "God's Estimation of Men" (Sermon 41).

7. The final letters of the word "communion" trail into the margin.

8. Cf. Rom 12:10.

9. Cf. John 3:30; Phil 2:3.

10. "Firm; immovable" (Johnson's *Dictionary*, s.v. "fast").

11. In 1852, a newspaper article recorded that the River Cam in Cambridge had flooded its banks (see "The Floods," *The Cambridge Chronicle and University Journal, Isle of Ely Herald, and Huntingdonshire Gazette* [November 20, 1852]). Charles may have had a similar instance in mind when he wrote the line, "Trees are sometimes carried down rivers."

12. "'*And he shall be like a tree planted;*' not a wild tree, but 'a tree *planted*,' chosen, considered as property, cultivated and secured from the last terrible uprooting, for 'every plant, which my heavenly Father hath not planted, shall be rooted up.' Matthew xv. 13" (*TD* 1:2, italics in the original).

13. Cf. Luke 6:43.   14. Cf. Prov 3:34.

15. Cf. Jas 1:3.   16. Cf. Rom 5:3–4; 2 Pet 1:6.

17. "Not a tree in the desert, but placed where the rivulets come rippling to his roots" (*MTP* 57:475).

18. "It is chiefly here that the godly man differs from others. He does not consider first how the world regards a thing, but how God looks at it" (*MTP* 57:471). Cf. Ps 101:4.

19. Charles incorporated four types of ordering techniques in this sermon: Greek letters (alpha, beta, gamma), Roman numerals, English letters, and cardinal numbers. A previous example of his diverse ordering techniques is found in the sermon "Condescending Love of Jesus" (Sermon 5).

20. Charles originally wrote the word "on." He added a tittle above the letter "o" to correct the mistake and construct the word "in."

21. Cf. Ezek 18:34.   22. Cf. 1 Cor 5:9–11.

23. "One that contemns; a despiser; a scorner" (Johnson's *Dictionary*, s.v. "contemner").

24. The letter "n" in the word "religion" trails into the margin.

25. By using the word "Graduation," Charles was emphasizing the progressing postures of the sinner: one who walks, then stands, and finally sits.

26. The words "ungodly," "sinners," and "scorners" correspond to the one who "walks," "stands," and "sits." Charles changed the word "scornful" in Ps 1:1 to "scorners."

27. To begin his list, Charles wrote the number 1 and then the letter "a" before the word "Delight." His use of English letters in the remainder of the list suggests he intended the letter "a" to begin the list. It is not clear why Charles used this letter again two lines below; either he intended to expand on his first point or

replace it. If the former interpretation is correct, the second point should correctly be listed by the letter "b," and the third point should be listed by the letter "c." In 1864, Charles said, "David had not a fourth of what we possess; it was a very little Bible then, but it has gone on increasing like a majestic river, until it is the wondrous volume we have. We, therefore, should take ten times more delight in it than the Psalmist did" (*MTP* 57:473).

28. See "The Perpetuity of the Law of God" (*MTP* 28, Sermon 1660).

29. An alternative reading of this line is "Delight and love to the truth [are] necessary to prosperity."

30. An alternative reading of this line is "Meditat[ing] on divine things is like ruminating [on] it."

31. The letter "d" in the word "day" was smudged toward the bottom of the page. The smudge was likely the result of a malfunction of the writing instrument. A similar smudge is found beneath the letter "b" in the word "been" in the following sermon, "He Took Not Up Angels" (Sermon 52).

32. "He takes a text and carries it with him all day long; and in the night-watches, when sleep forsakes his eyelids, he museth upon the Word of God. In the *day* of his prosperity he sings *psalms* out of the Word of God, and in the *night* of his affliction he comforts himself with *promises* out of the same book" (*TD* 1:2, italics in the original). See also "Songs in the Night" (*MTP* 44, Sermon 2558).

33. The letter "d" in the word "order" was smudged.

Heb. 2.16. "He took not up angels." 52

We shall notice the two senses.

I. He did not appear in the form & nature of an angel. here was amazing condescension and wisdom.
1. He could not have died in any other nature
2. He could not have become a perfect pattern for us.
3. He would not be one with his Church & brethren and so
4. Could not have sympathized with us.
5. The human race would not have been so honoured
6. Nor should we have had a pledge of resurrection.

II. He did not save angels. here is sovereign grace.
They were both sinners, both deserving eternal wrath.
There was no reason why man & not Satan should be chosen
1. They were perhaps equal in sin. there was pride, discontent, evil thoughts, rebellion, robbery. Man was tempted but perhaps some devils were & the prize was greater. Satan had more light but man had light enough.
2. There was no more to excite mercy in one case than another Satan had even fallen farthest. Satan could not be more ungratefull Neither of them sued for mercy. Satan will suffer as much as if not more than man.
3. Satan had greater powers of mind and intellect than man he was not subject to the physical infirmities of man and consequently if saved, he could, humanly speaking, have served God better, and again there would not have been such obstacles to his sanctification, man could not have been such a tempter to the devil, owing to his nature, God's mightiest foe would have thus been conquered. His would have been only a restoration man's salvation is a sort of revolution. He would have been an apt scholar. Yet God to manifest the sovereignty of his grace chose man. Learn hence the justice of Election as well as its grace and in receiving the Sacrament let us consider these things.

75

52

HE TOOK NOT UP ANGELS
~~Rom~~[1] Hebrews 2:16[2]

"For verily he took not on him the nature of angels; but he took on him the seed of Abraham."

We shall notice the two senses:

I. HE DID NOT APPEAR IN THE FORM AND NATURE OF AN ANGEL.
    Here was amazing condescension[3] and wisdom.

    1. He could not have died in any other nature.[4]

    2. He could not have become a perfect pattern for us.

    3. He would not be one with his Church and brethren,[5] and so

    4. Could not have sympathized with us.[6]

    5. The human race would not have been so honoured.[7]

    6. Nor should we have had a pledge of resurrection.[8]

II. HE DID NOT SAVE ANGELS. Here is sovereign grace.
They were both sinners, both[9] deserving eternal wrath.[10] There was no reason why man and not Satan should be chosen.

1. They were perhaps equal in sin. There was pride,[11] discontent, evil thoughts, re-bellion, robbery. Man was tempted, but perhaps some devils were, and the prize was greater. Satan had more light,[12] but man had light enough.

2. There was no more to excite mercy in one case than another. Satan had even fallen farthest.[13] Neither of them sued for mercy. Satan could not be more un-grateful. Satan will suffer as much as, if not more than, man.[14]

3. Satan had greater powers of mind and intellect than man. He was not subject to the physical infirmities of man, and consequently, if saved, he could, humanly speaking, have served God better. And again, there would not have been[15] such obstacles to his sanctification. Man could not have been such a tempter to the devil, owing to his nature. God's mightiest foe would have thus been conquered. His would have been only a restoration.[16] Man's salvation is a sort of revolution. He would have been an apt scholar.[17] Yet God, to manifest the sovereignty of his grace, chose man.

Learn hence the justice of Election as well as its grace, and in receiving the Sacrament[18] let us consider these things.

75

1. Charles originally wrote the word "Rom" before striking through it. If he had intended to preach from Rom 2:16, the verse would read, "In the day when God shall judge the secrets of men by Jesus Christ according to my gospel."

2. On March 18, 1856, Charles preached an additional sermon on Heb 2:16 entitled "Men Chosen—Fallen Angels Rejected" (*NPSP* 2, Sermon 90). The structural similarities suggest Charles used the outline above when writing his later sermon. For additional sermons on angels, see "Angels Charged with Folly" (Notebook 8, Sermon 360); "The Angelic Life" (*MTP* 14, Sermon 842); "Angelic Studies" (*MTP* 16, Sermon 933); "Mahanaim, or Hosts of Angels" (*MTP* 26, Sermon 1544); "Fallen Angels a Lesson to Fallen Men" (*MTP* 31, Sermon 1820); "Angelic Interest in the Gospel" (*MTP* 46, Sermon 2697); and "Angelic Protection in Appointed Ways" (*MTP* 52, Sermon 2969).

3. "[H]*e did not stoop to the intermediate step of angel-ship, but he stooped right down and became a man*" (*NPSP* 2:290, italics in the original).

4. "Gabriel, if I were in thy dress I could not fight with death; I could not sleep in the tomb; I could not feel the pangs and agony of dissolution, therefore, I must, I will, become a man" (ibid., 2:291).

5. "Once more, Christ became a man, and not an angel, *because he desired to be one with his dear church.* Christ was betrothed to his church ere time began; and when he came into the world he virtually said, 'I will go with thee, my bride, and I will delight myself in thy company[.] Angels' garments were not a fitting wedding dress for me to wear'" (ibid., italics in the original).

6. "Sweetly, also, let us remember that if Christ had been an angel, *he could not have sympathised with us.* In order to sympathise with our fellow-creatures we must be something like them. Suppose a man made of iron, or of brass; could he sympathise with our wearied lungs, or with our aching bones?" (ibid., italics in the original)

7. "Again, if Christ had not taken upon him the nature of man, *then manhood would not have been so honorable or so comfortable as it is.* I consider that to be a Christian man is to be the greatest thing that God has made. Little as I am, I can say of myself, if I am a child of God, I am next to my Maker" (ibid., 2:292, italics in the original).

8. "[H]ad [Christ] been an angel, the resurrection would not have had that great and glorious proof, nor should we have been so content to be human, seeing there would be death, but no immortality and life" (ibid., 2:292). Cf. Rom 8:11; 1 Cor 15:20.

9. Two illegible letters are found beneath the letters "b" and "o" in the word "both." Charles may have originally written the word "each." If this interpretation is correct, the sentence would read, "They were both sinners, each deserving eternal wrath."

10. Cf. Jude 6.

11. Cf. Isa 14:12–15.

12. Cf. 2 Cor 11:14.

13. Cf. Luke 10:18.

14. The handwriting in this line, and also that in the line above, suggests these two sentences were added after Charles wrote his second point.

15. A smudge is found beneath the letter "b" in the word "been." A similar smudge is found beneath the letter "d" in the word "day" in the previous sermon, "Christian Prosperity and Its Causes" (Sermon 51).

16. "If Satan had entered heaven, it would have been like a restoration—an old king come back to his ancient throne; but when man goes there, it is like a king going to a new dynasty—a new kingdom" (*NPSP* 2:295).

17. "The devil is a greater scholar than you, and a nimbler disputant" (*Lectures* 1:11).

18. Charles preached the above sermon prior to leading his congregation in the observance of the Lord's Supper (see also "Slavery Destroyed" [Sermon 73]). This is the only time Charles used the word "Sacrament" in Notebook 1. In his later ministry, he used this word interchangeably with "ordinance" to refer to the Lord's Supper. See also "Baptism and the Lord's Supper" in the following sermon, "Pleasure in the Stones of Zion" (Sermon 53).

53. Psalm 102.14. Pleasure in the stones of Zion.

This Psalm written towards the end of the Captivity either by Daniel or Nehemiah, bears the impress of a deep love of his country. The Jews as well as all people have an intense love to their own land, they desire to be buried in it, and always have some of its dust put into the grave with them.
but the psalm is applicable to the spiritual Israelites they love the stones and dust of Jerusalem. – what are they

I. The Doctrines, by which every scriptural truth is meant they must be cared for, churches cannot flourish where doctrines are corrupt – Popery – Arminian – Soc. Antinom &c God's people love the truth and search out of the Scriptures. Election. depravity. perseverance, just by faith – grace &c – we shall not be indifferent but study them.

II. The Saints. are living stones, they will love, assist & pray for each other – we love to see newborn souls, 'tis an evidence of conversion – we shall not despise the meanest dust.

III. The Ordinances. the pillars of strength, the services of the Sabbath our delight, Baptism & the Lords Supper. together with all meetings for prayer are our delight even the dust which we think not so much of we favour.

IV. The Agencies, Preaching the word here & every where, brethren who speak in the villages, Sunday School, Missionary efforts, the Churches universally – and wherever the walls are falling we shall want to build them up. we take an interest in every thing good.
1. He who takes no interest is not a Christian.
2. We should be ready to show our love to it.
Appeal for the particular cause &c –
76

53

PLEASURE *in the* STONES *of* ZION
Psalm 102:14[1]

"For thy servants take pleasure in her stones, and favour the dust thereof."

This Psalm, written towards the end of the Captivity either by Daniel or Nehemiah,[2] bears the impress[3] of a deep love of his country. The Jews, as well as all people, have an intense love to their own land.[4] They desire to be buried in it and always have some of its dust put into the grave with them.[5] But the psalm is applicable to the spiritual Israelites. They love the stones and dust of Jerusalem. What are they?

I. THE DOCTRINES, by which every scriptural truth is meant. They must be cared for. Churches cannot flourish where doctrines are corrupt. Popery,[6] Arminian,[7] Soc,[8] Antinom,[9] etc. God's people love the truth and search out of the Scriptures. Election, depravity, perseverance, just[10] by faith, grace, etc. We shall not be indifferent, but study them.

II. THE SAINTS ARE LIVING STONES.[11] They will love,[12] assist,[13] and pray for each other.[14] We love to see newborn souls. 'Tis an evidence of conversion. We shall not despise the meanest dust.

III. THE ORDINANCES, the pillars of strength. The services of the Sabbath, our delight, Baptism and the Lord's Supper, together with all meetings for prayer, are our delight.[15] Even the dust which we think not so much of, we favour.

IV. THE AGENCIES. Preaching the word here and everywhere.[16] Brethren who speak in the villages,[17] Sunday School,[18] Missionary efforts, the Churches universally.[19] And wherever the walls are falling, we shall want to build them up. We take an interest in every thing good.
1. He who takes no interest is not a Christian.
2. We should be ready to show our love to it.

Appeal for the particular cause, etc.

76

1. This is the only time Charles preached a sermon on Ps 102:14 specifically. However, in 1856, he preached a sermon on Ps 102:13–14 entitled "Zion's Prosperity" (*MTP* 44, Sermon 2576). There is insufficient structural similarity or overlapping content to suggest he had the above outline in mind when writing his later sermon. Similarities are found, however, in his exposition of Ps 102:14 (see *TD* 4:422–23). In the Scripture reference above, Charles originally wrote the number 4 beneath 2. There is no evidence to suggest he intended to preach on Ps 104:14. In the index at the beginning of this notebook, Charles listed the correct Scripture reference. Given the absence of this sermon in the index at the end of this notebook, a question remains regarding how he might have listed the reference.

2. In his exposition, Charles departed from specifying when in Israel's history this Psalm was written or used. "*It is in vain to enquire into the precise point of Israel's history which thus stirred a patriot's soul, for many a time was the land oppressed, and at any of her sad seasons this song and prayer would have been a most natural and appropriate utterance*" (*TD* 4:417, italics in the original).

3. "1. Mark made by pressure;" "2. Effects of one substance or another;" "3. Mark of distinction; stamp" (Johnson's *Dictionary*, s.v. "impress").

4. "They delight in her so greatly that even her rubbish is dear to them" (*TD* 4:422).

5. On this point Charles may have been influenced by John Gill: "[S]uch great reverence and respect have the greatest of the wise men among the *Jews* for the land of *Israel*, literally understood, that they kiss the borders, the stones of it, and roll themselves in its dust" (John Gill, *An Exposition of the Old Testament, in Which Are Recorded the Original of Mankind, of the Several Nations of the World, and of the Jewish Nation in Particular: The Lives of the Patriarchs of Israel; the Journey of That People from Egypt Through the Wilderness to the Land of Canaan, and Their Settlement in that Land; Their Laws Moral, Ceremonial, and Judicial; Their Government and State Under Judges and Kings; Their Several Captivities, and Their Sacred Books of Devotion. In the Exposition of Which, It Is Attempted to Give an Account of the Several Books, and the Writers of Them; a Summary of Each Chapter; and the Genuine Sense of Every Verse: And Throughout the Whole, the Original Text, and the Versions of It, Are Inspected and Compared; Interpreters of the Best Note, Both Jewish and Christian, Consulted; Difficult Places at Large Explained; Seeming Contradictions Reconciled; and Various Passages Illustrated and Confirmed by Testimonies of Writers, as Well Gentile as Jewish, Vol. IV. Containing, Psalms, the Latter Part, Proverbs, Ecclesiastes, and Song of Solomon* [London: printed for the author; and sold by George Keith, at the Bible and Crown in Grace-church-street, 1765, The Spurgeon Library], 4:123, italics in the original).

6. "There has been much stir here about the late Popish Aggression,—the clergy seem to be very anxious about it" (*Autobiography* 1:192). During the same year in which Charles preached the sermon above, two articles appeared in *The Blackburn Standard* revealing the widespread resistance to "Popish Aggression" that extended from Dublin, Ireland, to St. Andrews, Scotland, in the east. In St. Andrews, the public burning of a nine-foot statue of the pope occurred near the castle ruins. According to the article, "orders were given for his Holiness to be taken from the cart, and fastened to the stake; this occupied a little time, and during its performance, a student of divinity delivered a speech, which, however, was but little heard" ("'Burning of the Pope' in Fife—Extra-Ordinary Crowd of Citizens," *The Blackburn Standard* [January 29, 1851]).

7. Abbr., "Arminianism." From the Puritan tomes in Stambourne to the Calvinist cook in Newmarket (Mary King), anti-Arminian sentiment had been baked into Charles's childhood and education. Charles was converted in an Arminian church in Colchester but did not join for theological reasons. In his diary for April 7, 1850—only three months after his conversion—Charles wrote, "Arminianism does not suit me now" (*Autobiography* 1:129). He later wrote, "And what is the heresy of Arminianism but the addition of something to the work of the Redeemer? Every heresy, if brought to the touchstone, will discover itself here. I have my own private opinion that there is no such thing as preaching Christ and Him crucified unless we preach what nowadays is called Calvinism. It is a nickname to call it Calvinism; Calvinism is the gospel, and nothing else" (*Autobiography* 1:172). Charles once called Arminianism "Pelagianism under another name" (*ST* April 1887:166). Charles's alignment with the Particular Baptist tradition must be brought into balance with his appreciation of Wesleyan worship and piety. In his 1861 lecture "The Two Wesleys," Charles said, "As for John and Charles Wesley, they seemed to fly with all the speed of seraphs,—they had never a moment's rest; they were, from early morning till late at night, incessantly engaged in the good cause. As I have read their lives . . . I have felt as if I had not yet begun to live (C. H. Spurgeon, "The Two Wesleys: On John and Charles Wesley" [London: Alabaster, Passmore, & Sons, 1861; repr., Eugene, OR: Wipf & Stock, 2014], 62). He also said, "In studying the life of Mr. Wesley, I believe Whitefield's opinion is abundantly confirmed—that Wesley is near the eternal throne, having served his Master, albeit it with many mistakes and errors, yet from a pure heart, fervently desiring to glorify God upon the earth" (ibid., 6). With regard to maintaining friendship despite theological differences, a rough comparison may be seen between Whitefield's relationship with Wesley and Charles's relationship with Chicago evangelist D. L. Moody, about whom Charles said, "I appreciate probably more than anybody else" (C. H. Spurgeon, *Eccentric Preachers* [London: Passmore &

Alabaster, 1879], 31). In 1873, Charles's attitude toward Arminianism can be summarized in the words, "At the present day, if you speak to a man about his soul, he will ask you, 'Are you an Arminian or a Calvinist?' To this we reply, 'Dear fellow, are you saved? That is your matter'" (*MTP* 19:55). In 1858, Charles said, "I am persuaded that neither the Church of England, nor the Wesleyans, nor the Independents, nor the Baptists, have got all the truth. I would not belong to any one of these denominations, for all the land that is beneath the sky, if I had to endorse all that is held by them. I believe the church ought to be governed by an Episcopalian Presbyterian Baptist Independency. I believe we are all right in a great many of our doctrines, but that we all have something yet to learn" (*MTP* 46:105). See also Iain H. Murray, *Spurgeon v. Hyper-Calvinism: The Battle for Gospel Preaching* (Edinburgh: Banner of Truth Trust, 1995; repr., 2000) and "The Path of the Just" (Sermon 35).

8.   Abbr., "Socinianism." Socinianism was an anti-Trinitarian intellectual movement that emerged from sixteenth-century Italian Reformers Lelio Sozzini and his nephew Fausto Socinus. Socinians refuted the idea that Christ could simultaneously possess two substances while dwelling in one person (see Andrew Fuller's interaction with Socinianism in Andrew Fuller, *The Calvinistic and Socinian Systems Examined and Compared, as to Their Moral Tendency; in a Series of Letters Addressed to the Friends of Vital and Practical Religion, Especially Those Amongst Protestant Dissenters* [London: W. Harrod, 1793]). Charles equated Socinianism with "theological leprosy" (*ST* April 1887:168) and claimed, "[T]he tadpole of Darwinism was hatched . . . [in] the pew of the old chapel in High Street, Shrewsbury, where Mr. Darwin, his father, and we believe his father's father, received their religious training" (168). See also Charles's comment about Socinianism in "The Minister's Commission" (Notebook 2, Sermon 110).

9.   Abbr., "Antinomianism." From αντι–νομος, translated "against law," Antinomianism is the "general name for the view that Christians are by grace set free from the need of observing any moral law" (E. A. Livingstone, *The Oxford Dictionary of the Christian Church* [3rd ed.; ed. F. L. Cross; Oxford: Oxford University Press, 2005], s.v. "Antinomianism"). In 1864, Charles described Antinomianism in the following words: "I am not under the law of God, therefore I will live as I like. . . . I am not under the law, therefore will I live and fulfil my own lusts and pleasures. . . . I am God's elect: Christ shed his blood for me: I shall never perish " (*MTP* 10:223). Approximately half a century before Charles preached the above sermon, Andrew Fuller had noted the influence of the Antinomian movement in England (see Robert W. Oliver, *History of the English Calvinistic Baptists, 1771–1892: From John Gill to C. H. Spurgeon* [Edinburgh: The Banner of Truth Trust, repr. 2006], 29). In a letter to his

mother on November 12, 1850, Charles wrote, "I hope yet, one day, to prove myself no Antinomian, though I confess my daily sins and shortcomings; yet I would not willfully sin, and I feel some hatred to it. I desire to hate it more" (Angus Library and Archive, Regent's Park College, Oxford University, D/SPU 1, Letter 8).

10. Abbr., "justification."

11. Cf. 1 Pet 2:5.

12. Cf. John 15:12.

13. Cf. Gal 6:2.

14. Cf. Jas 15:16. See also "Intercession of the Saints" (Sermon 48).

15. In his 1850 diary, Charles recorded that he attended prayer meetings on the following dates: April 15, 22, 29; May 5, 6, 9, 20; June 2, 3, 6, 10, 13 (*Autobiography* 1:127–45; see also Charles's letter to his father on September 19, 1850 [Angus Library and Archive, Regent's Park College, Oxford University, D/SPU 1, Letter 7]). Charles attended prayer meetings at Waterbeach Chapel (*Autobiography* 1:238), New Park Street Chapel (*Autobiography* 1:365), and the Metropolitan Tabernacle (*MTP* 60:409).

16. For an additional instance in which Charles separated the two words "every" and "where," see "Jesus, the Shower from Heaven" (Sermon 43). See also "Preaching! Man's Privilege and God's Power!" (*NPSP* 6, Sermon 346).

17. "There is a Preachers' Association in Cambridge, connected with St. Andrew's Street Chapel. . . . A number of worthy brethren preach the gospel in the various villages surrounding Cambridge, taking each one his turn according to plan" (*Autobiography* 1:200).

18. From May 5 to October 2, 1850, Charles taught Sunday school on a regular basis at St. Andrew's Street Chapel in Cambridge. In the main the content of his teachings is unknown with the exception of his June 2 lesson. In his diary Charles wrote, "Had a large class at Sunday-school, gave an address upon Death—the dreadful sword hanging by a single hair above the head of the ungodly" (*Autobiography* 1:141). See also "The Sunday-School Teacher—a Steward" (*NPSP* 4, Sermon 192); "The Sunday-School and the Scriptures" (*MTP* 31, Sermon 1866); and Charles's comment about "Sabbath Schools" in "The Little Fire and Great Combustion" (Sermon 54).

19. For Charles's ecumenism, see "Can Two Walk Together Unless They Are Agreed?" (Sermon 76); *ST* February 1892:52; *MTP* 27:198; 28:628; and 58:150.

James 3. 5.   The little fire & great combustion.   54

The apostle speaking of the influence of so small as member as the tongue compares it to a fire — small in beginning but none can tell how great in the end.

thus it may be said of the influence both of good & evil.

I Good — many useful things, river, mustard seed &c do so.

1. In the world all great and good enterprizes have had small beginnings as the Gospel, Missionary Society, Sabbath Schools — establishment of churches in heathen countries

2. In the man, Grace is small & weak at first, little love little knowledge, but it spreads & fires the whole. on earth 'tis but the smoking flax in heaven eternal noon.

3. By a man individually little can be done but that little is a little fire. Newton's mother. Luther, John Berridge in Waterbeach — Praying men. By the word in season, by work for God, by prayer.

II. Evil like fire increases — Fires. In America.

I. In the world — Adam & Eve, did a small action & yet how great as earth's sin & hell's torment witness. Mahometanism —

2. In the man. evil is progressive. Great crimes succeed to small. Hazael. anger. wars. vile murders — men do habitually what they once trembled at

3. Individual influence for evil is great — Tom Paine. John Smith — priest in Lucerne.

+ Let us not fear for the cause of God.

2. Let the humble rejoice in what God does in them and by them.

3. Let us beware of sin. —

77

Mr Charles (converted)

54

The LITTLE FIRE
and GREAT COMBUSTION
James 3:5[1]

*"Even so the tongue is a little member, and boasteth great things,
Behold, how great a matter a little fire kindleth!"*

The apostle, speaking of the influence of so small a[2] member as the tongue, compares it to a fire, small in beginnings but none can tell how great in the end. Thus it may be said of the influence both of good and evil.

I.[3] GOOD. MANY USEFUL THINGS:

river,[4] mustard seed,[5] etc., do so.

1. In the world. All[6] great and good enterprizes have had small beginnings [such] as the Gospel, Missionary Society,[7] Sabbath Schools,[8] establishment of churches in heathen countries.

2. In the man. Grace is small and weak at first. Little love, little knowledge, but it spreads and fires the whole. On earth 'tis but the smoking flax.[9] In heaven, eternal noon.[10]

3. By a man. Individually, little can be done. But that little is a little fire. Newton's mother.[11] Luther,[12] John Berridge[13] in Waterbeach, Praying men. By the word in season, by work for God, by prayer.

II. EVIL, LIKE FIRE, INCREASES. Fires. In America.[14]

1.[15] In the world. Adam and Eve did a small action,[16] and yet, how great as earth's sin and hell's torment witness. Mahomet<u>anism</u>.[17]

2. In the man. Evil is progressive. Great crimes succeed to small. Hazael,[18] anger, wars, vile murders.[19] Men do habitually what they on[c]e trembled at.[20]

3. Individual influence, for evil is great. Tom Paine,[21] John Smith,[22] Priest in Lucerne.[23]
    1.[24] Let us not fear for the cause of God.
    2. Let the humble rejoice in what God does in them and by them.
    3. Let us beware of sin.

77

Mr. Charles converted[25]

1.	This is the only time Charles preached a sermon on Jas 3:5. For additional sermons on fire, see: "Brand Plucked from the Fire" (Notebook 5, Sermon 242); "Perpetual Fire" (Notebook 8, Sermon 363); "Fire! Fire! Fire!" (*MTP* 7, Sermon 397); "The Ship on Fire—a Voice of Warning" (*MTP* 10, Sermon 550); "The Barley-Field on Fire" (*MTP* 10, Sermon 563); "Fire—the Want of the Times" (*MTP* 15, Sermon 854); "The World on Fire" (*MTP* 19, Sermon 1125); "God's Fire and Hammer" (*MTP* 42, Sermon 2460); "Lessons from the Malta Fire" (*MTP* 55, Sermon 3136); and "God's Firebrands" (*MTP* 57, Sermon 3233).

2.	Charles originally wrote the word "as." He may have originally intended to write, "The apostle, speaking of the influence of so small as [the] member [of] the tongue." Given his use of the word "as" again on the next line, this may have been accidental, the result of dittography.

3.	The size and location of Roman numeral I suggests Charles added it after he had written the word "God."

4.	Cf. Isa 35:6; John 7:38.	5.	Cf. Matt 17:20; Luke 17:6.

6.	An illegible letter, likely "m," appears beneath the letter "A" in the word "All." Charles may have intended to write the line, "Most great and good enterprizes have had small beginnings."

7.	Originally titled "Particular Baptist Society for the Propagation of the Gospel Amongst the Heathen," the Baptist Missionary Society was founded on October 2, 1792, by William Carey and thirteen others, including Andrew Fuller. Charles may have been familiar with the account of the origins of the Baptist Missionary Society in Francis Augustus Cox, *History of the English Baptist Society, 1792 to 1842* (Boston, MA: Isaac Tompkins, 1844). Charles addressed the Baptist Missionary Society on numerous occasions throughout his ministry, including on April 28, 1858, when he preached a sermon entitled "The Desolations of the Lord, the Consolations of His Saints" (*NPSP* 4, Sermon 190). See also "Gospel Missions" (*NPSP* 2, Sermon 76) and "The Model Home Mission and the Model Home Missionary" (*MTP* 15, Sermon 929).

8.	Charles taught Sabbath school, also called Sunday school, at St. Andrew's Street Chapel (*Autobiography* 1:38; 1:191). See notes in the previous sermon, "Pleasure in the Stones of Zion (Sermon 53).

9. Cf. Isa 42:3; Matt 12:20. See also "Smoking Flax" (*MTP* 31, Sermon 1831).

10. An alternative reading of this line is "Our earth 'tis but the smoking flax in heaven['s] eternal noon."

11. Elizabeth Newton played a significant role in the spiritual formation of her son, John (see Dennis R. Hillman, ed., *Out of the Depths by John Newton* [Grand Rapids, MI: Kregel Publications, 2003], 20). For additional references to John Newton in Charles's later ministry, see *NPSP* 1:143, 147, 259; and *MTP* 24:181.

12. It is unclear to what episode in Martin Luther's life Charles was referring. Given the previous reference to John Newton's mother, Charles may have been thinking of Luther's mother, Margarette. More likely Charles's line of thinking shifted here to the contrast between Luther's humble origins and the widespread Reformation he sparked. For additional references to Luther, see "Free-Will—a Slave" (*NPSP* 1, Sermon 52); "A Luther Sermon at the Tabernacle" (*MTP* 29, Sermon 1749); and "The Luther Sermon at Exeter-Hall" (*MTP* 29, Sermon 1750).

13. John Berridge (1716–1793) was an Anglican preacher, vicar of Everton, and contemporary of George Whitefield. Of Berridge, Charles said, "He was a man of remarkable learning, being as familiar in the learned languages as in his mother tongue, and well instructed in theology, logic, mathematics, and metaphysics: he was not, therefore, eccentric because he was ignorant. He possessed a strength of understanding, quickness of perception, depth of penetration, and brilliancy of fancy beyond most men, while a vein of innocent humour ran through all his public and private discourses" (C. H. Spurgeon, *Eccentric Preachers* [London: Passmore & Alabaster, 1879], 125). Charles likely first encountered Berridge's writings in his grandfather's attic in Stambourne. If not, he would have become familiar with his legacy in Waterbeach where, like Charles, Berridge had ministered. See also Richard Whittingham, *The Works of John Berridge with an Enlarged Memoir of His Life* (London: Simpkin, Marshall, and Company, 1838).

14. Charles may have had in mind the fires that broke out in Philadelphia, New York, and New Jersey in 1850. Articles about these fires were published in British newspapers such as "Destructive Fires in America," *Dundee, Perth, and Cupar Advertiser* (July 26, 1850).

15. If Charles had been consistent with his ordering technique, the number 1 would have been written here instead of Roman numeral I.

16. Cf. Gen 3:6.

17. The word "Mahometanism" was a reference to Islam—the religion of the prophet Mahomet, or Muhammad. Four years after Charles preached the sermon above, John Gibson Cazenove noted the increasing rise in popularity of Islamic literature: "If, gazing upon the shelves of a well-stocked modern library, we should observe a large and increasing proportion of volumes, which, more or less directly, bore reference to the person and the creed of Mahomet" (John Gibson Cazenove, *Mahometanism: An Article Reprinted from "The Christian Remembrancer of January, 1855"* [London: J. and C. Mozley, 1856], 9). With regard to the Koran, Charles later said, "A man must have a strange mind who should mistake that rubbish for the utterances of inspiration" (*MTP* 37:45). See also Charles's reference to Islam in "What Think Ye of Christ?" (Sermon 71); *MTP* 27:253; 34:322; 36:246; and *ST* July 1882:352.

18. Hazael was the king of Damascus whom God instructed the prophet Elijah to anoint (1 Kgs 19:15).

19. See "The Men Possessed of the Devils" (Sermon 70).

20. Charles likely added afterward the letters "ed" at the end of the word "trembled" and also "at" above the line.

21. Thomas Paine (1737–1809) was an American political activist and philosopher who, in his book *The Age of Reason*, critiqued institutional religion. For a recent treatment of Paine, see Harvey J. Kaye, *Thomas Paine: Firebrand of the Revolution* (Oxford: Oxford University Press, 2000). Additional references to Paine are found in *MTP* 7:373; 9:518; 12:174; 14:347; 24:333; and 44:522.

22. Charles likely used the name "John Smith" in the generic sense to serve as a placeholder. For additional examples, see *MTP* 35:286; 36:364; and 42:567. An exception is "John Smith," the editor of *The Glasgow Examiner*, who indirectly called Charles a "quack" (*Autobiography* 2:112). An alternative interpretation is that Charles was referencing John Smyth (1570–1612), founder of the General Baptists in Holland.

23. The "Priest in Lucerne" could be a reference to Constantin Siegwart-Müller

(1801–1869), a politician affiliated with the ultramontane party in Switzerland and, later, the chief magistrate of the Lucerne state council. Though not a priest, Siegwart-Müller reestablished conservative Catholicism, which benefited Jesuits returning to Lucerne (*Encyclopædia Britannica Online,* Encyclopædia Britannica Inc., 2016, s.v. "Constantin Siegwart-Müller"). Charles may have read about Siegwart-Müller in newspapers covering Switzerland's civil war of 1847 (Sonderbund War), which ended approximately four years before he preached the sermon above. In his later ministry Charles traveled to Lucerne with his wife and two friends. Charles wrote, "In the church at Lucerne, I think they had the head of John the Baptist, with some of the blood in a dish, and other relics innumerable; yet I was expected to go on Sunday, and worship there! I could not do it, for I should have kept on thinking of John the Baptist's head in the corner. Though I have a great respect for that Baptist, and all other Baptists, I do not think I could have controlled myself sufficiently to worship God under such circumstances" (*Autobiography* 2:370).

24. Charles either wrote the first stroke of Roman numeral III before the word "Let" (cf. "Adoption" [Sermon 1]), or he wrote the number 1 to signal the beginning of a list. If the latter interpretation is correct, the horizontal crossbar may have served as an em dash (cf. "Adoption" [Sermon 1]). It is unlikely Charles intended to strike through the number 1.

25. "Mr. Charles" was the first recorded convert of Charles's ministry at Waterbeach Chapel. His conversion occurred on the seventy-seventh time Charles preached, which is problematic given Charles's later remarks that his first convert was the wife of an agricultural farmer, likely the "Mrs. Spalding" who was converted approximately three months later on the 100th time Charles preached (see "Sinners Must Be Punished" [Sermon 9]). Who was "Mr. Charles," and why did Charles not identify him as his first convert? The likely answer is that Mr. Charles apostatized. In his autobiography Charles described a "tall, fine, big fellow" named "Tom So-and-so" who "caused [Charles] many bitter tears" at Waterbeach (see *Autobiography* 1:238–39). Charles identified him as "the ringleader in all that was bad . . . the terror of the neighbourhood . . . [who] . . . would be drunk for two or three weeks at a spell, and then he raved and raged like a madman." Charles recalled, "That man came to hear me; I recollect the sensation that went through the little chapel when he entered. He sat there, and fell in love with me; I think that was the only conversion that he experienced, but he professed to be converted. He

had, apparently, been the subject of genuine repentance, and he became outwardly quite a changed character; he gave up his drinking and swearing, and was in many respects an exemplary individual. All the parish was astonished. There was old Tom So-and-so weeping, and it was rumoured about that he felt impressed; he began regularly to attend the chapel, and was manifestly an altered man. The public-house lost an excellent customer; he was not seen in the skittle-alley, nor was he detected in the drunken rows that were so common in the neighbourhood. After a while, he ventured to come forward at the prayer-meeting; he talked about what he had experienced, what he had felt and known. I heard him pray; it was rough, rugged language, but there was such impassioned earnestness, I set him down as being a bright jewel in the Redeemer's crown. He held out six, nay, nine months he persevered in our midst. If there was rough work to be done, he would do it; if there was a Sunday-school to be maintained, six or seven miles away, he would walk there. At any risk, he would be out to help in the Lord's work; if he could but be of service to the meanest member of the Church of Christ, he rejoiced greatly. I remember seeing him tugging a barge, with perhaps a hundred people on board, whom he was drawing up to a place where I was going to preach; and he was glorying in the work, and singing as gladly and happily as any one of them. If anybody spoke a word against the Lord or His servant, he did not hesitate a moment, but knocked him over." However, "... the jeers and scoffs of his old companions,—though at first he bore them like a man,—became too much for him. He began to think he had been a little too fanatical, a little too earnest. He slunk up to the place of worship instead of coming boldly in; he gradually forsook the week-night service, and then neglected the Sabbath-day; and, though often warned, and often rebuked, he returned to his old habits, and any thoughts of God or godliness that he had ever known, seemed to die away. He could again utter the blasphemer's oath; once more he could act wickedly with the profane; and he—of whom we had often boasted, and said, in our prayer-meetings, 'Oh! how much is God glorified by this man's conversion! What cannot Divine grace do?'—to the confusion of us all, was to be seen sometimes drunk in our streets, and then it was thrown in our teeth, 'This is one of your Christians, is it?—one of your converts gone back again, and become as bad as he was before?' Before I left the district, I was afraid that there was no real work of grace in him." If "Mr. Charles" was the same man who Charles described, then his apostasy may explain the priority given to "Mrs. Spalding" as being Charles's first convert. The 1851 Census recorded "Thomas Charles," a thirty-one-year-old man who was born in 1820 and worked as an agricultural laborer in Histon, Cambridgeshire, which was only five miles from Waterbeach. The handwriting of "Mr. Charles converted" differs from that of the outline above. Also, Charles may have intended the vertical stroke after the word "converted" to serve as a closing parenthesis.

55 .–   Matt 11. 28 .   Rest for the weary .

Little of this now a days and many false rests.

I . The weary who they are not and who they are

1 . Not those who think themselves good enough .

2 . Not those who love worldly pleasures .

3 . Not those who are indifferent to religion .

But .

1 . Those to whom past sins are burdensome .

2 . Those who mourn over the sin in them ;

3 . Those who are longing for Jesus in his grace ,

II . The coming . "come unto me".

1 . It is not a proud, self righteous, come .

2 . It is not a single cry , or groan, or hasty prayer,

But .

1 . A humble, dependant, sorrowful trust in Jesus .

2 . It is an earnest and continued invocation of him

III . The rest – is glorious here but far more

glorious is the rest that remaineth –

IV . A hearty exhortation .

1 . To burdened Christians to roll their burdens on h.

2 . To poor sinners to trust in him .

Oh Divine spirit give life, energy fire & a blessing

78

55

REST *for the* WEARY
Matthew 11:28[1]

"Come unto me, all ye that labour and are heavy laden, and I will give you rest."

Little of this now a days, and many false rests.[2]

I. THE WEARY. Who they are not, and who they are.
   1. Not those who think themselves good enough.
   2. Not those who love worldly pleasures.[3]
   3. Not those who are indifferent to religion.

   But

   1. Those to whom past sins are burdensome.[4]
   2. Those who mourn over the sin in them.[5]
   3. Those who are longing for Jesus in his grace.[6]

II. THE COMING. *"Come unto me."*
   1. It is not a proud, self-righteous, come.
   2. It is not a single cry, or groan, or hasty prayer.

   But

   1. A humble, dependant,[7] sorrowful trust in Jesus.
   2. It is an earnest and continued invocation of him.

III. THE REST IS GLORIOUS HERE,[8] BUT FAR MORE GLORIOUS IS THE REST THAT REMAINETH.[9]

IV. A HEARTY EXHORTATION.
   1. To burdened Christians, to roll their burdens on him.[10]
   2. To poor sinners, to trust in him.[11]

   Oh Divine spirit, give life, energy, fire[12] and a blessing.[13]

78

1. Charles preached five additional sermons on Matt 11:28: "Christ's Word with You" (*MTP* 28, Sermon 1691); "The Christ-Given Rest" (*MTP* 39, Sermon 2298); "The Old Gospel for a New Century" (*MTP* 47, Sermon 2708); "Jesus Calling" (*MTP* 48, Sermon 2781); and "A World-Wide Welcome" (*MTP* 59, Sermon 3352). Charles also preached a sermon on Matt 11:27–28 entitled "Powerful Persuasives" (*MTP* 62, Sermon 3502) and three sermons on Matt 11:28–30: "The Meek and Lowly One" (*NPSP* 5, Sermon 265); "Rest, Rest" (*MTP* 17, Sermon 969); and "Rest for the Labouring" (*MTP* 22, Sermon 1322). The two sermons that most resemble the outline above are "Rest, Rest" (cf. "I. The weary" with *MTP* 17:14; "II. The coming" with 16; "III. The rest" with 17–18) and "Rest for the Labouring." In the latter sermon Charles followed the contours of the outline above more closely, suggesting he may have had it in mind when writing his later sermon. For additional sermons on rest, see "Heavenly Rest" (*NPSP* 3, Sermon 133); "Rest" (*MTP* 15, Sermon 866); "Rest in the Lord" (*MTP* 23, Sermon 1333); "Christ's Rest and Ours" (*MTP* 43, Sermon 2542); "The Saviour Resting in His Love" (*MTP* 47, Sermon 2720); "Rest as a Test" (*MTP* 47, Sermon 2748); "The Believer's Present Rest" (*MTP* 55, Sermon 3169); and "The Lord's Eternal Rest" (*MTP* 58, Sermon 3294).

2. An alternative reading of this line is "[There is] little of this now a days, and [there are] many false rests."

3. Cf. 1 John 2:15.   4. Cf. Ps 38:4.

5. Cf. Matt 5:4; Jas 4:9.   6. Cf. John 7:37.

7. Charles originally wrote the letter "t" in the word "dependant" prematurely. An additional interpretation, though less likely, is that he intended to write the word "dependable" instead.

8. "All the rest that God gives we may safely take. No man ever rested too long on the bosom of Jesus. I believe many Christian workers would be better if they enjoyed more. . . . It is astonishing what a difference a night's rest makes with our troubles" (*MTP* 58:572).

9. Cf. Matt 25:46; Heb 4:3.

10. The stem and arc in the letter "m" in the word "him" was not distinguished (cf. "him" four lines above and also in the line below). Cf. Matt 11:29; 1 Pet 5:7.

11. Cf. Prov 3:5; Isa 12:2.

12. The mention of "fire" may suggest Charles had in mind his previous sermon, "The Little Fire and Great Combustion" (Sermon 54).

13. This is the first of numerous prayers Charles wrote at the conclusion of his sermons in his early notebooks. It is not known if he verbalized these prayers during the service. More likely they were intended to be private. For additional prayers in this notebook, see "What Think Ye of Christ?" (Sermon 71); "Slavery Destroyed" (Sermon 73); "The Physician and His Patients" (Sermon 74); and "Can Two Walk Together Unless They Are Agreed?" (Sermon 76).

Gal. 1. 24. God glorified in the saved –

Paul had established the Galatian church, they had rece_d
him kindly. but through certain false teachers they had been
let to despise both Paul and his doctrine – Paul prove him_
self to be an apostle of the Lord, and declare justification to
be of faith – Paul's was not boasting when he said this. –

I. In his as well as other's conversion we see reason to
    glorify God – we know it is his work, his only – in
Paul's conversion there were several circumstances which
specially glorified –.

1 God's grace. He rejected the gospel, hated & persecuted the good
2 God's sovereignty. in that though Paul was so vile he saved
him and passed by many others – why not Agrippa or Gamaliel,
3. God's power. violently opposed he was and a very rigid Pharisee,
in the very act of rebellion saved not by some sickness bringing
him low, not by Peter or eloquent preachers. not even by the truth.

So also in every sinner's conversion the same is manifest
1. God's grace. at least to the soul converted this is evident enough
2. God's sovereignty. if rich since so few rich are chosen. If poor that
God should notice the poor. if learned or unlearned, if virtuous or vicious,
if old or young – sovereignty will be always manifest.
3. God's power. the will has to be turned, the affection taken
off one object and put on another – habits conquered – impossibility
are performed. – no education, science, morality could do this.
preachers and angels would be powerless without the spirit

II. In his after conversation. Paul an apostle, taught by direct revelation
a most eloquent and successful preacher possessed of charming grace,
So also we all should endeavour that men may glorify God in us.

1. By a generally consistent walk.   we should impute all our progress
2. By activity in God's service   to Jesus. the author & finisher of them
3. By patience and submission under trial   both in ourselves & others. –

79

56

GOD GLORIFIED
in the SAVED
Galatians 1:24[1]

"And they glorified God in me."

Paul had established the Galatian church. They had rece[d][2] him kindly, but through certain false teachers they had been le[d][3] to despise both[4] Paul and his doctrine. Paul prove[d] himself to be an apostle of the Lord[6] and declare[d] justification to be of faith.[7] Paul's[8] was not boasting when he said this.

I. IN HIS, AS WELL AS OTHER[S']][9] CONVERSION, WE SEE REASON TO GLORIFY GOD.
    We know it is his work,[10] his only. In Paul's conversion, there were several circumstances[11] which specially glorified:

    1. God's grace. He rejected the gospel, hated and persecuted the good.[12]

    2. God's sovereignty. In that, though, Paul was so vile. He saved him and passed by many others. Why not Agrippa or Gamaliel?[13]

    3. God's power. Violently[14] opposed he was, and a very rigid[15] Pharisee in the very act of rebellion.[16] Saved, not by some meekness bringing him low, not by Peter or eloquent preachers, not even by the truth.

    So, also, in every sinner's conversion the same is manifest.

    1. God's grace. At least to the soul converted, this is evident enough.

    2. God's sovereignty. If rich, since so few rich are chosen.[17] If poor, that God should notice the poor.[18] If learned or unlearned, if virtuous or vicious,[19] if old or young, sovereignty will always manifest.

    3. God's power. The will has to be turned. The affection[20] taken off one object and put on another. Habits conquered. Impossibilities are performed. No education,[21] science,[22] morality could do this. Preachers and angels would be powerless without the spirit.[23]

II. IN HIS AFTER CONVERSATION. Paul an apostle, taught by direct revelation.[24]

A most eloquent and successful preacher.[25] Possessed of charming graces.[26]

So, also, we all should endeavour that men may glorify God in us.

1.	By a generally consistent walk	We should impute all our graces
2.	By activity in God's service.	to Jesus, the author and finisher of them,[27]
3.	By patience and submission under trial[28]	both in ourselves and others.[29]

79

1. This is the only time Charles preached a sermon on Gal 1:24. For additional sermons on glory, see "The Glory of God in the Face of Jesus Christ" (*MTP* 25, Sermon 1493); "God Glorified by Children's Mouths" (*MTP* 26, Sermon 1545); "Glory!" (*MTP* 29, Sermon 1721); "A View of God's Glory" (*MTP* 54, Sermon 3120); and "God's Glory and His Goodness" (*MTP* 61, Sermon 3448).

2. Abbr., "received."

3. Charles may have intended to write the word "led" instead of "let." For an additional example, see "The Wise Men's Offering" (Sermon 58).

4. An illegible letter, likely "e," was written after the word "both." It is possible Charles originally misspelled the word.

5. Cf. Gal 2:4; 5:7.   6. Cf. Gal 1:1.   7. Cf. Gal 2:16.

8. Charles may have intended to write the words "Paul's boasting."

9. Charles originally inserted the apostrophe between the letters "r" and "s" in the word "others." However, the context suggests he intended the word to be plural possessive and not singular possessive.

10. Cf. Phil 1:6.

11. A yellow stain, likely the result of the aging process of the manuscript, appears beneath the word "circumstances." The origin of the stain can be found in "The Wise Men's Offering" (Sermon 58) and can be seen surrounding the word "longing" in the following sermon, "The Affliction of Ahaz" (Sermon 57).

12. Cf. 1 Cor 15:9.

13. Herod Agrippa (10 BC–AD 44) was the king of Judea (cf. Acts 12:1–5). Gamaliel was the well-respected Pharisee of Jerusalem who trained Saul (cf. Acts 22:3).

14. The letter "g" was written at the end of the word "violently." Charles likely intended this letter to be "y" instead.

15. The placement of the tittle above and before the letter "i" makes the word "rigid" difficult to discern.

16. An alternative reading of this sentence is "Violently opposed he was, and a very rigid Pharisee [who was] in the very act of rebellion."

17. Cf. 1 Cor 1:26.   18. Cf. Jas 2:5.

19. The final letters in the word "vicious" trail into the margin.

20. An illegible letter, likely "b" or "h," was written beneath the letter "a" in the word "affection." Charles originally may have intended to write the word "brain" or "heart."

21. "Soon after I had begun to preach the Word in the village of Waterbeach, I was strongly advised to enter Stepney, now Regent's Park, College, to prepare more fully for the ministry" (*Autobiography* 1:241).

22. Eight years after Charles preached this sermon, Charles Darwin published *On the Origin of Species* (1859). Charles publicly critiqued the theory of evolution in his lecture on October 1, 1861, "The Gorilla and the Land He Inhabits" (see *Autobiography* 3:51–54). However, in the above sermon, Charles likely used the word "science" to speak more broadly, as he did in his later ministry: "Begin with any other science you like, and truth will seem to be all awry. Begin with the science of Christ crucified, and you will begin with the sun, you will see every other science moving round it in complete harmony. The greatest mind in the world will be evolved by beginning at the right end. The old saying is, 'Go from nature up to nature's God;' but it is hard work going up-hill. The best thing is to go from nature's God down to nature; and if you once get to nature's God, and believe Him, and love Him, it is surprising how easy it is to hear music in the waves, and songs in the wild whisperings of the winds, to see God everywhere, in the stones, in the rocks, in the rippling brooks, and to hear Him everywhere, in the lowing of cattle, in the rolling of thunders, and in the fury of tempests. Christ is to me the wisdom of God. I can learn everything now that I know the science of Christ crucified" (*Autobiography* 1:166).

23. See "And only skeletons without the Holy Ghost" on the title page of this notebook. See also the prayer at the conclusion of the previous sermon, "Oh Divine spirit, give life, energy, fire and a blessing" ("Rest for the Weary" [Sermon 55]).

24. Cf. 2 Cor 12:2–4; Gal 1:17.   25. Cf. 1 Cor 2:1–4.

26. An alternative reading of this line is "Paul, an apostle [who was] taught by direct revelation [was] a most eloquent and successful preacher [who was] possessed with charming graces."

27. Cf. Heb 12:2.   28. Cf. Jas 1:2.

29. The handwriting in these three lines differs from that in the body of the outline; the lines were likely added after the writing of the list on the left.

57   2 Chron. 28. 22.   The affliction of Ahaz.

Affliction since the fall the common lot of all men, universal as its cause, sin. It has become a law of nature and it is useless to attempt avoiding sorrow we must see in what way it tends to our advantage.

I. To the godly afflictions in the hand of the Spirit are useful. for 1 They shake our earthly prospects and set us longing for glory. 2. It is like correction it keeps us from destruction. 3. It manifests our graces 4 Tries and confirms our faith by experience and so sanctifies us and meetens us for heaven.

But II. To the ungodly they are not necessarily useful. They are used by God sometimes as Manasseh, jailor, but are they are not necessarily useful for
1. We might then expect nurses, doctors, sextons, sailors &c to be very holy.
2. Ahaz, Pharoah, Israelites, and many inst wherein it was not, The fruits of sickness are temporary, evanescent fears. —Nor is sickness the best time for repentance.
1. For the mind is apt to deceive itself & take fear for convers
2. The pain &c of the disease distract the soul.
3 Death bed repentances seldom genuine and it is highly improbable that he who has lived in sin should be willing to give it up at the last moment
1. How we ought to strive that affliction may be sanctified
2. How foolish those who rely on sickness.
3. How wicked those who sin more in trouble

80

The AFFLICTION *of* AHAZ
2 Chronicles 28:22[1]

"And in the time of his distress did he trespass yet more
against the Lord. *This is that king Ahaz."*

Affliction since the fall,[2] the common lot of all men.[3] Universal as its cause, sin.[4]
It has become a law of nature and it is useless to attempt avoiding sorrow.[5]
We must see in what way it tends to our advantage.[6]

I.   TO THE GODLY, AFFLICTIONS IN THE HAND OF THE
   SPIRIT ARE USEFUL.[7] For

   1.   They shake our earthly prospects[8] and set us longing[9] for glory.[10]

   2.   It is like correction.[11] It keeps us from destruction.

   3.   It manifests our graces.[12]

   4.   Tries and confirms our faith[13] by experience, and so sanctifies us
      and meetens[14] us for heaven.[15]

But II.   TO THE UNGODLY, THEY ARE NOT
   NECESSARILY USEFUL.
   They are used by God sometimes as Manasseh,[16] jailor,[17] but[18] they are not
   necessarily useful,[19] for
      1.   We might then expect nurses, doctors, sextons, sailors, etc., to be very holy.[20]
      2.   Ahaz, Pharaoh,[21] Israelites,[22] and many inst[23] wherein it was not. The
         fruits of sickness are temporary, evanescent[24] fears.
   —Nor is sickness the best time for repentance.
      1.   For the mind is apt to deceive itself and take fear for conversion.[25]
      2.   The pain, etc., of the disease distract the soul.[26]
      3.   Death bed repentances [are] seldom genuine,[27] and it is highly improbable
         that he who has lived in sin should be willing to give it up at the last moment.

1.   How we ought to strive that affliction may be sanctified.

2.   How foolish [are] those who rely on sickness.

3.   How wicked [are] those who sin more in trouble.[28]

80[29]

1. On March 8, 1863, Charles preached an additional sermon on 2 Chron 28:22 entitled "That King Ahaz" (*MTP* 52, Sermon 2993). The similarities in the first and second Roman numerals of the later sermon (see *MTP* 52:302–3) suggest Charles likely had the above outline in mind when writing this later sermon. For additional references to Ahaz, see "Ruins" (*MTP* 44, Sermon 2565) and "The House of Morning and the House of Feasting" (*MTP* 54, Sermon 3108).

2. Cf. Genesis 3.

3. "The road to heaven is rough, and the path to hell is not always smooth" (*MTP* 52:301). Cf. Rom 3:23. An alternative reading of this line is "Since the fall, affliction [is] the common lot of all men."

4. Charles may have intended to combine this phrase with the previous sentence. If this interpretation is correct, an alternative reading of this line is "Just as the cause of sin is universal, the common lot of all men since the fall is affliction."

5. "Since, then, dear friends, the stream of sorrow is here, and we cannot make it flow in any other direction" (*MTP* 52:301).

6. The final letters in the word "advantage" trail into the margin. The cluster of dots above the word was imprinted symmetrically onto the next page (see "The Wise Men's Offering" [Sermon 58]).

7. Cf. Pss 66:10; 119:67.

8. "Trials cut the ropes which fasten our souls to earthly things" (*MTP* 52:302).

9. The series of yellow stains surrounding the word "longing" are likely the result of the aging process of the manuscript and can also be found beneath the word "circumstances" in the previous sermon, "God Glorified in the Saved" (Sermon 56). The source of the stains can be found in the following sermon, "The Wise Men's Offering" (Sermon 58)

10. Cf. Col 1:24.   11. Cf. Prov 15:32.

12. "I must confess that I have often felt unusual spiritual power when coming up to preach to you after a season of sickness; and there have been times when I have heard some of you say, 'Our minister speaks more sweetly now than he did before

he was laid aside.' Yes, the olives must go into the press if the oil is to be squeezed out of them, and the grapes must be trodden upon with loving feet before the wine flows forth from them. The file must be used upon us to bring out the true quality of the metal. There is no hope that we shall ever be made into much fine gold unless we are often put into the crucible, and unless that crucible be put into the midst of the glowing coals. So I say that we get much good from our trials" (*MTP* 52:302–3). The words "It manifests our graces" may have been inspired by the phrase, "We should impute all our graces" in the previous sermon ("God Glorified in the Saved" [Sermon 56]).

13. Cf. 1 Pet 1:7.

14. From "meet," which Samuel Johnson defined as "fit; proper; qualified" (*Johnson's Dictionary*). See also "Regeneration" (Sermon 7).

15. Cf. 2 Cor 4:17.   16. Cf. 2 Chron 33:1–20.

17. Cf. Acts 16:25–31.

18. As an example of dittography, Charles originally wrote the word "are" before and after "they." The context suggests he did not intend to write "but are they?" The correct reading of this line is "but they are not necessarily useful for."

19. "[S]orrow will not of itself be beneficial to us. It is possible to endure afflictions on earth, and afterwards to endure eternal damnation in hell. Sinners may go from beds of languishing to beds of flame" (*MTP* 52:301).

20. The words "to be very holy" were written above the line. Charles likely did not intend to say that nurses, doctors, sextons, and sailors cannot be holy. Rather, his point was that affliction by itself cannot sanctify. If it could, those who work in these occupations would possess the greatest amount of holiness given the difficulties inherent to their jobs.

21. Charles misspelled the word "Pharaoh" by reversing the letters "a" and "o." For additional examples, see "Meekness of Moses" (Notebook 3, Sermon 179); "The New Song on Mount Zion" (Notebook 5, Sermon 250); "Christian Citizenship" (Notebook 7, Sermon 343); and "Pentecost" (Notebook 8, Sermon 374). In 1863, Charles said, "Affliction did not soften him; on the contrary, it hardened him" (*MTP* 52:305). Cf. Gen 12:17.

22. "The children of Israel, too, though they were smitten many times, yet revolted again and again" (*MTP* 52:305).

23. Abbr., "instances." Cf. 2 Kgs 13:14.

24. For an additional instance in this notebook in which Charles used the word "eva-nescent," see "Josiah" (Sermon 66).

25. The final letters of the word "conversion" trail into the margin.

26. Later in his ministry the sentence "The pain, etc., of the disease distract the soul" took on greater meaning for Charles when he suffered from a variety of physical and mental diseases including gout, kidney disease, and depression. Susannah wrote that he "was a true comforter of the suffering and sorrowing; his frequent personal afflictions, added to his own sympathetic disposition, made him 'a succourer of many'" (*Autobiography* 4:113; see also "The Christian's Heaviness and Rejoicing" (*NPSP* 4, Sermon 222). For a recent academic treatment of Charles's suffering, see William Brian Albert, "'When the Wind Blows Cold': The Spirituality of Suffering and Depression in the Life and Ministry of Charles Spurgeon" (PhD diss., The Southern Baptist Theological Seminary, 2015). See also Kim-Hong Hazra, "Suffering and Character Formation in the Life and Sermons of Charles Haddon Spurgeon 1834–1892" [PhD diss., Regent College, 1986] and Zach Eswine, *Spurgeon's Sorrows: Realistic Hope for Those Who Suffer from Depression* [Ross-shire, Scotland: Christian Focus Publications, 2014]). For a primary source of Charles's personal correspondence about his suffering, see Hannah Wyncoll, ed., *The Suffering Letters of C. H. Spurgeon* (London: The Wakeman Trust, 2007).

27. "[T]here may have been some few persons who have been saved on a death-bed, but my own conviction is that they have been very, very, very, very, very few" (*MTP* 52:308).

28. An alternative reading of this line is "How wicked [are] those who sin more [when they are] in trouble."

29. The number 80 was written in a different color of ink and is comparable to the number 81 in the following sermon, "The Wise Men's Offering" (Sermon 58).

Matt. 2. 11. The wise men's offering.

Just before Jesus' birth there was a general expectation of the Messiah both by Jews & Gentiles — The Jews knew it from the prophets especially Daniel, & Simeon and Anna both prophesied it, the sceptre had now departed, and from these things one of their Rabbi's positively declared his advent.

The Gentiles knew it partly by tradition, the Arabians by their descent from Ishmael, Balaam one of their prophets had foretold it, the Persians were taught it doubly by Zoroaster the servant of Daniel, the Romans lords of the Jews, had heard of it and there are allusions to it in Virgil, Suetonius, Tacitus, &c — other nations were acquainted with it both by the books and intercourse of the Jews, that nation being found in all countries — Even the Sybils, and oracles, false though they were, had been constrained to foretel it. These Magians were wise men, probably of some court like Daniel and that company, they were students of astronomy (often astrology), natural history and theology. They may possibly have practised wicked arts but even then how wonderful the power that could make them seek Jesus.

They took particular notice of the heavenly bodies, and on this occasion observed a new luminary, some have con- jectured that this was the light which shone round the shepherds but this luminary was a permanent and moving light. They had been in the habit of associating the appearance of a new star, with the birth of some important personage and knowing Jesus was expected they concluded it was "his star" Led by God; who willed that his own should be honoured by wise men as well as shepherds, seeing that he was lord of all, they set out guided by this star or remarkable luminary — If they started from Arabia

* They were probably favored with divine communications like Melchizedek, Job.

58

The WISE MEN'S OFFERING[1]
Matthew 2:11[2]

*"And when they were come into the house, they saw the young child with
Mary his mother, and fell down, and worshipped him: and when they had opened
their treasures, they presented unto him gifts; gold, and frankincense, and myrrh."*

Just before Jesus'[s] birth, there was a general expectation of the Messiah, both by
Jews and Gentiles. The Jews knew[3] it from the prophets, especially Daniel.[4] Simeon[5] and Anna[6] both prophesied it. The sceptre had now departed, and from these
things one of their Rabbis[7] positively declared his advent.

The Gentiles knew it partly by tradition. The Arabians, by their descent from Ishmael.[8] Balaam, one of their prophets, had foretold it.[9] The Persians were[10] taught
it doubtless by Zoroaster, the servant of Daniel. The Romans, lords of the Jews,
had heard of it, and there are allusions to it in ~~Virgil~~ Suetonius,[11] Tacitus,[12] etc.
Other nations[13] were acquainted with it, both by the books and intercourse of the
Jews. That nation being found in all countries.[14] Even the Sybils[15] and oracles, false
though they were, had been constrained to foretell[16] it. These Magians were wise
men, probably of some court like Daniel and that company.[17] They were students
of astronomy (often astrology),[18] natural history, and theology.*[19] They may possibly have practised wicked arts. But even then, how wonderful the power that could
make them seek Jesus.

They took particular notice of the heavenly bodies, and on this occasion observed
a new luminary. Some have conjectured that this was the light which shone round
the shepherds,[20] but this luminary was a permanent and moving light. They had
been in the habit of associating the[21] appearance of a new star with the birth of
some important personage,[22] and knowing Jesus was expected they concluded it
was "his star." Led by God, who willed that his son should be honoured by wise
men as well as shepherds, seeing that he was lord of all, they set out, guided by this
star or remarkable luminary.[23] If they started from Arabia, [cont'd]

*They were probably favored[24] with divine communications like Melchizedek,[25] Job.[26]

which is often called the east (Judg 6.3. Job. 1.3.) they must have traversed deserts and encountered dangers. Arabia was noted for wise men.

They were led by the star to Judea, but there probably the star forsook them and they had to enquire at Jerusalem for the place where the king was born. they had such strong faith that they did not doubt it but said "Where is he that is born". this going to Jerusalem was providential for.

1 By this means Herod knew it, his malice was excited and our Lord was driven to Egypt & Nazareth.

2. The whole Jewish nation would notice their coming, and would thus have evidence of the birth of the Messiah, even the great Sanhedrim, knew it and gave their opinion that he was born in Bethlehem.

Again the star appeared and let them to the house they worshipped "him" not Mary, and gave presents as men do in the east when they visit princes. this money supported the Holy Family in Egypt — they on their return would publish these things and thus the nations would be prepared to receive Jesus.

Was their adoration spiritual?

1. Here is a tale of providence.

2. The wise men set us an example of worship to Jesus in adoration and offering the best.

3. Here is a type of that promise "all nations shall bow before him". ————

81

which is often called the east (Judg 6:3,[27] Job 1:3[28]), they must have traversed deserts and encountered dangers. Arabia was noted for wise men.[29]

They were led by the star to Judea.[30] But there, probably the star forsook them and they had to enquire at Jerusalem for the place where the king was born. They had such strong faith that they did not doubt it, but said, "Where is he that is born?"[31] This going to Jerusalem was providential, for

1. By this means, Herod knew it.[32] His malice was excited and our Lord was[33] driven to Egypt and Nazareth.[34]

2. The whole Jewish nation would notice their coming and would thus have evidence of the birth of the Messiah. Even the great Sanhedrin[35] knew[36] it and gave their opinion that he was born in Bethlehem.[37]

Again the star appeared and le[d][38] them to the house.[39] They worshipped "him," not Mary,[40] and gave presents as men do in the east when they visit princes.[41] This money supported the Holy Family in Egypt. They, on their return, would publish these things, and thus the nations would be prepared to receive Jesus.

Was their adoration spiritual?

1. Here is a tale of providence.

2. The wise men set us an example of worship[42] to Jesus in adoration and offering the best.

3. Here is a type[43] of that[44] promise, "all nations shall bow before him."[45]

81[46]

1. Charles departed from his usual outline style in this sermon with longer sentences. This progression reached full maturity in Notebook 9 when Charles's sermons occupy eight to twelve pages each. After accepting the pastorate of the New Park Street Chapel in London, however, Charles reverted to writing mere outlines as he does in the main in Notebook 1 (see *Autobiography* 3:293).

2. This is the only time Charles preached a sermon on Matt 2:11. However, on December 24, 1882, Charles preached a similar sermon on Matt 2:10 entitled "The Star and the Wise Men" (*MTP* 29, Sermon 1698). For additional references to the wise men, see "The Sages, the Star, and the Savior" (*MTP* 16, Sermon 967); *MTP* 39:434; and *Lectures* 1:14.

3. The letter "n" was written beneath the "k" in the word "knew." Charles likely wrote the word "new" before correcting the misspelling.

4. See Daniel's "seventy weeks" prophecy (Dan 9:24–27).

5. Cf. Luke 2:26.   6.   Cf. Luke 2:36–38.

7. Charles inserted an apostrophe between the letters "i" and "s" in the word "Rabbi's." The context suggests, however, he intended the word to be plural, not possessive.

8. Cf. Gen 25:13.   9.   Cf. Num 24:17.

10. The yellow stains surrounding the word "were" are likely the result of the aging process of the manuscript and can be found in the previous two sermons, "God Glorified in the Saved" (Sermon 56) and "The Affliction of Ahaz" (Sermon 57). The stain covers a total of five pages in length, the most extensive in Notebook 1. Cf. "was" in the following sermon, "The First Promise" (Sermon 59).

11. It is not clear why Charles struck through the name of the Roman poet Virgil (70 BC–19 BC), whose Fourth Eclogue has been interpreted by Augustine and subsequent scholars as being an allusion to Jesus Christ. Modern scholarship often traces Virgil's Fourth Eclogue to "Sibylline writings originating in a south Italian culture that had come under Phoenician influence" ("Virgil's Fourth or Messianic Eclogue" in Margaret Drabble, Jenny Stringer, and Daniel Hahn, eds., *The Concise Oxford Companion to English Literature* [3rd ed.; London: Oxford University Press, 2007, online ed., 2013]). Charles may have struck through Virgil's name

because he could not locate an allusion to Jesus Christ in Virgil's works. An additional interpretation is that Charles had been influenced by the scholarship of his day that departed from a traditional interpretation of Virgil. Either way, in *Lives of the Twelve Caesars*, Roman historian Suetonius (AD 69–c. AD 120) offered a more compelling allusion to Jesus Christ in his reference to the Roman dispute over the name "Chrestus," a name believed to be a corrupt spelling of "Christ" (see C. Suetonius Tranquillus, *The Lives of the Twelve Caesars; to Which are Added, His Lives of the Grammarians, Rhetoricians, and Poets* [trans., Alexander Thomson; ed., T. Forester; London: George Bell and Sons, 1890], 318). For a modern translation of Suetonius's work, see Gaius Suetonius Tranquillus, *The Twelve Caesars* (trans. Robert Graves; ed. J. B. Rives; rev. ed.; London: Penguin Group, 2007).

12. The Roman historian Publius Cornelius Tacitus (c. AD 56–c. AD 118) offered the following reference to Jesus Christ in *The Annals of Imperial Rome*: "Therefore, to squelch the rumor [that the burning of Rome had taken place by order], Nero supplied (as culprits) and punished in the most extraordinary fashion those hated for their vice, whom the crowd called 'Christians.' Christus, the author of their name, had suffered the death penalty during the reign of Tiberius, by sentence of the procurator Pontius Pilate. The pernicious superstition was checked for a time, only to break out once more, not merely in Judea, the origin of the evil, but in the capital itself, where all things horrible and shameful collect and are practiced" (Tacitus, quoted in Craig Evans, *Jesus and His Contemporaries: Comparative Studies* [Leiden, The Netherlands: Brill, 2001], 42). For a modern translation of Tacitus's work, see *Tacitus: the Annals of Imperial Rome* (trans. Michael Grant; rev. ed.; London: Penguin Group, 1996).

13. Charles likely added the letter "s" to the end of the word "nations" afterward.

14. An alternative reading of this line is "Because the Jewish nation is found in all countries, other nations were acquainted with it, both by the books and intercourse of the Jews."

15. See John J. Collins, *Seers, Sibyls and Sages in Hellenistic-Roman Judaism* ([Leiden, The Netherlands: Brill, 2001], 181–210).

16. This is the only time in Notebook 1 that Charles spelled the word "foretel" with one "l."

17. Cf. Daniel 1.

18. Samuel Johnson defined "astronomy" as "a mixed mathematical science, teaching the knowledge of the celestial bodies." He defined "astrology" as "the practice of foretelling things by the knowledge of the stars" (Johnson's *Dictionary*, s.vv. "astronomy" and "astrology"). For additional references to astronomy in Charles's later sermons, see *MTP* 12:103–4 and 46:499–500. For additional references to astrology, see *MTP* 20:617 and 39:436.

19. Charles intended the asterisk after the word "theology" to signal the footnote that can be found at the bottom of the page.

20. Charles was likely referencing the English biblical scholar John Lightfoot (1602–1675), who was quoted in John Gill's commentary on Matthew: "[I]t was the light or glory of the Lord, which shone about the shepherds, when the angel brought them the news of Christ's birth, and which at so great a distance appeared as a star to these wise men" (Gill, *An Exposition of the New Testament*, 1:10). Charles sided with Gill's interpretation that the light "seems to be properly a star, a new and an unusual one" over against Lightfoot's conjecture.

21. An illegible letter, likely "a," can be found beneath the letters "t" and "h" in the word "the." Charles likely began writing the word "appearance" prematurely.

22. In Charles's personal copy of *The Voices of the Stars*, Oxford professor J. E. Walker compared the Babylonian god Nebo, as recorded in Isa 46:1, to the planet Mercury. He wrote, "As the brightness of Mercury wanes in the first glow of sunrise, so the star of Nebo, in its false light, pales and vanished in the golden dawn of Christ's Nativity" (J. E. Walker, *The Voice of the Stars; or, the Supernatural Revealed in the Natural Science of the Heavens* [London: Elliot Stock, 1894, The Spurgeon Library], 96).

23. An alternative reading of this sentence is "Led by God, who willed that his son should be honoured by wise men as well as shepherds, [and] seeing that he was Lord of all, they set out, guided by this star or remarkable luminary." The lines may also read, "[They were] led by God, who willed that his son should be honoured by wise men as well as shepherds. Seeing that he was Lord of all, they set out, guided by this star or remarkable luminary."

24. Typically, Charles used the traditional British spelling, "favoured." For additional examples of his use of this word, see "No Condemnation to Christians"

(Notebook 3, Sermon 174); "Leaning on Jesus Bosom" (Notebook 3, Sermon 183); and "The Church Is to Be Purged" (Notebook 4, Sermon 219).

25. Cf. Gen 14:18; Heb 7:1–28. See also "King of Righteousness and Peace" (Sermon 42).

26. Cf. Job 38–42.

27. Judges 6:3, "And so it was, when Israel had sown, that the Midianites came up, and the Amalekites, and the children of the east, even they came up against them."

28. Job 1:3, "His substance also was seven thousand sheep, and three thousand camels, and five hundred yoke of oxen, and five hundred she asses, and a very great household; so that this man was the greatest of all the men of the east."

29. The handwriting in this sentence differs in size from that in the body of this sermon and may have been written afterward.

30. Cf. Matt 2:1.

31. Matt 2:2, "Where is he that is born King of the Jews? for we have seen his star in the east, and are come to worship him."

32. Cf. Matt 2:3.

33. The source of the yellow stain that surrounds the word "was" can be found on the reverse side of the page. The stain is likely the result of the aging process of the manuscript.

34. Cf. Matt 2:13.

35. Charles wrote the letter "m" instead of "n" at the end of the word "Sanhedrin." There is no evidence to suggest he corrected the misspelling.

36. An illegible letter, possibly "f," was written beneath the "k" in the word "knew." Charles may have originally intended to write the line, "Even the great Sanhedrin knew it . . ."

37. Cf. Matt 2:4–6.

38. Charles may have intended to write the word "led" instead of "let." This is the second such instance in this notebook (see also "God Glorified in the Saved" [Sermon 56]).

39. Cf. Matt 2:9.

40. Matt 2:11, "And when they were come into the house, they saw the young child with Mary his mother, and fell down, and worshipped him: and when they had opened their treasures, they presented unto him gifts; gold, and frankincense and myrrh." With regard to Mariology, Charles said, "Worship is due to the Lord alone, and if rendered to the most blessed among women it is idolatrous. This superstition robs God of his glory and ensnares the souls of men" (*MTP* 32:506). In 1864, Charles noted, "[F]or every prayer offered to Jesus Christ, I believe there are fifty, at the present moment, offered to the Virgin Mary. At all events, in the Romanist's rosary, there are nine beads for the 'Hail Mary' to every one for 'Our Father'" (*MTP* 52:602).

41. On this point Charles might have consulted Matthew Henry's exposition: "In the Eastern nations, when they did homage to their kings, they made them presents" (Henry, *An Exposition of the New Testament*, 1:21).

42. An alternative reading of this line is "The wise men set [for] us an example of worship."

43. See also "The Peculiar People" (Sermon 25).

44. Charles struck through the word "that" with a diagonal line that intersected with another line to construct a crisscrossing pattern resembling the letter "X." The size of the intersecting lines suggests Charles likely intended to strike through the content of his third point.

45. Psalm 72:11, "Yea, all kings shall fall down before him: all nations shall serve him." Cf. Ps 86:9.

46. The handwriting of the number 81 is similar to that of the number 80 in the previous sermon, "The Affliction of Ahaz" (Sermon 57). The base of the number 1 was smeared to the left.

Gen. 3. 15   The first promise.   59

This is a most glorious promise, the first and only one
untill the time of Abraham, we will notice.

I. The occasion of its gift by making some remarks
on the preceeding verses.

II. The Characters mentioned. Jesus and his elect, the seed
of the woman. all who believe on & partake the spirit of Jesus.
Satan and the wicked who bear a likeness to him.
Scoffers. Sinners. Self righteous. Rejecters of the gospel.
between these two parties there is a conflict.

III. The bruising of the heel or the inferior nature.
1. In the temptation, suffering and death of Jesus.
2. In the persecution of God's people.
3. In the struggle of every Christian's heart.
"bruising the heel"; is painful, difficult it makes the way,
but it is not fatal — distress but not death.

IV. The bruising of the head of the serpent & his seed.
1. In the triumph of Jesus & Satan's confinement in the pit.
2. In the salvation of all the elect.
3. In the overthrow of hell's dominion in the world
and the establishment of the kingdom of righteousness.

1. We must look for trial.

2. And as surely as that comes will final triumph come.

82. 480.

The FIRST PROMISE
Genesis 3:15[1]

"And I will put enmity between thee and the woman, and between thy seed and her seed; it shall bruise thy head, and thou shalt bruise his heel."

This is a most glorious promise, the first and only one[2] until[3] the time of Abraham.[4] We will notice:

I.   THE OCCASION OF ITS GIFT BY MAKING SOME REMARKS ON THE PRECEDING[5] VERSES.

II. THE CHARACTERS MENTIONED.
Jesus and his elect, the seed of the woman,[6] all who believe on and partake [of] the spirit of Jesus, Satan and the wicked who bear a likeness to him, Scoffers, Sinners, Self righteous, Rejecters of the gospel. Between these two parties there is a conflict.[7]

III. THE BRUISING OF THE HEEL[8] OR THE INFERIOR NATURE.
1. In the temptation,[9] suffering, and death of Jesus.[10]
2. In the persecution of God's people.[11]
3. In the struggle of every Christian's heart. "Bruising the heel" is painful. Difficult it makes the way. But it is not fatal. Distress, but not death.[12]

IV. THE BRUISING OF THE HEAD OF THE SERPENT[13] AND HIS SEED.
1. In the triumph of Jesus[14] and Satan's confinement in the pit.[15]
2. In the salvation of all the elect.[16]
3. In the overthrow of hell's dominion in the world[17] and the establishment of the kingdom of righteousness.[18]

1.[19] We must look for trial.

2. And as surely as that comes will final triumph come.

82. 480.

1.   An illegible number was written beneath the 3 in the Scripture reference "Gen 3:15." The indices at the beginning and end of this notebook contain no evidence as to what number Charles may have written. On November 26, 1876, Charles preached an additional sermon on Gen 3:15 entitled "Christ the Conqueror of Satan" (*MTP* 22, Sermon 1326). On September 21, 1890, he preached a sermon on Gen 3:14–15 entitled "The Serpent's Sentence" (*MTP* 36, Sermon 2165). Both sermons contain overlapping content; however, it does not appear Charles had the outline above in mind when writing either. Additional sermons on the fall include "Human Inability" (*NPSP* 4, Sermon 182); "Christ the Conqueror of Satan" (*MTP* 22, Sermon 1326); and "The Serpent's Sentence" (*MTP* 36, Sermon 2165).

2.   "This is the first gospel sermon that was ever delivered upon the surface of this earth. . . . There lie within it, as an oak lies within an acorn, all the great truths which make up the gospel of Christ" (*MTP* 22:661–62).

3.   This is the only time in Notebook 1 in which Charles spelled the word "until" with two "l's." Cf. "preceding" two lines below.

4.   See "Abraham Justified by Faith" (Sermon 3).

5.   As in Charles's spelling of the word "untill" two lines above, he added an additional letter—in this case "e"—to the word "preceding." Samuel Johnson spelled the word "preceding" (Johnson's *Dictionary*). This is the only time in this notebook that Charles misspelled this word.

6.   "That seed of the woman, that glorious *One,*—for he speaks not of seeds as of many but of seed that is one" (*MTP* 22:664, italics in the original).

7.   "This putting of the enmity between the two seeds was the commencement of the plan of mercy, the first act in the programme of grace" (*MTP* 22:664).

8.   "Satan will be howling at you, and perhaps he will be nibbling at your heel, barking and biting at you; so climb into the Rock Christ, and he will not be able to reach you, and you will scarcely hear his howling" (*MTP* 47:252).

9.   Cf. Matt 4:1–11.   10.   Cf. John 19:17–30.

11.   Cf. Matt 24:9; 2 Tim 3:12.

12. An alternative reading of these sentences is "'Bruising the heel' is painful and makes the way difficult, but it is not fatal. [It causes] distress, but not death."

13. "I see the serpent rise above me. This great python, with opened jaws, gapes upon me as though he would swallow me up quick. But I am not afraid. . . . This bruise upon the head of the evil is a mortal stroke. If he had been bruised upon the tail, or upon the neck, he might have survived; but the Lord shall utterly slay the kingdom of evil, and crush out its power" (*MTP* 36:527).

14. Cf. Col 2:15.

15. Cf. Rev 20:3. Due to a lack of space in the margin, Charles did not separate the word "the" from "pit."

16. See "Election" (Sermon 10). Cf. Eph 1:4; 2 Thess 2:13.

17. Cf. John 16:33.   18. Cf. John 18:36.

19. Charles likely intended the line of dots above the number 1 to signal his final remarks. See also "Necessity of Purity for an Entrance to Heaven" (Sermon 2); "Condescending Love of Jesus" (Sermon 5); and "The Fight and the Weapons" (Sermon 37a).

60.　　　Phil 4. 7 .　　The peace of God . —

We who dwell in England in times of peace know little of its value.
War is one of the most awful scourges of the world: it is
the destroyer of every holy thing; peace the angel of heaven.
The apostle hear speaks of a wondrous peace.

I. Internal peace, the peace which God causes, there is no
civil war in the renewed soul. — the soul is at war with
the enemies in its walls but not with itself.　　of the word
　1. Peace of mind or intellect. the soul finds rest in the doc & precepts
　2. Peace of the affections. there is a holy content and satisfaction
　3. Peace of the emotions. fear and dread are banished.
　4. Peace of conscience, by obedience to its dictates, & giving its demands

II. External peace or peace with others. —
　1. With all men we are at peace. Jesus gives us love even to
　　our enemies, humility, calmness, and holiness secure this
　2. Peace with God — so necessary since God is so mighty
　　and we so weak.　　it is a peace.
　a. Profound and Perfect — there are not the slightest bickering
　no truce, nor superficial peace like the peace of France with its
　president or parties bound to keep the peace but a peace
　arising from moral conformity, sympathy, & love
　b. Unbroken Peace. Justice breaks it not, Holiness cannot.
　Truth cannot, yea these are all engaged to defend it.
　God will not and we cannot for the covenant is in Jesus and
　　afflictions cannot.
　c. Eternal peace. Justification & Sanctification are eternal
　The covenant making and keeping God is eternal
　d. Heavenly peace. as the babe and its mother, the lamb
　and the shepherd, the peace of man with his maker
　on earth is as great as that in heaven. —

III. The triune God its author
　1. God the Father. the planner. the giver of the son.
　2. God the Son. the procurer, the covenant fulfiller & sustainer
　3. God the Spirit. the executor in our soul

83

THE PEACE *of* GOD
Philippians 4:7[1]

"And the peace of God, which passeth all understanding, shall keep
your hearts and minds through Christ Jesus."

We who dwell in England in times of peace know little of its value.[2] War is one of the most awful scourges of the world. It is the destroyer of every holy thing. Peace, the angel of heaven.[3] The apostle here[4] speaks of a wondrous peace.

I. INTERNAL PEACE, THE PEACE WHICH GOD CAUSES.

There is no civil war in the renewed soul. The soul is at war with the enemies in its walls, but not with itself.

1. Peace of mind or intellect. The soul finds rest in the doc[5] and precepts of the word.[6]

2. Peace of the affections. There is a holy content[7] and satisfaction.

3. Peace of the emotions. Fear and dread are banished.[8]

4. Peace of conscience. By obedience to its dictates[9] and giving its demands.

II. EXTERNAL PEACE, OR PEACE WITH OTHERS.[10]

1. With all men we are at peace.[11] Jesus gives us love even to our enemies.[12] Humility, calmness,[13] and holiness secure this.

2. Peace with God. So necessary since God is so mighty and we so weak.[14]
   It is a peace:
   a. Profound and Perfect. There are not the slightest bickerings. No truce nor superficial peace, like the peace of France with its president,[15] or parties bound to keep the peace, but a peace arising from moral conformity, sympathy, and love.
   b. Unbroken Peace. Justice breaks it not. Holiness cannot. Truth cannot. Yea, these are all engaged to defend it. God will not and we cannot, for the covenant is in Jesus.[16] And afflictions cannot.[17]
   c. Eternal peace. Justification and Sanctification are eternal. The covenant making and keeping. God is eternal.[18]
   d. Heavenly peace. As the babe and its mother, the lamb and the shepherd.[19] The peace of man with his maker on earth is as great as that in heaven.

III. THE TRIUNE GOD, ITS AUTHOR.

1. God the Father. The planner, the giver of the son.[20]

2. God the Son. The procurer,[21] the covenant fulfiller[22] and sustainer.

3. God the Spirit. The executor[23] in our soul.

83

1. Charles preached two additional sermons on Phil 4:7: "How to Keep the Heart" (*NPSP* 4, Sermon 180) and "The Peace of God" (*MTP* 24, Sermon 1397). On January 12, 1888, he preached a sermon on Phil 4:6–7 entitled "Prayer, the Cure for Care" (*MTP* 40, Sermon 2351). All three sermons share overlapping themes with the above outline; however, only his sermon "The Peace of God" was an expansion of the above outline (cf. *MTP* 24:76–77). For additional sermons on peace, see "King of Righteousness and Peace" (Sermon 42); "Blessed Are the Peacemakers" (Notebook 5, Sermon 269); "The God of Peace" (*NPSP* 1, Sermon 49); "The Peacemaker" (*MTP* 7, Sermon 422); "The God of Peace and Our Sanctification" (*MTP* 23, Sermon 1368); "Peace: A Fact and a Feeling" (*MTP* 25, Sermon 1456); "Peace: How Gained, How Broken" (*MTP* 35, Sermon 2112); "The Peace of the Devil, and the Peace of God" (*MTP* 36, Sermon 2157); and "Christ Our Peace" (*MTP* 59, Sermon 3386).

2. When Charles wrote this notebook in 1851, Britain was not engaged in any major domestic or international combats. However, in the following year, the Second Anglo-Burmese War began, followed in 1853 by the Crimean War (see *ST* April 1878:145; *MTP* 26:524; 33:720). On October 7, 1857, Charles was invited to preach to a crowd of 23,654 at the Crystal Palace in Sydenham in response to the Indian Rebellion, also called India's First War of Independence (see "Fast-Day Service" [*NPSP* 3, Sermons 154–155]). For the context of this political sermon, see *Autobiography* 2:239.

3. An alternative reading of these lines is "War is one of the most awful scourges of the world. It is the destroyer of every holy thing [while] peace [is] the angel of heaven."

4. Charles originally wrote the word "hear." The context suggests, however, he intended to write the word "here."

5. Abbr., "doctrines."

6. The phrase "of the word" was written above the word "precepts." Cf. Ps 119:165.

7. Cf. Phil 4:12.

8. Cf. Deut 31:6; Ps 56:3; Isa 41:10; 2 Tim 1:7.

9. Cf. Acts 23:1; 1 Tim 1:5,19; 1 Pet 3:16.

10. "Dear friends, it is very essential that we, as Christian people, should not only talk about this peace, and believe in it, but that we should enjoy it, and exhibit it" (*MTP* 55:606).

11. Cf. Rom 12:18; Heb 12:14.

12. Cf. Matt 5:44. See also "Intercession of the Saints" (Sermon 48).

13. "I believe that, to some of you, the best way in which you can honour God, and win others to Christ, is by exhibiting a quiet, cheerful frame of mind, especially in sickness. Nothing is so convincing to ungodly men as to see Christians very calm in time of danger, very resigned in the hour of affliction, very patient under provocation, and taking things altogether, as Christian men should take them, as from the hand of God" (*MTP* 55:606).

14. An alternative reading of this line is "Peace with God [is] so necessary since God is so mighty and we are so weak."

15. Charles may have been referencing Louis Napoléon Bonaparte's coup d'état that occurred on December 2, 1851 (see Walter Bagehot, *The Works and Life of Walter Bagehot* [9 vols.; ed., Mrs. Russell Barrington; London: Longmans, Green, and Co., 1915], 1:77–137). The coup d'état was publicized throughout British newspapers (see "Foreign Intelligence," *The Cambridge Independent Press* [December 13, 1851]).

16. It is unclear why Charles wrote the letter "h" at the end of the word "Jesus." He possibly intended to write the words "Jesus' hand." However, it is more likely the letters "a," "n," and "d" constituted the article "and." If this interpretation is correct, the word "and" should belong with the words "afflictions cannot" on the next line. A less likely interpretation is that the words "and afflictions cannot" were added later, and Charles assumed the word "Jesus" was instead "Jewish," thus necessitating the addition of the letter "h."

17. The words "afflictions cannot" were written beneath the line. They likely belong with the word "and" in the line before. In 1878, Charles said, "I know what it is to suffer from terrible depression of spirit at times; yet at the very moment when it has seemed to me that life was not worth one single bronze coin, I have been perfectly peaceful with regard to all the greater things" (*MTP* 24:79).

18. Charles may have intended the words "covenant-making-and-keeping" to be compound adjectives that describe "God." If this interpretation is correct, the sentence should read, "The covenant-making-and-keeping God is eternal." Cf. Ps 102:12; 1 Tim 1:17; Rev 1:8.

19. An alternative reading of this line is "Heavenly peace, [such] as the babe and its mother, the lamb and the shepherd." Cf. Psalm 23; Luke 15:1–7.

20. Cf. Matt 3:17.

21. See "Salvation in God Only" (Sermon 24).

22. Cf. Matt 5:17.

23. The word "executor" comes from the verb "execute" which means "to perform; to practise." In this context the best meaning of the word is "to put in act; to do what is planned or determined" (Johnson's *Dictionary*). See also "Effectual Calling" (*NPSP* 2, Sermon 73) and "Effectual Calling—Illustrated by the Call of Abram" (*MTP* 14, Sermon 843).

Matt 25. 19 — The improvement of our talents. 61.

This cannot refer to saints alone for one is condemned.
But must apply to all men — God has given to all men talents
to improve, the wicked do not do so and are condemned
God gives his saints grace to improve them, and then
rewards them for so doing — not for so doing but through Jesus.

I. God has given to all so powers to glorify him.
1. for he has made nothing in vain — beasts, plants, insects,
much less man superior to all — lord vicoregent of the earth.
endowed with high faculties — specially Xn man who
is the superbest work of God, his crowning piece.
2. Is this not one reason why men are spared.
God might have damned men at once but he lets them go on.
He could have taken all his elect to heaven at once as he does
elect infants — the reason is he wishes them to glorify him.
3. The Scriptures contain no instance of an untalented believer.
4. We may learn from the talents this fact.
Wealth, learning, ability, courage, prudence, wisdom
Influence in society, the family,
Use of reason, revelation, our time, prayer.

II. God expects us to improve them.
For our own and others good —   Not to please ourselves.
No spiritual sloth is allowable.   Nor to seek any other object than God's glory
In so doing they will be increased. Nor to spend ourselves in sin —

III. He will call us to a reckoning. — this will be conducted
with justice, the books of judgment will be opened —
there will be a scrupulous examination. men their own
accusers — according to their talents. he will require at their
hand.   Let us examine ourselves and see if during this
year we have done so. — If not are we not guilty of ingratitude
the wicked punished for sin. the righteous rewarded by grace alone
84.

61

The IMPROVEMENT
of OUR TALENTS
Matthew 25:19[1]

"After a long time the lord of those servants cometh, and reckoneth with them."

This cannot refer to saints alone, for one is condemned. But must apply to all men. God has given to all men talents to improve. The wicked do not do so and are condemned. God gives his saints grace to improve them and then rewards them ~~for~~ on[2] so doing. Not for so doing, but through Jesus.

I. GOD HAS GIVEN TO ALL SO[ME][3] POWERS TO GLORIFY HIM.

1. For he has made nothing in vain: beasts, plants, insects.[4] Much less man, superior to all, lord, viceregent[5] of the earth,[6] endowed with high faculties.[7] Specially Xn[8] man, who is the superbest work of God, his crowning piece.

2. Is this not one reason why men are spared? God might have damned men at once, but he lets them go on.[9] He could have taken all his elect to heaven at once as he does elect infants.[10] The reason is he wishes them to glorify him.

3. The scriptures contain no instance of an untalented believer.[11]

4. We may learn from the talents this fact. Wealth, learning, ability, courage, prudence, wisdom, Influence in society, the family, Use of reason, revelation, our time, prayer.

II. GOD EXPECTS US TO IMPROVE THEM.

For our own and others['] good.   Not to please ourselves.[12]

No spiritual sloth[13] is allowable.   Nor to seek any other object than God's glory.[14]

In so doing, they will be increased.   Nor to spend ourselves in sin.

III. HE WILL CALL US TO A RECKONING.[15]

This will be conducted with justice. The books of judgment will be opened.[16]
There will be a scrupulous examination.[17] Men [will be] their own accusers
according to their talents [that] he will require at their hand.

Let us examine ourselves and see if during this year[18] we have done so. If not,
are we not guilty of ingratitude? The wicked, punished for sin. The righteous,
rewarded by grace alone.[19]

84.

1. This is the only time Charles preached a sermon on Matt 25:19. However, on January 31, 1858, he preached a sermon on Matt 25:22–23 entitled "The Two Talents" (*NPSP* 4, Sermon 175). Thematic overlap exists; however, the differences in the structure of the later sermon suggest Charles did not have the above outline in mind when writing "The Two Talents."

2. Charles may have struck through the word "for" and replaced it with "on" for theological reasons. If, by using the word "for," the sentence underscored the earning of God's merit in the improving of talents, then the strikethrough was likely intended to redirect the emphasis away from the propagation of a works-based righteousness. By changing the word "for" to "on," Charles exchanged the cause of the reward for the timing of the reward and thus redirected the emphasis back to the grace of God that enabled the action. This shift in emphasis from "why" to "when" is subtle, but it may shed light onto the reason for Charles's prepositional redaction. It was likely for this reason that Charles further clarified his point in the following phrase: "not for so doing, but through Jesus." See also the final sentence of the outline, "The righteous, rewarded by grace alone."

3. The context suggests Charles intended to use the word "some" instead of "so."

4. Charles's admiration and appreciation for the natural world is evidenced by the books he owned in his personal library, such as J. G. Wood, *Sketches and Anecdotes of Animal Life* (4th ed.; London: George Routledge and Co., 1857, The Spurgeon Library); William Kirby, *The Bridgewater Treatises on the Power, Wisdom, and Goodness of God as Manifested in the Creation of Animals and in Their History, Habits, and Insects,* vol. 1 (London: William Pickering, 1835, The Spurgeon Library); and Robert John Thornton, *A New Family Herbal; or a Popular Account of the Natures and Properties of the Various Plants Used in Medicine, Diet, and the Arts* (London: Richard Phillips, 1810, The Spurgeon Library).

5. One who is "governing; ruling" (Johnson's *Dictionary*, s.v. "regent"). However, Johnson did not supply a definition for the word "vice-regent." According to Joseph Worcester, the word "vice-gerent" comes from the Latin words *vice*, which is translated "in the place of," and *gero*, which is translated "to carry on, to administer," and is defined as "an officer acting as deputy or lieutenant of another" (Worcester's *Dictionary*). The word "viceroy" may also function as a synonym to "vice-regent" or "vice-gerent." Worcester defined "viceroy" as "one who governs in place of a king, with a delegated

regal authority; an officer representing a king in a dependency; a vice-king." In Johnson's Dictionary a "viceroy" was defined as "he who governs in place of the king with regal authority." The context surrounding Charles's use of the word "vice-regent" suggests that any of these definitions can apply in the sentence "Man . . . [is] viceregent of the earth." In other words, man is the delegated authority over earth who represents God, the King. An article in *The Cork Examiner* adds cultural context to Charles's statement: "What the future government of India may be, it is early to predicate, but the inevitable conclusion is, that it must be governed somewhat in the same manner as Ireland; viz., that there shall be a principle Secretary of State for India and a Lord-Lieutenant, or Vice-Regent, who, under the crown, shall have all but regal power" ("The Future and Present of India," *The Cork Examiner*, [August 12, 1857]). For additional uses of the word "vice-regent" in Charles's sermons, see "Oh That Men Would Praise the Lord" (Notebook 2, Sermon 105); *NPSP* 1:351; and *MTP* 29:454.

6. Cf. Gen 1:26.

7. An alternative reading of these sentences is "Much less man [who is] superior to all—[the] lord [and] vice-regent of the earth [who is] endowed with high faculties."

8. Abbr., "Christian." For additional instances in which Charles abbreviated this word, see "Necessity of Purity for an Entrance to Heaven" (Sermon 2); "The Path of the Just" (Sermon 35); and "Imitation of God" (Sermon 69).

9. Cf. 1 Tim 2:4.

10. Throughout his ministry Charles believed persons who died in infancy were counted as among God's elect. See "Infant Salvation" (*MTP* 7, Sermon 411) and *TD* 1:106. For additional references to David's son, Absalom, see "The Barley-Field on Fire" (*MTP* 10, Sermon 563) and "An Anxious Enquiry for a Beloved Son" (*MTP* 24, Sermon 1433).

11. "*Simon Peter was worth ten Andrews*, so far as we can gather from sacred history, and yet Andrew was instrumental in bringing him to Jesus. You may be very deficient in talent yourself, and yet you may be the means of drawing to Christ one who shall become eminent in grace and service. Ah! dear friend, you little know the possibilities which are in you. You may but speak a word to a child, and in

that child there may be slumbering a noble heart which shall stir the Christian church in years to come. Andrew has only two talents, but he finds Peter. Go thou and do likewise" (C. H. Spurgeon, *Evening by Evening*, February 19, italics in the original).

12. Cf. Phil 2:3.

13. For additional references to sloth, see "Despisers Warned" (Sermon 26); "The Fight and the Weapons" (Sermon 37a); and "The Fight" (Sermon 37b).

14. "You will never glory in God till first of all God has killed your glorying in yourself" (*MTP* 20:348).

15. Cf. Isa 2:12; 10:3.

16. Cf. Rev 20:12.

17. Cf. Matt 12:36.

18. Charles did not record a date for his preaching of this sermon. However, if December 2, 1851, is the correct date of the coup d'état he referenced in the previous sermon (see "The Peace of God" [Sermon 60]), then he likely preached the above sermon at the end of December 1851. If this interpretation is correct, it would explain Charles's call for reflection at the end of the year.

19. An alternative reading of this line is "The wicked [will be] punished for sin [and] the righteous [will be] rewarded by grace alone." Cf. Rom 3:28.

62   Ps. 73. 24 ...   God the guide of his saints.

Man is not intended for earth, he is only a pilgrim through it to eternal happiness. this he seeks for, but to gain it

I Man needs a guide, at all times, in all stages of growth.

1. If we consider <u>man</u> we shall see this - the swallow flies across the ocean by instinct, animals migrate, ants store food by instinct man has none. he has no foresight - he cannot see far before him he has no prudence, no wisdom, little strength, is inclined to death
<small>never went the way before</small>
<small>to death</small>

2. The way is full of difficulties and beset with dangers. mountains rivers, forests, flowery allurements, bypaths, ambush, hiding robbers

3. Many are ruined who have made a fair shew.

II. This Guide should be well chosen. He must have experience, foresight, acquaintance with the way, prudence. might. fidelity. ability to go all the way,

Many Guides men choose are useless. Guide Passion, Guide Reason, is often a self conceited fool. Guide Priest is an impostor. Guide Philosopher. Guide Moralist of this world

III God is the only Guide who answers to this description He has eternal experience, omniscience, prudence, omnipotence faithfulness, eternity -- the saints redeemed witness this Heaven belongs to him & he will give admittance ...

+

1. All should implicitly trust themselves in his hand.

2. Christians who have done so should rely on him.

3. Eternal glory should cheer the road.

+ He guides his people   1 By the precepts of the Bible.
                           2 By providence
                           3. By Spiritual Influence in prayer.

85.

62

GOD, *the* GUIDE *of* HIS SAINTS
Psalm 73:24[1]

"Thou shalt guide me with thy counsel, and afterward receive me to glory."

Man is not intended for earth.[2] He is only a pilgrim through it to eternal happiness.[3] This he seeks for, but to gain it:

I. MAN NEEDS A GUIDE AT ALL TIMES,
    IN ALL STAGES OF GROWTH.

1. If we consider <u>man</u>, we shall see this. The swallow flies across the ocean by instinct.[4] Animals migrate.[5] Ants store food by instinct.[6] Man has none. He has no foresight. He cannot see far before him. [He] never went the way before.[7] He has no prudence,[8] no wisdom, little strength, is enclined[9] to death.[10]

2. The way is full of[11] difficulties and beset with dangers: Mountains, rivers, forests, flowery allurements, bypaths, ambush, highway robbers.[12]

3. Many are ruined who have made a fair shew.[13]

II. THIS GUIDE SHOULD BE WELL CHOSEN.
    He must have experience, foresight, acquaintance with the way, prudence, might, fidelity, ability to go all the way. Many Guides men choose are useless: Guide Passion. Guide Reason is often a self-conceited fool. Guide Priest is an impostor. Guide Philosopher. Guide Morality of this world.

III. GOD IS THE ONLY GUIDE WHO ANSWERS TO THIS DESCRIPTION.

He has eternal experience, omniscience,[14] prudence, omnipotence,[15] faithfulness,[16] eternity.[17] The saints, redeemed witness.[18] This Heaven belongs to him, and he will give admittance.

x[19]

1. All should implicitly trust themselves in his hand.[20]

2. Christians who have done so should rely on him.

3. Eternal glory should cheer the road.[21]

x   He guides his people:

1. By the precepts of the Bible.[22]
2. By providence.
3. By Spiritual Influence in prayer.[23]

85.

1. On October 4, 1888, Charles preached an additional sermon on Ps 73:24 entitled "Guidance to Grace and Glory" (*MTP* 40, Sermon 2389; see also *MTP* 52:338). Overlapping content exists; however, it is unlikely Charles had the above outline in mind when writing the later sermon. See the heavily annotated 1864 Psalter that he used during his writing of *The Treasury of David: The Book of Psalms, Translated out of the Original Hebrew; and with the Former Translation Diligently Compared and Revised, by His Majesty's Special Command* ([rev. ed.; London: George E. Eyre and William Spottiswoode, 1864, The Spurgeon Library], Psalm 73).

2. A cluster of yellow dots surrounds the space between the words "earth" and "he." These dots are likely the result of the aging process of the manuscript and do not appear to hold significance for the text. The imprint of these dots can be found beneath the letter "G" in the word "Gethsemane" in the following sermon, "Gethsemane's Sorrow" (Sermon 63).

3. Given the specific reference to John Bunyan's *The Pilgrim's Progress* in "The Fight and the Weapons" (Sermon 37a), Charles likely had this allegory in mind. Cf. Ps 84:5; Heb 11:10; 2 Pet 2:11.

4. The following explanation for swallow migration was taken from Charles's personal copy of *The Bridgewater Treatises* by English entomologist William Kirby (1759–1850): "[I]t is not only the increasing heat of the southern regions which induces the *swallow* to seek a less ardent clime to transact her loves and rear her young; but also a stimulus, caused by the heat, acting upon her organization, which aids to accomplish that important purpose, and is the leading star by which her Creator impels her to the land of her own nativity, and which is destined to be that of her offspring" (Kirby, *The Bridgewater Treatises*, 1:102, italics in the original).

5. "But, besides the insectivorous emigrators, many of the higher and more powerful tribes are accustomed to change one country for another. When the carcasses of animals putrify, and birds multiply under the influence of the northern sun, vultures, eagles, falcons, hawks, &c. leave the south and go to partake of the feasts provided for them in higher latitudes" (ibid., 1:103).

6. In Charles's personal copy of *The Wonders of Animal Instinct* by French zoologist Ernest Menault (1830–1903), the following observation can be found: "The intelligence of ants has been a subject of remark for many ages. . . . The females are at all times

surrounded by a respectful court, are even carried in triumph when fatigued, and nourished by the richest food" (Ernest Menault, *Wonders of Animal Instinct: With Illustrative Anecdotes from the French of Ernest Menault* [London: Cassell, Petter, and Galpin, n.d., The Spurgeon Library], 1–2). Cf. Prov 6:6; 30:25.

7.   The phrase "never went the way before" was written above the line. The context suggests Charles likely intended to insert it after the line, "he cannot see far before him."

8.   Charles wrote the words "never went the way before" above the line. If he intended to insert this phrase after the word "has," then the sentence would read, "man has never went the way before." It is also possible Charles intended to insert it after the word "none" in the line above.

9.   "To bend; to lean; to tend toward any part" (Johnson's *Dictionary*, s.v. "encline"). Charles's use of the letter "e" instead of "i" in this spelling is unusual but not exclusive to this sermon (see also "The Downfall of Pride" [Notebook 4, Sermon 200]).

10.   The words "to death" were written above the line. If Charles intended them to belong with the phrase above, the sentence would read, "he cannot see far before him to death." More likely Charles intended these words to follow "is enclined."

11.   The words "full of" were written above the line and indicated with a caret between the words "is" and "difficulties."

12.   Cf. Luke 10:30.

13.   In Victorian England the word "shew" was a common spelling of the word "show." During the same year that Charles wrote Notebook 1, the two words were used interchangeably in an article about the Great Exhibition in *The Cambridge Chronicle*: "I do not doubt, that while this Great Exhibition shall shew to foreign countries the marvels of our industry—shall show to us, also, the marvels of the industry of our foreign competitors" ("Lord Stanley on the Exhibition," *The Cambridge Chronicle and University Journal, Isle of Ely Herald, and Huntingdonshire Gazette* [June 14, 1851]).

14.   Cf. Ps 147:5; 1 John 3:20.

15.   Cf. Jer 32:27; Matt 19:26.

16.   Cf. Ps 36:5; 1 Cor 1:9.

17.   Cf. Job 36:26; Ps 102:12; Isa 41:4.

18.   An alternative reading of this line is "The saints [are] redeemed witness[es of] this."

19.   Charles may have intended this "x" to serve as a footnote like the asterisk halfway through his previous sermon, "The Wise Men's Offering" (Sermon 58). If this interpretation is correct, then the phrase, "He guides his people" and the following three points should precede the line that begins with the first point: "1. All should implicitly trust . . ." However, the "x" also might have represented the fourth point or the conclusion of the body of the sermon. The first interpretation is the most likely and suggests Charles added this information afterward, thus necessitating the footnote.

20.   Cf. Prov 3:5.

21.   "There is no true glory for any man who takes his own course; but glory is for those of you who put your hand into the hand of the great Father, and pray him to forgive all your iniquities for Christ's sake, and to lead you in the way everlasting" (*MTP* 40:571).

22.   "Nine times out of ten, look to the Ten Commandments, and you will at least know what you must not do; and knowing what you must not do, you will be able to conclude what you may do. There are some wonderfully plain directions in God's Word as to all manner of circumstances and conditions" (*MTP* 40:569). Cf. Ps 119:105.

23.   On July 4, 1869, Charles preached a sermon entitled "An Assuredly Good Thing" (*MTP* 15, Sermon 879). In this sermon he expounded on the spiritual influences that occur during the practice of prayer and, in particular, how to draw near to God: "Prayer is the *modus operandi*, it is the outward form of drawing near to God; but there is an inner spiritual approach which is scarcely to be described by language. Shall I tell you how I have sometimes drawn near to him? I have been worn and wearied with a heavy burden, and have resorted to prayer. I have tried to pour out my soul's anguish in words, but there was not vent enough by way of speech, and therefore my soul has broken out into sighs, and sobs, and tears. Feeling that God was hearing my heart-talk, I have said to him, 'Lord, behold my affliction; thou knowest

all about it, deliver me. If I cannot exactly tell thee, there is no need of my words, for thou dost see for thyself. Thou searcher of hearts, thou readest me as I read in a book; wilt thou be pleased to help thy poor servant! I scarce know what help it is I want, but thou dost know it. I cannot tell thee what I desire, but teach me to desire what thou wilt be sure to give. Conform my will to thine.' Perhaps at such a time there may be a peculiar bitterness about your trouble, a secret with which no stranger may intermeddle, but you tell it all out to your God. With broken words, sighs, groans, and tears, you lay bare the inmost secret of your soul. Taking off the doors of your heart from their hinges, you bid the Lord come in, and walk through every chamber, and see the whole. I do not know how to tell you what drawing near to God is better than by this rambling talk. It is getting to feel that the Lord is close to you, and that you have no secret which you wish to keep back from him, but have unveiled your most private and sacred desires to him. The getting right up to Jesus, our Lord, the leaning of the head, when it aches with trouble, upon the heart that always beats with pity, the casting of all care upon him, believing that he cares for you, pities you, and sympathises with you—this is drawing near unto God" (*MTP* 15:376–77, italics in the original). See also "Elijah's Faith and Prayer" (Sermon 44).

Matt 26..38   Gethsemane's Sorrow.—

The Garden's of Eden and Gethsemane are places of great interest
Jesus retired and suffered temptation both in the commencement
and close of his public ministry.   His human nature was perfect
both body and soul. they both suffered in the work of atonement.
I. We shall consider a few of the causes of his grief.   Of course the
first cause was his bearing the sins of his people & God's wrath for sin
1. His ill-treatment by the world. Unfaithfulness of friends, treachery
of Judas, murder by the nations — added to this his heavenly love.
2. The Shock given to his unsullied purity by his standing in
the room of sinners, and bearing their guilt away; about to be charged
with blasphemy; and to be the innocent victim of ~~cruel~~ earthly foulest crime
3. The Indignities he was about to endure in being sold as a slave
tried before the court, held up to public scorn, and ignominious death
4. His foresight would increase the pain — man cannot foresee
    nor the brute and happy is it but Jesus could foresee it all
    He could hear the rabble accusing him, feel the blinding cloth, & their
buffetings, Herod & his mighty men. the crown of thorns.
    the horrid flagellation, — (soldiers cutting his throat). The cry "crucify him"
His going through the streets, fainting. nailing to the cross — forsaken of
his God, his death.
5 — A Sense of Loneliness without help, Hopelessness certain was his death
II. The Reason to satisfy justice and save sinners.—
We may infer 1. The Son's & Father's love to men.
            2. The Justice of God
            3. Man's hardness of heart
          — 4. The sinner's fearful doom

86

63

GETHSEMANE'S SORROW
Matthew 26:38[1]

"Then saith he unto them, My soul is exceeding sorrowful, even unto death:
tarry ye here, and watch with me."

The Gardens[2] of Eden and Gethsemane[3] are places of great interest. Jesus retired and suffered temptation, both in the commencement[4] and close of his public ministry. His human nature was perfect,[5] both body and soul. They both suffered in the work of atonement.[6]

I. WE SHALL CONSIDER A FEW OF THE CAUSES OF HIS GRIEF.

Of course, the first cause was his bearing the sins of his people and God's wrath for sin.[7]

1. His ill treatment by the world,[8] Unfaithfulness of friends,[9] treachery of Judas,[10] murder by the nations.[11] Added to this, his heavenly love.[12]

2. The Shock[13] given to his unsullied purity by his standing in the room of sinners[14] and bearing their guilt away.[15] About to be charged[16] with blasphemy.[17] And to be the innocent victim of ~~cruel~~ earthly, foulest crime.[18]

3. The Indignities he was about to endure in being sold as a slave,[19] tried before the court,[20] held up to public scorn, and ignominious[21] death.

4. His foresight would increase the pain.[22] Man cannot forsee, nor the brute, and happy is it. But Jesus could forsee it all. He could hear the rabble[23] accusing him, feel the blinding cloth[24] and their buffetings,[25] Herod and his mighty men, the crown of thorns,[26] the horrid flagellation[27] (soldier cutting his throat),[28] the cry, "crucify him,"[29] his going through the streets,[30] fainting,[31] nailing to the cross,[32] forsaken of his God,[33] his death.[34]

5. A sense of Loneliness, without help, Hopelessness. Certain was his death.[35]

II. THE REASON.[36] TO SATISFY JUSTICE AND SAVE SINNERS.[37]

We may infer: 1. The Son's and Father's[38] love to men.[39]
               2. The Justice of God.
               3. Man's hardness of heart.
               4.[40] The sinner's fearful doom.

86

1. This is the only time Charles preached a sermon on Matt 26:38. For additional sermons on Gethsemane, see "Gethsemane" (*MTP* 9, Sermon 493); "The Garden of the Soul" (*MTP* 12, Sermon 693); "The Agony in Gethsemane" (*MTP* 20, Sermon 1199); "Jesus in Gethsemane" (*MTP* 48, Sermon 2767); and "Christ in Gethsemane" (*MTP* 56, Sermon 3190).

2. Charles inserted an apostrophe between the letters "n" and "s" in the word "Gardens"; however, the context suggests he intended this word to be plural, not possessive.

3. A cluster of yellow stains surrounds the letter "G" in the word "Gethsemane." The source of the stains can be found in the previous sermon, "God, the Guide of His Saints" (Sermon 62), and is likely the result of the aging process of the manuscript.

4. Cf. Matt 4:1–11; Luke 4:1–13.

5. "[W]hatever Satan may have suggested to our Lord, his perfect nature did not in any degree whatever submit to it so as to sin" (*MTP* 9:76).

6. "[T]here was agony between the attributes of his nature, a battle on an awful scale in the arena of his soul. The purity which cannot bear to come into contact with sin must have been very mighty in Christ, while the love which would not let his people perish was very mighty too. It was a struggle on a Titanic scale, as if a Hercules had met another Hercules; two tremendous forces strove and fought and agonised within the bleeding heart of Jesus. . . . I marvel not that our Lord's sweat was as it were great drops of blood, when such an inward pressure made him like a cluster trodden in the winepress" (*MTP* 20:597).

7. "The woe that broke over the Saviour's spirit, the great and fathomless ocean of inexpressible anguish which dashed over the Saviour's soul when he died, is so inconceivable . . . the very spray from that great tempestuous deep, as it fell on Christ, baptised him in a bloody sweat. He had not yet come to the raging billows of the penalty itself, but even standing on the shore, as he heard the awful surf breaking at his feet, his soul was sore amazed and very heavy" (*MTP* 20:594). Cf. 2 Cor 5:21.

8. Cf. John 15:18.   9. Cf. Matt 26:69–75.

10. Cf. Matt 26:47–49.

11. It is unclear why Charles bolded the letters "tions" in the word "nations." The same pressure from his writing instrument can be found in the word "his" two lines above.

12. Cf. John 17:26.

13. An illegible letter, possibly "m," appears beneath the letter "h" in the word "Shock." Charles may have originally written the word "mock."

14. Cf. 1 Pet 3:18. 15. Cf. Rom 8:3.

16. The letters "ed" in the word "charged" trail into the margin.

17. Cf. Matt 26:65. 18. Cf. Luke 23:41.

19. Cf. Matt 26:14–16. 20. Cf. Luke 23:7,11; John 18:19–24.

21. "Mean; shameful; reproachful; dishonourable" (Johnson's *Dictionary*, s.v. "ignominious").

22. With reference to Christ's bleeding in Gethsemane, Charles wrote, "No need to put on the leech, or apply the knife; [his blood] flows spontaneously" (C. H. Spurgeon, *Morning by Morning; or, Daily Readings for the Family or the Closet* [New York: Sheldon and Company, 1866, The Spurgeon Library], March 23).

23. "A tumultuous crowd; an assembly of low people" (Johnson's *Dictionary*, s.v. "rabble").

24. Cf. Luke 22:64. 25. Cf. Mark 14:65.

26. Cf. Matt 27:29; John 19:2. 27. Cf. Matt 27:26; John 2:15.

28. Charles may have been referring to the Roman practice of cutting the necks of criminals. In *Antiquities of the Jews*, Roman-Jewish historian Josephus (AD 37– c. AD 100) recounted: "[Alexander] brought [the Jews] to Jerusalem, and did one of the most barbarous actions in the world to them: for as he was feasting with concubines, in the sight of all the city, he ordered about eight hundred of them to be crucified, and while they were living, he ordered the throats of their children and wives to be cut before their eyes" (Flavius Josephus, *The Works of Flavius Josephus, the Learned and Authentic Jewish Historian, and Celebrated Warrior, to*

Which Are Added, Three Dissertations Concerning Jesus Christ, John the Baptist, James the Just, God's Command to Abraham ([trans. William Whiston; 4 vols; London: William Allason and J. Maynard, 1818, The Spurgeon Library], 2:251).

29. Cf. Mark 15:13; Luke 23:21; John 19:15.   30. Cf. John 19:17.

31. Cf. Mark 15:21.   32. Cf. Luke 23:33; John 19:18.

33. Cf. Matt 27:46; Mark 15:34.   34. Cf. Matt 27:50; Luke 23:46.

35. Charles wrote the word "death" above the line. The handwriting in the phrase "was his death" differs from that in the body of the sermon and was likely added afterward. The word "certain" may have been coupled with "Hopelessness." An alternative reading of this line is "Hopelessness [was] certain."

36. Charles underscored the words "The Reason" with a line of dots and dashes.

37. "His bones are every one of them dislocated, and his body is thus torn with agonies which cannot be described. 'Tis manhood suffering there; 'tis the Church suffering there, in the substitute. And when Christ dies, you are to look upon the death of Christ, not as his own dying merely, but as the dying of all those for whom he stood as the scapegoat and the substitute. . . . When you die you will die for yourselves; when Christ died, he died for you, if you are a believer in him" (*NPSP* 4:69). Cf. 1 Tim 1:15.

38. An illegible stroke, possibly the tittle of the letter "I," can be found to the left of the apostrophe in the word "Father's."

39. Cf. John 3:16.

40. The em dash preceding the number 4 does not appear to hold significance for the text. Cf. horizontal stroke to the right of the number 5, five lines above.

64   Matt 13 . 25 .   Parable of the bad & good seed.

How plain all our Lord's discourses were . so plentifully interspersed with allusions to passing events , (tale of a man who
sowed garlic in a farmer's field.

I. What is meant by the good seed , the wheat –

He sower is Jesus . and the gospel minister . the wheat are they
who receive the truth . and are real Christians, they are
compared to wheat in many places in Scripture –

I. Because of their preciousness, being chosen of God. the excellent of the earth . redeemed, regenerated.

2. Because of their usefulness to the world, & absolute necessity.

3. They have life, they grow. they die before they live, they have
weight and permanence not as chaff. fulness in Jesus.

4. Great care is required in sowing, manuring, weeding, hoeing,
and threshing – so God's people are God's peculiar care.

These sons of God are in the church and some in the world.

II. The Evil seed, the tares, sown by the enemy of Christ,
his saints & his Church, even the devil, the seed are

1. Evil men, who are found in the world, the congregation, the church.
2. All discord, heresy, scism, and sin.

III. The persons who allowed the seed to be sown & their sleep.
1 all Christians 2 the Ministers. 3. The Church.
they sleep. by neglect , by lukewarmness, by indolence
caused by worldly care, the old man, outward ease, neglect of ordinance.

We may learn.

1. There is a mixture of good & evil here, but a separation
shall come . even professors must be examined .

2. Churches should be awake , Christians should be awake,
since the enemy does not sleep. but goes his way to do
mischief in other fields . where men are asleep. –

87.

PARABLE *of the* BAD *and* GOOD SEED
Matthew 13:25[1]

"But while men slept, his enemy came and sowed tares among the wheat, and went his way."

How plain[2] all our Lord's discourses were, so plentifully interspersed with allusions to passing events[3] (tale of a man who sowed garlic in a farmer's field).[4]

I. WHAT IS MEANT BY THE GOOD SEED, THE WHEAT.
The sower is Jesus and the gospel minister. The wheat are they who receive the truth and are real Christians. They are compared to wheat in many places in Scripture:[5]

1.[6] Because of their[7] preciousness,[8] being chosen of God,[9] the excellent of the earth,[10] redeemed, regenerated.

2. Because of their usefulness to the world and absolute necessity.

3. They have life, they grow, they die before they live,[11] they have weight and permanence. Not as chaff. Fulness in Jesus.

4. Great[12] care is required in sowing,[13] manuering, weeding, hoeing, and threshing. So God's people are God's peculiar care. These sons of God are in the church and some in the world.

II. THE EVIL SEED, the tares, sown by the enemy of Christ,[14] his saints, and his Church, even the devil.[15]
The seed[s] are:[16]

1. Evil men who are found in the world, the congregation, the church.

2. All discord, heresy, scism,[17] and sin.

III. THE PERSONS WHO ALLOWED THE SEED TO BE SOWN AND THEIR SLEEP:[18]

1. All Christians.

2. The Ministers.

3. The Church.
    They sleep by neglect, by lukewarmness,[19] by indolence caused by worldly care, the old man,[20] outward ease, neglect of ordinances.[21] We may learn:
    1. There is a mixture of good and evil here,[22] but a separation shall come.[23] Even professors must be examined.
    2. Churches should be awake. Christians should be awake since the enemy does not sleep but goes his way to do mischief in other fields where men are asleep.

87.

1. This is the only time Charles preached a sermon on Matt 13:25. See also "The Parable of the Sower" (*NPSP* 6, Sermon 308) and "Wheat in the Barn" (*MTP* 60, Sermon 3393). In the final years of his life, Charles began writing a devotional commentary on Matthew that "specially [called] attention to the Kingship of the Lord Jesus Christ" (*Autobiography* 4:315–17). Charles died before completing his commentary; however, not wanting "his last literary work to stand like a broken column," Susannah and a private secretary finished the work for publication (see C. H. Spurgeon, *The Gospel of the Kingdom: A Popular Exposition of the Gospel According to Matthew: With Introductory Note by Mrs. C. H. Spurgeon, and Textual Index of Sermons, &c, by C. H. Spurgeon, on Various Passages in the Gospel According to Matthew* [London: Passmore & Alabaster, 1893]). The Bible Charles used during the writing of this commentary is housed at The Spurgeon Library and contains copious notes, shedding light onto Charles's later understanding of Matthew.

2. "Now, in these days, there are some who would be glad if we would preach anything except Christ crucified. Perhaps the most dangerous amongst them are those who are continually crying out for intellectual preaching, by which they mean preaching which neither the hearers nor the preachers themselves can comprehend, the kind of preaching which has little or nothing to do with the Scriptures, and which requires a dictionary rather than a Bible to explain it" (*MTP* 56:482). See also "The Eloquence of Jesus" (Sermon 49).

3. For additional references to current events, see *Autobiography* 4:128; *NPSP* 3:342; and 3:381.

4. In August 1859, approximately eight years after Charles preached the sermon above, American abolitionist Harriet Tubman delivered a political speech in Boston in which she recounted the following story: A man "sowed onions and garlic to feed his cows, having heard that this would increase his dairy production and bring him greater profits. But once the garlic and onions had settled in the cows' bellies, the milk took on their flavors and the butter churned up with too strong a taste. Nobody would buy it. And so the farmer returned to the old method and went back to sowing clover. But it was too late. The wind had blown onions and garlic over his fields, and they sprouted once again. And the clover came up tasting of them, as did the butter. There was no going back" (Beverly Lowry, *Harriet Tubman: Imagining a Life* [New York: Anchor Books, 2007], 249); this story is also recounted in Jean M. Humez, *Harriet Tubman: The Life and the Life Stories* [Madison, WI: The University

of Wisconsin Press, 2003], 38). Charles did not reference this story again; however, he often spiritualized the unsavory bitterness of garlic with the sweetness of Jesus Christ: "'If so be ye have tasted that the Lord is gracious,' *abhor the garlic flavour of the world's vices*" (*MTP* 36:563, italics in the original). See also *MTP* 8:389.

5. Cf. Matt 3:12; Luke 22:31.

6. For consistency, Roman numeral I should be replaced with cardinal number 1.

7. The size and location of the letters "ir" in the word "their" suggest Charles added them afterward. The original line likely read "Because of the preciousness."

8. Cf. Isa 43:4.   9. Cf. Jer 1:5; Gal 1:15.

10. Cf. Ps 16:3.   11. Cf. Luke 9:23; Gal 2:20.

12. An illegible letter, likely "t," was written beneath the "G" in the word "Great." Charles may have originally begun writing the word "they" as he did in the line directly above.

13. In the Bible Charles used for his commentary on Matthew, he underscored the phrase "a sower went forth to sow" in Matt 13:3.

14. "We know who the enemy is. His time for work is in the night. He sleeps not when watchmen are steeped in slumber; but then is he specially active. Quietly, cunningly, without observation, that malicious one sowed the darnel, the bastard wheat; a something so like wheat that no one could tell the difference till they began to ripen. He brought in those who loved 'modern thought', and worldly amusements, who were by their talk Christian, and by their boasts profoundly spiritual; and having introduced them cunningly, he departed" (Spurgeon, *The Gospel of the Kingdom*, 102).

15. An alternative reading of this sentence is "The evil seed—the tares—[who are] sown by the enemy of Christ, his saints, and his Church, even the devil."

16. Depending on whether Charles intended the word "seed" to be singular or plural, the line could read "The seed[s] are" or "The seed [is]." See also the subject/verb disagreement in "The Saints' Justification and Glory" (Sermon 68).

17. This is the only time in Notebook 1 that Charles spelled the word "schism" without inserting the letter "h" between the "c" and "i." Samuel Johnson defined the word as "a separation or division in the church of God" (Johnson's *Dictionary*, s.v. "schism").

18. "The servants are all too apt to sleep. There is a season when nature requires them to do so, and there are other times when sinful sloth persuades them to the same indulgence. Good, easy men, they cannot believe that anyone would do harm to their master's field; besides, watching and driving away trespassers is unpleasant work. 'Heresy-hunting' is the nickname for watchfulness. 'Rigid Puritanism' is the contemptuous title for careful discipline. 'Bigotry' is the title by which faithfulness is described. '*While men slept*' could any cultured person resist the spirit of the times, and keep awake?" (Spurgeon, *The Gospel of the Kingdom*, 102, italics in the original).

19. Cf. Rev 13:16.

20. Cf. Rom 6:6; Eph 4:22; Col 3:9.

21. For additional references to ecclesial ordinances in this notebook, see "God's Estimation of Men" (Sermon 41); "Christian Prosperity and Its Causes" (Sermon 51); "Pleasure in the Stones of Zion" (Sermon 53); "Josiah" (Sermon 66); and "Can Two Walk Together Unless They Are Agreed?" (Sermon 76).

22. "It is a great sorrow of heart to some of the wheat to be growing side by side with tares. The ungodly are as thorns and briars to those who fear the Lord" (*MTP* 60:74).

23. Cf. Matt 3:12; 25:32–33.

Prov. 28.26 _ Trust not the heart. 65

Solomon the wisest of men both by divine gift, and actual experience, as well as extensive observation.

The heart sometimes means the affections, here it means the man, the secret, inner man. _ this we must not trust.

I. Why should we not trust the heart

1. Because it is depraved, desperately wicked, a villain.
2. Because it is selfish, partial, and is not able to judge truly.
3. It is deceitful, we do not know it, or understand ourselves
4. There is a curse upon the man who does it.
5. It has done harm to us already & to millions more.

II. Who do trust the heart.

1. Those who believe in its purity, think that they can withstand temptation, and stay their career of sin.
2. Those who follow their own inclinations.
3. Those who believe the suggestions of their hearts.

III. What are its false suggestions.

1. Religion is of no consequence
2. I am no worse than my neighbours, we shall die together
3. I can be saved at anytime, very easily.
4. I am waiting for the Spirit.
5. I have sought him but have not found him

88

65

TRUST NOT *the* HEART
Proverbs 28:26[1]

"He that trusteth in his own heart is a fool: but whoso walketh wisely, he shall be delivered."

Solomon, the wisest of men, both by divine gift[2] and actual experience, as well as extensive observation.[3] The heart sometimes means the affections.[4] Here, it means the man, the secret, inner man. This, we must not trust.

I. WHY SHOULD WE NOT TRUST THE HEART?

1. Because it is depraved,[5] desperately wicked, a villain.

2. Because it is selfish,[6] partial, and is not able to judge truly.

3. It is deceitful.[7] We do not know it or understand ourselves.[8]

4. There is a curse upon the man who does it.

5. It has done harm to us already and to millions more.

II. WHO DO TRUST THE HEART?

1. Those who believe in its purity, [who] think that they can withstand temptation and stay their career of sin.

2. Those who follow their own inclinations.

3. Those who believe the suggestions of their hearts.

III. WHAT ARE ITS FALSE SUGGESTIONS?

1. Religion is of no consequence.

2. I am no worse than my neighbours. We shall die together.

3.[9] I can be saved at anytime very easily.

4. I am waiting for the Spirit.

5. I have sought him, but have not found him.[10]

88

1. This is the only time Charles preached a sermon on Prov 28:26. For additional sermons on the heart, see: "A Divided Heart" (*NPSP* 5, Sermon 276); "Believing with the Heart" (*MTP* 9, Sermon 519); "Faith Purifying the Heart" (*MTP* 23, Sermon 1349); "Exhortation—'Set Your Heart'" (*MTP* 32, Sermon 1884); "Christ the Cure for Troubled Hearts" (*MTP* 41, Sermon 2408); "The Cure for a Weak Heart" (*MTP* 42, Sermon 2455); "The Deceived Heart" (*MTP* 46, Sermon 2686); "God's Writing on Man's Heart" (*MTP* 52, Sermon 2992); "The Cause and Effect of Heart Trouble" (*MTP* 54, Sermon 3076); "Binding Up Broken Hearts" (*MTP* 54, Sermon 3104); and "The Divided Heart" (*MTP* 62, Sermon 3527).

2. Cf. 2 Chron 1:10–12.

3. An alternative reading of this line is "Solomon [was] the wisest of men, both by divine gift and actual experience, as well as [by] extensive observation." See also "Despisers Warned" (Sermon 26).

4. On this point Charles may have consulted Jonathan Edwards. See Jonathan Edwards et al., *The Works of Jonathan Edwards*: "True religion, in great part, consists in holy affections (1:236). . . . If we do but consider what the hearts of natural men are, what principles they are under, what blindness and deceit, what self-flattery, self-exaltation, and self-confidence reigns there, we need not at all wonder that their high opinion of themselves, and confidence of their happy circumstances, are as high and strong as mountains, and as violent as a tempest. For what should hinder, when once conscience is blinded, convictions are killed, false affections high, and those forementioned principles let loose? When, moreover, these principles are prompted by false joys and comforts, excited by some pleasing imaginations impressed by Satan, transforming himself into an angel of light?" (1:257).

5. Cf. Rom 1:24.

6. Cf. Ps 119:36; Jas 3:14.

7. Cf. Jer 17:9.

8. Cf. Rom 7:15.

9. The bolded number 3 was likely the result of a malfunction of Charles's writing instrument and not an attempt to draw attention to the third point. Cf. "3. Strong piety" and "6. Humble" in the following sermon, "Josiah" (Sermon 66).

10. Cf. Matt 7:7.

·

66.　　　　2 Kings 22 - 2　　　Josiah.

All Scripture characters intended either as beacons
or examples, Josiah eminently adapted for imitation

I. Josiah's piety, its most eminent characteristics.
　1. Youthful piety, when he was 12 years old.
　2. Singular piety, the whole nation was corrupt.
　3. Strong piety. he had no book of the law,
　4. Zealous, he was not content with reforming Judah,
　　he must reform Israel, he builds the house of God.
　5. Steady, it was not effervescent or changeable
　　　　　　　　　　　(?) evanescent
　6. Humble, tender hearted piety.

II. The effects of Josiah's piety.
　1. Destruction of idolatry — he hated idols.
　2. Reverence for God's house & ordinances,
　3. Reverence for God's holy word, a dread of
　　the anger of the Eternal one, and fear of him
　4. Conscientious dealing with all men,
　Cæsar has his due, he keeps his treaty with
　Babylon and dies fighting Necho.

III. The means for attaining such piety. —
　1. Earnest Prayer. ⎫
　2. Study of the Bible, ⎬　Who can tell what evils
　3. Faith & repentance ⎭　he escaped or the blessings he enjoyed

89

66

JOSIAH
2 Kings 22:2[1]

"And he did that which was right in the sight of the LORD, and walked in all the way of David his father, and turned not aside to the right hand or to the left."

All Scripture characters [were] intended either as beacons or examples.[2] Josiah [is] eminently adapted for imitation.

I.   JOSIAH'S PIETY. Its most eminent characteristics:

  1.   Youthful piety. When he was 12 years old.[3]

  2.   Singular piety. The whole nation was corrupt.[4]

  3.   Strong piety. He had no book of the law.

  4.   Zealous. He was not content with reforming Judah. He must reform Israel. He builds the house of God.

  5.   Steady. It was not effervescent[5] or changeable.

  6.   Humble.[6] Tender hearted piety.[7]

II. THE EFFECTS OF JOSIAH'S PIETY.

  1.   Destruction of idolatry.[8] He hated idols.

  2.   Reverence for God's house and ordinances.[9]

  3.   Reverence for God's holy word,[10] a dread of the anger of the Eternal one, and fear of him.

  4.   Conscientious dealing with all men. Caesar has his due.[11] He keeps his treaty with Babylon and dies fighting Necho.[12]

III. THE MEANS FOR ATTAINING SUCH PIETY.

  1.   Earnest Prayer.
  2.   Study of the Bible.   } Who can tell what evils he escaped
  3.   Faith and repentance.   or the blessings he enjoyed?

89

1. This is the only time Charles preached a sermon on 2 Kgs 22:2. For additional sermons on Josiah, see "Self-Humbling" (*MTP* 13, Sermon 748); "The King-Priest" (*MTP* 25, Sermon 1495); and "Cheer Up, My Comrades" (*MTP* 26, Sermon 1513).

2. An illegible letter, likely "l," was written beneath the letter "p" in the word "examples." It is possible Charles prematurely wrote the letter before he corrected the misspelling of the word.

3. According to 2 Kgs 22:1 and 2 Chron 34:1, Josiah was eight years old, not twelve, when he became king. Charles may have confused Josiah with Manasseh, who became king of Judah at the age of twelve (2 Kgs 21:1).

4. Cf. 2 Kgs 22:13.

5. The word "evanescent" was written in pencil above the word "effervescent." The question mark contained within the parentheses before the word suggests the redactor questioned whether or not the correct word should be "evanescent," which Samuel Johnson defined as "vanishing; imperceptible; lessening beyond the perception of the senses" (Johnson's *Dictionary*). The following words in the line, "or changeable," suggest the redactor was correct. The word "evanescent" satisfies the context of the line better than "effervescent," which Johnson defined as "the act of growing hot" (Johnson's *Dictionary*). See also Charles's use of the word "evanescent" in his sermon "The Affliction of Ahaz" (Sermon 57).

6. The boldness of the ink was likely the result of a malfunction of the writing instrument. For similar instances, see the words "of idolatry" two lines below and also the number 3 in the previous sermon, "Trust Not the Heart" (Sermon 65).

7. Cf. 2 Chron 34:27.   8.   Cf. 2 Kgs 23:10–15.

9. See "Parable of the Bad and Good Seed" (Sermon 64).

10. Cf. 2 Kgs 22:18; 23:2.   11.   Cf. Mark 12:17.

12. Cf. 2 Kgs 23:29–30; 2 Chron 35:20–24.

Mark IX. 42.   Offending God's little ones.   67

The people of God are represented as sheep in the midst of wolves.
Jesus has taken special care however that those who
bless them shall be blessed and cursers cursed.

I. The Characters – "little ones" "that believe in me".

Believers are called little ones because they have
Simplicity. they receive the word as children without dispute
Weakness. requiring strength, guidance, teaching, food.
Humility. thinking nothing of themselves
Dependance. absolute upon their heavenly Father.

II. The Crime against them " to offend ":–

1. By a scandalous life, false professors, hireling preachers,
and hypocritical men of religion do this.

2. Despising Gospel ministers, criticising, telling faults,
calumniating them, and rejecting their message.

3. Jesting at the saints, scorning their actions,
speaking ill of them and persecuting them.

4. Discouraging the young.

5. Misleading by sophistry and false doctrine,
persuading and decoying the good to sin and causing
offence to the sons of God (causing them to offend)
making strife, impairing usefulness. opposing.

III. Why so great a crime " it were better &c ".

1. Because they are Jesus purchase

2. He made them.

3. He loves them, they are united to him.

91

67

OFFENDING GOD'S LITTLE ONES[1]
Mark 9:42[2]

"And whosoever shall offend one of these little ones that believe in me, it is better for him that a millstone were hanged about his neck, and he were cast into the sea."

The people of God are represented as sheep in the midst of wolves.[3] Jesus has taken special care, however, that those who bless them shall be blessed, and cursers cursed.[4]

I. THE CHARACTERS: *"little ones" "that believe in me."*
    Believers are called little ones because they have:
    Simplicity.[5] They receive the word as children, without dispute.[6]
    Weakness. Requiring strength, guidance, teaching, food.[7]
    Humility. Thinking nothing of themselves.[8]
    Dependance. Absolute upon their heavenly Father.[9]

II. THE CRIME AGAINST THEM: *"to offend."*
    1. By a scandalous life, false professors, hireling[10] preachers, and hypocritical men of religion do this.
    2. Despising Gospel ministers, criticising, telling faults, calumniating[11] them, and rejecting their message.
    3. Jesting at the saints,[12] scorning their actions, speaking ill of them, and persecuting them.
    4. Discouraging the young.
    5. Misleading by sophistry and false doctrine,[13] persuading and decoying[14] the good to sin, and causing offence to the sons of God[15] (causing[16] them to offend), making strife, impairing usefulness, opposing.

III. WHY SO GREAT A CRIME? *"it were better," etc.*[17]
    1. Because they are Jesus['s] purchase.[18]
    2. He made them.[19]
    3. He loves them.[20] They are united to him.[21]

91

1. This is the only time Charles preached a sermon on Mark 9:42. For references to Mark 9:42 in his later sermons, see *MTP* 39:551; 48:250; 50:533; and 60:346–47.

2. Charles originally wrote Roman numeral IX instead of the number 9 in the Scripture reference. Charles also displays this tendency in "Christ About His Father's Business" (Sermon 15); "Love Manifest in Adoption" (Sermon 16); "Imitation of God" (Sermon 69); and "The Men Possessed of the Devils" (Sermon 70).

3. The word "wolves" trails into the margin. Cf. Matt 10:16; Luke 10:3.

4. Cf. Gen 12:3.

5. It appears Charles intentionally bolded the words "Simplicity," "Weakness," "Humility," and "Dependance" for emphasis.

6. Cf. Matt 18:3; Luke 18:17; 2 Tim 3:15.

7. Charles founded two orphanages later in his ministry that provided for the material, educational, and spiritual needs of London's disenfranchised children. The inspiration for the Stockwell Orphanage has origins in the ministries of George Müller (1805–1898). In 1855, Charles traveled to Müller's orphan-house on Ashley Down in Bristol and said, "I never heard such a sermon as I saw in my life there" (*NPSP* 1:378). After Müller preached, Charles was asked to say a few words but declined because he had "been crying all the while to think how God had heard this dear man's prayer, and how all those three hundred children had been fed by my Father through the prayer of faith." Charles reflected, "Simply by asking of God in his way, [Müller] has raised (I believe) £17,000 towards the erection of a new orphan-house. When I consider that, I sometimes think we will try the power of faith here, and see if we should not get sufficient funds whereby to erect a place to hold the people that crowd to hear the Word of God. Then we may have a tabernacle of faith as well as an orphan-house of faith. God send us that, and to him be all the glory" (*NPSP* 1:378). Approximately eleven years later, a donation of £20,000 was given to Charles for the construction of the Stockwell Orphanage by a Mrs. Hillyard, the widow of an Anglican clergyman (*Autobiography* 3:167, 172). On September 9, 1869, the orphanage for boys officially opened, followed ten years later by the girls' wing. The Stockwell Orphanage thrived throughout Charles's ministry and continued to function after his death. The current website for "Spurgeons," a children's charity in the United Kingdom, provides a brief but helpful history of the orphanage's development in the twentieth century. At the beginning of World War II in 1939, the orphans were evacuated from Stockwell and

sent to live at St. David's in Reigate, Surrey. The damage caused by German bombs prevented the reopening of the orphanage, and by 1953, all the children were sent to live in a new complex of buildings in Birchington, Kent. After that location closed in 1979, foster families housed the remaining children. In 1991, the orphanage became an international charity. "Today Spurgeons helps 37,071 children and young people and 78,643 parents and carers every year through its work with children's centres, young carers, struggling families and families affected by the criminal justice system" (www.spurgeons.org/about/our-history, accessed May 28, 2016). See notes in "Adoption" (Sermon 1).

8. Cf. John 3:30; Phil 2:3.

9. Two alternative readings of this line are: "Absolute [dependency] upon their heavenly Father" and "[They are] absolute[ly] dependant upon their heavenly Father." Cf. 2 Cor 1:9.

10. "One who serves for wages" (Johnson's *Dictionary*, s.v. "hireling").

11. "To accuse falsely; to charge without just ground" (Johnson's *Dictionary*, s.v. "calumniate").

12. Cf. 2 Kgs 2:23–25.   13. Cf. Rom 16:17; 2 Pet 2:1.

14. "To lure into a cage; to entrap; to draw into a snare" (Johnson's *Dictionary*, s.v. "decoy").

15. "[T]here is a chain, in hell, of hot iron that shall be bound around thy waist; there are fiends that have whips of fire, and they shall scourge thy soul throughout eternity, because thou darest to put a stumbling block in the way of God's children" (*MTP* 50:533).

16. An illegible letter, likely "m," was written beneath the "c" in the word "causing." Charles may have begun writing the word "make" or "making." Cf. the following phrase, "making strife."

17. Charles inserted quotation marks around the etc.; however, it has been relocated to reflect his likely intention.

18. Cf. Acts 20:28; 1 Cor 6:20.   19. Cf. Eph 2:10.

20. "Our Father loves them, and he that touches them touches the apple of his eye" (*MTP* 48:250). Cf. 1 John 4:19.

21. Cf. 1 Cor 6:17; Eph 5:31–32.

68   Isaiah 46. 25 —   The saints justification & Glory.

The seed of Israel are all elect, praying, believing men, to whom the promises are all given. They in God have every thing.

I. Justification –

1. They shall be justified in all they say of God.

2. Their persons shall be justified. By God.
The Son by his death and merits procuring.
The Father giving the Son & accepting them
The Spirit revealing the sentence of justification
all the seed, not one excepted, all.
there is no other plan of Justification.

II. Glory.

1. A Christian now glories in his God, in all his attributes, and actions & delights to glorify him, it is his only business.

2. The Christian shall share the glories of heaven and glory after God –

This will be needed on a sick bed and at the final judgement. —

90

68

The SAINTS'[1]
JUSTIFICATION *and* GLORY
Isaiah 45:25[2]

"In the LORD *shall all the seed of Israel be justified, and shall glory."*

The seed of Israel are[3] all elect,[4] praying, believing men to whom the promises are all given. They, in God, have every thing.

I. JUSTIFICATION.

1. They shall be justified in all they say of God.

2. Their persons shall be justified. By God

   The Son. By his death and merits procuring.[5]

   The Father. Giving the Son[6] and accepting them.[7]

   The Spirit. Revealing the sentence of Justification.[8]

All the seed, not one excepted.[9] All. There is no other plan of Justification.

II. GLORY.

1. A Christian now glories in his God, in all his attributes[10] and actions, and delights to glorify him. It is his only business.

2. The Christian shall share the glories of heaven[11] and glory after God.

This[12] will be needed on a sick bed and at the final Judgment.[13]

90

1. The absence of an apostrophe in the word "Saints" is problematic. Is the word plural or singular possessive? Both interpretations contain theological significance. If the word is singular, Charles intended to emphasize the justification of the individual. If the word is plural, the emphasis shifts to the church universal. An examination of the pronouns within the body of the outline suggests the correct placement of the apostrophe is after the word: "The Saints' Justification and Glory." A similar example is found in the title "The Saints' Love to God" (*MTP* 51, Sermon 2958). For an instance in which Charles used the singular possessive for this word, see "The Saint's Trials and the Divine Deliverances" (*MTP* 63, Sermon 3548).

2. This is the only time Charles preached a sermon on Isa 45:25 specifically. However, on September 15, 1878, he preached a sermon on Isa 45:24–25 entitled "Five Divine Declarations" (*MTP* 48, Sermon 2793). There is insufficient overlapping content or structural similarity to suggest he used the above outline in writing his later sermon. For additional sermons on justification, see: "Justification, Conversion, Sanctification, Glory" (Notebook 2, Sermon 102); "Justification by Imputed Righteousness" (Notebook 2, Sermon 117); "Justification by Grace" (*NPSP* 3, Sermon 126); "Justification and Glory" (*MTP* 11, Sermon 627); "Justification by Faith—Illustrated by Abram's Righteousness" (*MTP* 14, Sermon 844); "A Vindication of the Doctrine of Justification by Faith" (*MTP* 21, Sermon 1239); "Perfect Justification and Perfect Pardon" (*MTP* 48, Sermon 2789); "False Justification and True" (*MTP* 51, Sermon 2932); "Pardon and Justification" (*MTP* 53, Sermon 3054); "Justification by Faith" (*MTP* 60, Sermon 3392); and "Justification, Propitiation, Declaration" (*MTP* 61, Sermon 3488). In the Scripture reference for this sermon, the number 5 was written in pencil above 6. The correct Scripture reference is Isa 45:25, not 46:25. Isaiah 46:25 does not exist (chapter 46 contains only thirteen verses). In the index at the beginning of this notebook, Charles did not correct the mistake.

3. As demonstrated in his previous sermon, "Parable of the Bad and Good Seed" (Sermon 64), it is not clear if Charles intended the word "seed" to be singular or plural. Alternative readings of this phrase are: "The seed[s] of Israel are" and "The seed of Israel [is]."

4. See "Election" (Sermon 10).

5. Cf. "Regeneration" (Sermon 7); Rom 5:1.

6. Cf. 1 John 4:14.   7. Cf. Eph 1:6.

8. The final letters in the word "Justification" trail into the margin. Cf. 1 Cor 6:11.

9. Cf. John 6:39; Rom 8:38–39.

10. One of Charles's most prized books in his library was *The Divine Attributes of God* by English Puritan Stephen Charnocke (1628–1680). For Charles's personal copy, see Stephen Charnocke, *Discourses upon the Existence and Attributes of God* (London: Henry G. Bohn, 1849, The Spurgeon Library).

11. Cf. Rom 8:17.

12. The yellow stain above the word "This" is likely the result of the aging process of the manuscript.

13. Charles used the spelling "judgment" ten times in this notebook and "Judgement" only twice (see the original title of his sermon "Future Judgment" [Sermon 6]). Samuel Johnson did not include the letter "e" between the "g" and "m" in his definition of the word "judgment" (Johnson's *Dictionary*). Cf. Matt 25:31–46; 2 Cor 5:10; Heb 9:27; 2 Pet 3:10.

Epes. V. 1 —   Imitation of God.

Man is a creature formed for Society, and for imitation.

He will imitate something. but there is nothing perfect or so worthy of imitation as that which Paul gives us "God"

Some of his attributes are inimitable. others it would be foolish to profess to have as for instance,

Power, over the elements, and over mind. Canute, rainmakers, persecutors

Knowledge of things to come, of secrets, of the heart, gipsies. silly books

Sovereignty, belongs to him only, not to thrones; or rulers. Universal dominion

Eternity, we must die. we may not strive to live for ever.

Nor can we imitate any of his attributes on his own scale. neither his justice, holiness, mercy nor goodness. we make a small picture — I. Justice. He is exactly just, his law, his acts, he did not destroy Sodom or the world without enquiry, nor will he men he does not save without justice —   so we must be just to our country, to all men, and to God —

II Holiness. God can do no wrong, he hates all sin, he exerts himself to further holiness — so we should be consistently holy, hating sin &

III. Truth & Faithfulness — no exaggeration, equivocation in him No breach of promise — so let the X'ns word be his oath.

IV. Mercy to those who offend, forbearance under injuries, longsuffering with others and forgiveness to seventy times seven

V. Goodness — to the saints love, to the world pity, kindness. benevolence, wide liberality.

The argument for such conduct is adoption, Election, redemption, Effectual calling and all acts of grace are the most powerful arguments for holiness,

Let us see if we have the evidence of being "dear children

Imitation of our dear Father.

92

69

IMITATION *of* GOD
Ephesians 5:1[1]

"Be ye therefore followers of God, as dear children."

Man is a creature formed for Society[2] and for imitation. He will imitate something, but there is nothing perfect or so worthy of imitation as that which Paul gives us: "God."[3] Some of his attributes are inimitable.[4] Others it would be foolish to profess to have. As for instance:

Power over the elements[5] and over mind.[6] Canute,[7] rainmakers,[8] persecutors. Knowledge of things to come,[9] of secrets,[10] of the heart,[11] gipsies,[12] silly books.[13] Sovereignty belongs to him only, not to thrones or rulers. Universal dominion.[14] Eternity. We must die.[15] We may not strive to live for ever.

Nor can we imitate any of his attributes on his own scale. Neither his justice, holiness, mercy, nor goodness. We make a small picture:

I. JUSTICE. He is exactly just.[16] His law, his acts. He did not destroy Sodom or the world without enquiry.[17] Nor will he. Men he does not save without justice.[18] So we must be just to our country,[19] to all men, and to God.

II. HOLINESS.[20] God can do no wrong but hates all sin.[21] He exerts himself to further holiness. So we should be consistently holy, hating sin,[22] etc.

III. TRUTH AND FAITHFULNESS. No exaggeration, equivocation in him. No breach of promise.[23] So let the Xⁿ's[24] word be his oath.

IV. MERCY to those who offend,[25] forbearance under injuries, longsuffering with others,[26] and forgiveness to seventy times seven.[27]

V. GOODNESS. To the saints, love. To the world, pity, kindness, benevolence, wide liberality.

The argument for such conduct is adoption,[28] Election,[29] redemption, Effectual calling, and all acts of grace are the most powerful arguments for holiness.[30]

Let us see if we have the evidence of being "dear children."[31]
Imitation of our dear Father.

92

1. On June 10, 1883, Charles preached an additional sermon on Eph 5:1 entitled "Imitators of God" (*MTP* 29, Sermon 1725). Overlapping content exists; however, Charles departed from the content in the Roman numerals in the above outline. For additional sermons on imitating God, see "Christ's People Imitators of Him" (*NPSP* 1, Sermon 21) and "Portraits of Christ" (*MTP* 7, Sermon 355). Charles wrote Roman numeral V instead of the cardinal number 5 in his Scripture reference. This tendency is also found in "Offending God's Little Ones" (Sermon 67) and "The Men Possessed of the Devils" (Sermon 70).

2. The dark inkblot that appears on the terminal of the letter "S" in the word "Society" may have been the result of a malfunction of the writing instrument. If Charles had written the word "formed" twice, it would constitute an error in dittography. When the letter "r" is compared with that in the word "for" in the following phrase, Charles's pen lift becomes more noticeable.

3. "Listen to me, ye aspiring minds: if ye must needs be original, the most wonderful originality in this world would be for a man's character to be a precise copy of the character of God: in him there would be novelty indeed" (*MTP* 29:328).

4. "Above imitation; not to be copied" (Johnson's *Dictionary*, s.v. "inimitable"). In 1883, Charles said, "Creatures cannot imitate their Creator in his divine attributes, but children may copy their Father in his moral attributes. By the aid of his divine Spirit we can copy our God in his justice, righteousness, holiness, purity, truth, and faithfulness. We can be tenderhearted, kind, forbearing, merciful, forgiving; in a word, we may walk in love as Christ also hath loved us" (*MTP* 29:330).

5. Cf. Exod 14:21; Mark 4:25–41. 6. Cf. Ps 139:2.

7. King Cnut the Great, also called King Canute (AD 985 or 995–AD 1035), was the Danish king who conquered England in the early eleventh century. According to legend one of his courtiers told him that the ocean would obey him. Believing this, Canute placed his throne on the beach in his attempt to stop the tide, but the water continued to rise. He scolded the courtier by saying, "Let all men know how empty and worthless is the power of kings. For there is none worthy of the name but God, whom heaven, earth, and sea obey" (Michael McHugh, *Story of the Middle Ages* [Arlington Heights, IL: Christian Liberty Press, 2002], 43); see also David Hughes, *The British Chronicles* ([Westminster, MD:

Heritage Books, 2007], 1:296–98), and Timothy Bolton, *The Empire of Cnut the Great: Conquest and the Consolidation of Power in Northern Europe in the Early Eleventh Century* (Leiden, The Netherlands: Brill, 2009). For additional references to Canute in Charles's later sermons, see *MPT* 7:286; 20:604; and 54:499.

8.　"The Rain-maker is found in every idolatrous country, but I think scarcely anybody believes in him now. What antics and tricks the Rain-makers go through to produce rain, but it does not come, neither can their gods create a cloud!" (*MTP* 35:633).

9.　Cf. Jer 1:5; Acts 2:23; 4:27–28; Rom 8:29.

10.　Cf. Deut 29:29.

11.　Cf. Ps 44:21. Charles inserted a comma after the word "secrets." However, he may have intended the line to read, "Of secrets of the heart."

12.　For additional references to Gypsies, see "Justification, Conversion, Sanctification, Glory" (Notebook 2, Sermon 102); *MTP* 23:287; 27:322; 36:616; and 39:291. In his personal library Charles owned a copy of George Smith, *Gipsy Life: Being an Account of Our Gipsies and Their Children, with Suggestions for Their Improvement* (London: Haughton & Co., 1880, The Spurgeon Library). Only months after Charles preached the sermon above, an article appeared in *Bell's Weekly Messenger* about a scandalous marriage between a Gypsy and a "town-bred" English woman. According to the account, the Gypsies were "a class whose appearance in our young days was a source of painful alarm, connected as they were with stories of kidnapping children, selling them to brutal captains, who again transferred them to cruel planters in South America." After a lengthy history of the Gypsy ethnicity, the writer attempted to "account for the declination of the gypsy class from the useful to the questionable character which they bear at present." The writer added, "[I]n England we regard them as doomed to become soon only a subject of historical remembrances to perplex future antiquaries" ("Who and What are Gypsies?" *Bell's Weekly Messenger*, [August 7, 1852]). One of Charles's greatest admirers and champions of his preaching was British evangelist Rodney "Gypsy" Smith (1860–1947), founder of the Gipsy Gospel Wagon Mission. Rodney's father served in the enquiry rooms at the Metropolitan Tabernacle (see Rodney Smith, *Gipsy Smith: His Life and Work* [4th ed.; New York: Fleming H. Revell, 1906], 321).

13. "Be much with the silly novels of the day, and the foolish trifles of the hour, and you will degenerate into vapid wasters of your time" (*MTP* 17:600). It is worth noting that Charles owned and read many nineteenth-century novels. A selection in The Spurgeon Library includes those written by Charles Dickens, Herman Melville, Mark Twain, and Lord Byron.

14. The final letters in the word "dominion" trail into the margin.

15. Cf. Heb 9:27.   16. Cf. Isa 61:8.

17. Cf. Gen 18:26.

18. An alternative reading of this line is "He does not save men without justice."

19. See "Intercession of the Saints" (Sermon 48).

20. "Imitation of God is the sincerest form of admiring him; neither can we believe that you know God, and are at all charmed with his holiness, unless you endeavour, as he shall help you, to imitate him as dear children" (*MTP* 29:326–27).

21. Cf. Prov 6:16–19.   22. Cf. Amos 5:15; Rom 12:9.

23. Cf. Deut 7:9.

24. Abbr., "Christian's." In this notebook additional examples of this abbreviation are found in "Necessity of Purity for an Entrance to Heaven" (Sermon 2); "The Path of the Just" (Sermon 35); and "The Improvement of Our Talents" (Sermon 61).

25. Cf. 1 Pet 1:3–4.   26. Cf. 2 Pet 3:9.

27. Cf. Matt 18:22.   28. Cf. Eph 1:5.

29. See "Election" (Sermon 10).

30. An alternative reading of this line is "The argument for such conduct is adoption, Election, redemption, Effectual calling, and all acts of grace. [These] are the most powerful arguments for holiness."

31. The word "children" was smeared toward the right side of the page.

70   Mark V. 15.   The men possessed of the devils.

Gadara & Gergesa two adjacent cities or the Girgashites the ancient
and Gadarenes the modern inhabitants. One is mentioned
as being more ferocious than the other, they lived in the outer caves
of the tombs, compelled to do so by the devils that men might
be deluded into the believe of necromancy, and that souls are changed
into devils or to render the persons more uncomfortable.

The devil is no fancy how he will afflict men in hell
what a fool Satan was to let the man come near Jesus Christ.
The devil's confession an evidence of Jesus divinity.
He asks Christs permission in every thing, he knew & trembled at it.
He thought to defeat Jesus by rendering him obnoxious to the people
but Christ did it to punish the Jews, to manifest the reality of the
possession. — what a mercy Satan is not allowed to afflict us now.
~~I. The Power~~ — the Gadarenes besought him to leave them.
he hears theirprayer, that of the devils and not the poor mans.
Jesus is God for he says "tell how great the Lord" &c "How great things Jesus"
    I. The terrible power of sin. In Satan's fall, in his now
intensely evil nature, the maladies man suffers, possession
by real devils then & by devilish principles now. the devil
of lust cannot be bound, devil Lucifer pride cannot be tamed,
devil hatred will cut himself, devil sloth dwells among the tombs
devil rebellion breaks chains & fetters in sunder.
    II. The wonderful power of Christ. In keeping his people,
conquering sin & Satan, curing maladies, casting devils out
casting out all the devils of lust, pride, &c which are legion.
and makes the man "sit" and learn with humility
"clothes" him with morality & holiness — puts him in his right mind
cures the lunacy of sin — Jesus can save the vilest, he is a
strong deliverer. he transforms heathens, drunkards, whoremongers
robbers, murderers, incendiaries and makes them saints.

70

The MEN POSSESSED
of the DEVILS
Mark 5:15[1]

"And they come to Jesus, and see him that was possessed with the devil,
and had the legion, sitting, and clothed, and in his right mind: and they were afraid."

Gadera[2] and Gergesa,[3] two adjacent cities. Or, the Girgashites the ancient and Gadarenes the modern inhabitants. One is mentioned as being more ferocious than the other.[4] They lived in the outer caves of the tombs, compelled to do so by the devils that men might be deluded into the belief[5] of necromancy,[6] and that souls are changed[7] into devils, or to render the persons more uncomfortable.[8]

The devil is no fancy[9] how he will afflict men in hell. What a fool Satan was to let the man come near Jesus Christ. The devil's confession,[10] an evidence of Jesus['s] divinity. He asks Christ's permission[11] in everything.[12] He knew and trembled at him. He thought to defeat Jesus by rendering him obnoxious to the people, but Christ did it to punish the Jews, to manifest the reality of the possession. What a mercy Satan is not allowed to afflict[13] us now.

I. THE POWER[14] The Gadarenes besought him to leave them.[15] He hears their[16] prayer, that of the devils and not the poor man['s].[17] Jesus is God, for he says, "tell how great the Lord,"[18] etc. "How great things Jesus."[19]

I. THE TERRIBLE POWER OF SIN. In Satan's fall,[20] in his now intensely evil nature, the maladies man suffers. Possession by real devils then, and by devilish principles now.[21] The devil of lust[22] cannot be bound. Devil Lucifer, pride cannot be tamed.[23] Devil hatred will cut himself.[24] Devil sloth[25] dwells among the tombs. Devil rebellion breaks chains and fetters in sunder.[26]

II. THE WONDERFUL POWER OF CHRIST. In keeping his people,[27] conquering Sin and Satan,[28] curing maladies, casting devils out, casting out all the devils of lust, pride, etc., which are legion,[29] and makes the man "sit" and learn with humility, "clothes"[30] him with morality and holiness, 93[36] puts him in his right mind,[31] cures the lunacy of sin. Jesus can save the vilest.[32] He is a strong deliverer.[33] He transforms heathens, drunkards, whoremongers, robbers, murderers,[34] incendiaries, and makes them saints.[35]

1. This is the only time Charles preached a sermon on Mark 5:15. For additional sermons on demons, see: "Mary Magdalene" (*MTP* 14, Sermon 792); "The Devil's Last Throw" (*MTP* 29, Sermon 1746); and "Satan, Self, Sin, and the Saviour" (*MTP* 58, Sermon 3306). Charles originally wrote Roman numeral V instead of the number 5 in the Scripture reference. For additional examples, see the Scripture references in "Offending God's Little Ones" (Sermon 67) and "Imitation of God" (Sermon 69).

2. Gadara is located approximately five miles to the southeast of the Sea of Galilee beneath Emmatha. Mark and Luke recorded this event as having taken place "at the country of the Gadarenes" (Mark 5:1; Luke 8:26).

3. Gergesa is located on the eastern side of the Sea of Galilee across from Magdala. Matthew described this event as having taken place in "the country of the Gergesenes" (Matt 8:28).

4. On this point Charles may have consulted John Gill (see Gill, *An Exposition of the New Testament*, 1:364).

5. Charles originally wrote the word "believe." The letters "ve" are struck through in pencil and replaced with the letter "f" to construct the word "belief."

6. "The art of revealing future events, by communication with the dead" (Johnson's *Dictionary*, s.v. "necromancy").

7. The word "changed" trails into the margin.

8. "[T]he persuasion some had, that the souls of the men after death, are changed into devils; or rather, to establish a notion which prevailed among the *Jews*, that the souls of the deceased continue for a while to be about their bodies; which drew persons to necromancy, or consulting with the dead. . . . Or the devil chose these places, to render the persons possessed, the more uncomfortable and distressed; to make them wilder and fiercer, by living in such desolate places, and so do more mischief to others: which was the case of these, who were *exceeding fierce*, wicked, malignant, mischievous, and troublesome, through the influence of the devils in them" (Gill, *An Exposition of the New Testament*, 1:76, italics in the original).

9. The word "fancy" predated the nineteenth century and was used, according to Samuel Johnson, in at least nine ways: "1. Imagination;" "2. An opinion bred rather by

the imagination than the reason;" "3. Taste; idea; conception of things;" "4. Image; conception; thought;" "5. Inclination; liking; fondness;" "6. In *Shakespeare*, it signifies love;" "7. Caprice; humour; whim;" "8. False notion;" and "9. Something that pleases or entertains without real use or value" (Johnson's *Dictionary*, s.v. "fancy"). Charles used the first and second meanings of the word "fancy" in this line. A modern translation of this line could be, "It is no mere imagination that the devil will afflict men in hell" or "That the devil will afflict men in hell is *real*, not imaginative." Charles used the word "fancy" in a similar way in 1855: "Beloved, it is no fancy that we are condemned for our sins, it is a reality" (*NPSP* 1:398). For additional uses of this word in his later sermons, see *MTP* 24:477; 27:128; and 36:134.

10. Mark 5:7, "And cried with a loud voice, and said, What have I to do with thee, Jesus, thou Son of the most high God? I adjure thee by God, that thou torment me not."

11. It is unclear why Charles bolded the letter "i" in the word "permission." It is possible he prematurely wrote the letter "o" before correcting the misspelling.

12. Mark 5:12, "And all the devils besought him, saying, Send us into the swine, that we may enter into them."

13. The dark inkblot above the word "afflict" was likely accidental and not intended to draw undue attention to the word "reality" above.

14. It is unclear why Charles struck through the first Roman numeral and its title, "I. The Power." The revised Roman numeral three lines below reflects a change in the direction of the sermon from the power and divinity of Jesus Christ to the power of sin and Satan.

15. Mark 5:17, "And they began to pray him to depart out of their coasts."

16. Charles likely added the letters "ir" in the word "their" after the line was written. Originally, it may have read "He hears the prayer."

17. Charles originally did not insert apostrophes in the words "devils" and "mans." The context suggests, however, he intended these words to be in the possessive, not the plural.

18. Mark 5:19, "Howbeit Jesus suffered him not, but saith unto him, Go home to thy friends, and tell them how great things the Lord hath done for thee, and hath had compassion on thee."

19. Mark 5:20, "And he departed, and began to publish in Decapolis how great things Jesus had done for him: and all men did marvel."

20. Cf. Luke 10:18.

21. Charles was inconclusive about the authenticity of alleged demonic possession in the nineteenth century. In 1883, he said, "I suppose that we have never seen Satanic possession, although I am not quite sure about it; for some men exhibit symptoms which are very like it. The present existence of demons within the bodies of men I shall neither assert nor deny; but certainly, in our Saviour's day it was very common for devils to take possession of men and torment them greatly. It would seem that Satan was let loose while Christ was here below that the serpent might come into personal conflict with the appointed seed of the woman, that the two champions might stand foot to foot in solemn duel, and that the Lord Jesus might win a glorious victory over him. Since his defeat by our Lord, and by his apostles, it would seem that Satan's power over human bodies has been greatly limited; but we still have among us the same thing in another and worse shape, namely, the power of sin over men's minds. That this is akin to the power of the devil over the body is clear from holy Scripture" (*MTP* 29:577–78). Charles was not ignorant of the occult in his city, as seen in his personal copy of *Mystic London* (see Charles Maurice Davies, *Mystic London; or, Phases of Occult Life in the Metropolis* [London: Tinsley Brothers, 1875, The Spurgeon Library]). From 1928 to 1931, a series of séances was conducted under the supervision of Canadian surgeon and paranormal researcher Dr. Thomas Glen Hamilton in which a clairvoyant claimed the spirit of Charles Spurgeon took possession of her body (see Christian T. George, "Raising Spurgeon from the Dead," Desiring God, December 5, 2015, accessed May 28, 2016, http://www.desiringgod.org/articles/raising-spurgeon-from-the-dead).

22. Cf. Job 31:1; Matt 5:28.

23. An alternative reading of this line is "Devil Lucifer's pride cannot be tamed" or "[For] Devil Lucifer, pride cannot be tamed."

24. Cf. Mark 5:5.

25. For additional references to sloth in this notebook, see "The Fight and the Weapons" (Sermon 37a); "The Fight" (Sermon 37b); and "The Improvement of Our Talents" (Sermon 61).

26. Cf. Mark 5:4.

27. Cf. Num 6:24.

28. Cf. Col 2:15.

29. Cf. Mark 5:9.

30. Mark 5:15, "And they come to Jesus, and see him that was possessed with the devil, and had the legion, sitting, and clothed, and in his right mind: and they were afraid."

31. Charles originally wrote the word "minds." However, the context suggests he intended the word to be singular, not plural.

32. In a letter to his father on May 15, 1851, Charles wrote, "I am very comfortable and I may say happy. Were it not for my vile heart, I might rejoice" (Angus Library and Archive, Regent's Park College, Oxford University, D/SPU 1, Letter 9).

33. Cf. Ps 140:7.

34. In his 1892 address in Nashville, Tennessee, entitled "The Death of Spurgeon," B. H. Carroll recounted the impact of Charles's sermons and said, "A bush ranger in Australia was converted by reading one, blood-stained, which he had taken from the body of a man he had murdered" (Cranfill, 29).

35. In this sentence Charles may have been reflecting on the spiritual transformation that occurred in the village of Waterbeach during his pastorate. "There went into that village a lad, who had no great scholarship, but who was earnest in seeking the souls of men. He began to preach there, and it pleased God to turn the whole place upside down. In a short time, the little thatched chapel was crammed, the biggest vagabonds of the village were weeping floods of tears, and those who had been the curse of the parish became its blessing. Where there had been robberies and villainies of every kind, all round the neighbourhood, there were none, because the men who used to do the mischief were themselves in the house of God, rejoicing to hear of Jesus crucified. I am not telling an exaggerated story, nor a thing that I do not know, for it was my delight to labour

for the Lord in that village. It was a pleasant thing to walk through that place, when drunkenness had almost ceased, when debauchery in the case of many was dead, when men and women went forth to labour with joyful hearts, singing the praises of the ever-living God; and when, at sunset, the humble cottager called his children together, read them some portion from the Book of Truth, and then together they bent their knees in prayer to God. I can say, with joy and happiness, that almost from one end of the village to the other, at the hour of eventide, one might have heard the voice of song coming from nearly every roof-tree, and echoing from almost every heart. I do testify, to the praise of God's grace, that it pleased the Lord to work wonders in our midst. He showed the power of Jesu[s]'s name, and made me a witness of that gospel which can win souls, draw reluctant hearts, and mould afresh the life and conduct of sinful men and women" (*Autobiography* 1:228). The stippling above the word "saints" could suggest a pause in Charles's thinking, as is also evidenced above the numbers "9. 51" at the conclusion of his sermon "Condescending Love of Jesus" (Sermon 5).

36. The number 93 was written before the word "cures" in the left margin and not, as usual, at the bottom of the page. For an additional example, see "An Exhortation to Bravery" (Sermon 72).

Matt. 22. 42.   What think ye of Christ?   71

Jesus did not ask if they expected the Messiah but what were
their views of his person, nature, office & Kingdom. we may
gain something by asking ourselves the same question.
The Gospel regenerates nations and the world by individuals
other schemes profess to act on each man through the mass.
Jesus asks this question of each one of us. tis he, who has authority,
Great teachers often teach by question, this is one on the most
important of all sciences and a vital one in that science.
The Heathen cannot answer they know him not.
The Jew will not, through obstinacy accept him. The
Mahometan & Mormonite think him a prophet but not supreme
The atheist rejects all thought of God & his son also.
The deist disbelieves revelation. but we do not,
though there are many practical atheists let us hope you are not
Nor are we Arians denying his divinity or Socinians
thinking him to be a God by office — but though we
may not fall into their errors, it is necessary for us
to be right — for our views of Jesus will affect.

I. our closing with the gospel, if we doubt his suitableness
    his power, willingness, faithfulness, love.

II. Our consecration to him — unless we think highly
    of him we shall not give up all and follow him.

III. Our doctrinal sentiments — this is the point of sight

IV. Our faith will not grow to assurance & confidence
    without a correct thought of Christ.

V. Our conduct — our pride, & so on can only be
    humbled by him —

Let us study Jesus — our lord. Our God —

94.692.
            Bless me — amen —

WHAT THINK YE *of* CHRIST?[1]
Matthew 22:42[2]

"Saying, 'What think ye of Christ? whose son is he?' They say unto him, 'The son of David.'"

Jesus did not ask if they expected the Messiah. But what were their views of his person,[3] nature,[4] office,[5] and kingdom?[6] We may gain something by asking ourselves the same question.

The Gospel regenerates nations and the world by individuals. Other schemes[7] profess to act on each man through the mass. Jesus asks this question of each one of us. Tis he who has authority.[8] Great teachers often teach by question.[9]
This is one o[f][10] the most important of all sciences, and a vital one in that science.

The Heathen cannot answer.[11] They know him not.[12]

The Jew will not through obstinacy accept him.

The Mohametan[13] and Mormonite[14] think him a prophet, but not supreme.

The atheist rejects all thought of God, and his son also.

The deist disbelieves revelation, but we do not.

Though there are many practical atheists, let us hope you are not. Nor are we Arians,[15] denying his divinity. Or Socinians,[16] thinking him to be a God by office. But though we may not[17] fall into their errors, it is necessary for us to be right, for our views of Jesus will affect:

I.   OUR CLOSING[18] WITH THE GOSPEL, if we doubt his suitableness, his power, willingness, faithfulness, love.[19]

II. OUR CONSECRATION TO HIM. Unless we think highly of him, we shall not give up all and follow him.[20]

III. OUR DOCTRINAL SENTIMENTS.[21] This is the point of sight.

IV. OUR FAITH will not grow to assurance[22] and confidence without a correct thought of Christ.

V.   OUR CONDUCT, our pride, and so on, can only be humbled by him.

Let us study Jesus, our Lord, Our God.[23]

94. 692.   Bless me. Amen.

1.   For this sermon Charles likely consulted a sermon on Matt 22:42 entitled "What Think Ye of Christ?" by George Whitefield (1714–1770). For Charles's personal copy of this sermon, see George Whitefield, *The Works of the Reverend George Whitefield, M. A., Late of Pembroke-College, Oxford, and Chaplain to the Rt. Hon. the Countess of Huntingdon. Containing All His Sermons and Tracts Which Have Been Already Published: With a Select Collection of Letters, Written to His Most Intimate Friends, and Persons of Distinction, in England, Scotland, Ireland, and America, from the Year 1734, to 1770, Including the Whole Period of His Ministry. Also Some Other Pieces on Important Subjects, Never Before Printed; Prepared by Himself for the Press. To Which Is Prefixed, an Account of His Life, Compiled from His Original Papers and Letters* ([London: Edward and Charles Dilly, 1772, The Spurgeon Library], 5:353–72). Charles held Whitefield in the highest esteem and said, "[I]f there were wanted two apostles to be added to the number of the twelve, I do not believe that there could be found two men more fit to be so added than George Whitefield and John Wesley" (*Autobiography* 1:176). In a sermon preached at Whitefield's Tabernacle in 1856 entitled "Spiritual Revival, the Want of the Church" (*MTP* 44, Sermon 2598), Charles said, "God had clothed Whitefield with power; he was preaching with a majesty and a might of which one could scarcely think mortal[s] could ever be capable; not because he was anything in himself, but because his Master girded him with strength. . . . You will not think him eloquent; you cannot think so. His expressions were rough, frequently unconnected; there was very much declamation about him, it was a great part indeed of his speech; but wherein lay his eloquence? Not in the words he uttered, but in the tones in which he delivered them, in the earnestness with which he spoke them, in the tears which ran down his cheeks, and in the pouring out of his very soul. . . . If you had heard him preach, you could not have helped feeling, that he was a man who would die if he could not preach" (*MTP* 44:572–73; see also *ST* September 1870:426–27). On April 18, 1855, *The Essex Standard* compared Charles to "Whitefield stirring the breasts of the thousands in Hyde Park" (*Autobiography* 2:47). The comparison was further popularized in the first biography written of Charles entitled *"The Modern Whitefield": Sermons of the Rev. C. H. Spurgeon, of London; with an Introduction and Sketch of His Life* by E. L. Magoon (New York: Sheldon, Blakeman & Co., 1856). Charles objected to this comparison, saying, "I have been puffed off as being a Whit[e]field, the greatest preacher of the age, which certainly I am not, and never professed to be" (xxvi; see also Morden's comparison in *Communion with Christ and His People*, 70–71). In the above outline Charles did not follow Whitefield's primary divisions; however, the overlapping content is noted below.

2.   On January 26, 1873, Charles preached an additional sermon on Matt 22:42 enti-
     tled "Questions of the Day and the Question of the Day" (*MTP* 19, Sermon 1093).
     Overlapping content is found throughout the second Roman numeral of his later
     sermon (see *MTP* 19:57–58) and suggests Charles may have had Whitefield's ser-
     mon in mind when writing his later sermon.

3.   "*First*, What think you about the person of Christ? 'Whose Son is he?'" (White-
     field, 356, italics in the original). In his 1873 sermon, Charles said, "We speak of
     the Lord's teachings and doings, but we ought more often to remember that he is
     a real personage, not a name, or a fiction; not a shadow that has passed across the
     historic page, but a man of whom we may ask the question—'Whose Son is he?' as
     the Master asked it here" (*MTP* 19:57). For additional references to the personhood
     of Jesus Christ, see *TD* 2:367; 4:440; *MTP* 9:698; and 21:386. Concerning the
     hypostatic union, Charles said, "God and man in one person is the Lord Jesus
     Christ! This brings our manhood near to God and by so doing it ennobles our
     nature, it lifts us up from the dunghill and sets us among the princes; while at the
     same time it enriches us by endowing our manhood with all the glory of Christ
     Jesus in whom dwelleth all the fulness of the Godhead bodily" (*MTP* 18:713; see
     also 22:290).

4.   "We can never forget that Jesus Christ is God. The church has given forth many a
     valiant confession to his deity; and woe be to her should she ever hesitate on that
     glorious truth!" (*MTP* 26:161; see also 19:132 and 30:26).

5.   Throughout his sermons Charles spoke to the three offices of Jesus Christ. With
     regard to Christ's prophetic office, Charles said, "Jesus Christ is the Prophet
     of Christendom. His words must always be the first and the last appeal. . . . He
     comes not as a prophet who assumes office, but God hath anointed him to preach
     glad tidings to the poor, and to come among his people with the welcome news
     of eternal love" (*MTP* 15:6–7; see also 29:352). With regard to Christ's priestly
     office, Charles said, "Come, then, and learn of the great High Priest. His office is
     a compassionate one, and you may learn all of God from him the more readily be-
     cause he is meek and lowly of heart, and will count it no drudgery to teach you the
     very ABC of divine truth" (*MTP* 36:316; see also 47:52). With regard to Christ's
     kingly office, Charles said, "I dread men who say, 'We believe, and therefore we
     are saved,' and then do not live in holiness; for these divide our Lord's offices,

setting up his priesthood and denying his kingship. Half a Christ is no Christ—a Christ who is a priest but never a king is not the Christ of God" (*MTP* 28:94; see also 25:304 and 33:93).

6. The final book Charles wrote, though he died before its completion, was a commentary on Matthew entitled *The Gospel of the Kingdom* (see notes on "Parable of the Bad and Good Seed" [Sermon 64] and also *Autobiography* 4:315–17).

7. Charles originally spelled this word "scemes." He corrected the misspelling by inserting the letter "h" above the word and between the letters "c" and "e."

8. Cf. Matt 28:18.

9. Charles may have been thinking of the Socratic model of education, a teaching style attributed to the Greek philosopher Socrates (469/470 BC–399 BC). In 1888, Charles said, "Socrates was wont, not so much to state a fact, as to ask a question and draw out thoughts from those whom he taught. His method had long before been used by a far greater teacher. Putting questions is Jehovah's frequent method of instruction" (*MTP* 34:229). For an example of the Socratic method, see the ethical discussion between Socrates and Euthyphro (*Plato, with an English Translation 1. Euthypro, Apology, Crito, Phaedo, Phaedrus* [trans. Harold North Fowler; Cambridge, MA: Harvard University Press, 1914; repr., 1960], 1–60). For Charles's personal copy of *Aristotle's Treatise on Rhetoric*, see Theodore Buckley, *Aristotle's Treatise on Rhetoric: Literally Translated from the Greek. With an Analysis by Thomas Hobbes, and a Series of Questions[,] New Edition, to Which Is Added, A Supplementary Analysis Containing the Greek Definitions. Also the Poetic of Aristotle, Literally Translated with a Selection of Notes, an Analysis, and Questions* (ed. Thomas Hobbes; London: Henry G. Bohn, 1857, The Spurgeon Library). Charles favored and implemented the question-answer educational model as seen in his 1855 editing and republication of the "Baptist Confession of Faith" (see *NPSP* 1:354).

10. The context suggests Charles likely intended to write the word "of" instead of "on."

11. "Mere heathen morality, and not JESUS CHRIST, is preached in most of our churches" (Whitefield, 356).

12. Cf. John 10:27.

13. This is the second time in this notebook that Charles referenced the religion of Islam. See also "The Little Fire and Great Combustion" (Sermon 54).

14. "One of the most modern pretenders to inspiration is the Book of Mormon. I could not blame you should you laugh outright while I read aloud a page from that farrago" (*MTP* 37:45). Charles also said, "In the base counterfeit of the book of Mormon, a mere child, fresh from the Sunday-school, can discover marks and lines which are manifestly far from divine " (*ST* May 1865:266). For additional references to Mormonism, see "The Mind of Christ" (Notebook 7, Sermon 330); "Angels Charged with Folly" (Notebook 8, Sermon 360b); *NPSP* 2:182; *MTP* 18:429–30; and 21:35.

15. Arius (AD 250–336) was a heretic in the early church who believed Jesus Christ was the first creation of God and therefore less than equally God (see Harry R. Boer, *A Short History of the Early Church* [Grand Rapids, MI: Eerdmans, 1976], 167). Charles summarized Arius's Christology in the following words: "There was Arius; he would receive Christ as a good man, but not as God" (*MTP* 41:161). See also Lewis Ayres, *Nicaea and its Legacy: An Approach to Fourth-Century Trinitarian Theology* (Oxford: Oxford University Press, 2004). Charles likely read about Arius in his personal copy of Henry B. Smith and Philip Schaff, eds., *Theological and Philosophical Library: A Series of Text-Books, Original and Translated for Colleges and Universities: The Creeds of the Greek and Latin Churches* (London: Hodder and Stoughton, 1878, The Spurgeon Library). For additional references to Arius, see *ST* March 1887:123 and April 1887:166.

16. "But I think it no breach of charity to affirm, that an *Arian* or *Socinian* cannot be a [C]hristian" (Whitefield, 357, italics in the original). In 1862, Charles said, "Dear friends, Socinianism must be utterly abhorred of us, for it strikes at once at the Deity of our blessed Lord and Master. We cannot give to such persons even the name of Christians" (*MTP* 8:462). He also said, "Only preach Socinianism, and what a splendid hunting-ground this tabernacle will be for the spiders!" (*MTP* 7:206). For additional references to Socinianism, see "Pleasure in the Stones of Zion" (Sermon 53); "The Minister's Commission" (Notebook 2, Sermon 110); "The Corner Stone" (Notebook 2, Sermon 128); "The Certain Judgment" (Notebook 3, Sermon 136); *MTP* 13:567; and 61:451.

17. The excessive stippling above the word "not" was likely the result of a malfunction of the writing instrument.

18. This is the only time Charles used the word "closing" in a soteriological sense. The word was common in Whitefield's day: "[Satan] will fight and strive hard to keep the soul from closing with Jesus" (Whitefield, 328). Sang Hyun Lee noted that Jonathan Edwards also used this phrase: "Our salvation, according to Edwards, is effected in 'closing' with Christ, in his cleaving to us and our cleaving to him" (Sang Hyun Lee, ed., *The Princeton Companion to Jonathan Edwards* [Princeton, NJ: Princeton University Press, 2005], 73). Though commonly used in the eighteenth century, the phrase predated Whitefield and Edwards, as evidenced in John Durant's 1660 publication *A Cluster of Grapes*: "Oh! when should wee ever let out all our souls to the utmost, if not then when wee come to close with Jesus Christ?" (John Durant, *A Cluster of Grapes Taken Out of the Basket of the Woman of Canaan. Or, Counsel and Comfort for Beleeving Soules, Comming to Christ and Meeting with Discouragements: Being the Summe of Certain Sermons Preached upon Matthew 15. from Verse 22. to Verse 29. Wherein Among Other Things, Is Declared More Particularly, I. What Seeming Harsh Entertainment the Soul May Find from Christ. II. What Holy, and Humble Behaviour the Soul Ought to Have Under That Entertainment. III. How Blessed and Comfortable a Conclusion Christ Will Make with the Soul at Last* [London: printed for L. C. and are to bee sold by H. Mortlocke at the Phoenix in Paul's church-yard neer the little north-door, 1660, The Spurgeon Library], 7). Mark Noll found that the phrase "closing with Christ" was part of a post-Reformational reaction in Europe against "preaching as learned discourses about God" (Mark A. Noll, *The Rise of Evangelicalism: The Age of Edwards, Whitefield, and the Wesleys* [vol. 1 of A History of Evangelicalism: People, Movements and Ideas in the English-Speaking World; Downers Grove, IL: InterVarsity, 2003], 52).

19. "And now, What think you of this love of Christ? Do not you think it was wondrous great? Especially when you consider, that we were Christ's bitter enemies, and that he would have been infinitely happy in himself, notwithstanding we had perished for ever" (Whitefield, 359).

20. Cf. Matt 19:21; Luke 18:22.

21. For the "doctrinal sentiments," Charles may have referenced, as did Whitefield, the doctrine of justification (see Whitefield, 362, 365, 366).

22. "For CHRIST came not only to save us from the guilt, but from the power of our sins: till he has done this, however he may be Saviour to others, we can have no assurance or well-grounded hope, that he has saved us: for it is by receiving his

blessed Spirit into our hearts, and feeling him witnessing with our spirits, that we are the sons of God, that we can be certified of our being sealed to the day of redemption" (ibid., 368).

23. "Behold, I have told you before; and I pray God, all you that forget him may seriously think of what has been said, before he pluck you away, and there be none to deliver you" (ibid., 372).

72.   Deut 20.1 —   An Exhortation to bravery.

Horses & Chariots forbidden to the Israelites, and much dreaded because they were unaccustomed to them. the chariots armed with scythes, made of iron, bearing soldiers with javelins did great execution, —   the "people more than thou"

I   yet "be thou not afraid of them." we may fear in one sense but not in another. we may.
  1. Fear to give them cause to blaspheme.
  2. Lest we should cease to fight & be enticed by them.
But we may not.
  1. Dread Persecution, this is and must be the lot of all f. us.
  2. Distrust God's providence in temporal affairs.
  3. Nor his power, mercy, faithfulness & willingness to save.

II. He has not told us to be bold without giving some ground.
  1 Because, God is with us. — Jesus has conquered once. the cause is as much God's as ours, His honor would be tarnished by our defeat. Consider "he brought us out of Egypt" what miracles he wrought. Gideon, Barak, David, Hezekiah. what he has done for us. "he led us through the wilderness." fed us and clothed us till this moment.

III. Some seasons when this courage is specially required
  1. Under conviction to enable us to trust in Jesus.
  2. In baptism, that we may witness a good confession
  3. In company with worldlings, amid jeers, in spreading the gospel and doing good.
  4. Under temptations of Satan, with a sight of our depravity, a prospect of a dreary way
  5. In expectation of death & judgment.

IV. Some further exhortation.
  1. Because lose this all is lost.
  2. The prize is heaven, the Captain Jesus.
  3. "Ye have not yet resisted unto blood"
  4. Consider many have won already. Amen. & may I.

72

An EXHORTATION *to* BRAVERY[1]
Deuteronomy 20:1[2]

"When thou goest out to battle against thine enemies, and seest horses,
and chariots, and a people more than thou, be not afraid of them:
for the Lord thy God is with thee, which brought thee up out of the land of Egypt."

Horses and Chariots [were] forbidden to the Israelites, and much dreaded because they were unaccustomed to them. The chariots, armed with scythes,[3] made of iron, bearing soldiers with javelins, did great execution. The "people more than thou."

I. YET, *"be though not afraid of them."* WE MAY FEAR IN ONE SENSE, BUT NOT IN ANOTHER. We may:

    1. Fear to give them cause to blaspheme.

    2. Lest we should cease to fight and be enticed by them.

But we may not:

    1. Dread Persecution. This is and must be the lot of all of us.[4]

    2. Distrust God's providence in temporal affairs.

    3. Nor his power,[5] mercy,[6] faithfulness,[7] and willingness to save.[8]

II. HE HAS NOT TOLD US TO BE BOLD WITHOUT GIVING SOME GROUND:

    1. Because God is with us.[9] Jesus has conquered once.[10] The cause is as much God's as ours. His honor would be tarnished by our[11] defeat. Consider, "he brought us out of Egypt." What miracles he wrought: Gideon,[12] Barak,[13] David,[14] Hezekiah.[15] What he has done for us: "He led us through the wilderness," fed us,[16] and clothed us[17] till this moment.

III. SOME SEASONS WHEN THIS COURAGE IS SPECIALLY REQUIRED:

1. Under conviction, to enable us to trust in Jesus.

2. In baptism, that we may witness a good confession.[18]

3. In company with worldlings, amid jeers, in spreading the gospel and doing good.

4. Under temptations of Satan, with a sight of our depravity, a prospect of a dreary way.

5. In expectation of death and judgment.[19]

[20]

IV. SOME FURTHER EXHORTATION:

1. Because lose this, all is lost.[21]

2. The prize is heaven, the Captain Jesus.[22]

95[25] 3. "Ye have not yet resisted unto blood."[23]

4. Consider, many have won already.[24]   Amen. So may I.

1. This is the only time Charles preached a sermon on Deut 20:1. Additional references to courage and boldness are found in *MTP* 9:149; 24:162; 24:488; 57:556; and 60:152.

2. An illegible number, likely 2, appears beneath the number 0 in the Scripture reference, Deut 20:1. There is no evidence in the indices at the beginning or end of this notebook to confirm what this number might have been. If Charles had intended to preach from Deut 22:1, his text would have read, "Thou shalt not see thy brother's ox or his sheep go astray, and hide thyself from them: thou shalt in any case bring them again unto thy brother."

3. Throughout his ministry Charles used the words "scythe" and "sickle" interchangeably. According to Samuel Johnson, a "sickle" was "the hook with which corn is cut; a reaping hook" (Johnson's *Dictionary*). For additional references to both words in Charles's later sermons, see *NPSP* 1:324; 3:191; *MTP* 10:577; 50:392; and 53:41.

4. See Charles's account of his great grandfather's grandfather, Job Spurgeon, a Quaker from Dedham who was imprisoned for almost four months for not paying the fine demanded of him for his attendance at a nonconformist meeting (*Autobiography* 1:8; see also the notes in "Salvation in God Only" [Sermon 24]). For additional sermons on persecution, see "Consolation in the Furnace" (*MTP* 11, Sermon 662); "Prosperity under Persecution" (*MTP* 17, Sermon 997); "A Word for the Persecuted" (*MTP* 20, Sermon 1188); and "Persecuted, but Not Forsaken" (*MTP* 44, Sermon 2574). Cf. 2 Tim 3:12.

5. Cf. Ps 62:11; 1 Cor 6:14.

6. Cf. Ps 145:9; Eph 2:4; 1 Pet 1:3.

7. Cf. Pss 86:15; 89:8; 1 Cor 1:9.

8. Cf. 1 Tim 2:3–4.

9. Cf. Josh 1:9; Isa 41:10; Matt 28:20.

10. Cf. 1 Cor 15:57.

11. A dark stain, likely the result of the aging process of the manuscript, appears beneath the line and between the words "by" and "our." The imprint of this stain can be found surrounding the letters "ple" in the word "pleasantness" in the following sermon, "Slavery Destroyed" (Sermon 73).

12. Cf. Judges 6–8.

13. Cf. Judges 4.

14. Cf. 1 Samuel 17.

15. Cf. Isaiah 38.

16. Cf. Exodus 16.

17. Cf. Exod 12:35–36; Deut 8:4; 29:5.

18. Charles's description of baptism as "a good confession" correlates to the title of the fourteenth chapter in the first volume of his autobiography: "A Good Confession—Baptism" (*Autobiography* 1:147). On April 6, 1850, Charles wrote the following words in a letter to his father: "I did not sit down at the Lord's table, and cannot in conscience do so until I am baptized. To one who does not see the necessity of baptism, it is perfectly right and proper to partake of this blessed privilege, but were I to do so, I conceive would be to tumble over the wall, since I feel persuaded that it is Christ's appointed way of professing him" (Angus Library and Archive, Regent's Park College, Oxford University, D/SPU 1, Letter 5). In Charles's diary entry for that day, he recorded, "Had some serious thoughts about baptism" (*Autobiography* 1:129). He was baptized less than one month later. On May 3, 1850, fifteen-year-old Charles woke early in Newmarket before departing at 11:00 AM for the village of Isleham some eight miles away. "What a walk it was!" Charles reflected. "What thoughts and prayers thronged my soul during that morning's journey!" (ibid., 1:151). At 1:00 PM, he arrived at the River Lark. The site had been used first for baptism in 1798. In Charles's day, five churches in the area used the location for baptisms. Charles described the River Lark as "a beautiful stream, dividing Cambridgeshire from Suffolk, and is dear to local anglers" (ibid.). He claimed to have forgotten the content of the service because "my thoughts were in the water, sometimes with my Lord in joy, and sometimes with myself in trembling awe at making so public a confession" (ibid., 1:152). After he escorted two women into the water, he himself was baptized by Mr. Cantlow. He reflected, "It was a new experience to me, never having seen a baptism before, and I was afraid of making some mistake. The wind blew down the river with a cutting blast, as my turn came to wade into the flood; but after I had walked a few steps, and noted the people on the ferry-boat, and in boats, and on either shore, I felt as if Heaven, and earth, and hell, might all gaze upon me; for I was not ashamed, there and then, to own myself a follower of the Lamb. My timidity was washed away; it floated down the river into the sea, and must have been devoured by the fishes, for I have never felt anything of the kind since. Baptism also loosed my tongue, and from that day it has never been quiet. I lost a thousand fears in that River Lark" (ibid.). That same day Charles recorded the following words in his diary: "Blest pool! Sweet emblem of my death to all the world! May I, henceforward, live alone for Jesus! Accept my body and soul as a poor sacrifice, tie me unto Thee; in Thy strength I now devote myself

to Thy service for ever; never may I shrink from owning Thy name!" (*Autobiography* 1:135). For additional sermons on baptism, see "Faith Before Baptism" (Notebook 9, Sermon 396); "Baptismal Regeneration" (*MTP* 10, Sermon 573); "Baptism—a Burial" (*MTP* 27, Sermon 1627); and "Baptism Essential to Obedience" (*MTP* 39, Sermon 2339). See also *NPSP* 4:170 and *MTP* 17:156.

19. Cf. Matt 25:31–46; 2 Cor 5:10; Heb 9:27; 2 Pet 3:10.

20. This line is unusually located. Charles may have originally intended to conclude the sermon after the third Roman numeral before appending Roman numeral IV.

21. An alternative reading of this line is "Because [if you] lose this, [then] all is lost."

22. See "Christ About His Father's Business" (Sermon 15).

23. Heb 12:4, "Ye have not yet resisted unto blood, striving against sin."

24. An alternative reading of this line is "Consider [the] many [who] have won already."

25. The number 95 was written in the left margin between the numbers 3 and 4 and not, as usual, at the bottom of the page. Additional examples are found in "The Men Possessed of the Devils" (Sermon 70) and "The Church and Its Boast" (Sermon 75).

Rom. p. 17 ~   Slavery destroyed.   73

The Table of our Lord is a fitting place for taking a
view of ourselves and God's dealings with us, we may
I. See our former state "slavery"
1. A State of restraint from good, & constraint to ill.
the man sins with hell before him, the slave toils in
feverish atmospheres _ a state of degredation, ruled
by our own passions, our companions. Satan.
2. A state of uneasiness, fear, remorse, pain.
3. A toil for nought, death the wages, hell the end.
This slavery was hopeless, from our own inability
to pay or escape, and our Master's strength.
II. But now our present state "servants of God"
1. This perfect freedom :
2. Joyful existence.   { = ways of pleasantness
3. Fervent prospect _   { gift of God ...
III. The means ....
Unfeigned obedience to pure doctrine.
The Scriptures are our guide & Jesus we wish to serve.
"obedience" to the doctrine, not hearing only but doing, & it
is from the heart, not outward merely, but inward
IV The Glory must be given to God. "God be thanked"
   He did it 1. By redemption with price
              2. Deliverance with power.
He melts us & delivers us into the mould __
Let us thank him in our words, actions, prayers _
   and be desirous that all do so do _
96. 97. 269
              Help. Amen.

73

SLAVERY DESTROYED
Romans 6:17[1]

*"But God be thanked, that ye were the servants of sin, but ye have obeyed
from the heart that form of doctrine which was delivered you."*

The Table of our Lord is a fitting place for taking a view of ourselves and God's
dealings with us.[2] We may:

I. SEE OUR FORMER STATE: *"slavery."*

1. A State of restraint from good and constraint to ill. The man sins with hell
   before him. The slaves toil in feverish atmospheres.[3] A state of degradation,
   ruled by our own passions,[4] our companions, Satan.[5]

2. A state of uneasiness, fear, remorse, pain.

3. A toil for nought. Death the wages.[6] Hell the end.[7] This[8] slavery was hopeless, from our own inability to pay[9] or escape, and our Master's strength.

II. BUT NOW, OUR PRESENT STATE: *"servants of God."*[10]

1.[11] This perfect freedom.
2. Joyful existence.   } Ways of pleasantness. Gift of God.[12]
3. Heavenly[13] prospect.

III. THE MEANS:

Unfeigned obedience to pure doctrine. The Scriptures are our guide, and Jesus
we wish to serve. "Obedience" to the doctrine. Not hearing only, but doing.[14]
And it is from the heart. Not outward merely, but inward.[15]

IV.[16] THE GLORY MUST BE GIVEN TO GOD.

"God be thanked."[17]
He did it:

1. By redemption with price.[18]
2. Deliverance with power. He melts us and delivers us into the mould.

Let us thank him in our words, actions, prayers, and be desirous that all do so do.[19]

<u>Help. Amen.</u>

96. 97. 269

1. An unusual stroke, possibly the number 7, was attached to the base of the number 6 in the Scripture reference, Rom 6:17. There is no evidence in the indices at the beginning or end of this notebook to suggest what this stroke might have represented. The diagonal crossbar might have served as a strikethrough. This is the only time Charles preached a sermon on Rom 6:17. For additional references to slavery, see "The Tower of Babel" (Notebook 3, Sermon 140); "The Three Fold Spirit" (Notebook 6, Sermon 312); "Christ Destroying the Works of the Devil" (Notebook 8, Sermon 355); "The Lord Reigneth" (Notebook 8, Sermon 371); and "Our Change of Masters" (*MTP* 25, Sermon 1482).

2. For additional references to the Lord's Supper in this notebook, see "God's Grace Given to Us" (Sermon 14); "Salvation in God Only" (Sermon 24); "God's Estimation of Men" (Sermon 41); "He Took Not Up Angels" (Sermon 52); "Pleasure in the Stones of Zion" (Sermon 53); and "An Exhortation to Bravery" (Sermon 72).

3. Charles may have had Gen 3:19 in mind. More likely, however, his thoughts were directed to the "feverish atmospheres" in which slaves had to work. In his personal library Charles owned Edward Underhill's *The West Indies* in which the story of one Maria Jones is told: Jones was kidnapped as a child in Africa, forced onto a slave ship, scourged by her owner, sold to a planter in Trinidad, and "was driven to daily toil in the cane field" until she was at last emancipated (Edward Bean Underhill, *The West Indies: Their Social and Religious Condition* [London: Jackson, Walford, and Hodder, 1862, The Spurgeon Library], 22).

4. Cf. Rom 6:12; 2 Pet 3:3.

5. An alternative reading of this line is "[It is] a state of degradation [in which we are] ruled by our passions, [those of] our companions, and [those of] Satan."

6. Cf. Rom 6:23.

7. An alternative reading of this line is "Death [is] the wages [and] hell [is] the end."

8. Charles originally wrote what appears to be the number 1 before the word "This." If this interpretation is correct, it would explain the presence of the number 2 that Charles struck through three lines below. An additional interpretation is that instead of the number 1, Charles may have intended to write the number 4 or Roman numeral II.

9. See Charles's inscription "Gave to a poor Black man" in his personal inventory of expenses (Angus Library and Archive, Regent's Park College, Oxford University, D/SPU 1).

10. Romans 6:22, "But now, being made free from sin, and become servants to God, ye have your fruit unto holiness, and the end everlasting life." Cf. 2 Cor 6:4.

11. Charles originally wrote the number 2 beneath 1. This may correspond to the number 1 three lines above.

12. The location of the phrase "gift of God" suggests Charles intended to use these words to describe "Heavenly prospect."

13. A dark inkblot, likely the result of a malfunction of the writing instrument, appears over the letters "Hea" in the word "Heavenly." There is no evidence the inkblot bled through the page.

14. Cf. Jas 1:22.   15. Cf. Rom 2:29.

16. Charles originally wrote Roman numeral V before changing it to IV.

17. Romans 6:17, "But thanks be to God that, though you used to be slaves to sin, you have come to obey from your heart the pattern of teaching that has now claimed your allegiance" (NIV).

18. Cf. Eph 1:7.

19. An alternative reading of this line is "and be desirous that all do [who] so do."

74   Mark 2.17. The Physician and his patients

Publicans counted the vilest of all men. Matthew, whose Hebrew
name was Levi was one of them, but while engaged in this
work & in bad company, Jesus calls him & constraining grace
makes him follow, he was afterwards the Evangelist. Upon
his conversion (though he modestly omits to mention it) he made a
great feast, not in the toll house, but in his own house, partly
out of respect to Jesus & also that his evil companions
might come under the sound of the Gospel — How love invents plans,
Jesus comes & sits down, the Pharisees seeing this complain
to his disciples, not himself, perhaps they were afraid of him
and also to weaken the faith of his disciples for say they.
"a man who can associate with these bad men is not very
good himself." For they themselves would not touch a Publican
Jesus knowing their evil thoughts turns on them, and draws
himself. "I am a physician, these need me, therefore I am here".
Much of valuable Scripture was drawn out of Christ by enemies

I. Jesus is a physician and a good one for he has.
1 Knowledge. A of anatomy, for he made man, of all secret
parts, all peculiar constitution. B of disease, its cause,
progress, symptoms, this he acquired by experience on earth. all, all.
Y Of chemistry, he understands remedies, time for plasters or
cuts, cordials or bitters. he has abundance blood & water are
the two catholicons. at all hours he is prepared. —
2. Care. His love to man proves this. the numerous saints are
living testimonials of his skill. all are cured. wholly cured
no relapse a total cure.

II. The Patients, are all sick. — those who shall be cured will be
only the sick, others will die of their disease, and no wonder.
men in health need not wonder if the doctor does not send
any medicine. And even if he did they would not take
them for they are bitter potions. repentance. deep sorrow,
cutting out of proud flesh, cutting off legs and arms,

74

The PHYSICIAN *and* HIS PATIENTS[1]
Mark 2:17[2]

"When Jesus heard it, he saith unto them, They that are whole have no need of the physician, but they that are sick: I came not to call the righteous, but sinners to repentance."

Publicans [were] counted the vilest of all men. Matthew, whose Hebrew name was Levi,[3] was one of them.[4] But while engaged in this work and in bad company, Jesus calls him,[5] and constraining grace[6] makes him follow. He was afterward the Evangelist. Upon his conversion (though he modestly omits to mention it), he made a great feast,[7] not in the toll house but in his own house,[8] partly out of respect to Jesus and also that his evil companions might come under the sound of the Gospel. How love invents plans.[9] Jesus comes and sits down. The Pharisees, seeing this, complain to his disciples, not [to] himself.[10] Perhaps they were afraid of him,[11] and also to weaken the faith of his disciples. "For,"[12] say they, "a man who can associate with these bad men is not very good himself."[13] For they, themselves, would not touch a Publican.[14] Jesus, knowing their evil thoughts, turns on them and excuses himself. "I am a physician. These need me. Therefore, I am here."[15] Much of valuable Scripture was drawn out[16] of Christ by enemies.

I. JESUS IS A PHYSICIAN, AND A GOOD ONE, for he has:

   1. Knowledge:

      α.[17]Of anatomy, for he made man of all secret parts,[18] all peculiar constitution.

      β.[19]Of disease. All, all.[20] Its cause, progress, symptoms. This he acquired by experience on earth.[21]

      γ. Of chemistry. He understands remedies,[22] time for plasters[23] or cuts, cordials[24] or bitters.[25] He has abundance. Blood and water are the two catholicons.[26] At all hours, he is prepared.

   2. Care. His love to man proves this. The numerous saints are living testimonials of his skill. All are cured,[27] wholly cured. No relapse.[28] A total cure.

plucking out of eyes, sickness of sin, short diet, hunger and thirst, this regimen men will not submit to . They must not take Christs medecine and the devil's poison . but must avoid all this.
But to those feeling their need, inability, poverty, Jesus is just the one, medecine gratis, attendance free, certain cure even for the worst.

III. The way he cures. "calls to repentance".

this is not the medecine but it is the water it must be taken in. a sense of sin, sorrow for it, shame on its account, & avoiding of it in future. He calls in the preaching of the gospel on all but specially the sick. but this is unavailing without the effectual call of the Holy Spirit. this will be given only to sinners, it is accompanied with power.

1. The Folly of self righteous persons . they refuse the only good, they are suicides, just as much as the man was who sick refuses medecine, as much as he who takes poison or a dagger.
Think not to cure thyself or to go to heaven in sickness.

2. A Blow at unbelief. - This will kill us as much as the other to deny the power of Jesus is as bad as to deny our need
But come, come, sick! dying!! dead!!! health, recovery life —

Lord, constrain us to come.

99. 127. 194.

II. THE PATIENTS ARE ALL SICK.

Those who shall be cured will be only the sick.[29] Others will die of their disease, and no wonder. Men in health need not wonder if the doctor does not send any medicine.[30] And even if he did, they would not take them, for they are bitter potions: repentance, deep sorrow, cutting out of proud flesh, cutting off legs and arms,[31] plucking out of eyes, sickness of sin, short diet, hunger and thirst. This regimen, men will not submit too.[32] They must not take Christ[']s medicine and the devil's poison, but must avoid all this. But to those feeling their need, inability, poverty, Jesus is just the one. Medicine gratis,[33] attendance free, certain cure, even for the worst.

III. THE WAY HE CURES: *"call to repentance."*[34]

This is not the medicine, but it is the water.[35] It must be taken in.[36] A sense of sin, sorrow for it, shame on its account, and avoiding of it in future. He calls in the preaching of the gospel on all, but specially the sick. But this is unavailing without the effectual call of the Holy Spirit. This will be given only to sinners. It is accompanied with power.

1. The Folly of self righteous persons. They refuse the only good. They are suicides, just as much as the man was who [is] sick [and] refuses medicines, as much as he who takes poison or a dagger. Think not to cure thyself or to go to heaven in sickness.

2. A Blow at unbelief. This will kill us as much as the other. To deny the power of Jesus is as bad as to deny our need. But come, come, sick! dying!! dead!!! Health, recovery, life.

Lord, constrain us to come.

99. 127. 194.[37]

1. Charles consulted John Gill's commentary on Mark 2:13–17 for the introductory paragraph of this sermon (Gill, *Exposition of the New Testament*, 1:350–51). The overlapping content is noted below.

2. On March 25, 1877, Charles preached an additional sermon on Mark 2:17 entitled "For Whom Is the Gospel Meant?" (*MTP* 23, Sermon 1345). There does not appear to be any overlapping content between the above outline and the later sermon. The sermon that most resembles the above outline is "The Great Physician and His Patients" (*MTP* 11, Sermon 618). See also "The Faculty Baffled—the Great Physician Successful" (*MTP* 14, Sermon 827); "The Chief Physician and the Centurion's Servant" (*MTP* 24, Sermon 1422); "The Physician Pardons His Palsied Patient" (*MTP* 39, Sermon 2337); and "Patients for the Great Physician" (*MTP* 49, Sermon 2835).

3. Matthew was the only Gospel writer to self-identify with the name "Matthew" (Matt 9:9); Mark and Luke called him "Levi" (Mark 2:14; Luke 5:27–28).

4. "[I]t is thought, by some, probable, that he was a loose, extravagant young man, and so might depart from his father's family, and enter into this scandalous employment of a publican" (Gill, *Exposition of the New Testament*, 1:350).

5. Cf. Mark 2:14.

6. "Christ knew him: his eye was upon him as he passed by him, and his time was a time of love, and so a time of life; he looked upon him, and said unto him, live; quickening power went along with his words, and he arose, and left all, and followed him. . . . How powerful is efficacious grace! what is it, it cannot do! it turns the heart of a sinner at once, enclines it to Christ, and causes it to leave all for his sake; it at once fills a soul with love to Christ, faith in him, and obedience to him; it works powerfully, and yet freely; it always obtains, and effects what it designs, yet puts no force upon the will: *Levi*, under the drawings of divine grace, followed Christ most willingly and chearfully" (Gill, *Exposition of the New Testament*, 1:350, italics in the original). In 1877, Charles later said, "Constraining grace goeth out into the midst of the world to fetch in the wandering sheep and lambs; and therein the greatest love is revealed, even the love which puts forth its strength while yet we go astray" (*MTP* 23:604). He also said, "The Holy Ghost rests like a dove upon that blood-stained tree, and through him constraining

grace comes streaming down to human hearts" (*MTP* 13:571). See also "Constraining Love" (*NPSP* 6, Sermon 325).

7. Cf. Mark 2:15.

8. "In the house of *Levi*; not in the custom-house, or toll-booth, for that he left; but in his house in the city of *Capernaum*, where he had him, and made an entertainment for him, in token of gratitude, for the high favour bestowed on him" (Gill, *Exposition of the New Testament*, 1:350, italics in the original).

9. The word "plans" trails into the margin. It is possible, though unlikely, that this word is "places."

10. The stem of an unfinished letter, possibly "t," is found above the arc of the letter "m" in the word "himself."

11. The words "of him" trail into the margin and might have been added later.

12. Charles did not originally insert quotation marks around the word "For." However, the context suggests this word belongs with the quotation that follows. An alternative reading of this line is "For they say, 'A man who can associate . . .'"

13. This is a paraphrase of Mark 2:16, "And when the scribes and Pharisees saw him eat with publicans and sinners, they said unto his disciples, How is it that he eateth and drinketh with publicans and sinners?"

14. For additional references to publicans in this notebook, see "Election" (Sermon 10) and "Pharisees and Sadducees Reproved" (Sermon 39).

15. This is a paraphrase of Mark 2:17, "When Jesus heard it, he saith unto them, They that are whole have no need of the physician, but they that are sick: I came not to call the righteous, but sinners to repentance." Charles may have gleaned this technique from John Stephenson, who is cited in the following sermon, "The Church and Its Boast" (Sermon 75). See John Stevenson, *Christ on the Cross: An Exposition of the Twenty-Second Psalm* ([London: J. H. Jackson, 1844], 126–27). For additional examples of Charles's use of paraphrase, see "The Minister's Commission" (Notebook 2, Sermon 110); *MTP* 22:591; 35:187; and 46:401.

16. The stem of an illegible letter was attached to the letter "o" in the word "out." It is likely Charles prematurely wrote the letter "t" before he corrected the misspelling.

17. It appears Charles originally wrote the number 2 before changing it to the Greek letter alpha.

18. Cf. Ps 139:16.

19. It appears Charles converted the number 3 into the Greek letter beta by adding a stem.

20. Charles likely intended the words "all, all" to be inserted after the word "disease" as a reminder for him to list all the various diseases of which Jesus has knowledge. An alternative interpretation is that these words were intended to be placed after the word "experience" in the line below as a reminder to list all the diseases with which Jesus had experience. The former interpretation is more likely.

21. "Jesus did indeed enter into the woes of men. Walked the hospital! Why the whole world was an infirmary, and Christ the one only physician, going from couch to couch, healing the sons of men" (*MTP* 11:139).

22. "[God's promises] are to the believer a surgery in which he will find all manner of restoratives and blessed elixirs; he shall find therein an ointment for every wound, a cordial for every faintness, a remedy for every disease. Blessed is he who is well skilled in heavenly pharmacy and knoweth how to lay hold on the healing virtues of the promises of God" (*MTP* 8:97).

23. Samuel Johnson offered two uses of the noun "plaster." The first use comes from the French *plastre*, which is a "substance made of water and some absorbent matter, such as chalk or lime well pulverised, with which walls are overlaid or figures cast." The second use of the word comes from the Latin *emplastrum*, which is "a glutinous or adhesive salve" (Johnson's *Dictionary*). The context suggests Charles intended to use the second meaning of the word. Medicinal plasters were common in Victorian England. Three years before Charles preached the sermon above, a man with cholera was prescribed "a mustard plaster to be applied to his stomach" ("Another Rumoured Case of Cholera in Gloucester," *Gloucestershire Chronicle* [December 16, 1848]). See also *NPSP* 1:37.

24. "A medicine that increases the force of the heart, or quickens the circulation" (Johnson's *Dictionary*, s.v. "cordial"). Advertisements for cordials were common in Charles's day. One year prior to the writing of the outline above, an advertisement appeared in a newspaper for "Aromatic Cordial Medicine" that claimed to bring relief to those suffering from cholera and bowel complaints ("Cholera and Bowel Complaint," *The Birmingham Journal and Commercial Advertiser* [August 17, 1850]). See also "The Plant of Renown" (Sermon 20) and "The Gospel Cordial" (*MTP* 57, Sermon 3236).

25. "A very bitter liquor, which drains off in making of common salt, and used in the preparation of Epsom salt" (Johnson's *Dictionary*, s.v. "bittern"). In Charles's day bitters were often mixed with other ingredients such as in G. Oldham's "Aperient Family Pills," which offered "an efficacious and valuable remedy for Bilious derangement, Indigestion, Habitual Costiveness, or Nervous Affections.—They contain no mercurial preparation, being composed of vegetable aperients and bitters." ("Established Medicines, Prepared and Sold by G. Oldham and Co.," *The Weekly Freeman's Journal* [April 10, 1852]).

26. "An universal medicine" (Johnson's *Dictionary*, s.v. "Catholicon"). See also *MTP* 11:139.

27. Cf. Num 21:9; John 3:14.

28. "There is no relapse where Christ heals; no fear that one of his patients should be but patched up for a season, he makes a new man of him." (*MTP* 11:139).

29. An alternative reading of this line is "Only those who are sick will be cured."

30. Cf. *MTP* 11:142.

31. "The disease of sin is *deep-seated*, and has its throne in the heart. It does not lie in the hand or foot, it is not to be removed by amputation, much less by outward applications; no lancet can reach it, it is impossible to cauterize" (*MTP* 11:136, italics in the original).

32. Charles originally wrote the adverb "too." The final letter "o" was struck through in pencil to construct the correct word, "to."

33. Samuel Johnson defined the word "gratis" as "for nothing, without a recompense" (Johnson's *Dictionary*). The phrase "medicine gratis" can be translated "free medicine."

34. Mark 2:17, "When Jesus heard it, he saith unto them, They that are whole have no need of the physician, but they that are sick: I came not to call the righteous, but sinners to repentance."

35. Charles may have had John 4:14 in mind.

36. The medicinal practice of "taking the waters" was common in Victorian England. For instance, in *The Pickwick Papers*, Charles Dickens's character Mr. Pickwick systematically drank, or "took," the waters of Bath and "felt a great deal better" (Charles Dickens, *The Posthumous Papers of the Pickwick Club* [London: Chapman and Hall, 1856, The Spurgeon Library], 300). Later in his ministry Charles lived in Norwood, not far from the Crystal Palace in Sydenham. Near that location was the "Beulah Spa" which invalids frequented "to taste the waters, the medicinal properties of which are highly recommended by the faculty as most efficacious in many of those 'ills which flesh is heir to'" ("Beulah Spa, Norwood," *The Era,* November 7, 1852, 11).

37. The period after the number 194 was smudged toward the upper left side of the page.

75.　Ps. 22. 31 ...　　　　The Church and its boast.　　Stephenson

This Psalm written in the Spirit of prophecy, concerning Christ

Jesus commenced his death agonies with the expression in verse 1

He alludes to Gethsemane in verse 2 and his other praying nights

He remembers that in his sufferings God is righteously bruising

him for our sin .(4). He cites instances of God's deliverance of others

but remembers the opinion men had of him. (5. 6). He sees the wagging

of the heads (7. 8) He appeals to God's former love. (9. 10). He cries (11).

　Tell of his enemies. (12. 13) ... He sweat. he fainted. His bones were dislocated

by the fixing of the cross in its place. Heart fails, inflammation

comes over him , thirst, clamminess of the mouth. he is near death.

　He tells his crucifixion 16 ,... His emaciation and the impudent gaze 17.

His garment parted. 18.　　Here he importunes again 19 to 21

　Now comes the light in verse 21.　then gratitude . 22.

calls on all to praise him 23.　Aves a testimony & vow 24. 25

He refuses the vinegar & remembers the feast. 26 dwells on the effect of his death

　In the last verse we have him. consoling himself with

the thoughts

<u>I</u>. Of the glorious gathering "they shall come"

　All the covenanted ones, despite all opposition "shall come

　1. Into the world by birth, each in his time & season .

　2. Into grace by the newbirth, being quickened by the Spirit.

　3. Into glory everlasting, finally persevering

<u>II</u>　Their eternal theme. "and shall declare his righteous

　this is the object of their existence, conversion & glory.

1 God the Father's righteousness, in law, providence & grace

2. God the Son's in his perfect life. and painful death.

3. God the Spirit's in conversion, leaving sinners, dwelling with saints

<u>III</u>. The glorious argument "he has done it."

　All is fulfilled, law magnified, justice paid,

covenant fulfilled.　It is finished ...

98

　He Saviour's Soliloquy ...

75   Stephenson[1]

The CHURCH *and* ITS BOAST
Psalm 22:31[2]

*"They shall come, and shall declare his righteousness unto a people
that shall be born, that he hath done this."*

This Psalm [was] written in the Spirit of prophecy concerning Christ. Jesus commenced his death agonies[3] with the expression in verse 1.[4] He alludes to Gethsemane in verse 2,[5] and his other praying nights.[6] He remembers that in his sufferings God is righteously bruising him for our sin (4).[7] He cites instances of God's deliverance of others, but remembers the opinions men had of him (5, 6).[8] He sees the wagging of the heads (7, 8).[9] He appeals to God's former love (9, 10).[10] He cries (11).[11] Tell of his enemies (12,[12] 13).[13] He sweat. He fainted. His bones were dislocated[14] by the fixing of the cross in its place. Heart fails. Inflammation comes over him.[15] Thirst, clamminess of the mouth.[16] He is near death. He tells his crucifixion (16).[17] His emaciation and the impudent gaze (17).[18] His garment parted (18).[19] Here, he importunes[20] again (19 to 21[21]).[22]

Now comes the light in verse 21.[23] Then gratitude (22).[24] Calls on all to praise him (23).[25] Gives[26] a testimony and vow (24, 25).[27] He refuses the vinegar[28] and remembers the feast (26).[29] Dwells in the effect of his death.[30]

In the last verse,[31] we have him consoling himself with the thoughts:

I.   OF THE GLORIOUS GATHERING: *"they shall come."*
All the covenanted ones, despite all opposition, "shall come."[32]

1. Into the world by birth, each in his time and season.

2. Into grace by the new birth, being quickened by the Spirit.[33]

3. Into glory everlasting, finally persevering.

II. THEIR ETERNAL THEME: *"and shall declare his righteousness."*

This is the object of their existence, conversion, and glory.

1. [34] God the Father's righteousness: in law, providence, and grace.

2. God the Son's [righteousness] in his perfect life[35] and painful[36] death.

3. God the Spirit's [righteousness] in conversion, leaving sinners, dwelling with saints.[37]

III. THE GLORIOUS ARGUMENT: *"he has done it."*

All is fulfilled, law magnified, justice paid, covenant fulfilled. It is finished.[38]

The Saviour's Soliloquy.[39]

98[40]

1. For this sermon Charles borrowed heavily from nineteenth-century Anglican preacher John Stephenson (also spelled Stevenson), the perpetual curate of Curry and Gunwalloe, Cornwall, and Canon of Canterbury (not to be confused with J. H. Stephenson, the treasurer of Wells Cathedral [*Autobiography* 4:168], or G. Stephenson, the English mechanical engineer who used steam locomotion [*MTP* 14:219; 33:76; and 46:131]). The sermon above comes from Stephenson's work *Christ on the Cross: An Exposition of the Twenty-Second Psalm*. In the 1840s this commentary enjoyed wide reception and sold 6,000 copies in the first year of its publication (*The Church of England Quarterly Review* [London: William Edward Painter, 1843], 13:238). By 1850, 19,000 copies had been sold. Charles later said this commentary was "[t]he best of *Dr. Stevenson's* books. Exceedingly precious in its unveiling of the Redeemer's sorrows. We have derived personal spiritual benefit from the perusal of this gracious exposition, and are unable to judge it critically" (*Commenting and Commentaries*, 96, italics in the original.) In his exposition of Psalm 22 in *The Treasury of David*, Charles quoted Stephenson eighteen times, more than any other author (see *TD* 1:381–95).

2. This is the only time Charles preached a sermon on Ps 22:31. For additional sermons on the church, see "The Church of Christ" (*NPSP* 1, Sermon 28); "The Church-Conservative and Aggressive" (*MTP* 7, Sermon 393); "The Church's Love to Her Loving Lord" (*MTP* 11, Sermon 636); "The Church Aroused" (*MTP* 12, Sermon 716); "The Church as She Should Be" (*MTP* 17, Sermon 984); "Church Increase" (*MTP* 46, Sermon 2692); "The Church a Mother" (*MTP* 48, Sermon 2776); "Prayer for the Church" (*MTP* 48, Sermon 2788); "The Church Encouraged and Exhorted" (*MTP* 48, Sermon 2799); "The Church the World's Hope" (*MTP* 51, Sermon 2952); "The Church's Probation" (*MTP* 51, Sermon 2967); "The Church of God and the Truth of God" (*MTP* 54, Sermon 3093); and "The Church of the Firstborn" (*MTP* 56, Sermon 3206). See also *MTP* 11:349; 12:577; 46:433; 48:337; and 51:433.

3. "That voice was not more audible to the ears of his murderers, than it was piercing to the heart of his disciples, and of his Father" (Stephenson, *Christ on the Cross*, 3).

4. Ps 22:1, "My God, my God, why hast thou forsaken me? why art thou so far from helping me, and from the words of my roaring?"

5. Ps 22:2, "O my God, I cry in the day time, but thou hearest not; and in the night season, and am not silent."

6. "Many a night had he spent with God in prayer, but never one like that" (Stephenson, *Christ on the Cross*, 43).

7. Ps 22:4, "Our fathers trusted in thee: they trusted, and thou didst deliver them." Charles stopped using the word "verse" here (with the exception of "verse 21" eight lines below) and instead begun using parentheses. Stephenson wrote, "He perceived that his flesh was as helpless as a worm—powerless and passive—a creature crushed beneath the foot of man" (Stephenson, 79). He also wrote, "Though he hid his *face* from him as a Judge, he shut not his *heart* against him as a Father" (ibid., 280, italics in the original).

8. Ps 22:5–6, "They cried unto thee, and were delivered: they trusted in thee, and were not confounded. But I am a worm, and no man; a reproach of men, and despised of the people."

9. Ps 22:7–8, "All they that see me laugh me to scorn: they shoot out the lip, they shake the head, saying, He trusted on the LORD that he would deliver him: let him deliver him, seeing he delighted in him." Stephenson wrote, "They wag the head, shoot out the lip, make wide the mouth, draw out the tongue, wink with the eye, point with the finger, utter the jest, break forth with laughter, and jeer at him with bitterest scorn" (Stephenson, 115).

10. Ps 22:9–10, "But thou art he that took me out of the womb: thou didst make me hope when I was upon my mother's breasts. I was cast upon thee from the womb: thou art my God from my mother's belly."

11. Ps 22:11, "Be not far from me; for trouble is near; for there is none to help." See also "Jesus Wept" (*MTP* 35, Sermon 2091).

12. The beginning of an illegible number, likely 2, was written beneath 1. Charles may have prematurely written the number 2 before correcting the mistake.

13. Ps 22:12–13, "Many bulls have compassed me; strong bulls of Bashan have beset me round. They gaped upon me with their mouths, as a ravening and a roaring lion."

14   "We have remarked that our Lord's body was stretched, was transfixed with nails, was racked to dislocation" (Stephenson, 160). Cf. John 19:33.

15.   "INFLAMMATION must have commenced early, and violently, in the wounded parts" (Stephenson, 160; capitalization in the original).

16.   "So feeble had he become, so parched and dried up, that clamminess of the mouth, one of the forerunners of immediate dissolution, had already seized him" (ibid., 161).

17.   Ps 22:16, "For dogs have compassed me; the assembly of the wicked have inclosed me; they pierced my hands and my feet." Charles stopped using parentheses here and began listing only numbers. For consistency the parentheses will be retained throughout the remainder of the outline.

18.   Ps 22:17, "I may tell all my bones; they look and stare upon me." Stephenson wrote, "Immediately as they raised it, his emaciated frame was exposed to view. It was worn to skin and bone. He looked down upon it. He surveyed his wasted body" (Stephenson, 178).

19.   Ps 22:18, "They part my garments among them, and cast lots upon my vesture." An alternative reading of this line is "His garment [was] parted."

20.   "To seize; to harass with slight vexation; perpetually recurring; to molest" (Johnson's *Dictionary*, s.v. "importune").

21.   Charles originally wrote the number 22. He corrected the mistake by writing the number 1 over the final 2 to construct the number 21.

22.   Ps 22:19–21, "But be not thou far from me, O Lord: O my strength, haste thee to help me. Deliver my soul from the sword; my darling from the power of the dog. Save me from the lion's mouth; for thou hast heard me from the horns of the unicorns."

23.   "Now light is come—the true light of a Father's love—a Father's countenance of gracious approbation" (Stephenson, 228; see also 274).

24. Ps 22:22, "I will declare thy name unto my brethren; in the midst of the congregation will I praise thee."

25. Ps 22:23, "Ye that fear the LORD, praise him; all ye the seed of Jacob, glorify him: and fear him, all ye the seed of Israel."

26. The spelling of the word "Gives" is misleading. Charles originally wrote an illegible letter, likely an "S" or "F," before the "G" in the word "Gives" (Cf. the letter "G" in the word "God" nine lines above). The unfinished letter, combined with the corrected "G," forms the appearance of the letter "A." However, a closer inspection reveals Charles abandoned the original word and wrote "Gives." Stephenson used the verb "bears" instead of "gives" in his sentence "The Saviour bears his testimony" (Stephenson, 271).

27. Ps 22:24–25, "For he hath not despised nor abhorred the affliction of the afflicted; neither hath he hid his face from him; but when he cried unto him, he heard. My praise shall be of thee in the great congregation: I will pay my vows before them that fear him."

28. An illegible letter appears beneath the "g" in the word "vinegar."

29. Ps 22:26, "The meek shall eat and be satisfied: they shall praise the LORD that seek him: your heart shall live for ever."

30. The word "death" trails into the margin.

31. Ps 22:31, "They shall come, and shall declare his righteousness unto a people that shall be born, that he hath done this."

32. Charles did not include closing quotation marks after the word "come." The context suggests, however, that he was quoting from the same verse as seen in the line above.

33. "He quickened us by his Spirit from the death of sin, unto the life of righteousness" (Stephenson, 353–54).

34. The size and location of the number 1, and also the lack of punctuation, suggest Charles added this number after he had written the line.

35. Cf. 1 Pet 2:22.

36. An illegible word, likely "in," was written beneath the letter "p" in the word "painful." Charles may have written the words "and in."

37. Due to a lack of marginal space, the word "saints" was written above the line. Cf. Rom 8:11; 1 Cor 3:16.

38. Cf. John 19:30.

39. "A discourse made by one in solitude to himself" (Johnson's *Dictionary*, s.v. "soliloquy"). In his 1856 sermon "The Exaltation of Christ" (*NPSP* 2, Sermon 101), Charles used the word "soliloquy" in a similar way: "In the 22nd Psalm, which, if I read it rightly, is a beautiful soliloquy of Christ upon the cross" (*NPSP* 2:382). See also *MTP* 18:229 and 21:346.

40. The smudged number 98 was written in the left margin beneath the word "covenant" and not, as usual, at the bottom of the page. Additional examples of this habit are found in "The Men Possessed of the Devils" (Sermon 70) and "An Exhortation to Bravery" (Sermon 72).

Amos. 3. 3.   Can two walk together unless they are agreed.   76.

This question may be asked, in relation

I. To the Communion of saints.

There has been, is and will be still a great variety in their
states, tastes and views — yet they walk together, among
them there is an union of love, concern, enjoyment of each other
& this because & just in proportion as they are agreed in
their supreme love to one common Lord & in a consistent
manifestation of true holiness — these are the conditions of communion

II. To Communion with God.   That this was enjoyed by Adam
is evident, and by all saints, from numerous Scripture declarations
and from the experience of the saints in death, trouble & other
seasons.   It surpasses natural understanding, only the possessor
knows it.   It consists in   1. Mutual love
                              2. Mutual revelations
                              3. Common aims & interests

this cannot be enjoyed unless we are agreed with God — and just
in proportion as we are so.   the necessary agreement consists in

1. Reconciliation by the atonement of Jesus, the only ground of acceptance
2. Pardon & justification since perfection & sin is imperfection cannot agree
3. Regeneration Conversion & Sanctification making oneness of nature.

It is in meditation, prayer, the Scriptures, the ordinances, that we
come most into the secret of communion, but this depends
upon our previous agreement with God. (In our conversation)

Inf 1. Let none pretend to communion with God who are not like him
Inf 2. Let the Christian take heed lest he disagree with God
either by harboring sin, his own righteousness for if he does he cannot
"walk with God —
Inf 3. If holiness be necessary to a walk with him, how much more to
an everlasting dwelling with him

III. If sinners walk like Satan they agree with him.

Like effects spring from like causes. all sinners are brethren
in sin, our walk evidences our heart — Those whom
we walk with here we must live with for ever —

Bless me, Great God for Jesus.

101.

For 77 see 7

76

CAN TWO WALK TOGETHER UNLESS THEY ARE AGREED?

Amos 3:3[1]

"Can two walk together, except they be agreed?"

This question may be asked in relation:

I. TO THE COMMUNION OF SAINTS. There has been, is, and will be still a great variety in their states, tastes, and views. Yet, they walk together. Among them, there is [a] union of love,[2] concern, enjoyment of each other. And this, because and just in proportion, as they are agreed in their supreme love to one common Lord, and in a consistent manifestation of true holiness.[3] These are the conditions of communion.[4]

II. TO COMMUNION WITH GOD. That this was enjoyed by Adam is evident. And by all saints, from numerous Scripture declarations.[5] And from the experience of the saints in death,[6] trouble, and other seasons. It surpasses natural understanding. Only the professor knows it. It consists in:

1. Mutual love.

2. Mutual revelations.

3. Common aims[7] and interests.

This cannot be enjoyed unless we are agreed with God,[8] and just in proportion as we are so. The necessary agreement consists in:

1. Reconciliation by the atonement of Jesus, the only ground of acceptance.

2. Pardon and Justification, since perfection and sin is imperfection cannot agree.[9]

3. Regeneration, Conversion, and Sanctification, making oneness of nature. It is in meditation,[10] prayer,[11] the Scriptures,[12] the ordinances[13] that we come most into the secret of communion. But this depends upon our previous agreement with God. (In our conversation)

    Inf 1.[14] Let none pretend to communion with God who are not like him.

    Inf 2.   Let the Christian take heed lest he disagree with God, either by harboring sin, his own righteousness. For if he does, he cannot "walk with God.[”][15]

    Inf 3.   If holiness be[16] necessary to walk with him,[17] how much more to an everlasting dwelling with him?[18]

III. IF SINNERS WALK LIKE SATAN, THEY AGREE WITH HIM.

Like effects spring from like causes.[19] All sinners are brethren in sin.[20] Our walk evidences our heart. Those whom we walk with here, we must live with for ever.[21]

Bless me, Great God, for Jesus.[22]

101.

For 77, see 7[23]

1. Charles preached two additional sermons on Amos 3:3: "Preparation for Revival" (*MTP* 10, Sermon 597) and "Communion with Christ—a Baptizing Sermon" (*MTP* 46, Sermon 2668). On August 12, 1866, he preached a sermon on Amos 3:3–6 entitled "The Voice of the Cholera" (*MTP* 12, Sermon 705). Though in the context of baptism, the sermon that most resembles the outline above is "Communion with Christ—a Baptizing Sermon." There is enough overlapping content in this sermon to suggest Charles had the outline above in mind when writing the later sermon.

2. An alternative reading of this line is "[a] union of love."

3. Cf. Rom 12:1; 1 Pet 1:15–16.

4. If Charles intended the "conditions of communion" to be those he stated in the preceding paragraph, a period may be added after the word "communion." However, if Charles intended them to include those conditions outlined in the remainder of his sermon, a colon is best inserted. The former interpretation is preferred.

5. Charles may have had the following characters in mind: Elijah (2 Kgs 2:10–11), David (Psalms 42; 43), and Moses (Heb 11:24–26). See also Rev 19:1–8. The final letters of the word "declarations" trail into the margin.

6. "But what shall we do when we come to die, when the physician can no longer help us, and the beating of the pulse wax faint and few? Why then, 'he shall cover us with his feathers, and under his wings shall we trust.' Oh! it will be so blessed to go cowering down right under the shadow of the Almighty, hiding ourselves as the little chickens do in the hen's feathers, losing our own individuality in the realization of our union to Christ; finding that it is not death to die" (*MTP* 15:655). Charles was likely familiar with *Foxe's Book of Martyrs* during this season of his ministry. For a recent edition, see John King, ed., *Foxe's Book of Martyrs: Select Narratives* (Oxford: Oxford University Press, 2009). Cf. Heb 11:36–40.

7. "Two men cannot walk together if one turns his head in one direction, and another turns his head the opposite way. . . . But, the nearer they walk in precisely the same road, the more are they enabled to hold fellowship with one another" (*MTP* 46:146).

8. "We must be agreed with God *as to the end of our Christian existence*. . . . The main end of a Christian man is, that having been bought with precious blood, he may live unto Christ, and not unto himself" (*MTP* 10:615, italics in the original).

9. Alternative readings of this sentence are "since perfection and sin, [which is imperfection], cannot agree" and "since perfection, and sin is imperfection, cannot agree."

10. Cf. Josh 1:8; Pss 19:14; 119:97.

11. Cf. Luke 18:1; 1 Tim 2:8. See also "True Prayer—True Power!" (*NPSP* 6, Sermon 328).

12. Cf. Ps 119:11; Matt 5:18; 2 Tim 3:16.

13. See "God's Estimation of Men" (Sermon 41).

14. Abbr., "inference." For additional references to Charles's use of the word "inference" in this notebook, see "Future Judgment" (Sermon 6); "Free Grace" (Sermon 13); "Christ Is All" (Sermon 22); and "Regeneration, Its Causes and Effects" (Sermon 46). An em dash is found behind the number 1, suggesting Charles originally may not have intended to begin a list.

15. Charles was likely referencing Enoch, the man who "walked with God" (Gen 5:22). See also *MTP* 46:145. Charles did not include closing quotation marks after the word "God." However, quotation marks have been added since the context suggests Charles was quoting Gen 5:22.

16. The crossbar on the stem of the letter "b" is an example of dittography. Charles prematurely wrote the word "to" and corrected the mistake by changing the letter "t" to "b."

17. Cf. Gal 5:16.

18. An alternative reading of this line is "If holiness [is] necessary to walk with him, how much more [is holiness necessary] to [those in] an everlasting dwelling with him?" Charles said in a later sermon, "And, lastly, *be continually panting after more holiness.* Never be content with what thou art; seek to grow, seek to be more and more like Christ" (*MTP* 46:151–52, italics in the original).

19. The phrase "Like effects spring from like causes" was common in Victorian England. In 1862, English philosopher George Ramsey published the following words in his *Instinct and Reason*: "Like Effects spring from like Causes; The doctrines

of Natural and Revealed Religion are like to each other, and to the constitution and course of Nature; they are all like effects; therefore they had all the same cause or AUTHOR" (George Ramsey, *Instinct and Reason; or, The First Principles of Human Knowledge* [London: Walton and Maberly, 1862], 121, capitalization in the original).

20. Cf. Rom 3:23.

21. These words reflect Charles's budding ecumenism. His desire for denominational unity reached full blossom at the end of his ministry when, on New Year's Eve 1892, only days before his death, Charles told a group of friends, "During the past year I have been made to see that there is more love and unity among God's people than is generally believed. I speak not egotistically, but gratefully. I had no idea that Christian people, of every church, would spontaneously and importunately plead for the prolonging of my life. I feel myself a debtor to all God's people on this earth. . . . If anyone had prophesied, twenty years ago, that a dissenting minister, and a very outspoken one, too, would be prayed for in many parish churches, and in Westminster Abbey and St. Paul's Cathedral, it would not have been believed; but it was so. . . . In these days of infidel criticism, believers of all sorts will be driven into sincere unity. For my part, I believe that all spiritual persons are already one. When our Lord prayed that his church might be one, his prayer was answered, and his true people are even now, in spirit and in truth, one in him. Their different modes of external worship are as the furrows of a field; the field is none the less one because of the marks of the plough" (*ST* February 1892:52). This sentiment was shared by those like J. H. Stephenson who, in a letter to Charles dated July 8, 1890, wrote, "We may not belong to the same regiment of the great army, but our Captain is the same!" (*Autobiography* 4:168). In his 1858 sermon "The Great Revival" (*NPSP* 4, Sermon 185), Charles commented on the unity of London's churches: "[F]or we had last Sabbath evening, Exeter Hall full, Westminster Abbey full, and this place full too; and though we may not altogether agree in sentiment with all that preach, yet God bless them all! So long as Christ is preached, I rejoice, yea, and will rejoice; and I would to God that every large building in London were crowded too, and that every man who preached the Word were followed by tens of thousands, who would hear the truth" (*NPSP* 4:166). In his 1857 sermon "Heavenly Rest" (*NPSP* 3, Sermon 133), he said, "When the believer joins the church of God, and becomes united with them, he may expect to rest. . . . The church-member at the Lord's table has a sweet enjoyment of rest in fellowship with the saints; but ah! up there the rest of church fellowship far surpasses anything that is known here;

for there are no divisions there, no angry words at the church meetings, no harsh thoughts of one another, no bickerings about doctrine, no fightings about practice. There Baptist, and Presbyterian, and Independent, and Wesleyan, and Episcopalian, serving the same Lord, and having been washed in the same blood, sing the same song, and are all joined in one. There pastors and deacons never look coolly on each other; no haughty prelates there, no lofty-minded ministers there, but all meek and lowly, all knit together in brotherhood; they have a rest which surpasseth all the rest of the church on earth" (*NPSP* 3:213). For additional examples of Charles's ecumenism, see "Pleasure in the Stones of Zion" (Sermon 53); "David in the Cave of Adullam" (Notebook 2, Sermon 116); *MTP* 27:198; 28:628; and 58:150. Cf. John 17:21; 1 Cor 12:13.

22. An alternative reading of this prayer is "Bless me, great God, for Jesus['s sake]."

23. The phrase "For 77, see 7" was written as a cross-reference to indicate the location of the final sermon of this notebook, "The Lepers" (Sermon 77). Charles inserted his final sermon in the remaining blank space beneath the conclusion of "Regeneration" (Sermon 7). Charles also referenced this location in the index at the beginning of this notebook.

1.	Adoption	Ephes 1. 5
2.	Necesity of Purity to Heaven	Rev. 21.27
3.	Abraham justified by Faith	Gen 15. 6
4.	A Contrast	Eph 4. 8
5.	Condescending love of Jesus	2 Cor 8. 9
6.	Future Judgment	Col. 3. 25
7.	Regeneration	
8.	Final Perseverance	Ps. 94.14
9.	Sinners must be punished	Ps. 9.17
10.	Election	Eph. 1. 4
11.	Salvation to the utmost	Heb. 7. 25
12.	Death Consequence of Sin	Ezek. 18. 4
13.	Alpha and Omega	Rev. 21. 6
14.	God's grace given to us	Ros. 15. 11
15.	Christ about his Father's business	Luke 2. 49
16.	Love manifest in Adoption	John 3. 1
17.	Christian & his Salvation	Isa. 45. 17
18.	God's Sovereignty	Ps 10. 16
19.	An answer required	2 Sam 24. 13
20.	Plant of Renown	Ez. 34. 29
21.	Light of Christ	Matt 22. 25
22.	Christ is all	Col. 3. 11
23.	Precious Faith	2 Pet. 1. 1
24.	Salvation in God only	Jer. 3. 23
25.	Peculiar People	Deut. 14. 2
26.	Despisers warned	Prov. 29. 1
27.	Paul's renunciation	Phil. 3. 11
28.	Heaven's preparations	Joh. 14. 2
29.	Begin at Jerusalem	Luke 24. 47
30.	Salvation from Starvation	Prov. 10. 3
31.	Ignorance its evils	Prov. 19. 2
32.	Wrong Roads	Prov 14. 12
33.	Salvation from Sin	Matt. 1. 21
34.	Lamb & Lion	Rev. 5. 5. 6
35.	Path of the Just	Prov. 4. 18
36.	Certain fulfil of Promises	Josh. 21. 45
37.	The Fight	2 Cor. 10. 4

1. With the exception of a single-sermon index in Notebook 2 ("Self Deception," Sermon 78), this subject index was Charles's final attempt at categorizing his early sermons until he published the annually bound penny pulpit series in London as *The New Park Street Pulpit* (later called *The Metropolitan Tabernacle Pulpit*). Susannah noted: "at the end is a *subject* index, which bears a remarkable resemblance to those which set forth the contents of every volume of the *Metropolitan Tabernacle Pulpit*" (*Autobiography* 1:213–14, italics in the original).

2. Charles abbreviated the word "Ephesians" by writing "Ephes." This Scripture reference and those following have been spelled out for consistency. For an additional example of this abbreviation, see the third column of the index at the beginning of this notebook.

3. The correct title of this sermon is "Necessity of Purity for an Entrance to Heaven" (Sermon 2).

4. The correct Scripture reference for the sermon "A Contrast" (Sermon 4) is Eph 5:8, not Eph 4:8. Charles also made this mistake in the index at the beginning of this notebook. In the sermon itself, the number 5 was struck through in pencil and replaced with 4.

5. Charles did not use a scriptural reference in "Regeneration" (Sermon 7). See notes on the index at the beginning of this notebook.

6. The correct title of this sermon is "Salvation" (Sermon 11).

7. The correct title of this sermon is "Death, the Consequence of Sin" (Sermon 12).

8. The correct title of this sermon is "Free Grace" (Sermon 13).

9. Due to a lack of space, Charles abbreviated the word "Business" in the sermon "Christ About His Father's Business" (Sermon 15).

10. The correct biblical reference for the sermon "Love Manifest in Adoption" (Sermon 16) is 1 John 3:1, not John 3:1. In the sermon itself, the number 1 was written in pencil before the word "John." In the index at the beginning of this notebook, Charles wrote the correct Scripture reference.

11. The correct title of this sermon is "The Plant of Renown" (Sermon 20).

12. The correct title of this sermon is "Making Light of Christ" (Sermon 21).

13. The correct biblical reference for this sermon is Matt 22:5, not Matt 22:25.

14. Charles reversed the order of these two words, "Precious" and "Faith." The correct title of this sermon is "Faith Precious" (Sermon 23).

15. The correct title of this sermon is "The Peculiar People" (Sermon 25).

16. Charles inserted an apostrophe between the letters "r" and "s" in the word "Despisers." However, the context suggests he intended the word to be plural, not possessive. In the sermon itself, Charles correctly wrote "Despisers Warned" (Sermon 26).

17. The correct biblical reference for this sermon is Phil 3:9, not Phil 3:11. In the index at the beginning of this notebook, Charles wrote Phil 3:7. In the sermon itself Charles wrote the correct Scripture reference.

18. The correct title of this sermon is "Beginning at Jerusalem" (Sermon 29).

19. The correct title of this sermon is "The Wrong Roads" (Sermon 32).

20. The correct title of this sermon is "The Lamb and Lion Conjoined" (Sermon 34).

21. The correct title of this sermon is "The Path of the Just" (Sermon 35).

22. The correct title of this sermon is "Certain Fulfilment of Promises" (Sermon 36).

23. Absent from this list are the following forty-one sermons: "The Fight and the Weapons" (Sermon 37a); "The Son's Love to Us Compared with God's Love to Him" (Sermon 38); "Pharisees and Sadducees Reproved" (Sermon 39); "Christian Joy" (Sermon 40); "God's Estimation of Men" (Sermon 41); "King of Righteousness and Peace" (Sermon 42); "Jesus, the Shower from Heaven" (Sermon 43); "Elijah's Faith and Prayer" (Sermon 44); "The Authors of Damnation and Salvation" (Sermon 45); "Regeneration, Its Causes and Effects" (Sermon 46); "The Father and the Children" (Sermon 47); "Intercession of the Saints" (Sermon 48); "The Eloquence of Jesus" (Sermon 49); "Repentance and Salvation" (Sermon 50); "Christian Prosperity and Its Causes" (Sermon 51); "He Took Not Up Angels"

(Sermon 52); "Pleasure in the Stones of Zion" (Sermon 53); "The Little Fire and Great Combustion" (Sermon 54); "Rest for the Weary" (Sermon 55); "God Glorified in the Saved" (Sermon 56); "The Affliction of Ahaz" (Sermon 57); "The Wise Men's Offering" (Sermon 58); "The First Promise" (Sermon 59); "The Peace of God" (Sermon 60); "The Improvement of Our Talents" (Sermon 61); "God, the Guide of His Saints" (Sermon 62); "Gethsemane's Sorrow" (Sermon 63); "Parable of the Bad and Good Seed" (Sermon 64); "Trust Not the Heart" (Sermon 65); "Josiah" (Sermon 66); "Offending God's Little Ones" (Sermon 67); "The Saints' Justification and Glory" (Sermon 68); "Imitation of God" (Sermon 69); "The Men Possessed of the Devils" (Sermon 70); "What Think Ye of Christ?" (Sermon 71); "An Exhortation to Bravery" (Sermon 72); "Slavery Destroyed" (Sermon 73); "The Physician and His Patients" (Sermon 74); "The Church and Its Boast" (Sermon 75); "Can Two Walk Together Unless They Are Agreed?" (Sermon 76); and "The Lepers" (Sermon 77). The reason for Charles's truncation of his index is unclear.

24. Charles preached two sermons on 2 Cor 10:4: "The Fight and the Weapons" (Sermon 37a) and "The Fight" (Sermon 37b). The reason Charles did not include in this index "The Fight and the Weapons" (Sermon 37a) may suggest his preference for "The Fight" (Sermon 37b).

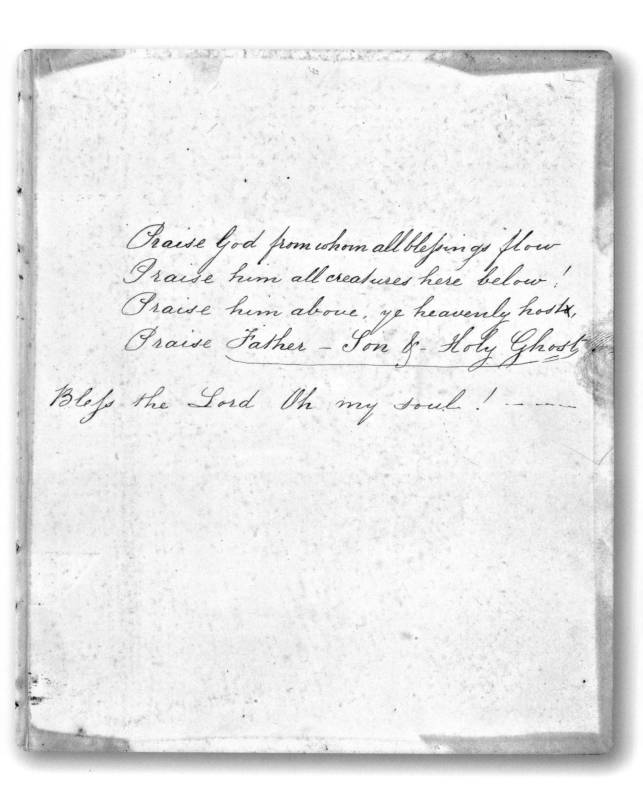

Praise God from whom all blessings flow
Praise him all creatures here below !
Praise him above, ye heavenly hosts,
Praise Father – Son & Holy Ghost,

Bless the Lord Oh my soul ! ———

Praise God from whom all blessings flow,[1]
Praise him all creatures here below!
Praise him above, ye heavenly hosts.[2]
Praise <u>Father, Son, and Holy Ghost</u>.[3]

Bless the Lord, Oh my soul![4]

1. In its modern form, the Doxology is attributed to Anglican bishop Thomas Ken (1637–1711). The four lines constituting the hymn were penned as the final stanzas of Ken's "An Evening Hymn" and "A Morning Hymn" (John Julian, *A Dictionary of Hymnology Setting Forth the Origin and History of Christian Hymns of All Ages and Nations with Special Reference to Those Contained in the Hymn Books of English-Speaking Countries. And Now in Common Use Together with Biographical and Critical Notices of Their Authors and Translators and Historical Articles on National and Denominational Hymnody, Breviaries, Missals, Primers, Psalters, Sequences, Etc. Etc. Etc.* [New York: Charles Scribner's Sons, 1892], 618–19). See also W. L. Bowles, *The Life of Thomas Ken: Viewed in Connection with Public Events, and the Spirit of the Times, Political and Religious, in Which He Lived, Including Some Account of the Fortunes of Morley, Bishop of Winchester, His First Patron, and the Friend of Isaak Walton, Brother-In-Law of Bishop Ken* (2 vols.; London: John Murray, 1830). Charles included the Doxology in the repertoire of hymns that were sung at the Metropolitan Tabernacle. In Charles's own hymnal Ken's 1697 version was cited (see hymn 153 in C. H. Spurgeon, *Our Own Hymn-Book: A Collection of Psalms and Hymns for Public, Social, and Private Worship* [London: Passmore & Alabaster, 1866; repr., 1885, The Spurgeon Library]). The Doxology was commonly set to "Old 100th," a tune originally composed by French Calvinist Louis Bourgeois (1510–1559) (see hymn 631 in John Rippon, *Comprehensive Edition. A Selection of Hymns, from the Best Authors, Including a Great Number of Originals, Intended to Be an Appendix to Dr. Watts's Psalms & Hymns. Containing All the Additional Hymns, with About Four Hundred, Now First Added, in All Upwards of Eleven Hundred and Seventy Hymns, in One Hundred Metres. With Copious Indices* [London: William Whittemore, Houlston and Stoneman, 1787, The Spurgeon Library]). The Doxology became a staple in Charles's ministry. One occasion stood out to him in particular. Approximately four years after Charles penned the words on this page, he wrote, "There were two evenings—June 22, and September 4, 1855,—when I preached in the open air in a field in King Edward's Road, Hackney. On the first occasion, I had the largest congregation I had ever addressed up to that time, but at the next service the crowd was still greater. By careful calculation, it was estimated that from twelve to fourteen thousand persons were present. I think I shall never forget the impression I received when, before we separated, that vast multitude joined in singing—'Praise God from whom all blessings flow.' That night, I could understand better than ever before why the apostle John, in the Revelation, compared the 'new song' in Heaven to 'the voice of many waters.' In that glorious hallelujah, the mighty waves of praise seemed to roll up towards the sky, in majestic grandeur, even as the billows of old ocean break upon the beach"

(*Autobiography* 2:92–93). Another memorable occasion occurred on September 23, 1890, when a violent storm beset the Stockwell Orphanage. After attempting to calm the children, Charles led them in the Doxology. "[T]here came another roll of drums in the march of the God of armies; and then, as an act of worship, we adoringly sang together, with full force, the words of the Doxology. . . . This was a grand climax. The heavens themselves seemed to think so, for there were no more thunder-claps of such tremendous force. I need not write more. The storm abated" (*Autobiography* 4:330). On February 8, 1891, after Charles returned to London from a three-month illness, the congregation of the Metropolitan Tabernacle—whose membership that month totaled 5,328—sang the Doxology "with thunderous effect" (G. Holden Pike, *Charles Haddon Spurgeon: Preacher, Author, Philanthropist, with Anecdotal References* [London: Funk & Wagnalls Company, 1892], 341). For references to the Doxology in Charles's later sermons, see *NPSP* 1:76; 3:31; *MTP* 12:124; 32:48; 33:636; 38:357; 39:21; and 51:520. Even today the Doxology continues to be sung at the Metropolitan Tabernacle. See "Awake, My Soul, and with the Sun" under the section "Public Worship and the Lord's Day" in the current church hymnal (see hymn 674 in *Psalms & Hymns of Reformed Worship* [London: The Wakeman Trust, 2008]).

2. Charles originally wrote the word "hosts" before he struck through the final "s" to form the word "host." Charles's correction from plural to singular is consistent with Thomas Ken's version of the Doxology. There may have been a connection in Charles's mind between the "heavenly host" in this line and the illustrated angels that appear in the front matter of this notebook (see title page).

3. A partial fingerprint, possibly a thumb, can be seen at the edge of the page after the word "Ghost." The source of the ink appears to be the period at the end of the line. If this is correct, then the print was stamped onto the page before the ink could dry, which would reveal that it belonged to Charles. An analysis is currently underway in The Spurgeon Library to compare the fingerprint on this page and others in the early notebooks, with those found on Charles's later sermon galleys. Whereas the source of the print above was ink, the prints on the later galleys were likely caused by the tar from the cigars Charles held while he redacted the sermons for publication. For additional examples of fingerprints in this notebook, see the two prints above the word "VOL. I" in the front matter on the page before the index.

4. Ps 103:1–2, "Bless the Lord, O my soul: and all that is within me, bless his holy name. Bless the Lord, O my soul, and forget not all his benefits." In his diary entry

for May 1, 1850, Charles wrote, "Another month now dawns on me. I have lived through one, I will bless the Lord for it, and trust Him for this also" (*Autobiography* 1:134). On May 2, he wrote, "Bless the Lord, O my soul; follow hard after Him, love and serve Him!" (ibid., 1:138). On May 25, he wrote, "Work, Lord, work! Thou hast encouraged me; may I not be disappointed! 'Bless the Lord, O my Soul'" (ibid., 1:140). In his annual letter to his congregation at the New Park Street Chapel, Charles wrote the following words in 1858 with regard to the raising of funds for the construction of the Metropolitan Tabernacle: "Another year of earnest effort, and the work will be nearing a conclusion. 'Bless the Lord, O my soul: and all that is within me, bless His holy name.' The Lord will prosper that which concerneth us; we shall continue in loving labour, knit together as the heart of one man; and, by-and-by, we shall raise the topstone to its place amidst the shouts of the people" (*Autobiography* 2:305). See also *Autobiography* 3:240; *MTP* 18:601; and 36:1.

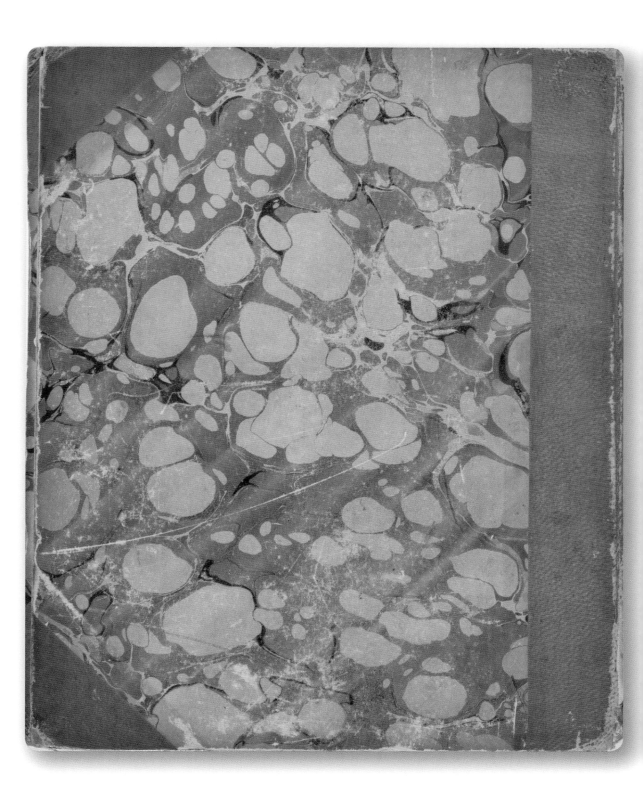

ABOUT THE EDITOR

CHRISTIAN T. GEORGE

(Ph.D., University of St. Andrews, Scotland) serves as curator of The Spurgeon Library and assistant professor of historical theology at Midwestern Baptist Theological Seminary in Kansas City, Missouri. For more information, visit *www.spurgeon.org*.

ABOUT THE PROJECT

Spurgeon's College (www.spurgeons.ac.uk) in London, England, where the original sermons were found; courtesy of Chris Gander

Chris Gander (Chris Gander Design Associates) and Rebecca George photographing the original notebooks at Spurgeon's College, London; courtesy of Christian George

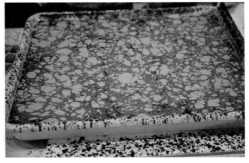

Lesley Patterson-Marx creates marbled paper using centuries-old techniques to replicate the original cover for Volume 1. Learn more about her process at www.bhacademic.com/spurgeon.

Charles Spurgeon's early sermon notebooks; courtesy of Chris Gander

SCRIPTURE INDEX

SUBJECT INDEX

W

Y

Z